11th October 1851.

Sketch of The Ballaarat Gold-Field.

AF593679

Commissioner's Tent.

Alfred Clarks Tent was afterwards erected here.

Golden Point

Lomax Claim.

Kavanah's claim yielded £3000.

Oddie's Tent.

Macdonald Sister & Co Claim.

Willis's claim.

Macdonald Sister & Champions claim.

Highett's claim.

Oddie's claim.

ISLAND

McLeod's Tent

YARROWEE

Cradle Macdonald's

Macdonald's Tent.

RIVER

RICH OPEN FLAT

Present site of the TOWNSHIP of BALLAARAT WEST. 1867.

Note

.... Indicating approximate extent of Present Gold field (1851)

—.—.— do do — do — at present covered with Tents.

[signature]

Copied from a sketch made by A. McDonald.

Mrs. N. Pescott

SOUVENIR PRESS

First published in Australia by Raphael Arts Pty., Ltd.

First British Edition published 1978 by
Souvenir Press Ltd, 43 Great Russell Street London WC1B 3PA

ISBN 0 285 62357 5

Printed photolitho in Great Britain by
Ebenezer Baylis and Son Limited
The Trinity Press, Worcester, and London

CONTENTS

PREFACE

There are still with us today sons and daughters of early settlers, who recall their parents' tales of living in Victoria in the mid-nineteenth century. Old miners, who sought the elusive gold with pan and windlass, can still be found. Their knowledge, learned from the first miners, has helped in the establishment of Sovereign Hill, which shows Ballarat's Main Street as it was in the middle of the last century.

Decendants of these early settlers have willingly provided their ancestors' cherished old recipes, hints, and homilies for inclusion in this book. They give us a picture of life as it was then in the cottages and mansions. It has been a fascinating labour, searching through early books of the colony, to complete the picture — now presented. Some came as a result of a letter on the subject, kindly published by Miranda of the Weekly Times.

My grateful thanks go to those ladies of the Sovereign Hill Interiors' sub-committee, who have given assistance with typing and word counts. Mention should be made of Mrs. J. Besemeres and Miss D. Ellis, who bore the brunt of the typing.

L. Pescott

Ballarat, Australia — October 1976

SOVEREIGN HILL, BALLARAT

Sovereign Hill is a re-created goldmining township covering the first ten years of Ballarat's exciting history.

Some of the buildings include the licensed United States Hotel, the Victoria Theatre with regular shows, restaurants — the New York Bakery and John Giloos, the Mechanics Institute and the Ballarat Times. About 120 people dressed in period costumes work at Sovereign Hill.

The township is open for inspection every day of the year.

Royalties from this book will assist with the future development of Sovereign Hill.

The first home for many early settlers was a tent in the bush, a wattle and daub or bark hut with one primitive chimney in which hung kettles over the fire. A camp oven would produce surprisingly good bread made with potato yeast. This was made from hops and potato cut up and boiled together. It was a relief from unending meals of damper. An improvement for cooking was the Colonial oven which needed a fire under and over the oven. Two saucepans and a kettle sat on two iron bars across the top fire. The colonial oven did not always produce better bread than the old camp oven.

The floors were often of pressed earth with chaff bags as rugs. As the children grew they graduated to sapling and hessian bunks with straw-filled mattresses, and maybe a crude patchwork quilt. Flour bags could become articles of wearing apparel. Nothing was wasted. Bread and dripping, bread and milk, fish, eels and local game provided the staple diet. Golden syrup and treacle when they could be bought were a luxury.

The next dwelling was a small wooden cottage with a verandah and a gable roof. As the family increased another gable would be added at the rear of this until there were up to four or five. Success from effort as a miner, storekeeper, haulage contractor or a squatter was reflected by the large homesteads and mansions that were built by these former settlers who had started out by building for themselves a log cabin hewn from local timber.

Many immigrants were from Scotland. They brought up their families with a strong religious background. On Sunday the household would appear in their best clothes in the kitchen, often the largest room in the house. The father read from the Bible and conducted a simple service. As neighbours increased a church was built and attendance became an adventure, the children double-dinking on their cart. The minister would return for a roast dinner with one of the parishioners. It would be the meal of the week, with all the trimmings. Children were expected to give of their best behaviour and be patient until it was over and permission given to leave the table, put on their pinafores and go out to play. There was no time for boredom with the cycle of preparations for jam-making, preserving of fruit, eggs to be "put down" in waterglass, butter to be made and clothes for the family.

Home-killed mutton was pickled in saltpetre and brine and was tender and pink to eat.

The hazards of bush life were taken in their stride. Pleasures were simple. What fun was had at gatherings in a farm kitchen, the men playing cards well into the night, or playing the fiddle or mouth organ. Songs around the fire, followed by a solid supper of scones and a large one layer cake made in the baking dish, and endless cups of tea.

The arrival of a mail order catalogue would give great pleasure. All the family would pore over it many times. A visit from an Indian hawker in a covered waggon was a great event. He sold spices, perfumes and all manner of materials and odds and ends. The most usual purchase was yards of calico and brightly coloured boiled sweets with the change.

Doing the weekly family wash was a major task. Said one pioneer, "Two wash tubs sat on a bench outside, and a copper was placed on an open fire nearby. Water had to be brought from a well or from the creek. It was carried in a barrel on a sledge drawn by a horse. A washing board was used to rub the clothes briskly up and down. They were of three kinds, made with wood or tin or thick corrugated glass. The corrugations of wood wore down with use, those of tin became flattened and cracked, so the ultimate was to own one of thick corrugated glass set in a wooden frame."

Without a wringer it was important to learn the art of hand-wringing correctly. To wring a sheet the hem was gathered into the upward-turned palm of the left hand. The rest of the sheet was swirled in the water anti-clockwise into a long twist. The right hand, palm uppermost, was placed under the twist about a foot from the left hand. By gripping and bringing the right hand over until the palm faced downwards, and pulling away from the left hand at the same time, the twist would be wrung as dry as possible. The left hand then moved down and the process was repeated to the end of the sheet, with the wrung part of the sheet curled up in the crook of the left arm. Handkerchiefs were always soaked in salt and water before being boiled. Articles washed would be rinsed twice in cold water. Water from wash-day activities was carried to water vegetables and fruit trees.

A number of heavy black irons kept hot on the stove ensured that ironing could proceed without pause.

The hard work shared by the whole family made strong links and gave happy memories to all its members. In time, the long hours of toil were not remembered as such but the happiness of working together.

The Ballarat gold-fields in their beginnings required great quantities of food for a large moving population of up to 150,000 souls. Until the early 1860's when the railway from Melbourne was constructed haulage teams from Geelong were the lifeline of the goldfields. A bullock team could pull up to 30 cwt. in winter, and 50 cwt. to 2½ tons in summer, on the upslope journey to Ballarat. In winter the time was eight to ten days and in summer four to five days. Teams camped along the way and there changed to fresh animals. The amount of churned up mud was almost defeating. In an effort to improve the track a plank road was constructed in the Buninyong area. the remains of which are still to be found. At the ford outside "Mount Buninyong" so huge was the log placed there to facilitate the crossing that when the modern highway was constructed recently it had to be left underneath the surface.

A census of conveyances (the first census?) was taken in the winter of 1854 at Batesford near Geelong. Despite poor weather, sixty carts, thirty-six bullock waggons, twenty horsemen, and ninety-eight walkers were counted going north to Ballarat in one day. South bound traffic was about the same. One horse dray would carry about 6 cwt. in poor weather, and in fine, half a ton. Horse fodder cost more than the equivalent weight of flour. At any one time on the 58 odd miles between Geelong and Ballarat on the track that wound over the Anakie and Brisbane ranges, there would be six hundred and fifty conveyances pulled by bullocks and some seven hundred and forty by horses.

Their loads would include tea from China, sugar from Mauritius and the West Indies, flour from the United States and Chile, oats from Britain, as well as clothing and footwear. The cost of transport was less for the long sea journey than for the last sixty miles to Ballarat. Those who could afford a coach fare would leave Geelong at 8 a.m. and arrive at Bath's Hotel in Ballarat at 5.30 p.m. There were stops at booths along the way. These institutions were hotbeds of wickedness. The answer to cheaper transport and food came towards the end of 1860 when Ballarat grew and milled grain and produced rolling stock for the new railway from its foundries.

To the west and north bullock teams were still the lifeline of the new settlers. The early waggons were of simple construction from locally hewn timber. Wheels came from the thick end of a large round log about one foot through with a hole burnt in the centre to accommodate the axle. Yokes for the bullocks were made from a slender log cut the width of two bullocks and shaped afterwards to fit their necks, then smoothed and oiled. The long whips came from skins tanned by a simple process. They were spread on the ground, fastened down with wooden pegs and spread with a mixture of salt and alum in hot water. As it dried the process would be repeated until it was tanned. Broken glass or anything at hand was used to scrape off the dried mixture. A sharp pocket-knife cut the leather into thin strips leaving a two inch strip at the top to hang on a hook on the fence. A rag soaked in linseed oil produced soft and pliable leather for plaiting — up to eight strands. A long strip of cloth with about ten pellets of lead in the centre was inserted into the "belly" of the whip to make a proper fall in size. Then the rolling of the whip began. It was placed on a solid bench, knee high and rolled with a heavy piece of timber about two feet long by twelve inches wide and three inches high, with notches in each end for the grip. A helper at each end to hold the whip as the maker with knees slightly bent and feet apart, slid the weight of timber from side to side making the whip roll with great speed until it was smooth and even. Remnants of silk from Coventry, England, rolled into little barrels sold well among the whip makers. They were put on the end of the whip, and as "whip crackers" made a noise like a pistol shot. Added to the whip, the bullocky urged his team on with the most colourful and down-to-earth language.

One of the most successful teamsters on the road between Geelong and Ballarat was John Dans. Well aware of the danger from bushrangers, he carefully put gold in the axles of his waggons and sealed it with tallow on the trips back from the goldfields. Gold was also carried in greasy old tallow barrels and well sealed with the tallow.

The number of bullocks in a team varied from two to twenty-two. Nothing was too much for the patient, plodding beasts. It was a great day on the out-back stations when the bullock team arrived with rations for up to six months. The mistress of the household would receive her flour in 150 pound bags, her sugar in 70 pound bags, her vinegar in barrels, great cheeses wrapped in cheesecloth, chests full of tea and kegs of liquor for the cellar. On the return haul the waggon would carry the wool clip or huge logs for fencing.

The first bulls were landed in 1787 at Botany Bay (Blair's "History of Australasia" 1879) from the Cape of Good Hope. Most died from disease or "went bush". New settlers pushing up the Nepean River some fifty miles from Sydney seven years later came across a herd of sixty cattle. Blair writes of the vital use made of bullock teams in exploration and settlement of the new country. Hume and Hovell found them invaluable. The Henty's brought thirty head of cattle from Tasmania to Southern Victoria in 1834. Mention is made of the waggons in early Melbourne in 1835.

In the early 19th century, Australian cooking was mainly a mixture of Irish, Scottish and English recipes. Due to distance from easy supplies, the wives of the early pioneers gave their food a rugged outback character. Their men had also to fend for themselves and learnt to cook in the outback with meat they had shot or trapped themselves. They learned much by observing the aboriginal way of living off the land. During the gold-rush days men from other countries flocked to Australia bringing with them recipes from their own backgrounds. Many were Chinese. Vineyards were established by early continental settlers. A Frenchman introduced asparagus to Australia. The Chinese were found throughout the gold-fields and many stayed on to produce succulent vegetables.

A chaplain on one of the early convict ships brought with him a few orange seeds to plant.

Elizabeth Farm at Parramatta produced marvellous vegetables, fruit and wine in the 1790's.

Salted meats were much used because of their ability to keep. In the early nineteenth century in Australia there was a difference between cooking in capital cities and that in country districts where supplies had far to come. Gold-seekers had to stock up in the cities before setting out for the gold-fields and hope they could buy fresh food-stuffs when they arrived. Eels were plentiful in the rivers around Ballarat.

Stockman's Equipment — . . . a tin pannikin, a good flat shovel, a wire hook, a billy to hold a quart, a flour sack to carry suet, corned beef, flour, salt, perhaps a tin of butter and a camp oven, tea and sugar. The bush cook dealt with meats at night to avoid the menace of flies. Ashes were used to clear muddy water and make it fit for use. Bottlebrush and red river gum was considered best for the pit style of cooking.

Bushland cooking is done in the hot embers of the camp fire made in a hole, the size of which depends on what has been produced by the hunters. Put in stones. Heat them for 2½ hours. Red river gum branches or those of the bottlebrush soaked in water put on the hot embers give off steam. Place meat or birds on these steaming branches. Cover with more of the same or a sack, and finally with earth to keep in the steam. Be careful, when removing the top layer when the food is cooked that the hot earth does not get on to the food. Chickens cooked in a row should have a hot stone inside wrapped in wet grass. Kangaroo tail unskinned, or beef about 4 inches thick will take about an hour.

"Scorch it at the top with a hot fire-shovel" is the rather alarming final injunction in an Eighteenth Century recipe for Savoury "Tosted" Cheese. While a cheese cake recipe of the same period begins grandly: "Take 12 quarts of milk, warm from the cow."

Early cookery writers had a fine scorn for exact measurements: "Take a tidy dollop of butter and a nice drop of parsnip wine". The pioneer wives brought their cook books with them, and for generations Australian cooking was essentially English in character. But time, climate and the availability of new ingredients gradually wrought their changes, and by the time cookbooks were being written and published in Australia, characteristic preferences — and dishes — had begun to emerge.

Mrs. Caroline Chisholm, the famous social worker, who accompanied her husband to New South Wales in 1838, was probably the first woman to prepare a collection of recipes for Australian housewives. She recommended dividing the week's ration of flour and meat into 7 equal parts, basing her recipes on this division. A dish made from stewed salt beef was called Stewed Goose. The same meat, boiled in paste for Sunday, was recommended as "a very nice pudding, known in the bush as Station Jack".

Food was cheap by present day standards. Fat sheep could be bought for 4/6d. each, fat ducks and fowls for 4d. a head — and rum cost 2/3d. per gallon.

But if the prices were low, the food was highly valued, and houses were sometimes burgled for a pound of flour. The penalty for stealing 3d. worth of flour (1½ lb.) was 200 strokes with the lash.

William Howitt writing in 1853.

Candy is dandy, but liquor is quicker — *Nash*

BREAKFAST LUNCH & SUPPER

William Howitt from Ballarat, May 20, 1854
. . . a whole host of shepherds are waiting, watching the result, and, of course, living at digging expenses, which is no trifle, especially when flour is from 12L. to 20L. a bag; meat 1s. a pound; onions, and potatoes 1s. 6d. per pound; brandy 1L. per bottle, and beer 10s. Many, having shepherded for six months, there are nine chances to one that the lead may make a bend, and they are off to shephered six months more, and quite as likely six months after that; and, finally, to put down a hole of one hundred and sixty feet, through sixty feet of water, and miss the prize by a few feet!

Some of the diggers in Eureka Gully, and other parts of the field, told me that they expected to get, when down, 1500L. a man, others 500L., and others 300L. — if they hit the lead! And I was assured here, too, that there was much destitution on the field. Still, Ballarat is one of those fields which displays an active and busy air, very different to Bendigo, Castlemaine, or the Ovens; and new ground is always breaking up.

Oats at 1L. 15s. and 2L. a bushel, and hay at from 60L. to 160L. a ton, as the carriage happens to be, are dreadful diminishers of profit.

CORNISH PASTY

1 lb. fillet of hogget, 2 leeks or medium-sized onions, ½ lb. skirt steak, 3 large potatoes, 1 large swede turnip, salt and pepper, 3 white turnips, a piece of young trombone about 1 inch thick.

For Pastry — 3 cups of plain Flour, 2 cups good Dripping, 1 cup Self-raising Flour, a pinch of Salt, juice of one lemon put into a cup, then water added to make 1 cup of liquid.

Mix in the usual manner and set aside. Cut meat into small pieces (do not mince it), peel and chip the turnips, potatoes and trombone (do not mince or dice) peel onions or leeks and chop finely. Mix meat and vegetables, then season well with pepper and salt, remembering that the use of sufficient salt ensures the flavour of a good pasty. With the palms of both hands, roll pastry on the board until it is smooth and not sticky. Cut into portions and with the rolling pin roll into rounds approximately 7 inches in diameter, and about one-eighth in thickness. In the centre of the round pieces place 6 to 7 heaping tablespoons of pasty filling. Brush edges with milk and bring pastry up to join just off centre top. Allow one quarter of an inch and trim off surplus pastry, particularly from the corners. Crimp, then make a small slit in the top of the pasty and into this put one teaspoon of melted butter. Brush pasty with milk and place on a lightly floured hot slide.

Bake in a hot oven for 45 minutes.

SCOTCH SCRAPPLE

1 cup oatmeal. ½ teaspoon salt.
1¼ cups water. ½ cup pork sausage meat

Add the oatmeal to the boiling, salted water. Cook for 20 minutes or until thick, stirring constantly to prevent sticking.

Stir in the crumbled sausage meat and mix thoroughly. Season to taste. Pour into a narrow dish and leave overnight. Cut into slices, dip the slices in flour and fry in a little fat until brown both sides. Served with fried tomatoes.

SCOTS PORRIDGE

2 pints cold water
2 teaspoons salt or to taste
½lb. coarse oatmeal

Combine water and salt in a medium saucepan. When almost boiling sprinkle in oatmeal, stirring continuously. Simmer 10-15 minutes. Cover and set aside in a warm place 4-5 hours or overnight if possible. Gently re-heat and serve with cream or milk.

Manners were often judged by the way porridge was eaten. It was considered bad manners to have sugar with porridge. Good manners dictated that one stood while eating porridge, or walked about the room with bowl in one hand and spoon in the other. Some ate their porridge with salt, and others with a large dollop of butter.

BUTTERMILK PORRIDGE

1 pint buttermilk
1 tablespoon plain flour
1 tablespoon sugar
Nob of butter
¾ cup rolled oats
1 tablespoon dark treacle

Melt butter in saucepan, add flour. Add buttermilk by half cupfuls, stirring all the time as when making white sauce. Add rolled oats and bring to the boil.

Keep stirring with a wooden spoon until mixture has boiled for two minutes. Let it cool down for a few minutes and stir in the sugar and treacle. Delicious in winter when still hot and in summer served icy cold.

CHEESE SOUFFLE

Melt butter in pan, add 1 oz. flour. Cook a moment, then add ¼ pint milk gradually. Cook well. Away from fire mix in 2 beaten egg yolks. Season highly with salt, pepper and cayenne. When cooler, add 4 ozs. grated cheese gently, first having beaten in tablespoon of egg white to soften mixture a little. Put in mould (greased) and bake ½ hour in hot oven. Tie greased paper higher than mould. Remove before serving. Eat immediately.

CHEESE STRATA

2 eggs
¼ lb. cheese
6 slices day-old bread
1¼ cups milk
¼ teaspoon dry mustard
1 dessertspoon minced onion
½ teaspoon salt
Pinch cayenne pepper

Remove the crusts from the bread and arrange three of the slices in a greased ovenproof dish. Cut the cheese into thin slices and arrange on the bread. Add remaining bread.

Beat the eggs and mix in the salt, pepper, mustard, milk and chopped onion. Pour over the bread in the dish and stand aside for 1 hour. Bake in a moderate oven for 50 minutes or until puffed and brown. Serve at once.

CHEESE PIES

Pastry:
8 ozs. (2 cups) plain flour
Pinch cayenne pepper
4 ozs. (4 tablespoons) butter
4 ozs. (½ cup) grated cheese
1 egg yolk
1 tablespoon lemon juice
1 tablespoon water

Sift flour and cayenne, rub butter into flour. Stir in cheese. Mix egg yolk, lemon juice and water together and mix with flour to form a firm dough. Place on floured board, roll out to 1/8 inch thickness. Using cutter, cut rounds to line individual pie tins and cut rounds for lids slightly smaller.

Filling:
1 small onion finely chopped
6 ozs. finely grated cheese
1 tablespoon milk
1 teaspoon butter
1 egg white

Finely chop onion and add to cheese, milk, butter and egg white. Mix together and place a teaspoon of mixture in each pie shell. Moisten rim of pie, cover with a lid and press edge together with fork. Make a small slit with a knife in the top, glaze with milk and bake in hot oven for 10-15 minutes.

CHEESE-TOPPED SCONE RING

8 ozs. S.R. Flour
¾-1 cup milk
½ teaspoon salt
1 tablespoon butter

For topping: 2 ozs. grated mature cheese
1 tablespoon melted butter

Sift the flour and salt together, rub in the butter and add sufficient milk to make into a soft dough. Turn on to a floured board and knead slightly. Roll out to ½ in. thickness and cut into rounds with a 2 in. cutter. Pack into a well-greased ring or sandwich tin, each scone overlapping the other by half. Pour the melted butter over the scones and sprinkle thickly with the grated cheese. Bake in a very hot oven for 15 minutes.

PARCELS

¾ lb. minced steak
4 tomatoes
Silver beet leaves
2 tablespoons rice
1 onion
Salt and Pepper

Cook rice and when cool mix with minced steak seasoned with salt and pepper. Cut white stems of silver beet leaves into small pieces and put into saucepan with chopped onion and tomato wedges seasoned with salt and a tablespoon of sugar.

Bring to boil. Pour boiling water over silver beet leaves to soften. Take a tablespoon of meat mixture and wrap in each leaf. Place in saucepan on top of tomato mixture and cook gently for about an hour.

MIXUM GATHERUM PIE

Put the remains of "this" with "those"; add "these" and "that". Mix all well together, moisten with a little of "that" (or milk will do if you haven't any of "that"). Season to taste. Put into pie dish, sprinkle with breadcrumbs, dot with butter and bake till nicely browned.

EGG AND HAM CAKES

8 ozs. ham
8 ozs. mashed potatoes
1 tablespoon chopped parsley
1 egg yolk
4 rashers bacon — rindless
4 eggs

Finely dice the ham. Mix together the mashed potato, ham and parsley, and add one egg yolk to bind. Divide the mixture into four. Shape into round flat cakes about one inch deep.

Wrap a rasher of bacon around each cake; fix with a toothpick. Place in an ovenproof dish and bake in a moderate oven — for 20 to 25 minutes. Poach the remaining eggs and serve on top of the ham cakes.

SHERRIED EGGS

Fry four slices of bread and keep hot. Grate the yellow rind from an orange and put aside. Break 6 eggs into a bowl, beat them, add just one tablespoon of sherry, beat again, add 3 level tablespoons of tomato, salt and a little cayenne pepper, and beat once more. Melt a good big egg of butter in your pan and scramble the eggs therein. Take from the stove while one third is still liquid, but continue to stir until set. Put on fried bread. Sprinkle well with grated orange peel. Serve at once.

CHEESE BREAD SOUFFLE

3 eggs
1 cup milk
3ozs. grated cheese
2ozs. butter
2 tablespoons breadcrumbs
salt to taste

Boil milk and pour over bread, cheese and butter. When cool, add beaten yolks of eggs and just before cooking fold in stiffly beaten whites. Bake souffle standing in dish of water for 30 to 40 minutes in moderate oven. One teaspoon of made mustard may be added if liked.

EGG PUFFS

Halve some hard-boiled eggs lengthwise. Dip them in melted butter on a plate, and sprinkle them with a mixture of finely chopped parsley, a little lemon thyme, grated lemon rind, a few chopped capers, a pinch of nutmeg, pepper and salt. Then roll out some scraps of pastry very thinly and cut out two ovals for each egg. Place one under and one over each piece, and pinch the edges together. Brush the puffs over with a little milk or beaten egg, and sprinkle them with finely grated cheese. Bake in a good oven until brown and crisp. These are good for high tea.

SCRAMBLED EGGS

. . . with asparagus tips. Mix with bouillon instead of milk.

DEVILLED SANDWICH BAKE

Make 4 sandwiches with ham and cheese. Place in greased tin.

Beat 3 eggs with — 2 cups of milk, salt, pepper, 1 teaspoon mustard, 2 teaspoons minced onion.

Pour over sandwiches. Allow to stand 1 hour. Bake in moderate oven until puffed and brown.

SCOTCH EGGS

Hard boiled eggs, shelled and coated with sausage meat, which is then crumbed and deep fried.

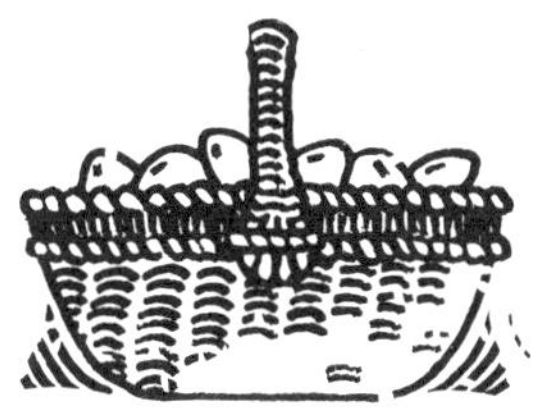

Does any man of common sense
Think ham and eggs give God offence?
Or that a herring has a charm
The Almighty's anger to disarm?
Wrapped in His majesty divine,
D'you think He cares on what we dine?
Dean Swift

BACON ROLLS

6 bacon rashers
1 lb. sausage mince
1½ level teaspoons mixed herbs
3 dessertspoons milk
pinch nutmeg
4 level teaspoons chopped parsley
1 medium onion, finely chopped
salt and pepper

Mix ingredients and add sufficient of the milk to moisten. Mould into twelve patties and wrap in a half rasher of bacon fastened with a toothpick. Place in a greased Swiss roll tin (or shallow dish) and bake in moderate oven ¾ to an hour. Serve with mashed potatoes and buttered peas.

UPSIDE-DOWN PIE

Vegetable and Bacon Topping:

½ lb. bacon rashers
1 cup grated cheese
3 cups cooked, drained and chopped spinach
1 cup thick white sauce
1 small onion (grated)
2 large tomatoes
Salt and pepper to taste
Finely chopped parsley
¾ cup soft breadcrumbs

Dough Base:

2 cups S.R. flour
½ cup grated cheese
Pinch salt
¼ teaspoon mustard
½ cup tomato puree
1 egg
1 oz. butter

Remove rind from rashers, cut them in half; fry in pan 1 or 2 minutes or just until fat is lightly transparent. Grease well an 8 in. square or oblong casserole. Arrange tomato slices on base, cover with overlapping slices of bacon. Combine spinach, parsley, cheese, white sauce, onion, breadcrumbs, salt and pepper, spread over bacon. Sift flour with salt and mustard, rub in butter, add cheese, moisten with tomato juice and beaten egg. Roll or pat out gently on lightly floured board to shape of casserole. Lift on top of spinach mixture. Bake in hot oven approximately 20 minutes or until well risen and brown. Let stand 5 minutes, then carefully turn out upside down on serving plate.

LUNCHEON DISH

3 ozs. melted butter
1 pint milk
12 slices day-old bread
4 ozs. semi-matured cheddar cheese, sliced
4 eggs
½ teaspoon salt
pinch pepper
1 teaspoon curry powder (optional)

Grease 2½ to 3 pint fireproof dish with butter. Cut bread into strips 1 to 1½ inches wide, after removing crusts. Brush one side with melted butter. Arrange slices on bottom and around sides of dish, placing buttered side to dish. Add layer of cheese slices, then more bread with buttered side towards the top. Beat eggs, add salt, pepper, curry and milk. Mix well and pour over bread and cheese. Stand one hour before baking for 45-50 minutes.

GRACE

For what we are about to receive, Lord make us truly thankful — Amen.

CHEESE FONDUE

3 ozs. white bread cut in small cubes
1 oz. margarine or butter, melted
2 eggs
¾ pint of milk
4 ozs. grated cheese
1 level teaspoon salt

Grease an ovenproof dish. Arrange in it alternate layers of bread cubes and grated cheese. Beat the eggs, add to them the milk, melted butter and seasoning. Pour into the dish. Leave to soak for 15 minutes. Put the dish in a baking tin with boiling water and bake in a moderate oven for 30 to 40 minutes till set. Serve at once.

GRUEL FOR INVALIDS

Mix 2 tablespoonsful of oatmeal very smooth in a little water or milk, making gradually to three quarters of a pint; add a little lemon peel, and half a blade of mace; set it over the fire for a quarter of an hour, stirring constantly. Strain it, add sugar to taste and a little white wine.

DEVILLED BISCUIT

Dip a captain's biscuit into boiling water, butter it well, spread over it ready made mustard, cayenne pepper, a good deal of black pepper and salt. Put it in the oven or on a gridiron. Bake or grill till brown. A relish with wine.

SCOTCH WOODCOCK

Three to four slices of bread, nine or ten anchovies, yolks of four eggs, half a pint of cream. Take three or four slices of bread cut in a pyramid form, toasted and buttered well on both sides, nine or ten anchovies washed, scraped and chopped fine (salt anchovies from a barrel, well soaked, not tinned anchovies), and put them between the slices of toasted bread. Have ready the yolks of four eggs, well beaten, half a pint of cream, which set over the fire to thicken but not to boil (stirring all the while), then pour it over the toast and send it to table as hot as possible.

Be not a collector of books without reading them

SAVOURY PANCAKES

4 ozs. plain flour   Salt   1 Egg
Approximately ½ pint Milk

Sieve into a basin the flour and coffee-spoonful of salt. Make a well in the centre and break in the egg. Add a little milk and water and mix with egg, using wooden spoon, gradually drawing in the flour and adding more milk. Once all the flour is stirred in, start beating, still adding more milk until batter is the consistency of fairly thin cream. Give a final good beating and leave it stand for an hour.

Butter or oil a hot frying pan before cooking each pancake. A 7 inch pan will take about 2 tablespoons of batter. Tilt the pan quickly as soon as the batter is in so that it covers all of it. Be sure to keep pancakes hot. As each is done, spread some of the filling down the centre and roll it up and place in hot dish. When all pancakes are filled, melt the rest of the butter. Pour over the pancakes. Sprinkle with grated cheese. Put in hot oven for 10 minutes to melt the cheese and brown it slightly.

SAVOURY PANCAKE FILLING

½ coffee cup of red wine
1 chicken's liver
1 bacon rasher
2 ozs. butter
½ coffee cup of stock
¼ pound ox kidney or 2 of lamb
1 shallot
1 oz. grated cheese

YORKSHIRE BUCK

1lb sharp Cheddar-type cheeese, shredded
1 tablespoon heavy cream
½ cup beer or ale
2 eggs slightly beaten
½ teaspoon salt
1 teaspoon sweet paprika
1 teaspoon Worcestershire sauce
Freshly ground pepper

Stir the cheese, cream, and beer over direct heat until the cheese is melted. Add the seasonings.

Add the eggs, beating constantly with a wire whisk until the mixture is thick and creamy. Serve over thin toast. In Yorkshire each serving is crowned with a poached egg.

BATTER BALLOONS

1 cup boiling water   1 tablespoon butter
1 cup flour   3 eggs

Place over fire saucepan containing water and add butter. Beat in flour and work till smooth and mixture leaves the sides of saucepan. Remove from heat and add eggs, beating in one at a time. Stand till cool. When ready to cook drop dessertspoonful at a time into hot fat. An average frying pan will cook about five at a time. Batter will puff into hollow balls and when ready will turn themselves over in the fat. Serve dredged with castor sugar and lemon. By adding chopped bacon and tomato and a pinch of salt these make a good breakfast dish.

MARROW TOAST

(A favourite breakfast of Queen Victoria)

Procure a marrow bone or get the butcher to chop one for you. Cut the marrow into small pieces the size of a filbert, and just parboil them in the boiling water with a little salt for a minute. The marrow must be drained instantly by standing it in a sieve. Season it with a little chopped parsley, pepper, and salt; squeeze a little lemon juice over it and the merest suspicion of chopped shallot. Toss lightly together and spread out on a square of hot, crisp, unbuttered toast. Serve immediately.

POACHED EGG STACK

¾ large white uncut loaf
1 teaspoon Worcestershire sauce
1½ tablespoons lemon juice
6 ozs. grated cheddar cheese
1 apple cored and sliced in rings
6 poached eggs

Slice the loaf into 1 inch thick slices and cut a 3 inch circle from each. Toast on both sides and sprinkle with cheese mixed with Worcestershire sauce. Grill for 1-2 minutes. Place ring of apple on top, dipped in lemon juice. Have the poached eggs ready, and on top of each apple ring. Serve hot.

SORREL AND EGGS

Take a quantity of sorrel, picked clean and washed, boil it with water and a little salt; and when it is cooked enough, drain it and butter it, and put in a little vinegar and sugar, then garnish it with eggs boiled hard and raisins.

That old English saying: After dinner sit a while, and after supper walk a mile.
Thomas Cogan

MEDIAEVAL KIDNEYS

2 veal kidneys
2 tablespoons chives or spring onions
2 tablespoons Madeira
6 bread rolls
2 tablespoons chopped parsley
2 egg yolks
6 dessertspoons butter
Salt and Pepper

Poach kidneys in salted water for 15 minutes, drain and chop into very small pieces. Slice the top crust off the rolls and scoop out the bread in the centre. Use half of this to mix with kidneys, parsley, chives, egg yolks and Madeira, salt and pepper. Butter the inside of the rolls, fill with mixture and bake in a hot oven for 20 minutes.

FRENCH BREAD

Beat an egg with 2 tablespoons milk, pepper and salt. Dip stale bread into the mixture. Fry both sides in a small amount of butter or dripping.

HUNTERS' DISH

2½ lb. potatoes (cooked)
¾ lb. cooked meat — ½ pint vegetable stock
3 ozs. onion — 1½ ozs. butter
½ lb. sour apples — Seasoning

Slice onions and apples, and fry lightly in fat. Slice cooked meat and potatoes. Place alternate layers of meat, potatoes, onion and apples in dish. Pour over stock, add a few pats of butter.

Bake in a moderate oven for 20 minutes.

BACON MUFFINS

½ pint milk 3 tablespoons melted bacon fat
2 rashers bacon salt to taste 1 egg
1½ dessertspoons sugar 2 cups plain flour
¼ teaspoon dry mustard
1½ teaspoons baking powder

Chop bacon finely and fry until softened. Drain well.

Beat egg, stir in milk and melted bacon fat. Mix together dry ingredients, make a well in the centre and add the liquid. Stir vigorously until flour is just moistened (batter should be lumpy). Stir in the bacon. Put heaped teaspoonful into greased muffin tins (push batter from side of spoon with another spoon).

POTATO AND HAM PIE

3 to 4 medium potatoes (sliced)
1 medium onion (chopped finely)
¼ lb. chopped ham or bacon — grated cheese
butter and milk — salt and pepper

Place a layer of potatoes in a casserole, sprinkle with a little chopped ham and onion, salt and pepper. Then another layer of potatoes, etc., finishing with a layer of potato. Cover with grated cheese, dot with butter and add enough milk to three quarters fill casserole. Bake in moderate oven about 1 hour until potatoes are soft.

HUBBLE BUBBLE

2 cooked potatoes sliced
3 tablespoons left over vegetables
2 tomatoes sliced — 1 large cup mushrooms
1 oz. grated cheese — 1 oz. butter
3 large eggs beaten — salt and pepper

Fry potatoes in butter, add mushrooms, cooked vegetables and tomatoes. Cook until heated through. Pour well seasoned eggs over the mixture and cook until they are set. Sprinkle cheese on top before serving.

FOR HAM PIECES

Mix finely chopped ham with an equivalent quantity of pureed spinach and blend with cream. Spice the mixture with nutmeg, salt and pepper. Take several squares of pastry, butter each one and place about three together. Make parcels of ham and spinach wrapped in the pastry and brown them in the oven.

POTATO BRIDIES

A good dish for Sunday night, potato bridies can be prepared beforehand then fried just before serving. Either cooked meat or cooked, flaked fish can be used for the filling.

You need 2 heaped tablespoonfuls smoothly mashed potatoes, 2 level tablespoons flour, salt and pepper to taste, some cooked minced meat or flaked fish, deep fat for frying.

Make potato paste by kneading the flour into the potatoes, seasoning with salt and pepper, then roll out to about ¼ inch thickness. Cut into rounds. Spread the meat or fish (well seasoned to taste but keeping the mixture dry) over half the round, then fold other half over the filling and pinch together all round. Carefully lower the bridies into smoking hot fat and cook until golden brown. Drain well and serve at once.

SCOTTISH GRACE BEFORE MEALS

Oh Lord, who blessed the loaves and fishes,
Look doon upon these twa bit dishes,
And though the taties be but sma',
Lord, mak 'em plenty for us a';
But if our stomachs they do fill,
'Twill be anither miracle.

WELSH RAREBIT

Grate about ½ lb. sharp cheese, place in pan on a medium fire, and stir. When it begins to melt, season highly with salt and pepper and cayenne pepper. Add ½ glass of ale and the yolk of egg well beaten, and 1 stiffly beaten egg white. Stir continuously until mixture begins to thicken. Add 1 heaped teaspoon of made mustard. Pour at once on to hot toast. Serve on very hot plates.

An egg beaten into the above becomes CHEESE MUFF.

SUPPER DISH

2 slices of toast (buttered), salt, pepper, 4 ozs. grated cheese, ¾ pint milk, 2-3 eggs.

Make a custard mixture with eggs, milk, 3 ozs. of the cheese, salt and pepper. Line a pie dish with sliced toast. Pour in mixture and sprinkle the rest of the cheese on top. Cook for about an hour in a moderate oven.

Chopped lean bacon and chopped parsley may be added if desired.

SINCE the Sabbath has to be observed very strictly, religious Jews are not allowed to light the fire or cook on that day. This dish has since time immemorial been invented as a typical Sabbath meal, which was prepared on the Friday and left in the oven till the following day.

THE CHOLENT (Jewish Bean Casserole)

1½ lb. dried beans	1 large onion
2 cloves garlic	3 tablspoons chicken fat
Salt	
10 Peppercorns	1 bayleaf
6-8 eggs	2 tablespoon plain flour

1 pint stock (or water — liquid off a smoked ox tongue)

Smoked beef, or tongue or smoked goose, or 2 lb. giblets.

Soak the dried beans overnight. Drain, mix in the flour, salt and carefully dilute with the stock or water. Add onion, garlic, peppercorns, bayleaf, and the whole uncooked eggs. Add also the chicken fat.

This dish owes its reputation as a delicacy to the smoked flavor it acquires from the smoked beef or goose. The meat cooks in with the beans and is eaten together — the tongue sliced and replaced in the casserole, the goose cut up. It is very nice made with fresh goose or duck.

Bring casserole to the boil on top of the stove, cover with lid tightly, place in low oven for about six hours.

JEWISH POTATO PANCAKES

Wash and peel 4 or more potatoes. Grate them (pour off juice). Mix with grated onion, 3-4 tablespoons flour, teaspoon salt, ½ teaspoon pepper, 2 beaten eggs. Fry tablespoonful of batter in chicken fat or butter, until well browned on both sides. Makes 8-12. Apple sauce adds to the serving.

CHEESE-SPINACH SOUFFLE

Mix 1 tablespoon of melted butter, one cup of spinach puree and two tablespoons grated parmesan cheese.

Bachamel: Two tablespoons butter, two tablespoons flour, ½ pint hot milk, pinch of salt, five egg yolks, six egg whites. Melt butter and add flour to make a paste. Add salt and hot milk in small quantities so sauce remains smooth. Stir constantly. Bring to boil and allow to simmer for seven minutes, allowing the flour to cook.

Add spinach mixture and beat with the egg yolks. Beat the egg whites until stiff but not dry. Fold into the mixture. Have a buttered souffle dish ready. Pour in the mixture and bake in a moderate oven for 35 to 45 minutes in a pan of hot water.

SAVORY CHEESE CUSTARD

6 eggs	6 tablespoons milk
¾ teaspoon salt	1 oz. butter

6 ozs. grated cheddar cheese
½ cup finely chopped shallots
½ cup finely diced ham
parsley garnish

Whisk the eggs lightly together with the milk and salt. Heat the butter in a heavy base frying pan and pour in the egg mixture. Sprinkle over the cheese, then top with the diced ham and shallots.

Cover the pan with a lid and put over a moderate flame for eight to ten minutes, or until the custard is firm, well risen and golden brown underneath. Serve immediately, cut into wedges. Garnish with parsley. 6 to 8 servings.

An alternative — Line baking dish with toasted buttered fingers of toast. Pour in custard and grate cheese on top. The toast floats to the top and forms a golden crust.

GRACE OF THE POOR

Heavenly Father bless us,
And keep us all alive;
There's ten of us for dinner
And not enough for five.

Anon.

TOAD-IN-THE-HOLE

6 ozs. flour, 1 pint of milk, 3 eggs, batter, a few slices of cold mutton, pepper and salt to taste, 2 kidneys.

Make a smooth batter of flour, milk, and eggs, in the above proportions; butter a baking-dish, and pour in the batter. Into this, place a few slices of cold mutton, previously well-seasoned, and the kidneys, which should be cut into rather small pieces; bake about 1 hour, or rather longer, and send it to table in the dish it was baked in. Oysters or mushrooms may be substituted for the kidneys, and will be found exceedingly good.

FRITTERS

2 heaped tablespoons plain flour with pepper and salt to taste. Mix with cold water to consistency of cream. Add and mix yolk of one egg, then 1 tablespoon melted butter. Let it stand — the longer the better — just before using, fold in beaten white of egg. Finally add chopped meat, ham or whatever you wish. Use fat or butter in which to fry.

CHICKEN LIVERS WITH RAISINS

1 lb. fresh chicken (or calf's) livers
4 tablespoons butter   Plain flour
Salt   Pepper
1 small glass sweet sherry (or better: Madeira)
3 tablespoons brandy
2 cups fresh muscatel or any grapes in season
Croutons of fried bread
½ cup chicken stock

Clean livers, but leave them whole (if using calf's liver, cut into thin medallions). Fry pieces of bread in butter and keep warm. Roll liver in flour, and fry in butter until crisp. Pour on the brandy and ignite. Transfer liver to warm platters and place on top of the fried bread. Meanwhile, add to the pan where livers were cooked, the grapes, the sweet sherry or Madeira, seasoning and the stock. Let it boil for five minutes till the sauce reduces. Pour this sauce over the livers and serve.

KIDNEYS IN WHITE WINE

This is a delicious luncheon dish.

Ingredients: The number of lamb kidneys required — allow two for each person. 1 glass of white wine, butter, a little flour, 1 bayleaf, salt, pepper.

Method: Remove the fat and skin from the kidneys, and cut in very thin slices. Melt the butter in a saute pan, and when very hot, put in the sliced kidneys, the bayleaf, and season with salt and pepper. Cook for a few minutes on a brisk fire, shaking the pan and turning the kidneys with a spoon. When nearly done (they should not take more than 8 to 10 minutes in all) sprinkle with a little flour, stir it in well, then remove the pan from the fire, and add the white wine. Replace on the fire, and stir a few minutes longer. Serve very hot.

APPLE AND ONION PIE

This is a good recipe to serve for Sunday night supper round the fire and was a popular "high tea" dish in Devon.

You need potatoes, apples and onions, salt, pepper, mace and nutmeg, butter, cider, and puff pastry. Slice raw, peeled potatoes and put a layer in the bottom of a pie dish, cover with a layer of sliced onion, season well and cover with sliced, peeled apples. Continue these layers, seasoning the onion layer well, until the dish is full. Dot the top layer liberally with butter and add two or three tablespoons of cider. Cover with pastry, crimping down well round the edge of the dish. Bake in a moderate oven for about one hour and a half.

PIGS IN BLANKETS

For Scones: Mix 1 lb. of cooked mashed potato and 8 ozs. self-raising flour to a stiff dough. Roll out on a floured board to ¼" thick. Cut into triangles and cook on both sides on a hot plate until light brown.

Fold each scone around a cooked sausage and fix with a toothpick. Serve these hot.

CASSEROLE OF CHICKEN LIVERS

Make a sauce by sauteeing ½ cup of chopped chicken livers with ½ cup of chopped shallots, and 1 cup of mushrooms, in ¼ lb. butter. Add salt, pepper, 1 cup of beef consomme and ½ cup of red wine. Thicken with 1 tablespoon of flour, stirring constantly until the sauce is smooth.

Have buttered casserole ready and pour in a layer of sauce, now break in 2 eggs for each person, add a light coating of sauce, and bake until the eggs are just set. Top with a little more sauce, a garland of parsley and serve with croutons or rusks.

Have a place for everything — and everything in its place.

SOUPS

"How sad it is to sit and pine,
The long half-hour before we dine!
But lo! the dinner now appears —
The object of our hopes and fears,
The end of all our pain!"

GIBLET SOUP

To each full set of duck or goose giblets (including head, neck, feet, wing-tips) allow 1 large carrot, small head of celery, 2 leeks, ½ lb. apples, ¼ lb. prunes, 1 oz. shortening, 2 ozs. flour, water, vinegar, parsley, sugar.

Clean giblets well, split heads and remove eyes and brains. Cut neck into three, remove windpipe and gullet. Cut each wing into two, wash heart, chop off claws and remove skin from the feet. Place cleaned pieces in cold salted water and bring to boil, skimming occasionally. Add flavourings such as a little parsley, top of leeks, celery and carrot. Simmer for 3 hours, then strain or sieve, leaving just a little liquid with the giblets. Cook sliced apples and prunes in small separate quantity of water until soft. Combine flour and shortening, add to sieved soup with 1 cup apple and prune liquor. Slice carrot, celery stalks and leeks, add to giblets and cook 10 minutes. Spoon in the apples and prunes with a little vinegar and sugar, then the sieved mixture. Serve hot.

If preferred, the sieved soup can be served as a separate dish to the giblet mixture.

MULLIGATAWNY SOUP

This recipe dates back to 1809.

Take four onions, sliced small, and a head of garlic. Fry them a light brown, then put them in a pan with the meat (fowl or any white meat is best). Three spoonfuls of curry powder and two of flour mixed together, likewise a spoonful of lemon juice and cayenne pepper to your taste. Pour over it a pint of boiling water and let it simmer slowly for a short time, then add a sufficient quantity of broth made without vegetables to make a tureen of Mulligatawny. The ingredients must then stew together an hour. To be served with a dish of rice (if you can get it) as for curry.

BARLEY BROTH — 1809 recipe

Put a quantity of barley with onions, carrots, turnips, and a sprinkling of salt and pepper, into a pot, with a quantity of water equal to the quantity of broth required, sufficient to boil a neck of mutton, which should be put into it, and let the whole boil slowly for five or six hours. During part of the time the mutton should be taken out, otherwise it will be overboiled. In place of a neck, a flap of mutton may be used, and grilled after it is boiled.

POTATO SOUP

1½ cups diced peeled potatoes
1 tablespoon coarsely grated onion
1 rounded teaspoon salt — pinch pepper
1½ level tablespoons butter
1 rounded tablespoon flour — 1½ cups milk
grated cheese and sippets
1½ cups hot water

Brown onion in butter in the cooker. Add flour and blend well. Add potatoes, salt, pepper and water. Cover with lid. Cook 15 minutes. Transfer to saucepan to be reheated with milk just before serving, topped with grated cheese and sprinkled with sippets.

SCOTCH BROTH

1½-2lbs. lean beef — 2 quarts water
salt and pepper — 1 medium carrot
2 leeks — 1½ oz. pearl barley
1 dessertspoon chopped parsley
2 oz. peas, turnip and onion

Put the meat in the pan with the water and seasoning, bring slowly to the boil and simmer gently for 1½ hours. Add the diced vegetables and barley. (To prevent barley from clouding soup, blanch it by placing it in cold water, bringing to the boil and straining). Simmer until the vegetables and barley are cooked — about 1 hour. Serve the meat separately on a dish with a little broth. Put the parsley in a tureen and pour the broth over it.

NETTLE BROTH

Chicken stock — barley
nettles — pepper and salt

Gather nettles and wash well and chop very finely. Have some good stock in which you have cooked a sufficient quantity of pearl barley. Add chopped nettles, simmer till tender and season to taste.

MINER'S BROTH

1 sheep's head — 3 quarts water
1 large carrot — 1 turnip
2 onions — 2 sticks celery
4 sage leaves — Pepper
½ cup rice or barley
2 tablespoons oat meal
1 dessertspoon salt

Wash head in cold, salted water. Remove nose bone, lay head in water to soak for 1 hour. Remove brains and soak separately. Put head, water and salt in pan, bring slowly to boil. Peel vegetables and cut into dice. When liquid boils, remove scum, add vegetables, pepper and rice or barley, simmer 3 hours. When soup has simmered for 2 hours, mix oat meal with a little cold water and add.

Tie brains and sage leaves in muslin and add. Remove head and brains, serve soup in a hot tureen. Cut meat off head, skin and split tongue, arrange on a hot dish. Chop brains, place on tongue and serve with white sauce.

KANGAROO TAIL SOUP

1 kangaroo tail — 2 pounds gravy beef
pepper and salt — 2 quarts water
2 carrots — 2 turnips
6 cloves — 1 small lemon
1 glass port wine

Chop the tail in small pieces. Put in deep saucepan with the beef cut small and with salt and pepper to season. Bring to boil and simmer two hours. Then strain. Put soup back in pan. Pick out the smaller pieces of the tail and add to the soup with the finely cut carrots and turnips, the pounded cloves and ginger, the juice of half the lemon and the wine. Cook until vegetables are tender. Serve with toast sippets.

MUSHROOM AND KIDNEY SOUP

1 ox kidney — ½ lb. mushrooms
2 quarts stock — 1 oz. dripping
1 oz. flour — 1 large onion
1 teaspoon each of salt, mustard and sugar,
a sprinkle of pepper — 1 tablespoon rice

Soak the kidney in warm salted water for 30 minutes. Wash the mushrooms (if necessary), peel them and cut into pieces, chop the stalks finely. Cut the kidney into small pieces, removing the hard core and fat. Peel and chop the onion. Heat the fat in a big saucepan and fry the onion and kidney and mushrooms for five minutes, turning to cook evenly. Push to one side and stir in the flour and seasonings, then stir in half the stock and stir until it boils. Cover and simmer gently for ¾ hour, then add the well washed rice and remainder of stock. Continue to simmer gently for 12 to 15 minutes more or until rice is tender. Skim if necessary and serve.

MOCK TURTLE SOUP

Put a cod's head in cold water, boil for 5 minutes. Take out and allow to cool, and take off the gelatinous part and the meat. Put the bones back into the saucepan with two quarts of fish stock or water, and let boil until the skin and gelatine left on them is dissolved. Strain the stock and take off the fat, add the pieces of gelatine and meat, thicken with one ounce and a half of flour, and lastly, add a gill of sherry and flavor to taste. Serve with egg-balls made thus: Mix together the yolks of two hard-boiled eggs and one raw yolk, a tablespoon each of flour and minced parsley, a little pepper, salt and nutmeg. Roll into tiny balls. Drop into fast boiling water and cook for a few minutes, then add to the soup.

VEGETABLE SOUP

Cut up about a pound of green French Beans, 3 or 4 Potatoes, 2 Tomatoes skinned. Pour over these vegetables 2 quarts of water, add salt and pepper, and cook all together on a moderate fire until nearly done. Just before serving the soup, crush 2 cloves of garlic in a wooden mortar with a wooden pestle. Add to it drop by drop, stirring as for mayonnaise, 4 tablespoons of oil. Keep stirring until the mixture forms a thin paste, then dilute with a cupful of soup, stirring and adding it little by little.

Pour this mixture into the soup proper. In the bottom of the tureen put 2 tablespoons of grated cheese. Pour soup over it, stir briskly, and serve.

BEER SOUP

1 bottle of beer — 4 egg yolks
4 ozs. sugar — 1 oz. butter

Mix beer with yolks and sugar in a jug. Pour into saucepan and beat with rotary whisk until it boils. Remove from heat at boiling point, add butter and serve with a garnish of parsley and paprika.

OX-TAIL SOUP

2 ox-tails, 2 slices of ham, 1 oz. of butter, 2 carrots, 2 turnips, 3 onions, 1 leek, 1 head of celery, 1 bunch of savoury herbs, 1 bayleaf, 12 whole peppercorns, 4 cloves, a tablespoonful of salt, ½ glass of port wine, 2 tablespoonsful of ketchup, 3 quarts of water.

Cut up the tails, separating them at the joints; wash them, and put them in a stewpan with the butter. Cut the vegetables in slices, and add them, with the peppercorns and herbs. Put in ½ pint of water, and stir it over a sharp fire till the juices are drawn. Fill up the stewpan with water, and, when boiling, add the salt. Skim well, and simmer very gently for 4 hours, or until the tails are tender. Take them out, skim and strain the soup, thicken with flour, and flavour with the ketchup and port wine. Put back the tails, simmer for 5 minutes, and serve.

CLEAR OX-TAIL SOUP

For a moderate sized tureen a couple of tails will suffice; but if you are about to entertain, let me recommend the same number to be used. Joint them and soak them in lukewarm water. Chop up a couple of Spanish brown onions, put these in a pot with half a drachm of cayenne pepper and the same quantity of allspice. Add the tails and pour in cold water until meat is covered; skim constantly as water boils. When scum has ceased to rise, cover pot close and simmer 2 hours. Strain liquor through a sieve, add 2 tablespoonsful of mushroom ketchup, a couple of glasses of sherry, season with salt to your taste, return meat to the soup. Serve with toasted bread.

PEA SOUP

¼ lb. of onions, ¼ lb. of carrots, 2 oz. of celery, ¾ lb. of split peas, a little mint shred fine; 1 tablespoon of coarse brown sugar, salt and pepper to taste, 4 quarts of water, or liquor in which a joint of meat has been boiled, or a long marrow bone, with herbs, mace, thyme, marjoram and sage.

Fry the vegetables for 10 minutes in a little butter or dripping, previously cutting them up in small pieces; pour the water on them, and when boiling add the peas. Let them simmer for nearly 3 hours, or until the peas are thoroughly done. Add the sugar, seasoning, and mint; boil for ¼ of an hour, and serve.

RICH VEGETABLE SOUP

Broad beans, carrots, celeriac, Jerusalem artichokes, spinach, turnips, swedes, can all be used to make soup in the following way.

Rub about 4 ozs. of the cooked vegetable through a fine wire sieve, also a very little cooked onion or shallot. Allow not more than one-eighth onion or the flavour will be spoilt. Reheat the mixture thinned with just a little milk and add a tablespoon of butter. When almost but not quite boiling add the yolk of an egg, a little butter, some finely chopped parsley and seasoning to taste. The soup must not boil after the egg has been added or it will curdle. If too thick add a little milk.

BARLEY CREAM SOUP

1 large teacup pearl barley

1 large onion	¾ pint milk
2 ozs. butter	3 pints white stock
2 egg yolks	½ blade mace
Pepper and salt	1 dessertspoon sugar

Wash barley and put in saucepan with enough cold water to cover it. Bring to the boil. Strain. Wash well in cold water. Put back in saucepan with peeled onion, mace and stock. Boil and simmer for three hours. Rub through sieve. Heat ½ pint milk and butter. Season with salt and pepper and sugar. Beat egg yolks with ¼ pint milk and stir into soup, which must be nearly boiling. Stir at side of fire for 2 minutes. Do not boil.

1. PUMPKIN SOUP

1 lb. pumpkin. Peel and cut, then cook in 2 pints water and lemon rind until tender, with 4 cloves and cinnamon stick.

Remove cinnamon, cloves and rind and sieve pumpkin. Brown flour in butter and stir in pumpkin and season. Flavour with white wine or wine vinegar.

2. PUMPKIN SOUP

Large lump butter	1 head celery
4 leeks	beef stock
1 onion	½ pint cream

6 medium sized potatoes
½ medium sized pumpkin or squash
Large lump of butter as finish to the soup

Mince the leeks and onion and add to the melted butter, simmer until golden brown; peel and mince the remaining vegetables, add to onion and leeks, cover pot, simmer 10 minutes.

Cover the ingredients with beef stock, add the second if necessary. Boil until the vegetables are tender. Strain through a sieve into a second pot. Bring to the boil, remove from the fire.

Add the butter, cream, taste for seasoning, adding salt and pepper as necessary.

LIVER DUMPLING SOUP

½ lb. minced pork	Slices of bread
½ lb. minced steak	chopped parsley
1 onion	salt and pepper
2 oz. minced calf's liver	
1 small clove garlic	
chicken or beef stock	

It is important all the meats be very finely minced.

Soak bread in water to cover 10 minutes, then squeeze dry. Chop onion, crush garlic. Combine all ingredients (except stock), mix together very well. Form into dumplings about the size of golf balls, using wet hands. Drop into 1 to 1½ quarts hot chicken or beef stock, bring to boil, reduce heat; simmer 5 to 10 minutes. Spoon 1 or two dumplings into each serving plate, ladle over the hot soup. Sprinkle with parsley.

CUCUMBER SOUP

1 large cucumber, a piece of butter the size of a walnut, a little chervil and sorrel cut in large pieces, salt and pepper to taste, the yolks of 2 eggs, 1 gill of cream, 1 quart of medium stock.

Pare the cucumber, quarter it, and take out the seeds; cut it in thin slices, put these on a plate with a little salt, to draw the water from them; drain, and put them in your stewpan, with the butter. When they are warmed through, without being browned, pour the stock on them. Add the sorrell, chervil, and seasoning, and boil for 40 minutes. Mix the well-beaten yolks of the eggs with the cream, which add at the moment of serving.

ARTICHOKE (JERUSALEM) SOUP

3 slices of lean bacon or ham, ½ a head of celery, 1 turnip, 1 onion, 3 ozs. of butter, 4 lbs. of artichokes, 1 pint of boiling milk, or ½ pint of boiling cream, salt and cayenne to taste, 2 lumps of sugar, 2½ quarts of white stock.

Put the bacon and vegetables, which should be cut into thin slices, into the stewpan with the butter. Braise these for ¼ of an hour, keeping them well stirred. Wash and pare the artichokes, and after cutting them into thin slices, add them with a pint of stock, to the other ingredients. When these have gently stewed down to a smooth pulp, put in the remainder of the stock. Stir it well, adding the seasoning, and when it has simmered for five minutes, taking care to skim it well, pass it through a strainer. Now pour it back into the stewpan, let it again simmer five minutes, taking care to skim it well, and stir it to the boiling milk or cream. Serve with small sippets of bread fried in butter.

CREAM OF POTATO SOUP

6 ozs. celery, turnip, onion (total amount 6 ozs.)

10 ozs. potatoes	2 tablespoons flour
1½ pints stock	5 ozs. milk
salt and pepper	2½ ozs. cream
1 oz. butter	12-18 croutons

Prepare the potatoes, celery, turnip and onion and chop roughly. Place in a large saucepan, adding the stock.

Bring to the boil and simmer 45 minutes or until all the vegetables are tender. Then puree the soup through a very fine sieve.

Make a roux with the butter and flour. Do not brown. Add the puree, stir until boiling and simmer 1 minute. Remove from the heat, add the milk, then the cream. Taste, flavour and adjust the consistency if necessary.

Reheat the soup without boiling and serve with the croutons.

Beautiful Soup, so rich and green,
Waiting in a hot tureen!

CREAM OF LETTUCE SOUP

Shred a fairly large head of lettuce as finely as possible. Chop 1 bunch watercress. Cream ¼ cup of butter until it is light and lemon-coloured. Gradually add to the butter, 1 teaspoon finely chopped taragon, and ½ teaspoon dried parsley, and blend well. Heat this herb butter in a soup kettle and add 3 tablespoons finely chopped onion and 2 tablespoons finely chopped green pepper. Cook for 3 or 4 minutes, stirring constantly, and add the chopped watercress and the shredded lettuce. Cook the mixture for 3 or 4 minutes, stirring constantly, add 1 quart beef stock, and cook for 20 minutes. Season to taste with salt and pepper and continue cooking for 15 minutes. Remove the mixture from the fire and stir in 1 cup scalded milk. Taste for seasoning, and just before serving, stir in 2 egg yolks, slightly beaten, mixed with 1 cup heavy cream.

SPINACH SOUP

1 lb. spinach
2 ozs. butter
1 oz. cornflour
1 pint hot milk
salt and pepper
nutmeg
¼ pint cream

Cook the spinach in a little salted water until tender. Rub through a sieve. Melt the butter in a saucepan, add the cornflour and cook gently for one minute. Gradually add the spinach puree and the milk. Season with salt, pepper and nutmeg. Stir in the cream just before serving. Serve with croutons of fried bread.

LEEK AND POTATO SOUP

Slice 2 good-sized leeks and dice 2 medium-sized potatoes. Drop them into 1½ pints of cold water. Cover and boil gently for 40 minutes. Season with salt and pepper, and add a walnut of butter. When the butter has melted, stir in half a pint of cold milk and re-heat, but do not boil. Add some meat extract just before serving.

POTAGE OF SPROUTS

1 lb. young Brussels sprouts, 1 tablespoon finely chopped onion, 2 tablespoons butter, 4 cups chicken broth, 2 good-sized potatoes sliced, ½ cup hot milk, salt and pepper.

Wash and trim the sprouts and cover with boiling water, boiling gently for 5 minutes, then drain. Melt the butter in a saucepan and cook the sprouts and onion in it for 2 minutes, turning gently. Add the potatoes and chicken broth, cover and simmer for 15 to 20 minutes or until vegetables are tender. Rub the vegetables through a fine sieve, reheat, then remove from heat and add the hot milk. Taste for seasoning. Croutons fried in butter can be served with this soup.

RICH STOCK

4 lbs. of shin of beef, 4 lbs. of knuckle of veal, ½ lb. of good lean ham; any poultry trimmings; 2 ozs. of butter; 3 onions, 3 carrots, 3 turnips (the latter should be omitted in summer, lest they ferment), 1 head of celery; a few chopped mushrooms when obtainable; 1 tomato, a bunch of savoury herbs, not forgetting parsley; 1½ ozs. of salt, 3 lumps of sugar, 12 white peppercorns, 6 cloves, 3 small blades of mace, 4 quarts of water.

Line a delicately clean pot with the ham cut in thin broad slices, carefully trimming off all its rusty fat; cut up the beef and veal in pieces about 3 inches square, and lay them on the ham; set it on the stove, and draw it down, and stir frequently. When meat is equally browned put in the beef and veal bones, the poultry trimmings, and pour in the cold water. Skim well, and occasionally add a little cold water to stop its boiling, until it becomes quite clear; then put in all the ingredients, and simmer very slowly for 5 hours. Do not let it come to a brisk boil, that the stock be not wasted, and that its colour may be preserved.

Strain through a very fine hair sieve, or cloth, and the stock will be fit for use.

ALMOND SOUP

1 tablespoon butter
2 tablespoons flour
1 tablespoon cornflour
1 cup cream
1½ quarts chicken or veal stock
2 ozs. almonds ground or chopped very finely

Cream together butter, flour and cornflour well. Add the hot stock, stirring constantly. Let boil for 5 minutes. Add cream and almonds. Serve very hot.

CREAMY LEEK SOUP

3 leeks (sliced finely) 1 onion (sliced) 3 tablespoons butter 3 potatoes (peeled and thinly sliced) 2 pints stock ¼ teaspoon nutmeg 1 teaspoon salt pepper ½ pint whipped cream (chilled for whipping) 1 tablespoon chopped chives or parsley

Saute leeks and onion in butter until soft, but do not brown. Add potatoes and stock and cook gently 45 minutes. Mash potatoes in the liquid and pass through fine sieve. Add milk and season with nutmeg, salt and pepper. Chill thoroughly. Fold cream into soup with chopped chives or parsley. This soup can be served piping hot or icy cold.

COCK-A-LEEKIE SOUP

A cock or fowl water or stock leeks salt

Cut off the roots and parts of the heads of 6 large leeks. Cut in pieces an inch long — split if liked. Wash very thoroughly in three waters to remove any earth. Place in pan and pour over water or stock, add the leeks, pepper and salt.

Cook until the flesh comes easily off the bird. Place pieces of fowl in the pan, heat thoroughly and serve with chopped parsley if liked.

JELLIED OR HOT PEA SOUP

Boil pea pods with a sliced onion, pepper and salt, and a sprig of mint. Strain. Boil with milk, thicken and serve. Add a few peas.

BROWN ONION SOUP

4 large onions	4 tablespoons butter
1 tablespoon sugar	2½ pints beef stock or
black pepper	water (or the two
salt	combined)
French bread	butter
freshly grated cheese	

Peel and slice onions thinly. Separate the rings. Heat butter in a large saucepan with a little sugar; add the onion rings and cook them very, very gently over low heat, stirring constantly with a wooden spoon, until the rings are an even golden brown. Add beef stock gradually, stirring constantly until the soup begins to boil. Then lower heat; cover pan and simmer gently for 30 minutes. Just before serving, correct seasoning. Serve in heated soup tureen or in individual serving bowls, each one containing toasted buttered rounds of french bread heaped with grated gruyere cheese.

Brown onion soup may also be served "gratinee". When ready to serve, place thin rounds of toasted and buttered bread in a casserole; cover with freshly grated cheese and pour onion soup over the toast. Sprinkle top with more cheese and place casserole under grill or in hot oven until golden. Serves 4 to 6.

CABBAGE SOUP with Liver Dumplings

Shred one or two cabbages and brown in a little hot oil. Sprinkle sparingly with flour, stir well and cook until flour starts to brown. Pour over the cabbage boiling beef or chicken stock, season and simmer for an hour. Drop the dumplings into the soup and continue boiling for twenty minutes.

Dumplings

Mince a pound of calf, beef or pork liver finely. Cube three slices of stale white bread, moisten in milk then squeeze dry. Saute two tablespoons finely chopped onion in four tablespoons of butter. Combine liver, bread and onions and mix well. Add two well beaten egg yolks, tablespoon of flour, salt and pepper. Fold in two stiffly beaten egg whites.

Flour hands and form mixture into walnut-sized balls. Cook 20 minutes in hot soup.

RED CABBAGE SOUP

1 Medium size red cabbage 3 medium onions 1 tart cooking apple 3 large potatoes 2 tablespoons butter pinch dried thyme pinch salt ½ bayleaf 1 medium ham or veal bone 2 quarts water salt and pepper to taste

Remove coarse outer leaves and hard core of cabbage, wash well and shred, then simmer for 15 minutes in 1 cup of water. In a large saucepan cook the sliced and peeled onions in the butter, until golden, then add the sliced apple, potatoes, seasonings, meat bone, the drained cabbage and water and cook slowly for 2 hours. Remove bone and put mixture through sieve, then reheat to serve.

CABBAGE SOUP

1 large cabbage, 3 carrots, 2 onions, 4 or 5 slices of lean bacon, salt and pepper to taste, 2 quarts of medium stock, lemon juice

Scald the cabbage, cut it up, and drain it. Line the stewpan with the bacon, put in the cabbage, carrots and onions; moisten with skimmings from the stock, and simmer very softly till the cabbage is tender; add the stock, stew softly for half an hour and carefully skim off every particle of fat. Season and serve. 8 persons.

GOLDEN CLEAR SOUP (CONSOMME)

The most perfect golden consomme (clear soup) can be made from the carcase of a duck. Just break it up, and cover well with cold water.

Bring to boil, skim, add a chopped onion and carrot. Simmer two hours at least, adding more water if necessary. Strain and cool.

Then clarify the liquid with the unbeaten white and crushed shell of an egg.

Bring liquid to boil — whisking all the time with an egg whisk. When it foams up, take off heat and stand aside for 5 minutes. Then put back over low heat and simmer 15 minutes. Strain through a scalded muslin.

Add quarter cup sherry — a tablespoon of lemon juice and one teaspoon meat extract (to give a deeper colour). Season with a little salt.

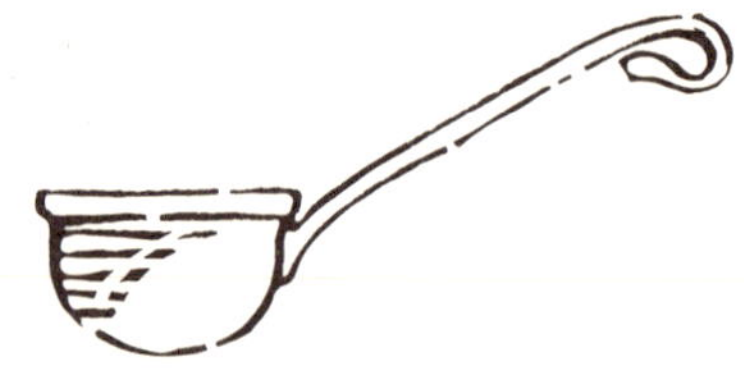

ROSEHIP SOUP

Soak 4 ozs. dried rosehips. Boil in pint water with lemon rind, cloves and cinnamon until they are soft, then sieve. Brown 1 oz. flour in 1 oz. fat and gradually add to soup. Sweeten, add wine and serve hot.

RED CURRANT SOUP (ICED)

To serve six:
1-1½ lbs. red currants (fresh)
1 rounded tablespoon plain flour
6 cups water — 1 cup plain sugar
Pinch salt — Juice of ½ lemon
½ pint sour cream

Wash red currants then boil for 10 minutes in six cups of water. Strain, but do not crush the fruit and while juice is still hot, add the sugar. Mix into a smooth paste the flour with the sour cream, carefully add this to the strained red currant juice, put into a saucepan and bring once to the boil. Turn off and squeeze in the lemon juice. Place in a glass jar. It should be thoroughly iced before the soup is ready to serve.

Instead of red currants you may use ripe apricots, stoned cherries, plums or, instead of fruit, simply peeled fresh cucumbers.

CREME VICHYSOISSE

Slice very thinly white parts of 4 leeks. Slice 1 medium-sized onion and cook the vegetables in 2 tablespoons butter until they just begin to turn golden. Add 5 medium-sized potatoes, peeled and sliced, 1 quart chicken broth or water, or a combination of both and 1 teaspoon salt. Boil for 35 to 40 minutes. Rub the liquid through a fine sieve. Return it to the fire and add 2 cups cold milk and 2 cups of cream. Season to taste and bring to a boil. Cool and rub the mixture through a very fine sieve. When it is cold add 1 cup cream. Strain again. Chill thoroughly and serve in bouillon cups, sprinkled with finely chopped chives.

GOLDEN BORTSCH

Cut into thin strips, white parts of 3 leeks, 1 onion, 2 carrots, 2 stalks of celery, 3 tender cabbage leaves, 4 small beets. Stew in ¼ lb. of butter for 10 minutes. Add 3 pints beef stock and carcase of fowl or duck, after breaking the bones. Add small bunch of fennel, salt to taste and simmer for 1 hour, covered. Strain. Take off fat. Before serving, add 1 pint sour cream and juice of grated large beet.

ASPARAGUS SOUP

1 lb. asparagus — 2 ozs. butter
Salt and pepper — ½ pint cream
1/3 cup flour — 2 sticks celery
1 medium sized onion
4 cups boiling chicken stock

Melt butter in pan. Fry chopped onion and celery until soft, but not brown. Stir in flour away from the heat. Cook a minute. Remove from heat, gradually add chicken stock and chopped asparagus. Simmer for 30-40 minutes. Sieve. Re-heat gently. Add cream. Season.

ELDERBERRY SOUP

½ lb. ripe elderberries
½ lb. apples
Juice and rind of lemon, sugar and salt

Cook berries in ½ pint water until soft. Sieve. Then puree with ¾ pint boiling water. Add apples cut up and sweetened. Add salt and rind. Just before serving, stir in lemon juice and rind.

FRIMSEL SOUP (Jewish)

3 or 4 quarts stock — 1 head celery
2 turnips — 1 bunch mixed herbs
3 carrots — 1 lb. frimsels
1 onion — 1 pinch saffron

Cut the vegetables as for Julienne soup, boil well in the stock until cooked. Half an hour before serving add the frimsels and saffron.

Frimsels: Beat the egg well with a pinch of salt, then add sufficient flour to thicken it enough to roll out. Roll as thin as wafer, allow to dry, then fold and cut as thin as vermicelli; add these to the soup.

ONION SOUP

Melt 1½ oz. butter in a saucepan. Add 4 sliced onions. Cook over slow heat, occasionally stirring, until clear, not brown. Add stock, salt, pepper and mace. Cover and simmer until onion is soft. Sieve. Thicken, add ½ pint milk. Serve with grated cheese.

ONION SOUP WITH DUMPLINGS

2 onions, ½ head celery, 1 oz. margarine or other fat, 1 dessertspoon plain flour, 2 pints stock, pepper and salt.

Dumplings: 2 ozs. self-raising flour, 1 oz. chopped suet, 2 teaspoons chopped parsley, water to mix.

1. Skin and chop onions; wash and chop celery. Melt fat and fry onions and flour gently in it, stirring continuously for a few minutes until pale gold. Add stock. Add celery and seasoning. Bring to boil, then cover and simmer gently for about three-quarters of an hour. Bring to boil just before adding dumplings.

2. Make dumplings while soup is cooking. Sieve flour, then mix in suet, chopped parsley and seasoning. Bind with a little cold water to make a light dough. Roll into small rounds on floured board. Add to soup, which should be boiling, and cook 15 minutes. Season soup again, if necessary, before serving.

TOMATO SOUP

3 ozs. rice	1 oz. butter
2 teaspoons salt	water
1 lb. tomatoes	1 tablespoon vinegar
Grated cheese	1 dessertspoon sugar

Wash rice well, put in saucepan with butter, salt, and 2 pints of water. Bring to boil. Reduce heat, cook slowly, uncovered, 30 minutes. Chop tomatoes roughly put into small saucepan with 1 tablespoon water, simmer gently until soft and mushy (approximately 10 minutes). Sieve, discard skins and seeds. Add tomatoes to rice with vinegar and sugar. Increase heat, boil together 2 minutes. Serve topped with grated cheese.

CAULIFLOWER SOUP WITH BREAD DUMPLINGS

1 medium-sized cauliflower

1 tablespoon salt	3 pints water
½ cup plain flour	2 ozs. butter
¼ teaspoon nutmeg	¼ teaspoon pepper

DUMPLINGS

2 cups soft, white breadcrumbs
1 tablespoon chopped parsley

2 tablespoons milk	1 teaspoon butter
1 egg	Salt and pepper

Boil water in large saucepan. Wash cauliflower, break into small florets, add to boiling water with salt. cook until just tender. Remove from saucepan and set aside; reserve liquid.

In separate saucepan melt butter, add flour, and cook, stirring, 1 minute. Gradually add reserved liquid; cook, stirring, until mixture boils and thickens slightly. Add nutmeg and pepper. Reduce heat and simmer 20 minutes, stirring occasionally. Increase heat and drop prepared dumplings, one at a time, into soup; cook, covered, 5 minutes. Add cauliflowers, cook 5 minutes longer. Adjust seasoning, serve hot.

Dumplings: Place breadcrumbs in mixing bowl, stir in softened butter, milk and parsley. Beat together egg and salt, add to breadcrumbs mixing well to form a firm mixture. Take dessertspoons of mixture and roll into small balls with wet hand. Cook in soup.

FISH SOUP

1 lb. fish (any variety, small fish will do).
1 good-size fish weighing 2-3 lbs. (best Murray cod, perch, schnapper).

5 medium onions	2 tablespoons lard
4 large potatoes	2 ripe tomatoes
8-10 black peppercorns	Salt

Scale and clean the inside of the small fish. Scale the Murray cod, clean, and cut into 1½ inch slices. Reserve the head.

Grease the saucepan either with lard or oil. Place the small fish on the bottom, salt, cover with a layer of finely sliced onion. Top it with the fish head. Make alternate layers now of the fish cutlets and the onion, season with salt add peppercorns. Lastly, add the peeled and sliced potato. Cover entirely with water. Bring to boil, then let it cook very, very slowly, barely bubbling, over the glowing coals for one hour. (Easiest way is to get the fire down low, bring the soup to boil on the kitchen stove, and leave to simmer slowly.)

BOULLABAISE

This Boullabaise a noble dish is —
A sort of soup, or broth, or brew.
Or hotchpotch of all sorts of fishes
That Greenwich never could outdo;
Green herbs, red peppers, mussels, saffron,
Soles, onions, garlic, roach and plaice,
All these you eat at Terre's Tavern
In that one dish of Boullabaise.

Thackeray

About 3 pound of any coarse, cheap fish — remove the fins and tail. Cut the fish into chunks, drop it into a big saucepan, and cover with at least 2 quarts of water. Split open the fish head and add that — it contains a large amount of gelatinous matter that will add to the consistency of the stock. Put on a low fire and bring slowly to simmer — never let it boil. Make hash of half a pound of onions, 2 peeled (and seeded, if possible) tomatoes, 1 or 2 shallots, clove of garlic, half a head of fennel, if possible celery tops, if not. Fry until golden in a gill of oil, then add to the simmering stock. Season with a dessertspoon of sweet pepper, a bayleaf, a clove, sprig of thyme, a bit of fresh orange peel, salt and pepper. Keep it all at simmer — boullabaise meaning low boil, until fish starts to separate from bone. At this moment a scant half teaspoon of saffron is added. Allow five minutes more.

Pour stock through the colander, and with a wooden spoon, rub, crush, and paddle until all the liquor is obtained. Cut fish you intend to eat into portions. Simmer, but do not let it fall apart. Add, if you can, a dozen or so fresh oysters and some prawns, just as the fish is nearly cooked.

In each soup plate put a slice of fried bread. On this put a fish portion. Thicken the soup very slightly. Pour into soup plates, and sprinkle with chopped parsley. Serve with a green salad and soft cheese.

FISH DISHES

There was a plentiful supply of eels in the creeks and rivers in Western Victoria. They still come from the Northern seas each year and swim up Mt. Emu creek to breed in Lake Carranballac. Being mud lovers it is best to put them, if it is possible, into a bucket of pure water. If they are especially muddy, the old method was to add salt and barley, soaked in red wine. Generally, an incision is made around the eels' necks, their skins pulled off. It is better first to lay them on a brazier of live coals, so that the skin sweels and folds. The charred skin can then be removed with a cloth, pulling from head to tail. This eliminates skin oil and improves the eel as to both flavour and digestibility.

EEL STEW

6 lbs. Eels — 1½ teaspoons Salt
2 ozs. Butter — 4 Onions
4 pieces Lemon Peel } if available
3 tablespoons Lemon Juice }
½ tablespoon grated Nutmeg
2 tablespoons fennel or caraway seeds
1 pint red Wine — ½ pint Port or Madeira
2 pints water or fish stock

Eels should be alive until used. Hang from a wire hook with string. Make a circular incision and peel back the skin just below the string, ripping it all off at once. Make a cut along the belly. Empty it and wash out the eel. Cut into pieces 2-3 inches long. Melt butter in a large heavy casserole and stir in onions. Cook for 5 minutes then add other ingredients. Stew gently for an hour. Add cream. 10 persons.

BROWN ITALIENNE SAUCE

Put into a pot chopped mushrooms, slices of lemon (no seeds), diced ham, 1 tablespoonful of chopped shallot washed and squeezed in a cloth, ½ bayleaf, 2 cloves, and ½ pint of oil. Heat. When you see your ingredients are about cooked, take out the lemon slices. Add 1 tablespoon of chopped parsley and 1 of espagnole sauce, 1 pint of good white wine, and a little pepper. Reduce. Skim. Remove the ham. When sufficiently reduced, take off the heat.

Mirepoix — a mixture of vegetables cut small, ham, bacon, put under the meat for braising, for example, onions, carrots, ham, with a bayleaf and a sprig of thyme.

MULLET in paper bags

Cook after cleaning, in separate bags, well greased inside. Season fish, sprinkle with lemon juice and knob of butter. Close bags. Cook ½ hour on hot coals beside the stream is best.

WALLY'S MURRAY COD or WILD TURKEY - (Aboriginal style)

(Recipe given by a former drover)

Leave feathers on and do not clean. If Murray cod, do not clean either. Cover with mud. Dig hole in wet sand about one foot deep. Light a fire in the hole. When all is glowing coals, damp down with more wet sand. Put in eucalyptus leaves, then prepared turkey or cod. Cover with eucalyptus leaves and another layer of damp sand. This generates hot steam. In half to three-quarters of an hour approximately, remove the bird or fish. The feathers will be gone. Sprinkle with salt.

BUSHRANGERS' TROUT

Clean fish, leaving on head and tail and wrap directly with clay mud about 1 inch thick. Then wrap with newspaper to hold clay in place.

Place on a bed of hot coals and cover with more hot coals. Keep fire burning on top so that hot coals are constantly fed down on to the fish. Bake for 2 hours, then remove from coals. The mud comes off easily, taking the skin with it, and leaving the fish clean and juicy.

To Smoke Hams, Eels and Fish at Home:

Take an old hogshead, stop up all the crevices, and fix a place to put a cross-stick near the bottom, on which to hang the articles to be smoked. Next, in the side, cut a hole near the top, to introduce an iron pan filled with sawdust and small pieces of green wood. Having turned the tub upside down, hang the articles upon the cross-stick, introduce the iron pan into the opening, and place a piece of red-hot iron in the pan, cover it with sawdust, and all will be complete. Let a large ham remain 40 hours, and keep up a good smoke.

JIM'S FISH

Don't clean fish.

Wrap in sheet of paper — or grass.

Get live coals — cover fish with fine ashes, above and below in layers. Finally place good covering of hot coals. 20-30 minutes for 1 lb. fish — cooking.

Take up and skin and remove inside of fish.

Redfin, Schnapper, Bream, Flathead — or other fish.

BILLABONG YABBIES

First find a shady dam or creek, then catch your yabbies with a small piece of meat on a string, or catch them with a net. Boil yabbies till tender in water with vinegar and sugar and salt (about 10 minutes). Beer may be added if liked. Best eaten under a gum tree with your mates. Another way — peel when cooked then heat for a few minutes in saucepan with butter.

They say that fish should swim thrice . . .
First it should swim in the sea
(do you mind me?),
Then it should swim in butter,
And at last sirrah,
it should swim in good claret.

Swift

INLET SCALLOPS

1½lbs. scallops (with the black portion removed)
½ doz. to 1 doz. oysters
2 dessertspoons butter
½ cup dry sherry or dry wine
½ cup cream
1 cup diced mushrooms
1 dessertspoon flour
lemon juice, ground pepper, salt and nutmeg (all to taste)

Slightly blanch scallops in salt water and drain. Melt one dessertspoon of butter in pan and slightly saute scallops. Add fresh diced mushrooms and oysters. Moisten with dry sherry or dry white wine, add cream and thicken with flour blended with the other dessertspoon of butter. Season to taste with lemon juice, ground pepper, nutmeg and salt. Cook for three to four minutes. Four servings.

SAILOR'S MUSSELS

Mussels should be well washed and scrubbed in several waters. Place 4 dozen in a large deep pot with ¼ pint of dry white wine, one sliced carrot, one finely chopped onion, a sprinkle of chopped parsley, a bayleaf, a sprig of thyme, a clove of garlic, sparing of salt and pepper and 3 ozs. butter.

Cover pot and cook quickly. When all mussels are open, remove their whiskery beards — keeping the others very hot. Remove mussels, discarding their top shell before laying in hot tureen. Save spare shell to scoop up the savoury juice. Strain over mussels in tureen court bouillon. Serve with crisp bread and a good red wine.

CUCUMBER AND SMOKED SALMON

Peel cucumbers and cut in halves lengthways. Scoop out seeds so that you have long basket shapes. Sprinkle with salt and drain upside down.

Cut slices of smoked salmon into strips about ½ inch wide by 2 inches long. Combine with sufficient cream cheese mixed with capers to fill cucumber halves. Sprinkle inside of cucumbers with a little white vinegar, salt and pepper and fill with cream cheese mixture. Garnish top with small bouquets of watercress or parsley.

PAPA BENJAMIN'S MUSSELS

2 lbs. mussels	½ lb. onions
2 tablespoons butter	½ lb. tomatoes
Salt and Pepper	Soft breadcrumbs
1 tablespoon mixed herbs	

Chop the onions finely and fry gently in the butter until brown, then add the tomatoes (cut in pieces) and the herbs. Cover pan and cook for 15 minutes. In another large pan put the mussels (very, very well washed to get rid of sand and grit), with a tea towl rung out in boiling water on top of them, and leave 2 to 3 minutes over fierce heat until their shells open (discard any that don't open). Remove shells. Strain the liquor and mix it with the mussels and onion and tomato puree. Add salt and plenty of pepper, and heat gently. Thicken the mixture by adding soft white breadcrumbs (don't use flour). Chill and serve.

KEDGEREE

½ lb. cold fish	¼ lb. boiled rice
2 hard-boiled eggs	1 oz. butter
Pepper and salt	

Flake up the fish, mix it with the rice. Shell the eggs and cut them in half. Put yolks on one side. Chop the whites and mix them with rice and fish. Season nicely and put into a saucepan with the butter and stir until thoroughly hot.

Pile on a dish and chop the egg yolks and sprinkle them over. Serve hot.

SALMON RECTORY

Place two salmon steaks (about half an inch thick) into a flat, buttered dish. Add four finely chopped shallots, one cup of sliced button mushrooms, the juice of half a lemon and season with salt and cayenne pepper. Pour over enough red wine to cover the salmon. Cover the whole with greasproof paper. Bring to the boil and continue to cook in a moderate oven for about 20 minutes. Take out the salmon and remove the skin and bones. Place the salmon in a warmed serving dish. Reduce the liquid in the pan over a quick flame and add two tablespoons of butter creamed with one tablespoon of flour. Blend in half a cup of thick cream and pour over salmon before serving.

FRESH SALMON STEAKS

Clean salmon and cut into steaks about ¼ inch thick. Dip in beaten egg and flour and fry in hot fat or butter 5-10 minutes. Remove from pan and keep hot. Stir a little flour into pan in which the fish was cooked, then add a little stock and seasonings. Pour over steaks and sprinkle with parsley.

SALMON MOULD

Take the fag end of a cold salmon. Remove all skin and bones. Pound it with two ordinary cracker biscuits. Beat up 2 eggs and add to the mixture. Melt about 1 tablespoon of butter in a small tea-cupful of milk with salt and black pepper, mixing this in with the salmon, biscuits and eggs. Put the whole into a well-greased mould and steam for 1½ hours. When it is cooked press with a weight of at least 4 pounds. Let it stand over-night. Serve with a hot or cold mayonnaise sauce and a green salad.

SOUSED FISH

1½ lbs. fish (couta, skipjack, mullet - anything inexpensive) 6 peppercorns ½ pint vinegar
¼ teaspoon spice ¼ teaspoon ground ginger
1 onion 4 cloves ½ teaspoon salt

Lay fish flat in dish, cover with chopped onion. Sprinkle rest of ingredients over, add vinegar. Cover and cook gently until just soft. Lift out, strain liquid over, and serve cold with lemon and tomato.

PRUNE-STUFFED WHOLE BREAM

3 lbs. Bream	2/3 cup cooked rice
Salt and pepper	Pinch grated nutmeg
Oil	

5 ozs. prunes, cooked, stoned and chopped
½ teaspoon finely grated orange rind

Mix the rice with the chopped prunes, orange rind, salt, pepper and nutmeg. Stuff the fish with the mixture and toothpick or sew edges together.

Brush both sides of fish with oil and put in baking dish. Bake in moderate oven until fish is tender. Serve with plenty of butter. Serves 6.

Dressed in batter or bathed in sauces,
Clothed in parsley for other courses!
To add one more to this fearful host,
The spectre appears — on cast-iron toast!
And in course of time, the remains we'll see
Dished up as salmon paste for tea!
(From 'Ode to a Salmon')

LOBSTER NEWBURG

Cook lobster meat in butter, then mix with sherry or brandy, egg yolks, cream and seasonings, served on toast or in pastry cases.

On china blue my lobster red
Precedes my cutlet brown,
With which my salad green is sped
By yellow Chablis down.
Sir Stephen Gaselee

FISH AND ALMOND CASSEROLE

12 ozs. fish	2/3 cup milk
1 oz. butter	salt and pepper
1 oz. flour	1 cup diced celery

1 tablespoon lemon juice
1/3 cup sherry (or stock)
1 tablespoon chopped parsley
¼ cup lightly toasted chopped almonds

Melt butter, stir in flour off the stove, add milk (previously heated with carrot, onion, peppercorns, then strained after ¼ hour). Stir till smooth. Cook 3 minutes. Season with salt and pepper. Add the sherry, lemon juice, parsley and celery. Stir gently. Put in casserole and top with almonds. Heat for 15 to 20 minutes before serving. Flavour is best if made the day before.

When buying a fish for baking allow about ½ lb. a person as a main dish. Schnapper or bream are both superb fish to stuff and bake. For 2 people a 1 lb. bay trout can be excellent. Leave head and tail on, or cut them off if preferred. Bone it if you wish. Rinse well and rub inside and out with salt and pepper. If using an overproof table dish grease it generously with butter. Lay fish down the centre. Fill the inside cavity with herb and breadcrumb stuffing using melted butter and beaten egg yolk to give moisture without wetness. Lay thin slices of lemon (rind left on) all down the opening. Slide some strings under the fish and tie (not too tightly) in three or four places, using the lemon as a binding over the stuffing. Pour a little wine (or wine and water) over the fish using just enough to moisten the bottom of the dish. White wine (sauterne, hock or chablis) is nicest for the finer fish, but red wine (claret or burgundy) has more flavour for dark fish such as trout. If you don't care for wine use water flavoured with lemon juice, a little minced onion and finely chopped parsley. Cover fish with a thickly buttered paper and bake in moderate oven heat allowing 10-15 minutes to the pound, and basting once or twice with the liquid in the pan. Crisp some bits of bacon over the fish just before it comes from the oven. Remove strings carefully when fish is done (test with a fine skewer). If the fish is large and is to be moved from a baking tin to a serving platter, lie on a piece of buttered muslin so you can lift it easily. Instead of strings a needle and strong thread can be used to sew the cavity together over the stuffing.

Liquid from a big fish can be thickened and used as a coating sauce. Fresh fish do not have sunken eyes. Delicate fish like flounder is overpowered by strong sauce. Melted butter is best.

STAR GAZY PIE (from a Cornish Miner)

Half a pound of good short pastry for pie top. When mixed wrap in a piece of greased paper and leave in a cool place whilst preparing the filling. Herrings are the usual fish used for this traditional Cornish dish, but Tommy Buffs make an excellent substitute.

Remove scales, fins and tails and heads from the 7 fish required, retaining the heads (from which the dish gets its name). With scissors slit all the way down the front of the fish opening it out, and remove the bones, sprinkle the inside of each filleted fish with a little salt, pepper and finely-chopped parsley. Then commencing at the tail, roll each fish. Grease the inside of your pie-dish or casserole with a generous amount of butter, then sprinkle over it some white bread-crumbs. Arrange the fish over breadcrumbs, and cover each layer with breadcrumbs. Remove the rind from 3 rashers, covering the top of the last layer with the rashers. Beat 2 large eggs and add 4 tablespoons of milk and carefully add 2 large tablespoons of good light vinegar. Stir and pour it over the pie contents. Roll the pastry to the size of the dish allowing a little for the drop of the pie when it cooks. It is a good idea to wet the rim of the dish to help the pastry to adhere. Cut a fairly large hole in the centre of the pie and retain the circle of pastry. In the hole, arrange the 7 well-washed fish heads, roll out the circle of pastry and cut strips to form a collar around the inside base of fish heads. Brush top with egg glaze and carefully lift your Star-Gazy pie on to centre shelf of moderate oven. Cook for 45 to 60 minutes. Serve with jacket potatoes slit at top and buttered and then sprinkled with finely chopped parsley.

COURT BOUILLON

Cook together white wine, red wine, butter, fine spices, bayleaf and herbs. Use to cook fish. Serve the fish with oil and vinegar sauce.

SHERRY-BAKED TROUT

Small whiting or mullet may be used instead.

4 small trout
2 tablespoons chopped parsley
½ cup soft breadcrumbs
Salt and pepper
2 tablespoons butter
1 small clove of garlic
Juice of half lemon
½ cup dry sherry

Clean and fillet the fish and rub with salt and pepper. Melt the butter and mix with the breadcrumbs, parsley and finely crushed garlic. Sprinkle half this mixture over the bottom of a well greased ovenproof dish. Arrange fish on top and sprinkle with remainder of breadcrumb mixture. Squeeze the lemon juice over them. Bake in a moderate oven for 10 minutes, then add the sherry and continue baking for another 10 to 15 minutes, depending on thickness of fish. If browning too much on top cover with a piece of buttered paper.

BAKED STUFFED FILLETS (sandwich style)

Fresh whiting fillets are suitable but buy the larger fillets and cut them in half across the middle, and "pair" them up. The one essential is to have flat, fairly thin fillets or they won't stuff neatly.

4 large fillets of whiting or
8 small fillets of flounder
¾ cup of very finely chopped celery
1 beaten egg
Pinch of dried thyme
Extra chopped parsley for garnish
2 brimming cups of fine stale breadcrumbs
1 tablespoon of finely chopped parsley
2 ozs. butter
½ cup dry sherry
Salt and pepper

Cook the chopped celery in the butter over low heat until the fat is practically absorbed and the celery is partly cooked but uncoloured. Put parsley and breadcrumbs in a basin. Pour on the celery and remaining butter. Add parsley and beaten egg. Toss lightly together. Add thyme (if used).

Sprinkle fish fillets with a little salt and pepper. Lay half the fillets in a well-greased baking pan. Spread with the stuffing keeping it neat. Place other fillets on top, "pairing" them to match. Put bits of butter on each sandwich. Moisten each with a dessertspoon of sherry. Run another spoonful or two of sherry into the dish to moisten bottom. Cover fish with buttered paper.

Bake in a fairly hot oven 35-40 minutes. Baste twice with a little extra sherry (you require half a teacup of sherry altogether). Test with a fine steel skewer. Lift carefully on a flat spatula or fish slice into warmed individual dishes. Sprinkle each with parsley.

For a family meal you can use thicker fillets of bream, mullet or other fish. Cook until tender to taste.

A good dish of trout is cooked in a fireproof dish with dabs of butter, salt, pepper and half a pint of cream. They are baked in a slow oven until the sauce is bubbling and in this you scatter dill or fennel, sage or winter savory finely chopped.

To remove the fishy smell from a pan, empty used tea leaves into it, fill with water and leave standing for 10 minutes.

AROMATIC PLANTS AND BEE PLANTS

An old fashioned garden to provide the lady of the house with herbs for her sachets and for her kitchen.

MEATS

HOW A GREAT-GRANDMOTHER WENT TO AUSTRALIA AND HOW SHE MADE SPICED BEEF FOR THE VOYAGE.

A hundred years ago a single 10 foot square cabin to Melbourne on a sailing ship cost £78 — and you provided your own bedding and your own pudding!

Great-grandmother sailed for Australia in the early 1860's. For her cabin door small bolt for inside, asp staple and padlock for outside. For her clothes: plenty of hooks with screws, gimlet and claw hammer to put them up. Strips of wood and a shelf with which to support her wash basin, plus extra stip to nail across corner to prevent water-can being upset. String to fasten across plates hung against side of berth and prevent them making a disagreable noise, to secure books, and to keep rations from being thrown off shelves by the motion of the vessel. Strips of tape: to tack in loops to hold cutlery. She also had to provide a mattress — the requirements being 20 inches wide for males, 18 inches wide for females and 36 inches wide for man and wife, not to mention bolsters, pillows, 3 pairs of sheets, 2 blankets and 1 dozen coarse towels per head.

Great-grandmother begged from friends and relatives any old clothes they could spare; and threw them overboard when dirty. The allowance of 3 quarts of water per day per person for drinking, cooking and washing, meant washing clothes was rarely possible. Great-grandmother took 4 pounds of marine soap per head and 6 pounds of candles to fit the family's lantern. Her medicine chest, contained yeast, castor oil, aperient pills (sic), calomel, ipecacuanha powders, bicarbonate of soda and cream of tartar for making effervescing drinks.

It was customary for passengers to be divided into 'messes' comprising about 8 adults, for cooking, eating and drawing rations. These small 'communes' each appointed a captain, or managing man. Typical rations provided by the ship per week were:

	2nd class	Steerage
Preserved meat	2½ lbs.	1 lb.
Fresh mess pork	1½ lbs.	1 lb.
Biscuit	1¼ lbs.	3½ lbs.
Raw sugar	1 lb.	1 lb.
Potatoes	4 lbs.	2½ lbs.
Lime juice	6 ozs.	6 ozs.
Tea	1½ lbs.	1½ lbs.

Flour allowed for the steerage was only enough for puddings and scones. Great-grandmother and her fellow 2nd class passengers had enough flour for a moderate supply of bread. She wrote home about sea-pie, and mentioned 'lobscouse' and 'dandyfunk'. I wonder what they were?

As extra rations the family took eggs smeared with lard, onions, dried apples, sago, arrowroot, coffee, preserves and pickles. But best of all they took Great-grandmother's spiced beef.

You buy a whole rib of beef, which usually weighs 14-17 lbs., though by the time the butcher has boned the rib it will weigh 3-4 pounds less.

Place the joint in a large bowl and rub well into it ½ lb. rock salt, 1 oz. each saltpetre, peppercorns, whole cloves, mace, allspice and cinnamon, and 1 lb. of raw sugar — demerara will do. Turn the beef daily — after about a couple of days it will be lying in thick spicy juice — and continue turning it once a day for 3 to 4 weeks.

Next, wash off all the spices, then roll and tie the beef tightly, cover with suet and rub well in. Tie-up in greaseproof paper, then in brown paper — just like a parcel. Put it in a large and deep baking tin in a moderate oven for 2 hours. Turn the parcel over, add a quart of water to the tin and bake for another 2 hours. Remove from the oven, take off the wrappings and place meat under weights for 24 hours.

In Great-grandmother's recipe book, she copied out quotations that caught her imagination. Perhaps most apt for all those who travel is:-

They must have a stout heart under all difficulties, a clear conscience under all temptations and trust in God for the result.

William Howitt, writing from Eutroa, on the Seven Creeks, December 1, 1852.

. . . We draw off to some distance from the highway — a welcome sign of stopping to the horses, and which they instantly understand. We place the cart so as to be convenient to get what we want out of it; then pitch our tent opposite to the fire, but so that the smoke shall blow from us. Charlton takes the horses, gives them water, and tethers them out where there is the best grass. Meantime Alfred and I make the beds up in the tent, and the two Edwards make a fire, get out flour, and prepare a damper or a leather-jacket for tea. The damper, the universal bread of the bush, is a mere unleavened cake of a foot diameter, and from an inch to an inch and a half thick, baked in the ashes. The leather-jacket is a cake of mere flour and water, raised with tartaric acid and carbonate of soda instead of yeast, and baked in the frying-pan; and is equal to any muffin you can buy in the London shops. A fat-cake is the same thing as a leather-jacket, only fried in fat, and is not only much sooner done, but is really excellent. After tea they bake in the camp-oven, in the embers of the fire, a loaf, raised also with acid and soda, and which is equal to any home-baked bread in England. A suet pudding, called a doughboy, or a dish of rice or potatoes, if we have them, are put into the fat, and when ready, beef steaks or mutton chops are fried; and our tea-dinner, you will admit, is not to be sneezed at, especially with the Spartan sauce of a day's travel. It is amazing what a quantity of tea is drunk in the bush. It comes upon the table everywhere in the bush or on the road. Two or three pannikins, that is, from a quart to three pints, are thought no extraordinary quantity for one person, after the copious perspiration of a day's travel in this warm, dry country.

After tea Alfred gets his cigar; we talk over our affairs, and retire early to bed. We are up at peep of day, that is, from four to five o'clock, breakfast again on tea, damper, and a fry; pack, and move on till noon, when we stop near some stream, get a luncheon pretty much like a dinner, lie down for a couple of hours, and then on again till four o'clock. That is our routine, except getting a bath, or good cool wash from head to foot, where bathing is impracticable, after we have camped.

If you could see us, however, now we are stationary, — if you could see all our pots, pans, pannikins, our buckets and tin dishes, for making loaves or puddings in, and our larger ones for washing in; our knives, forks and spoons lying about; our little sacks - pillowcases, in fact - of sugar, rice, salt, flour etc., standing here and there; our tea-chest, our tin tea-pot of capacious dimensions; our tea-kettle, in constant requisition; our American axes, for chopping firewood into suitable lengths; our lantern, at night suspended by a cord from the centre of the tent, or more commonly a crowbar stuck into the ground with a candle between its fork — a famous candelabrum — if you could see the whole interior of our tent, with its tarpaulin spread for a carpet, and the beds spread over part of the floor, covered with their gray rugs, that is at night, but in the day rolled up into a divan; the tent hung round with straw hats with veils on them, caps, etc., revolvers, daggers, travelling pouches; our guns standing in a corner, with books and portfolios lying about, you would say that it was a scene at once curious, yet comfortable-looking. It is amazing, however, since Bateman arrived, what an unvaried air of neatness the place has assumed. Things have fallen into order, and have been grouped so as to produce artistic effect. We have had four posts set down in front, and a roof made of boughs, so that we can sit out there in the air and the shade; and the ground under it is scattered with rushes, or the twigs of the sheoak, so that we are thus carpeted like the barons in their halls of old.

On our first day in camp we dig a pit approximately 2 ft. square and 2 ft. deep; then we light a large fire in this — the idea being to bake the earth, thus giving better heat reflection when we use it.

We buy either the loin or a leg of lamb. If we use a leg we insert a sharpening steel down by the bone and stuff the cavity made with rosemary and three cloves of garlic. We rub the outside of the leg with crushed rosemary and butter, pepper and salt. We then wrap the leg in anything up to 20 layers of paper.

Before preparing the lamb we light a biggish fire in our pit and allow it to burn down to coals. We put the lamb on the coals, and cover the pit with an earth lid, allowing only a very small aperture for oxygen to get to the coals.

On our return anything up to five hours later the lamb is beautifully cooked, juicy, pink and tender. After carefully unwrapping the leg we give it a quick brown on the barbecue fire.

From an early settler's letter.

SWAGGIE'S TEA

Fry 2 chops both sides in frying pan. Drain off fat and put layers of sliced onion and potatoes in, using one onion and one potato. Sprinkle with pepper and salt and a little flour, cover with water and boil until water is nearly gone.

OUTBACK HOT-POT

Take a pumpkin, slice off the top and hollow out the inside. Fill the pumpkin shell with joints of possum, kangaroo or trophies of the hunt, and replace the lid. Prepare a bed of hot coals and bury the pumpkin in them. Cook until done — time will vary, depending on the size.

Some of the dishes enjoyed by our forefathers would get a dubious reception today — and still others would be beyond the resources of the present-day housewife.

Wild-life, for example, was not only plentiful, but legally unprotected. Black swans, parrots, cockatoos, flying foxes, possums and goannas all went into the pot. So did the koala, on occasion. In the 1890's, "Gundaroo Bullock" was the name given to baked koala. And "Grabben Gullen Pie" was a hollowed-out pumpkin filled with possum meat and roasted.

SLIPPERY BOB

Take kangaroo brains, and mix with flour and water, and make into batter; well season with pepper, salt, etc., then pour a tablespoon at a time into an iron pot containing emu fat, and take them out when done. "Bush fare", requires a good appetite and excellent digestion.

One drover's cook actually made sausages while travelling, using some part of the sheep's entrails for casing and an affair made of hollow bamboo for forcing the sausage meat into it. He said he learnt that from a Chinaman, along with recipes for various kinds of sausages. They were wonderfully good eating.

Droving Days — H.M. Barker

HOW TO ROAST A LAMB OF 50 POUNDS IN THE GRAND STYLE

Open the belly and discard the intestines, put back the heart, liver and lungs. Then fill up the opening with dates, figs, dried raisins, honey, salt and pepper. Add rice if preferred — 2 cups. Sew up stomach again. Lay the lamb on a bed of coals in a pit 2 feet deep. Set fire to pile of dry wood on top of the sheep. When that is reduced to coals, cover them with some of the earth from the pit. After 2 hours haul out the cooked sheep. Scratched with a knife, the wool should fall away completely, revealing a golden skin. Carve.

COLONIAL GOOSE

Leg or a shoulder of mutton, boned
3 ozs. finely chopped bacon
1 teaspoon finely chopped parsley
3 ozs. fresh breadcrumbs
8 tablespoons finely chopped onion
1 teaspoon mixed herbs, thyme, sage and marjoram
½ teaspoon freshly grated nutmeg
½ teaspoon grated lemon rind
salt and pepper to taste
1 well beaten egg
milk

Mix all the ingredients together except the egg and milk. Add the egg and enough milk just to moisten the ingredients. Stuff the opening in the meat and tie securely.

Heat a little fat or butter in a roasting pan and brown the meat all over. Roast in a medium to hot oven, allowing 15 to 20 minutes to the pound depending on how well done you like it.

To serve, cut off strings and lay meat on a heated platter; surround with baby boiled potatoes or small roast potatoes. Serve with gravy handed separately in a sauce boat. Serves 8.

MUTTON AND SAGE PIE

1 cup plain flour
1 cup self-raising flour
3 ozs. dripping
1 teaspoon lemon juice
1 large onion
a little cold water to mix
a handful of fresh sage
4 or 5 cups cold cooked mutton, cut into cubes
3 cups of mutton, or beef stock
salt and pepper to taste

Sift flour together into a bowl. Rub dripping into flour with finger tips and mix to a pastry dough with lemon juice and water. Pick sage leaves from stalks and chop roughly. Place meat, sage, peeled and diced onion, stock and pepper and salt in a saucepan. Bring to boil and thicken with a little plain flour. Pour into pie-dish. Roll out pastry and cover meat. Decorate edge. Prick with fork and bake until brown. Serve hot with vegetables.

IRISH LAMB

Cover a leg of lamb with an ounce of butter mixed with a little chopped onion. The lamb goes into the roasting pan, resting on a dozen parsley stalks and beside it a carrot, an onion and a tablespoon of water. Roast in a moderate oven, reducing heat towards the end of cooking time (20 minutes per lb. and 20 minutes over). Baste occasionally.

Make gravy by pouring fat off sediment in pan. Sprinkle on sediment a dessertspoon of flour, mix well and brown. Mash together the cooked carrot and onion and a dessertspoon of mint jelly or mint sauce. Add to pan. Gradually add half a pint of beef stock or cold tea. Cook for 5 minutes. Season and strain.

OLD IRISH STEW

¼ lb. onions,	1 lb. forequarter chops
½ teaspoon salt	2 gills water
1¼ lbs. potatoes	Pepper

Take skin off chops and cut into big pieces, leaving some fat, in. Put in saucepan with water and simmer ¾ or 1 hour. Peel potatoes, cut onions in thick rings and put in basin, cover with boiling water and cover with plate till meat has cooked for ¾ or 1 hour. Add vegetables to the meat, onions first, then potatoes. Add an extra ¼ cup of water or stock and simmer for 1 hour.

Lift potatoes out of pot, place them round a hot dish, put meat in centre and pour onions and gravy over top.

CALF'S LIVER WITH ONIONS

3 tablespoons butter
5 ozs. thinly sliced onions
Salt and Pepper
2½ teaspoons white vinegar
½ teaspoon dried sage leaves, chopped
1 lb. calf's liver, cut crosswise, very thinly
2 tablespoons finely chopped, fresh parsley

Heat half of the butter in the frying pan. Add the onions and cook over a moderate heat, stirring frequently for 8 minutes. Then stir in the sage and cook a few minutes longer. Put aside off the stove. Pat the liver strips dry. Season with salt and pepper. Heat the rest of the butter in the frying pan. Drop in the sliced liver. Turn frequently for a few minutes. When lightly browned, stir in the onions and cook for 2 minutes. Put this all in a heated dish. Immediately pour the vinegar into the frying pan and heat quickly for 2 minutes. Pour contents of the frying pan over the liver and onions and sprinkle with chopped parsley. Serve at once.

TOASTED TONGUE

If a dried tongue steep it all night in water, if pickled, wash it well and soak it for several hours. Boil it slowly for three hours. If eaten hot (after trimming and peeling) stick it with cloves. Rub it with the yolk of an egg, strew crumbled bread over it. Baste it with butter and lightly brown it before the fire. Put brown gravy, a red wine sauce in the dish, and spoonfuls of red currant jelly round the rim.

Whoe'er has gone thro' any street,
Has seen a Butcher gazing at his meat,
And how he keeps
Gloating upon a sheep's
Or bullock's personals, as if his own;
How he admires his halves
And quarters — and his calves,
As if in truth upon his own legs grown;
His fat! his suet!
His kidneys peeping elegantly thro' it!
Thomas Hood

THICK OXTAIL STEW

Plain boiled potatoes go well with this dish, which looks most attractive when sprinkled with chopped parsley. A glass of port or red wine greatly improves the gravy and if liked 1 or 2 pickled walnuts may be laid on top of the stew in a silver entree dish as garnish. A tablespoon of the walnut juice should be stirred into the gravy. Triangles of toast, suet dumplings or forcemeat balls are generally put round as garnish.

Melt 2 oz. fat. Brown the pieces of oxtail, which then remove. Fry a sliced onion, carrot, turnip and stick of celery. Add 1 pint hot water, salt and pepper as desired and the oxtail. Cover and cook it slowly for about 2 hours, by which time the meat should be almost falling off the bones. Drain off surplus fat and thicken the stew with 1 dessertspoonful of cornflour mixed to a paste with the juice of a lemon and 1 dessertspoonful of Worcestershire sauce. Stir this into the stew and let it simmer for 15 minutes before serving.

Since the oxtail may very well be reheated without any loss of flavour, it is sometimes convenient to cook it the day before, then when it is cold, the fat can be lifted off. Before serving the stew should be brought to the boil and simmered for 15 minutes. The suet dumplings must be freshly cooked.

SMOKED BEEF

Cut beef into large pieces and cover with salt. After 2-3 days, press it and hang in a chimney, where only wood is burnt; at sufficient distance for fat not to be melted by the heat. Let it remain until it is dry. Eat in stew, sliced or grated.

There's just one bit of eating
Which I hold supremely great
An' that's good old bread and gravy
When I've finished up my plate.

STEAK AND KIDNEY PUDDING

Mix a pound of flour with half its quantity of finely ground suet. Add a large teaspoon of baking powder, chopped parsley and a seasoning of salt and black pepper. Make a thick paste with water. Line a bowl and put enough aside for the lid.

Inside place 2 pounds of rump steak and same amount of beef kidneys cut into shavings. The meat should be floured. Then add a dozen or more oysters, half a pound of fried mushrooms, five split hard-boiled eggs. Then add the following seasoning: A tablespoon of parsley, a chopped onion, whole black peppers, half-a-dozen cloves, pinch of mace. Then a cupful of claret and enough hot water to fill to the brim. The paste lid moistened at edges goes on. Then cap bowl with a sheet of parchment. A cloth is tied under the rim of the bowl, (the cloth covering bowl is floured) and knotted together on top. Then it is plunged into boiling hot water and allowed to simmer for 5 hours (never less than 4). Leave room for pudding to rise.

Add a dash of Worcestershire Sauce.

"Give them great meals of beef. They will eat like wolves and fight like devils.
Shakespeare

ROAST SADDLE OF MUTTON

Saddle of mutton a little salt

To ensure this joint being tender, let it hang for 10 days or a fortnight, if the weather permits. Cut off the tail and flaps, and trim off every part that has not indisputable pretensions to be eaten, and have the skin taken off and skewered on again. Put it down to a bright, clear fire, and, when the joint has been cooking for an hour, remove the skin and dredge it with flour. It should not be placed too near the fire, as the fat should not be in the slightest degree burnt, but keep constantly basted, both before and after the skin is removed. Sprinkle some salt over the joint; make a little gravy in the dripping-pan; pour it over the meat, which send to table with a tureen of made gravy and red-currant jelly. 8 persons.

CHOPS WITH WALNUT SAUCE

4 chops, 1 tablespoon potted turkey, or chicken and ham, 2 pickled walnuts 1 gill liquor from the jar of walnut pickles, a few drops of sherry.

Chop the walnuts very finely. Put the meat paste in a basin and add the walnut pickle liquor very slowly, stirring with a wooden spoon until all is thoroughly blended. Add the pickled walnuts. Then stand the basin in a saucepan half full of hot water, and stir.

Begin to grill the chops and while they are cooking, go on stirring the sauce, whilst adding the sherry in the basin until it boils. When the chops are done, put them in an earthenware dish. The pickle must not come into contact with metal; then pour the sauce round them.

The haunch was a picture for painters to study,
The fat was so white, and the lean was so ruddy.
Oliver Goldsmith

LEG OF LAMB IN PASTRY

1 small leg of lamb (3-4 lbs.)
Butter Thyme and rosemary
1-2 tablespoons good brandy
1 egg yolk, slightly beaten
2 lamb kidneys, diced
2½ ozs. sliced mushrooms
Salt and freshly ground pepper
Flaky pastry.

Have the butcher bone lamb. Saute kidneys in 2 tablespoons butter in a thick-bottomed frying pan for 1 minute. Add sliced mushrooms and season to taste with thyme, rosemary, salt and freshly ground black pepper. Simmer, stirring constantly, for 1 or 2 minutes more. Sprinkle with a good brandy.

Stuff leg of lamb with this mixture; reshape leg of lamb and stitch or tie opening with heavy thread. Sprinkle lamb with salt and freshly ground black pepper, and roast in a moderate oven for 20 to 25 minutes, or until half cooked. Cool; rub with 2 tablespoons softened butter; wrap in thinly rolled flaky pastry. Brush with cold water and bake in a hot oven for 15 to 20 minutes more. Brush with slightly beaten egg yolk and continue baking until the crust is browned.

TO DRESS A SHEEP'S HEAD

1 sheep's head, sufficient water to cover it, 3 carrots, 3 turnips, 2 or 3 parsnips 3 onions, a small bunch of parsley 1 teaspoonful of pepper 3 teaspoonfuls of salt, ¼ lb. of oatmeal.

Clean the head well, and let it soak in warm water for 2 hours, to get rid of the blood; put it into a saucepan with sufficient cold water to cover it, and when it boils, add the vegetables, peeled and sliced, and the remaining ingredients; before adding the oatmeal, mix it to a smooth batter with a little of the liquor. Keep stirring till it boils up; then shut the saucepan closely, and let it stew gently for 1½ or 2 hours. It may be thickened with rice or barley, but oatmeal is preferable.
For 3 persons.

"Meat eating tends to excite the passions. This is seen in the animal kingdom. The animals that are mild, patient, and docile, are generally herbivorous, such as the cow, the sheep, the horse; while the excitable, quick-tempered, and ferocious animals are meat-eaters, such as the lion, the tiger, the leopard. A meat diet also tends to constipation, the great scourge of the race.

"The Sabbath should not be made a day of feasting. The labour of the week being laid aside, a moderate amount of plain, wholesome food is all that is necessary. To gormandize on this day, as is the custom with man, causes the mind to become dull and stupid, and unfits it for spiritual devotion."
From "A Friend in the Kitchen"

Married women, more deeply versed in ballroom gossip than in the arts of boiling or frying, should set their faces against emigration, unless they intend to turn over a new leaf. Unmarried girls may emigrate, but they must condescend to become useful as well as agreeable. Many good, honest settlers have been ruined by having fine ladies for wives.
Emigrants Manual

MOCK VENISON
(made with leg of mutton)

Make a marinade of vinegar, salt, pepper, parsley, cloves, bayleaf, onion. Lay your joint in this, and keep for three days in a cool place, turning it twice a day. When ready to be cooked, lard it, roast and serve with a sauce made from the remains of the marinade, a little stock and a lot of pepper. Have red currant jelly handed separately.

HOMESTEAD CORNED BEEF

Soak corned meat for about one hour before cooking, then drain.

Put on to cook in fresh warm water to cover, and add a pinch of baking soda, ½ teaspoon of caraway seeds or cloves, 1 onion, 1 tablespoon of brown sugar and 1 tablespoon of vinegar or honey.

Bring slowly to boil, simmer until tender — about 40 minutes to the 1 lb. Leave in water until cold. Serve with mustard or onion sauce.

BARWON BEEF

Round of beef ham rind, spices, herbs, bacon, vegetables, brandy, red wine.

Make six small incisions in a 3 lb. piece of round of beef and insert small piece of onion in each one. In a casserole, place a piece of ham rind about 4 inches square, add the piece of beef and sprinkle it lightly with salt and pepper and a pinch each of nutmeg and cinnamon.

Add a boquet garni, three whole cloves, 1 slice of bacon, diced, four shallots, cut in halves, two medium onions, quartered and two carrots cut in long strips.

Then add ¼ cup of brandy, two cups of red wine, ½ cup of beef stock and enough water almost to cover the meat with liquid. Put a piece of heavy parchment paper over the casserole and tie it tightly around the rim.

Put the lid on the casserole and cook in a slow oven for about 6 hours. To serve, remove the beef to a deeper platter, surround it with the vegetables and pour the juices over it, first skimming from them as much fat as possible.

STUFFED GOANNA

2 large lamb flaps (boned)

Stuffing:

2 cups soft white breadcrumbs
1 tablespoon chopped butter
1 small finely chopped onion
1 tablespoon rosemary
1 tablespoon parsley
Beaten egg to bind
Salt and pepper to taste.

Mix all ingredients together. Place stuffing on one flap, cover with other flap.

Secure with skewers around edges. Place in baking dish, pour a little water around. Bake in a moderate oven for about an hour. Cover it if necessary. Serve with gravy and vegetables.

HOME CURING OF BACON

Cut up the pig, removing the spine and pelvis. Rub each piece well with salt, and pack in a cask or crock — not a metal container. Next morning, take the meat out and drain off liquid. Pour in brine when meat is again packed in the container, placing a heavy weight on top, as meat must be kept covered.

BRINE — To each 100 pounds of meat use 2 pounds of treacle or brown sugar, 1 oz. salt petre and enough salt stirred into boiling water to float a potato the size of an egg.

Approximately 8 pounds of salt to make 4 gallons of water into brine. Pour over the meat when cold. Turn meat every few days. Leave bacon in the brine for 3 weeks; hams and shoulders for 4 weeks. Then dry well in the sun. Hang in a dry cool place until thoroughly dry.

Smoke the meat for up to 2 days or the meat becomes the desired shade. Meat may be hung at room temperature for 30 days. This practice allows salt to equalise and improves the flavour. Finished meat may be rubbed lightly all over with vegetable oil to improve the appearance.

Beef can be cured in the same way, eliminating the use of pickle tubs.

Rice or oat husks can be bought from oatmeal manufacturers and most suitable for keeping meat packed in either bag or boxes.

MAKING A SMOKE HOUSE

There are several ways of smoking hams in your own back yard, usually done over a slow burning carpet of dried sawdust until the meat turns a light chestnut color.

An old outhouse makes a suitable smokehouse. In fact a smaller place will do so long as it is high enough to prevent the hams from being overheated by the smouldering sawdust.

A barrel placed on end on low brick walls is good enough for a few hams at a time.

TO ROAST A SUCKING PIG

After the pig has been scalded and prepared for the spit, wipe it as dry as possible and put into the body about ½ pint of fine breadcrumbs, mixed with 3 tablespoons of sage, minced, 3 ozs. of butter, a large saltspoon of salt and 2/3 as much of pepper or some cayenne. Sew it up with soft, but strong cotton; truss it as a hare, with the forelegs skewered back and the hind legs forward; lay it to a strong clear fire, but keep it at a moderate distance to save scorching. As soon as it becomes warm, rub it with a bit of butter tied in a fold of muslin and repeat this process constantly as it is roasting. When the gravy begins to drop from it, put under a deep oblong dish of suitable size to catch it in. As soon as the pig is of a fine light amber brown and the steam draws strongly towards the fire, wipe it quite dry with a clean cloth and rub a bit of cold butter over it. When it is half done, a pig iron, or a large flat iron should be hung in the centre of the grate, or the middle of the pig will be done long before the ends. When it is ready for the table, lay it into a very hot dish and before the spit is withdrawn, take off and open the head and split the body in two; chop together quickly the stuffing and the brains, put them into half a pint of good veal gravy, which has dropped from the pig; pour a small portion of this under the roast and serve the remainder as hot as possible in a tureen. A little powdered mace and cayenne and a squeeze of lemon juice may be added, should the flavour require heightening. Bread sauce and plain gravy should likewise be served with it. Some persons still prefer the old fashioned currant sauce to any other; and many have the brains and stuffing stirred into rich melted butter, instead of gravy; but the recipe which has been given has usually been so much approved, that we can recommend it with some confidence, as it stands.

In dishing the pig, lay the body flat in the middle and the head and ears at the ends and sides. When very pure oil can be obtained, it is preferable to butter for the basting; it should be laid on with a bunch of feathers. A pig of three weeks old is considered as best suited to the table and it should always be dressed if possible the day it is killed.

CASSEROLE TRIPE

2 lbs. tripe	3 small onions
2 large carrots	Some bayleaves
1 teaspoon thyme	6 whole cloves

a clove of garlic
4 bacon rashers cut in 2 inch pieces

Grease a casserole that can be closely covered and put a layer of bacon in it, then a layer of the vegetables, sliced, sprinkle with spices, also salt, pepper and a little cayenne. Then a layer of tripe. Repeat layers and cover with 3 cups of good broth. Cover casserole and put in oven. If cooking in a woodfire stove, can be left in a very moderate oven for 1½ hours.

TO BOIL A WHOLE HAM

The old fashioned way was to boil the ham in the kitchen copper, often with a bunch of hay in the water, a practise which goes back at least 200 years and was commended by all the best cooks. One purpose was to prevent the ham from sticking to the bottom of the cooking-pot. The bunch of hay, which is still used in France, is also thought to improve the flavour of the meat. The usual pot herbs, peppercorns, sweet herbs and a bayleaf may be added to the water in the cooking. The stock will make excellent pea soup.

First soak the joint depending on the type of cure and instructions of the suppliers. Usually 12 hours is enough, with several changes of water. Lay it in a ham-kettle or other large pan with cold fresh water to cover it. Bring slowly to the boil, clearing the scum as it rises, with a skimming spoon. Then reduce the heat and let it simmer for 20-25 minutes per lb. if it is a small joint. Large ones need less time. Allow 3 hours for a 10 lb. ham or gammon to 4½ hours for a 20 lb. ham. When a skewer can be stuck right through it, it is done.

HAM CURED WITH ALE

A ham weighing 10 to 12 lbs. 1 pint of old ale, 1 pint of stout, ¾ lb. of treacle, ¾ lb. of salt, ¾ lb. coarse salt, ¼ oz. saltpetre.

Put the ingredients into a saucepan and boil for about 5 minutes. While the mixture is boiling rub the ham with the coarse salt and put it in a large pickling pan. Then pour over the mixture whilst it is hot. Keep the ham in pickle for 3 weeks (adding the necessary water to make the pickle), turning and rubbing it every day. Then take it out, put it in a thin cotton bag and hang it in the kitchen to smoke.

TO DRESS A HAM FOR TABLE

When skinned, chop parsley (free from grit, but not wetted or washed) impalpably fine, scatter it over the ham, then grate a whole nutmeg over this. This will keep it almost any length of time, and adds a nice flavour.

BACON IN CIDER

1 corner bacon (6 lbs.)
1 pint cider 1 dozen cloves
1 bunch sweet herbs 2 ozs. brown sugar
1 teacupful brown breadcrumbs

Soak bacon overnight. Then bring to the boil, pour off water and add fresh herbs and simmer slowly, allowing 20 minutes to each pound, and pouring in the cider 1 hour before it is done. When cooked, let bacon cool and remove skin; cover with sugar and breadcrumbs, and stick with cloves. Bake till brown.

TO BOIL A HAM
(An eighteenth century recipe)

Steep your ham all night in water, then boil it. If it is a medium size it will take three hours' boiling, and a small one will take 2½ hours. When you take it off the fire, pull off the skin and smear it all over with beaten egg; strew on breadcrumbs, baste it with butter, set it to the fire until it is a light brown. If it is to be eaten hot garnish it with carrots and serve it.

Madeira is the accepted wine for braising ham and to reheat a substantial piece, press it into an oven dish that it just fits. Pour sufficient madeira on to the ham to keep it moist and heat in the oven. When the meat is ready, set it aside and add a handful of raisins to the wine and let it reduce on high heat. Season to taste and pour a little over each serving of ham.

CURING BACON AT HOME

Cut up the pig, removing the spine and pelvis. Rub each piece well with salt; and pack in cask, or crock (not metal).

Next morning, take the meat out and drain off liquid and discard the liquid. Pour on brine when meat is again packed in container. Place a heavy weight on top, as meat must be kept covered.

BRINE: To each 100 lb. of meat, use 2 lb. of treacle or brown sugar, 1 oz. salt petre and enough salt stirred into boiling water to float a potato the size of an egg.

It takes about 8 lb. of salt to make four gallons of water into brine.

Pour over meat when cold and turn meat every few days.

Leave bacon in the brine for three weeks; and hams and shoulders for four weeks.

Then dry well in the sun and hang in dry cool place.

YORKSHIRE PUDDING

The batter should always be made with plain flour, with no rising ingredient added. Do not use glass or enamel baking dish, causing "pudding" to become stodgy. Use a well used tin, a large square one, a 4 inch round tin or individual bun tins. The tins should be hot before the batter is put in. Bake on top browning shelf for 30 minutes in hot oven.

Gravy should be thickened with left over batter and some lightly fried onions.

ROAST BEEF

King Charles II is said to have honoured this joint with the accolade of knighthood, and hence the term of SIR-Loin.

Our Second Charles, of fame facete,
On loin of beef did dine;
He held his sword, pleas'd o'er the meat,
"Arise, thou famed Sir-Loin."
'Sir John Barleycorn's Ballad'

OLD BUCKINGHAMSHIRE BASTE

Roast the meat as usual. Baste every 30 minutes with a mixture of 2 tablespoonsful of Worcestershire Sauce, 2 tablespoonsful of any other thick piquant sauce, 1 teaspoonful of anchovy sauce or essence, 1 tablespoonful of mixed mustard, 2 small finely chopped onions.

The oven should be no more than moderately hot, after the joint has been basted as the gravy or sauce, which is made from the bastings with the fat and juices from the meat may burn. The flavour of this is excellent and it should be served with the meat.

TO CURE A ROUND OF BEEF IN HOT WEATHER, OR IF NEEDED FOR IMMEDIATE USE.

Rub in thoroughly a rather large quantity of fine salt, with a little saltpetre, then place it over a tub or pan of water on two sticks, placing a good quantity of salt on the upper side; turn it once after twelve hours, laying additional salt on the turned-up side; it will be cured in twenty-four hours. Should it be required at once, with a small squirt or syringe, if cold brine be at hand, it might be squirted into all the crevices, and then it could be cooked in twelve hours. If beef is not required in a hurry, a little sugar and less salt very much improves the flavour. This applies to curing hams.

THE IMPORTANCE OF CARVING

When meat is cooked let it "rest" for about 15 minutes before carving it. Gain is quality and flavour.

Meat is grained. Cut against the fibres.

Always put the fork into the heart of a sirloin.

Cherish your carving-knife as you would your razor. Never wash it in very hot water; clean with a damp cloth. Keep it sharp with a steel and a rub up on a stone back door step. Never put in the sink or drawer with other knifes.

A great deal of the comfort and satisfaction of a good dinner depends upon the carving. Awkward carving is enough to spoil the appetite of a refined sensitive person. Formerly in England there were regular teachers of the art of carving, and Lady Mary Wortley Montague confesses that she once took lessons of such a professor three times a week. In the seventeenth century carving was a science that carried with it as much pedantry as the business of school-teaching does in the present day; and for a person to use wrong terms in relation to carving was an unpardonable affront to etiquette.

HOT BOILED PIG'S TROTTERS

Hot boiled trotters with parsley sauce are served as a supper dish with bread and butter. Pig's feet, or trotters, take about 2½ hours to boil tender. Allow 1 trotter each, split in two by the butcher. Wash them well, put them in a pan with 2 peeled sliced onions, salt, pepper and a pinch of ground nutmeg and a strip of lemon peel: add 1 pint of white stock.

William Howitt, writing from Bendigo,
October 10th, 1853

Pork is almost as precious as eggs. The scarcity of pigs has made it any price that people please to ask. A Jew of the name of Lazarus, at the Ovens, was tempted by it to begin feeding pigs; but being taunted for it by a drunken fellow, one day when Charlton was by, he snatched up a whole litter of young ones, and in a rage flung them without any care, and subsequently with a terrific screaming, into a warehouse, where I suppose they would be kept close till they could be snugly disposed of. An old lady near here sold two little ones for 8L., and was congratulating herself on her good bargain when the butcher came back and said, "ah, Ma'am, I've made a very foolish bargain — I've sold the pigs for 15L.; and if I had kept them for only an hour longer I could have had 20L." (20L = £20). The poor lady was so struck by her own folly that she was very near taking to her bed, and lamented to us grievously her ill luck.

CARVING JOINTS

The best way to carve a ham in order that the fat and lean may be served evenly, is to begin in the middle of the ham and cut out thin, circular slices; though good carvers often begin at the large end of the ham, which is certainly the most saving way. In carving a sirloin of beef begin at either end, or in the middle. The outside should be sliced downward to the bone, while the inside or tender part should be sliced thin, lengthwise, and a little of the soft fat given with each piece. Ask whether the outside or inside is preferred; otherwise a small bit of the inside should be served with each plate, as this is generally regarded as the choicest portion.

But little skill is required in carving a round of beef. It should be cut in thin, smooth, and even slices.

A fillet of veal is cut in the same way as a round of beef. Ask whether the brown or outside is preferred. If it is stuffed, cut deep through the stuffing, and serve each plate with a thin slice, with a little of the fat also.

A leg of mutton should be sliced lightly, for if pressed too heavily the knife will not cut, but will squeeze out all the gravy. Begin to cut in the middle, as that is the most juicy part. Cut thin, deep slices, and help each person to a little of the fat and some of the brown, or outside.

In carving a fore-quarter of lamb, separate the shoulder from the breast and ribs by passing the knife under and through it; then separate the gristly part from the ribs, and help from that or the ribs, as may be chosen.

A haunch is the leg and a part of the loin. In carving, help to about equal parts of the fat of the loin and the lean of the leg. Cut each part directly down through, in slices about a quarter of an inch thick. A saddle of mutton should be cut in thin slices from tail to end, beginning close to the back-bone; help some fat from the sides.

A roast pig should be cut in two before being sent to the table. Begin to carve by separating the shoulder from one side, then divide the ribs; the joints may be divided or pieces cut from them. The ribs are considered the finest part, though some prefer the neck end.

PIG'S TROTTERS with SAUCE ROBERT

Boil 6 cloven pig's trotters very gently for several hours, until you can bone them with ease. Brush with egg and breadcrumbs. Fry until golden.

Soften chopped onions in butter, add nearly a wine glass of vinegar, when the onions have cooled, and reduce to half. Put in some wine, cook slowly for 10 minutes, then add chopped parsley and mustard.

PIGS EARS

Singe and clean with a nearly red-hot poker. Scrape, clean, blanch. Cook in a braising pot, fire under and cover. Let cool. Cut into thin strips and cover with sliced onions cooked in butter and veal broth, adding a dash of vinegar just before serving.

PIGS TROTTERS

Singe as many feet as a pig has. Scrape and wash in hot water. Split them in half. Tie the pieces together. Braise or cook in bouillon. Drain, cool, remove the tape. Separate the pieces. Dip in melted butter. Serve with parsley sauce, but with bread and salt in the summer.

PIG'S TROTTERS IN JELLY

Take two pig's feet, a little sage, salt and pepper. Split and wash the feet quite clean, place in a saucepan and cover with cold water. Simmer until the meat comes away easily from the bones, which takes about 2 hours. Cut the flesh into small pieces, return the bones to the pan and boil for another hour. Now remove the bones and put the meat back with a little chopped parsley and sage, or mixed herbs, simmer for a few minutes, then pour into a mould to set.

GALANTINE OF HAM AND TONGUE

1½ lbs. minced pork	10 rashers of bacon
2 parboiled onions	2 bayleaves
mixed spices	salt and pepper

½ lb. cooked tongue sliced into long strips
2 tablespoons of slivered almonds
½ lb. cooked ham sliced into long strips
1 small glass of sherry

Mince the pork meat with the parboiled onions. Season with pepper, salt, a pinch of mixed spices, sherry and nuts. Line a small meat press measuring approximately 8½ by 3½ by 4½ inches. If you do not have one, use a casserole with a weight on top for cooking. The pressing is important. Line the press with the bacon strips and bayleaf. Cover with a layer of pork forcemeat, then with a layer of the meat strips. Continue in this way until the press is filled. Cover with the rest of the bacon strips and the second bayleaf. Put on lid and press firmly. Place in oven in baking dish of hot water and bake in moderate oven for 1½ hours. When cool, chill. When serving, turn out and slice the galantine to show the different layers in profile.

BAKED HAM WITH ORANGE-HONEY GLAZE.

1 cooked ham ½ cup of orange juice
1 cup honey whole cloves
1 tablespoon grated orange rind

Place ham in roasting pan, fat side up, and bake in slow oven 25-30 minutes per pound. About 45 minutes before ham is done, remove rind, pour off all but 1 to 2 tablespoon of fat. Score ham diagonally with sharp knife and stick one clove in each diamond shaped area.

Blend the grated orange rind, orange juice and honey, spread mixture on ham. Return ham to oven and baste frequently with the glaze. Remove when ham is glazed and nicely browned.

GRAND PORK

Piece of fresh pork. Put in large dish. Cut up 2 large onions. Slice 2 inches of carrot thinly and drop them in, also 5 peppercorns crushed, a teaspoonful of chopped mint, a bayleaf, and a good sprig of thyme. Over all pour ¼ cup of strong vinegar, an equal quantity of water, and half a gill of good salad oil (not olive). In this mixture the pork must lie for 3 days being turned 3 or 4 times a day.

At the end of this time drain the meat and roast it basting with a little of the liquor of the marinade, the rest being boiled until slightly reduced, then strained. When roast is done, put aside and brown a little flour in the pan and make your sauce with the strained marinade plus a little mustard; this is a sauce and not a gravy.

DANDENONG PORK

Get the butcher to put half a pig's head — with the ear and tongue but minus the brains — and a long-cut pig's foot in brine for a couple of days. Other ingredients are approximately 1 lb. of a cheap and gelatinous cut of beef such as ox cheek or shin, a large onion, 4 large carrots, a bunch of parsley, 2 bayleaves, 8 to 12 whole peppercorns, 1 large leek or a couple of sticks of celery, 2 small cloves of garlic, lemon juice.

Soak the salted pig's head and foot in cold water to cover for a couple of hours. Put them in a very large saucepan with all the other ingredients except the lemon juice, cover with fresh cold water and simmer them very, very gently for a minimum of 4 hours. The slower the cooking the better the result will be, for if they are boiled too fast both beef and pig's head will be ragged and stringy.

When the head and foot are cooked — the meat should come away from the bones at a touch — remove them, with the beef, to a bowl. As soon as they are cool enough to handle, skin the tongue and also the rough parts of the head round the ear and snout where the skin is coarse. Remove all gristle — what you leave out of a brawn is as important as what you put in.

Chop the pig meat and skin which is left on, the boned foot, and the beef. Cut the tongue into neat slices. Taste to see if extra salt is needed. A brawn should always be fairly highly seasoned or it will be insipid and cloying, so it will probably need extra pepper, freshly milled, possibly salt, and the strained juice of a whole small lemon, a very important ingredient in dishes made of fat meat, but one not enough used by English cooks.

Now mix the sliced tongue with all the other chopped meat. There will be enough to fill a 3 to 4 pint mould, basin, terrine, or cake tin. Add about 3 soup ladles — approximately ¾ pint — of the hot stock and leave the whole thing to cool. Then cover with a piece of greased paper, a plate which just fits inside the tin or bowl, and a weight. Leave until next day. Before turning it out, stand the tin in a bowl of hot water for a few minutes. With a salad, brawn can serve as a main dish for a summer meal, or simply with toast or bread and a mustardy sauce it makes an excellent first course — like a paté.

Dash'd the bold fork through pies of pork;
O'er hard-boil'd eggs the saltspoon shook;
Leapt from its lair the playful cork:
Yet some there were, to whom the brook
Seem'd sweetest beverage, and for meat
They chose the red root of the beet.

C.S. Calverley

HONEY PORK

4 lbs. lean belly of pork or pork spareribs
1 dessertspoon Worcestershire sauce
3 tablespoons sweet sherry
3 tablespoons honey 2 medium onions
2 tablespoons lemon juice
½ teaspoon curry powder
¼ teaspoon chilli powder
¼ cup oil.

Remove rind and any excess fat from pork. Cut into 2 inch strips if using belly of pork. Combine peeled and finely chopped onion, worcestershire sauce, sherry, honey, lemon juice, pepper, salt, curry powder and chilli powder in bowl. Add pork pieces, marinate 2 hours. Drain marinade from pork; reserve.

Put pork and oil in baking dish, bake in moderately hot oven 45 minutes; brush frequently with marinade. Reduce heat to moderate, bake a further 30 minutes or until pork is tender. For last 20 minutes of cooking time pour marinade over pork, turning pork pieces occasionally.

When roasting pork, wash and place green apples in a dish in the oven to bake slowly below the roast. Serve instead of apple sauce.

COUNTRY BRAWN

1 sheep's trotter 1 pig's trotter
2 sheep's tongues ½ lb. pork fillet
Pepper and salt

A little Worcestershire sauce or two small spring onions improves the flavour.

Cover meats well with water. Cook for 2 or more hours. Take out bones before putting in mould to set.

BACON WITH RAISIN STUFFING

2 lbs. shoulder bacon (in the piece)
2 teacups breadcrumbs
salt and pepper to taste
½ teacup soft brown sugar
2 tablespoons butter
1 teaspoon crushed sage
½ cup seedless raisins
1 tablespoon cornflour

Soak bacon as necessary in cold water to cover. Remove, wipe over, then make a deep slit lengthwise in the bacon and stuff. Rub butter into breadcrumbs, add sage, seasoning and raisins. Mix well. Pack this stuffing into the bacon. Tie or skewer edges together.

Place on rack in baking pan and bake in moderate oven for 1 hour. Remove skin. Mix brown sugar with cornflour. Rub mixture well into fat side of bacon. Return to moderately-hot oven and bake 20 minutes until glazed. Serve cold with apple sauce.

BEEF WITH CELERY AND WALNUTS

1½ lbs. bladebone steak
*2 tablespoons plain flour
(may be increased to 3 tablespoons if a thicker sauce is desired)
bouquet garni (bayleaf, thyme,parsley)
1 pint stock (approximately)
2 teaspoons orange peel
1 oz. walnuts (shelled)
1½-2 ozs. butter 12 button onions
5 ozs. claret Salt, pepper
4 sticks celery ½ oz. butter

Cut the beef into large squares and brown in two lots in the hot butter, then remove. Meanwhile, blanch the onions, putting them into cold water and bringing to the boil, then simmer for a few minutes. Drain, then add the onions to the butter and cook slowly until a light golden brown. Remove from the stove. Add extra butter if required, and melt, to take up the flour.

* This being a thin sauce, most people prefer to use the increased quantity suggested.

Add the claret, bouquet garni, crushed with salt. Return the meat, cover with the stock and season with salt and pepper. Bring slowly to the boil, cover and simmer gently for about 1½ hours.

After cooking about one hour, add the following mixture to the casserole. Cook until tender.

Cut the celery in slices crossways. Heat ½ oz. of butter in a frying pan, add the walnuts and toss over the heat with salt until crisp. Add the celery and shake over the heat for a moment. Add to the casserole. Finely shred the orange peel, put in cold water and bring to the boil to remove the bitterness, then strain. Scatter the orange rind on top before serving.

SQUATTER'S CASSEROLE

1½ lbs. topside of beef cut very thin
1 tablespoon flour
1 tablespoon shortening
1 teaspoon grated lemon rind
1 tablespoon plum jam
3 rashers bacon 1 cup stock
¼ cup vinegar ¼ cup claret (optional)
Salt and pepper Prunes

Cut steak into 3 inch squares, place bacon and prune on steak and roll. Secure. Roll in seasoning and flour. Fry until browned. Place in casserole, add other ingredients.

Cook about 1½ hours. Thicken if necessary.

DUBLIN STEW

2 tablespoons butter 5 ozs. water
3 bayleaves Salt and pepper
1 large onion 8 ozs. carrot
2 tablespoons flour 5 ozs. stout
1½ lbs. bladbone steak
1 tablespoon chopped parsley
10-12 soaked prunes (optional)
10-12 hazelnuts (optional)

Heat half the butter and add the bayleaves; let them crackle. Cut the beef into cubes and brown in two lots, then remove. Slice the onion, add to the pan and cook till a light golden colour.

Add the remaining butter to the pan, sprinkle in the flour off the heat and work till smooth. Return to the heat, adding the stout and water. Season to taste and add the parsley and carrot, cut into circles.

Cover and braise in a moderately slow oven — 325 deg. — for 1½ to 1¾ hours.

In the 19th century, soaked and stoned prunes stuffed with toasted hazelnuts, were added half an hour before the meat was ready.

WAKEFIELD STEAK

1½ lbs. rump steak. Score steak. Mix together 1 teaspoon salt, 1 teaspoon sugar, ½ teaspoon pepper, 1 tablespoon chutney or tomato sauce, 1 tablespoon Worcestershire sauce, 1 tablespoon vinegar. Let steak stand in the mixture 2-3 hours. Put 1 oz. butter in pan. Drain steak, fry briskly in butter 10-12 minutes. Make gravy with rest of mixture.

Can be cooked in casserole.

BEEF CURRY

2 lbs. meat cut from shin
1 large green apple
2 medium-sized onions
1 tablespoon dripping
3 dessertspoons flour
1 dessertspoon curry powder
1 teaspoon brown sugar
1 tablespoon plum jam
1 tablespoon chutney
Squeeze lemon juice
1 skinned, chopped tomato
1½ cups stock or water
1 teaspoon salt Few sultanas

Peel and dice the apple and onions, fry until lightly browned in hot dripping; add chopped meat and brown slightly. Then stir in other ingredients in order given; place over low heat, stirring until boiling. Cover and simmer for 2-3 hours, stirring occasionally. Serve in a bed of rice, garnished with lemon and parsley.

OX HEART

This is an excellent dish if well basted and attended to. Stuff it in the centre with veal stuffing, and have a few stuffing balls in the dripping pan. Put paper on the heart at first, and afterwards take away the paper, and flour it so as to put a froth on. Serve hot, with hot water plates and currant jelly. It is very excellent cut in slices and hashed, but be sure to mind the fluid is not too watery. A dozen sheeps' hearts are very nice indeed dressed in this way.

SHEEP'S HEAD BAKE

2 sheep's heads 1-2 eggs
Onion, parsley, breadcrumbs a little milk

Boil sheep's heads until tender, then cut meat in small pieces. Add finely chopped onion and parsley, to taste. Put into buttered pie dish, moisten with a little stock and cover thickly with breadcrumbs moistened with 1 or 2 well-beaten eggs and a little milk. Dot small knobs of butter on top and bake for 30 minutes.

The rest of the stock can be used for broth.

MOCK GOOSE

Slice a sheep's liver and pour boiling water over it. Make some stuffing with bread, not fresh, pinch of herbs, onion, pepper and salt. (About 2 cups breadcrumbs would be enough.)

Grease a pie dish and put layer of stuffing on bottom, cover with a layer of finely sliced cooking apple, next a layer of liver and then a layer of parboiled potatoes.

Sprinkle with salt and pepper. Continue this way until dish is full. Sprinkle bacon pieces on top. Pour over ½ cup stock or hot water. Cover and bake 1 to 1½ hours in slow oven.

BALLARAT STUFFED MUTTON ROLLS

1½ lbs. mutton flaps 3 rashers bacon
1 egg Flour and mutton stock
Salt and pepper ¼ lb. stale breadcrumbs
pinch crushed herbs 1 peeled onion
teaspoon minced parsley
2 tablespoons dripping

Skin flaps, removing excess fat. Cut into neat pieces 3 x 4 inches. Mix crumbs with chopped bacon, parsley, herbs, salt and pepper to taste and beaten egg to bind. Place a small piece of stuffing on each flap and roll up. Skewer with toothpick or tie with string. Dip each roll in flour and fry until evenly browned in smoking hot fat. Drain and place in a casserole. Cover with mutton stock. Cover and simmer gently for 1¼ hours.

SEASONED LAMB'S FRY

1 large firm lamb's fry 3 cups of breadcrumbs
1 cup cold boiled rice 1 teaspoon mixed spice
½ teaspoon salt pinch of pepper
¼ teaspoon dry mustard
1 medium onion
½ teaspoon curry powder

Wash liver in salt and water, dry and trim if necessary. Cut a deep pocket with a sharp knife in thick side of liver.

Peel onion and dice finely. Blend together in a bowl, the breadcrumbs, onion, rice, mixed spice, curry powder, mustard, salt and pepper. Mix well together and press stuffing firmly into pocket. Tie up well with string. Place in hot fat to bake, surrounded with potatoes. Baste well while cooking. Serve in slices, with brown gravy, baked potatoes and green peas.

LAMB AS HAM

4-5 lb. leg of lamb — have the butcher pump the lamb 3 or 4 days before required.
2 lbs. plain flour ¼ cup vinegar
Rounded teaspoon mustard
¾ pint water to mix to a scone-like dough
buttered breadcrumbs

Roll out the dough made from the flour, mustard, vinegar and water and wrap the meat in it. Dot cloves over the dough and place in baking dish, without water or fat.

Cook for about 3½ hours in oven, not too hot. Remove the crust, cover with buttered breadcrumbs and put back in oven for about 15 minutes. Leave until cool to cut.

HASH MAGANDY

Fry a bit of salt pork in a big iron frying pan over the fire until done. Pour out most of the fat. Chop up the remains of the meat that was cooked the night before. Toss that in the pan and add a chopped onion or two. Cook this up a bit and toss in any left over vegetables such as carrots, beans or whatever. Left-over rice is good too. Add some water and thicken with flour.

LAMB

Roast a saddle of lamb on a bed of peeled onions, sprinkled with pepper and rosemary, but no salt.

CORROBOREE HOTPOT

1-1¼ lb. braising steak 1 oz. seeded raisins
2 onions ½ pint stock
2 cooking apples 1 tablespoon plain flour
2 tomatoes Salt
2 tablespoon dripping Brown sugar
2 ozs. sultanas Parsley
2 teaspoons curry powder 3 hard boiled eggs

Cut up the meat and slice the onions, apples and tomatoes. Heat the oil in a frying pan, add the meat, onion and apple and fry until golden brown. Add the tomatoes and curry powder fried in a little oil and cook for a few minutes longer. Place the mixture in a casserole, add the dried fruit and barely cover with stock. Place lid on the casserole and cook in a moderate oven for 1½ hours. Blend the flour with a little extra water and stir into the casserole. Season to taste with a little salt and brown sugar, garnish with parsley and sliced egg, and serve.

SCOTTISH HAGGIS

Procure the large stomach-bag of a sheep, also one of the smaller bags called "King's Hood", together with the pluck, which is the lights, liver and heart. The bags must be well washed, first in cold water, then plunged in boiling water and scraped. Great care must be taken of the large bag; let it lie and soak in cold water, with a little salt, all night. Wash also the pluck. You will now boil the small bag along with the pluck; in boiling, leave the windpipe attached and let the end of it hang over the edge of the pot, so that impurities may pass freely out. Boil for 1½ hours and take the whole from the pot. When cold, cut away the windpipe and any bits of skin or gristle that seem improper. Grate a quarter of the liver (not using the remainder for the haggis) and mince the heart, lights and small bag very small, along with ½ lb. of beef suet. Mix all this mince with 2 small teacupfuls of oatmeal, previously dried before the fire, black and Jamaica pepper and salt; also add ½ pint of the liquor in which the pluck was boiled, or beef gravy. Stir all together into a consistency. Then take the large bag, which has been thoroughly cleaned, and put the mince into it. Fill it only a little more than half full, in order to leave room for the meal and meat to expand. If crammed too full it will burst in boiling. Sew up the bag with a needle and thread. The haggis is now complete. Put it in a pot with boiling water and prick it occasionally with a large needle, as it swells, to allow the air to escape. If the bag appears thin, tie a cloth outside the skin. There should be a plate beneath it, to prevent it sticking to the bottom of the pot. Boil it for 3 hours. Serve in a napkin on a dish, without garnish or gravy, it being sufficiently rich in itself.

MOCK HAGGIS

½ to ¾lb. of any cooked meat, rabbit or chicken (or a mixture of all three if you have them)
1 cup of stock or water
¼ lb. minced suet
1 medium onion chopped small
1 handful of oatmeal
Salt and pepper

Mince the meat or chop if very fine, mix with other ingredients and put into a greased pudding basin. Cover with a cloth or two thicknesses of greaseproof paper and steam for two hours.

ORDERS OF HENRY VIII for refreshment and maintenance of dear Lady Lucy in her own room.

Idem: Every morning for breakfast one whole fillet of beef, a four pound loaf, a fruit tart and a gallon of strong beer.

Idem: At dinner a piece of salt beef, a slice of roast beef, some fricassee, a four pound loaf and a gallon of strong beer.

Idem: At supper a plate of vegetables, a joint of mutton, a plate of delicacies, a three pound loaf and a gallon of strong beer.

Idem: For late supper a two pound loaf, a cake, and half a gallon of wine.

What poor eaters we are now.

The discovery of a new dish does more for the happiness of man than the discovery of a star.

Brillat-Savarin.

ALMOND DUMPLINGS

1½ cups fine white biscuit crumbs
¼ cup blanched almonds, chopped fine
3 tablespoons butter, browned
1 teaspoon salt — Pepper, mace
½ cup milk — 1 egg, beaten

Roll biscuits very fine, add chopped almonds and seasoning, milk and egg. Mix well and add browned butter. Form little dumplings with a teaspoon. Cook in gravy five minutes.

DEVILLED JELLIED TONGUE IN PORT

2 calves' tongues or 4 lamb's tongues
1½ cups good meat stock
½ cup port — 4½ teaspoons gelatine
1 tablespoon mixed mustard
1 teaspoon Worcestershire sauce
1 teaspoon lemon rind finely grated
1 tablespoon lemon juice
2 hard-boiled eggs, chopped
1 tablespoon each onion, green pepper, parsley finely chopped
4 tablespons chopped pickles
cayenne, salt and pepper

Cook tongues, skin, trim, and cut into medium-sized pieces. Put meat stock and wine into saucepan and heat to boiling point (do not boil). Season with mustard, Worcestershire sauce, lemon juice and rind, a dash of cayenne, and salt and pepper to taste. Dissolve gelatine in 4 tablespoons cold water for 5 minutes, add to hot mixture, stirring constantly until mixture dissolves. Stir in other ingredients and pieces of tongue. Cool until lukewarm; put into greased container and chill thoroughly. When set, serve on crisp bed of shredded lettuce or water cress. Garnish with mayonnaise, radish roses, and tomato.

VEAL WITH CHEESE SCONE TOPPING

1½ lb. veal steak — ½ cup sour cream
2 ozs. butter — ½ cup tomato sauce
Seasoned flour — 1 cup water
1 large Onion — Salt and pepper

CHEESE SCONES

2 cups self-raising flour
2 ozs. grated cheese for topping
1 teaspoon salt — ¼ pint milk
2ozs. butter — Glazing
2 ozs. grated cheese — 1 egg

Cut veal into 1 inch cubes. Melt butter in saucepan; toss veal in seasoned flour, fry until brown. Add chopped onion, cook further 2 minutes. Add remaining ingredients; season to taste with salt, pepper. Bring to the boil, reduce heat, cover, simmer 8 to 10 minutes until meat is just tender. Transfer to greased casserole. Make up scones, arrange on top of veal. Brush top with milk or extra beaten egg. Sprinkle with 2 ozs. grated cheese. Place dish on baking tray, bake in hot oven 15 to 20 minutes until scones are crisp and golden brown.

Cheese scones

Sift together flour and salt into a bowl. Rub in butter; add 2 ozs. grated cheese. Beat together egg and milk, add to dry mixture to form soft dough. Turn on to floured board, knead lightly. Roll out to ½ inch thickness, cut out with 2 inch cutter.

SMOKED TONGUE WITH MADEIRA SAUCE

Soak the tongue 24 hours, changing the water frequently. Simmer, well covered with water, until a fork penetrates fairly easily. This process takes from 2 to 3 hours. Cool tongue, skin, and trim.

Place the tongue on a trivet in an earthenware pot.

Pour over it 4 cups of unsalted beef stock, and add 2 small onions chopped, 2 chopped carrots, a few sprigs of parsley, a small handful of celery tops, 1 small bayleaf or ½ large, a pinch of thyme, 6 peppercorns, crushed.

Seal the lid onto the pot and simmer 1 to 1½ hours, or until the tongue is very tender when pierced by a fork.

Strain the liquid off into a saucepan and reduce by boiling rapidly for several minutes. Taste. If the salt flavour is too strong, finely slice into the broth a peeled potato, boil up, taste, and remove the slices when sufficient salt has been absorbed. Add ½ cup well-washed seedless raisins and Madeira to taste — 3 or 4 ounces. Thicken with arrowroot and serve poured over the slices of tongue.

VEAL WITH VERMOUTH

2 lb. shoulder of veal	2 ozs. butter
4 onions	1-2 ozs. flour
1 glass white wine	½ gill dry vermouth
Bouquet garni	Seasoning
1 egg yolk	½ lb. mushrooms
¼ pint cream	1 teaspoon lemon juice

1-1½ pints veal stock or water

Cut the meat into 1½ inch cubes, melt the butter in a pan, add the veal and brown on all sides, then add the sliced onions and allow them to just take color. Stir in the flour and blend in the white wine and vermouth. Pour on enough stock to cover, season with salt and pepper and add the bouqet garni. Bring to the boil, cover the pan and simmer gently 1-1¼ hours, then add the sliced mushrooms and continue cooking for 15 to 20 minutes.

Just before serving, whisk the egg yolk with the lemon juice, stir in the cream. Add a little of the hot liquid to the yolk — cream mixture then add slowly to the pan. Allow to simmer for 1-2 minutes, then serve. Do not allow to boil.

LAMB CUTLETS MARIE-ANNE

For lamb cutlets Marie-Anne, you need a special cut of meat.

Cutlets are usually served with a cutlet frill over the end of the bone. They can be made simply by using double white paper fringed on one edge.

When making the sauce, add the hot sauce to the egg yolks carefully, so the mixture does not curdle. For this same reason, do not boil the sauce when re-heating it.

Most butchers will bone and roll the meat and you can cut your own.

2 lbs. best-end neck of lamb, chinned only

Divide into cutlets, taking a double bone if necessary, and trim well. For grilling it is essential to have a good plump cutlet.

Garnish:

Pint of broad beans, shelled.

About one dozen baby carrots, whole.

Boil the beans till tender, drain and keep hot. Cook the carrots in a covered pan with a spoonful or two of water, a knob of butter and a pinch of salt and sugar. By the time the carrots are cooked, the liquor should be reduced to a glaze.

Mix the beans and carrots together and bind with a light chicken stock. Grill the cutlets, arrange in a circle with the beans in the centre. Pour round a little gravy and serve the rest separately.

Sauce poulette:

½ oz. butter	Salt
½ oz. flour	1 egg yolk

¼ pint good veal or chicken stock
Squeeze of lemon juice
2 tablespoons cream or top milk
½ teaspoon chopped savory or parsley
Pepper

Melt the butter, blend in the flour and cook for two-three minutes. Add the stock, lemon juice and seasoning, stir until boiling, and then cook two-three minutes.

Beat the egg yolks with the cream and add one tablespoonful of the hot sauce.

Remove the sauce from the heat, add the egg-yolk mixture very slowly. Finally add the parsley and reheat carefully without boiling.

It's a very odd thing, as odd as can be,
That whatever Miss T. eats, turns into Miss T.
Porridges and apples, mince, muffins and mutton
Jam, junket and jumbles — not a rap, not a button
It matters; the moment they're out of her plate,
Though shared by Miss Butcher, and sour Mr. Bate.
Tiny and cheerful, and neat as can be
Whatever Miss T. eats, turns into Miss T.

Walter de la Mare

NOTES

SWEETMEATS

RICE SNOWBALLS (a pretty dish for Juvenile Suppers)

6 ozs. rice, 1 quart milk, flavouring of essence of almonds, sugar to taste, 1 pint custard.

Boil the rice in the milk, with sugar and a flavouring of essence of almonds, until the former is tender, adding, if necessary, a little more milk, should it dry away too much. When the rice is quite soft, put it into teacups, or small round jars, and let it remain until cold; then turn the rice out on a deep glass dish; pour over a custard, and on the top of each ball place a small piece of bright-coloured preserve or jelly. Lemon-peel or vanilla may be boiled with the rice, instead of the essence of almonds; but the flavouring of the custard must correspond with that of the rice.

TWISTED HAIR

4 level tablespoons Butter
¾ lb. Brown Sugar
2 level teaspoons Baking Soda
1½ lbs. Golden Syrup
3 tablespoons Vinegar

Heat the saucepan; add the butter and tip the pan to spread butter all over it, then add the syrup, sugar and vinegar and stir it over the fire until the sugar is dissolved, then boil without stirring to the thread stage. If it becomes a hard ball, then it is ready. Now add the baking soda. Stir while the mixture is foaming and then pour on to a buttered slab of marble or very large china dish (also buttered). Cool a little, then carefully lift up the edges and turn into the centre. Keep on doing this (known as pulling the toffee) until it becomes golden yellow in colour. Shape into curls and twists and plaits, and cut lengths with scissors.

LOVE APPLES

Make almond paste by mixing ½ lb. of almond meal with 2 ozs. of castor and icing sugars, well-sieved. Flavour with a few drops of almond essence, 2 drops of vanilla and a few drops of brandy (lemon juice can be substituted). Add sufficient raw egg to bind ingredients to a beautiful smooth paste (one yolk or one white usually is sufficient). Knead on a board well dusted with sieved icing sugar or cornflour.

Crumble an equal quantity of chocolate sponge cake moistened lightly with rum or sherry. Take a teaspoon of each. Sandwich between them a glacé cherry or small piece of glace apricot. Shape into a ball. Leave to dry out slightly. Coat the balls with thin almond paste. Roll in chocolate scrapings. Paint with heated apricot jam before rolling if chocolate does not stick.

MEDLAR COMFITS

Simmer 4 lbs. of ripe medlars in 1 pint of water until soft enough to press through a sieve. Weigh the resulting pulp and add an equal weight of sugar. Cook them slowly till the sugar melts, stirring continually, then let the mixture boil until it thickens into a paste, stir it all the time with a wooden spoon. When so thick that the bottom of the pan can be seen in stirring, the paste is done. It should now be rather like dough and no longer stick to the sides. Put it on a marble slab or pastry-board which has been sprinkled thickly with castor sugar. Smooth the mixture with a knife and leave it for some hours to dry. Sprinkle it with castor sugar, cut it in small squares, which roll in sugar. Store them in a tin.

These are pleasant to eat with coffee after dinner.

RATAFIAS

Good sultanas or sultana grapes, put into a wide mouthed jar, which is then filled with brandy. Securely stoppered, leave for several weeks. The sultanas swell. Serve in glasses with toothpicks.

CHRISTMAS RING

½ lb. puff pastry   4 ozs. ground almonds
4 ozs. castor sugar
½ beaten egg and 1 tablespoon of lemon juice

Roll out the pastry and cut a strip 5 x 20 inches long. Mix all other ingredients together, spread this mixture along the entire pastry strip and over half of its width. Fold over, seal well and form into a circle. Brush the top of pastry with beaten egg. Bake in a moderate oven for 15 to 20 minutes. When quite cold, ice with thin glace icing and sprinkle with chopped nuts and cherries.

MADEIRA CRUSTS

Cut several slices of stale bread into even lengths, about 3 inches by 1 inch. Dip in milk and fry in pan of boiling butter until brown. Drain and arrange on dish for serving.

Then pour on following syrup.

Boil small cup of sugar and ½ cup water about 15 minutes, add small cup of wine (sherry, madeira or port wine). Serve hot or cold. Raspberry jam may be added.

ALMACK

2 lbs. apples — 2 lbs. pears
2 lbs. plums — 1½ lb. sugar

Peel and core apples and pears. Stone plums, and boil together till tender. Rub through a sieve, add sugar and boil until stiff. Spread out thinly on dishes, and dry in the sun. When set, cut into squares, put in tins with paper between each layer. Nice for dessert. Peaches, quinces, apricots also can be used.

MARZIPAN DIAMONDS

Ingredients for the Marzipan:
4 ozs. ground almonds
4 ozs. sifted icing sugar
A little beaten egg

To complete the sweets:
3 ozs. glace cherries, chopped
A little pink colouring
2 teaspoons redcurrant jelly
Small diamonds of angelica
Small silver balls
A little extra sifted icing sugar
Paper cases for the Marzipan Diamonds

Mix the sifted icing sugar and the ground almonds together, then bind them to a firm paste with a little beaten egg. Work the chopped cherries and a little pink colouring into the mixture. Cut the marzipan in half and roll out each piece to about a quarter of an inch in thickness, making the two halves as near the same size as possible. Dust the board and rolling-pin with a little sifted icing sugar to prevent its sticking. Spread one of the pieces thinly with redcurrant jelly and sandwich it with the other. Cut the sweets into diamond shapes, each side measuring just over an inch.

Decorate each sweet with two small diamonds of angelica and a silver ball in the centre. Put the sweets into paper cases.

GOLDEN PRUNES

Soak prunes in weak tea for 2 hours and then in rum. Put in batter of 4 ozs. of flour, 3 tablespoons of melted butter, ¾ of a tumbler of tepid water, a pinch of salt, and the beaten white of an egg. Mix the flour and the butter, adding water gradually, keeping batter smooth and liquid. Make it some time before it is needed, adding the beaten egg-white at the last moment, and a tablespoon of rum. Fry the prunes. When golden roll them in powdered chocolate mixed with vanilla sugar.

CHOCOLATE FUDGE

2 dessertspoons of Cocoa
½ bottle of Milk
1 teaspoon of Vanilla Essence
1½ lb. of Sugar
4 ozs. of Butter

Soak sugar in the milk for an hour, then put 2 dessertspoons of cocoa and butter together. Mix and put in saucepan on to stove for 15 minutes until it bubbles. Put in greased tin. Cut when cool.

TREACLE TOFFEE

Rub the inside of a saucepan generously with butter, pour in required amount of treacle and boil gently till a little will break between the teeth, after being thrown into cold water.

Then immediately take pan from fire and pour toffee over blanched nuts of any description.

Now good digestion wait on appetite
And health on both
Shakespeare

AFTER DINNER SWEETMEATS

6 ozs. sugar — ¼ pint water
4 ozs. butter — 2 ozs. seeded raisins
2 ozs. almonds, ground
4 ozs. fine grated rind of an orange

Boil sugar and water until thick, but remove before it changes colour. Melt butter, stir in and brown slightly. Add raisins, rind of orange and almonds. Add mixture to syrup, stirring over low heat until thick. Pour into an oiled shallow pan. Mark into squares and chill. Brush with honey and sprinkle with chopped nuts.

THE VICAR'S BARLEY SUGAR

2 lbs. loaf sugar — 2 tablespoons vinegar
water — essence of lemon

Put vinegar into a ½ pint measure cup and fill up with water. Pour this into a saucepan, add the loaf sugar and, stirring all the time, boil for about 15 minutes, when the liquid should turn a lemon color.

When it will snap when tested by dropping in cold water, remove from heat and place bottom of saucepan in cold water to prevent the mixture from turning sugary.

Drop in 12 drops of essence of lemon. Butter a large flat dish and pour the mixture into it.

When it has cooled a little, cut into strips. Butter your fingers and shape the strips into twists.

If preferred, chopped almonds or walnuts can be added to the barley sugar, which can be cut into squares instead of twisting.

PENGELLES

For 6-8 slices of good white bread you will require the following: Cut razor-thin slices of lemon and orange, leaving the peel on. Divide into quarters. Put on a small plate, immerse in good liqueur. Break 2 eggs into a bowl, add 2-3 tablespoons of cream. Beat well. Heat 2 tablespoons of olive oil in a frying pan. Dip each slice of bread quickly but thoroughly into the egg mixture and fry until golden brown on both sides. Drain. (Add more oil from time to time as necessary.) Put the crisp fried bread on hot plates, decorate each slice with plenty of soaked fruit slices (plus remaining liqueur) and drench all in syrup. To be eaten with coffee.

ALMOND WAFERS

2 egg whites — 4 ozs. castor sugar
2 ozs. plain flour — 2 ozs. butter
Piece of vanilla pod
1 oz. shredded and blanched almonds

Beat egg whites and sugar until just melting — not too stiff — letting it run smoothly from the fork. Into that sieve flour. Melt butter, which should not be too hot when it goes into the mixture. Add almonds that are blanched and finely shredded. The mixture should be of a light and runny consistency.

Grease tin generously and let the grease set. Mixture must not go on a hot tray or it will stick. Fill the tip of a dessertspoon with the mixture, work this into a circle, getting the almonds more or less in the centre. Repeat until ingredients last. Bake in a hot oven for four minutes. Take tray out for a minute to dry out. Replace for another minute. When done, place over a rolling-pin and slightly curve.

NOTE: To be quite perfect, wafers should be crisp, curved and of a dark golden color, with the edges nicely browned.

BRANDY SNAPS

4 ozs. plain flour — 4 ozs. golden syrup
Pinch salt — 4 ozs. castor sugar
4 ozs. butter — Whipped cream
1 teaspoon ground ginger
1 dessertspoon lemon juice or water
Brandy

Sift the flour, salt and ginger. Melt the butter then add the sugar, golden syrup, lemon juice or water and cook until the mixture is blended. Add the sifted flour, salt and ginger and beat until smooth. Drop in teaspoonsful on a greased oven tray spacing well apart. Bake in a moderate oven for about 12 minutes.

Remove from the oven and leave for a few minutes to firm. Lift the biscuits from the tray with sharp knife, using a sawing movement. Turn the brandy snaps right side down, then roll round the handle of a wooden spoon. As soon as they are set, remove the spoon and cool on a wire rack. Store in an air-tight tin as soon as cold.

Serve filled with whipped cream, flavoured with a little brandy.

TOFFEE APPLES

1 lb. sugar
¼ pint water
2 tablespoons malt vinegar
red colouring
12 small red apples
skewers

Wash apples, dry and polish. Place a skewer firmly in each apple. Put water, sugar, vinegar and colouring in saucepan, stir over moderate heat until sugar is dissolved. Boil quickly until a little will set hard when tested in cold water. Remove from heat. Allow bubbles to subside. Dip apples, tilt saucepan, twist apples around in toffee, allow to drain for a moment and put on greased slide. Work as quickly as possible. If toffee starts to thicken before apples are done, return to low heat.

FINSKA good with champagne or wine

Blanch 12 almonds and put through a nut grinder.

Combine with 1 cup butter, 1¼ cups pastry flour, 2 tablespoons sugar. Work all together on a pastry board. Roll out in finger-thick lengths, cut into 2 inch pieces, dip in beaten egg white, sprinkle with sugar and chopped almonds.

Bake in moderate oven until light brown.

FLORENTINES

3¾ ozs. butter
1¾ oz. flaked almonds
4 ozs. castor sugar
Scant ounce glace cherries
3¾ ozs. finely chopped almonds
3¾ ozs. candied orange peel
2 large tablespoons cream
4 ozs. plain chocolate

Grease a tray with a little melted butter. Melt the butter in a saucepan, add the sugar and bring it slowly to the boil. Stir in the cherries, cut in quarters, the chopped and flaked almonds, and the finely chopped candied peel.

Whip the cream until thick, fold it into the mixture, then leave to cool and set. Drop the mixture in teaspoonful on to the prepared tray, leaving plenty of space between, as the biscuits spread during cooking. Bake in a moderate oven for about 10-12 minutes. After five minutes, remove the tray from the oven and pull together the edges of each biscuit with a plain pastry cutter. Return the biscuits to the oven to finish cooking. Allow the biscuits to cool on the baking tray and then remove with a thin sharp knife.

Melt the chocolate on a plate over a pan of hot water, remove from the heat, allow to cool to a thick but runny consistency working it well with a palette knife to keep it glossy.

When the biscuits are quite cold, dip or spread the smooth side with the prepared chocolate, and when on the point of setting, make wavy lines.

CHERRY AND NUT NOUGAT

6 ozs. granulated sugar
½ gill water (¼ pint)
1 level teaspoon honey
1 egg white
A few drops of lemon juice
1 oz. halved glace cherries
1 oz. chopped walnuts
A sheet of rice paper
A tin six inches square will be required.

Line the tin with half the rice paper. Dissolve the sugar in the water in a medium-sized pan over gentle heat. Make sure every grain of sugar is dissolved before the mixture comes to the boil. Add the honey. Bring the mixture to a rapid boil and boil it continuously, without stirring, for 3 or 4 minutes until the syrup seems thicker. To test for the right consistency drop a little of the syrup into a cup of cold water and when it is ready it should roll into a firm ball between the fingers. As soon as this stage is reached, take the pan off the heat. Quickly whip the egg-white stiffly, then beat the syrup into the egg white. Stir in the lemon juice, cherries and nuts and pour the nougat into the lined tin. Cover the nougat with the rest of the rice paper. Leave the nougat overnight or until it is absolutely cold. Cut the nougat into rectangles.

BUTTERSCOTCH

½ lb. butter
½ cup water
1 lb. sugar

Place the sugar and water in saucepan. Stir over low heat until sugar dissolves; add butter and melt. Bring to the boil. Boil until thick and darkening in color (approximately 30 minutes). Pour into oiled 8 inch sandwich tin. Cut into squares when almost cold.

ORANGE CREAMS

1 orange
1 egg white
10 ozs. sifted icing sugar
½ teaspoonful orange curacao (optional)
A very little candied orange peel
Paper cases for the Orange Creams

Grate the rind off the orange with a very fine grater (none of the white pith should be used). Beat the egg white in a fairly large bowl, then add the finely grated orange rind and sifted sugar. Add the orange curacao at this stage if you are using it. Beat the mixture well and add just enough orange juice, if necessary, to make the mixture a piping consistency. It must be fairly stiff so that it will hold its shape. Fill a forcing bag, which has a large star pipe attached, with the mixture and pipe it in stars on to a sheet of waxed paper. The mixture should make about 32 creams. Cut tiny squares of candied orange peel and decorate the centre of each cream with a piece.

Leave the creams for at least twelve hours to set, then lift them off paper and place in paper cases.

An apple a day keeps the doctor away.

FRENCH JELLIES

1 oz. gelatine
1 lb. sugar
1¼ cups water
peppermint flavouring
green food colouring or
squeeze lemon juice and red food colouring.

Mix gelatine with sugar in saucepan. Pour in water and soak for 30 minutes. Bring to boil, stirring until sugar and gelatine dissolve. Simmer together for 5 minutes. Flavour with peppermint and colour green or use lemon juice and colour red. Pour into wet tin approximately 11 x 7 inches. Chill. When firmly set, dip tin in hot water for a second, turn on to castor sugar. Cut into squares. Best kept in air-tight tin.

MARZIPAN

8 ozs. lump sugar
1 small beaten egg
⅜ pint water
5 ozs. ground almonds
1 pinch cream of tartar
a drop of vanilla essence (if you care for it)

Soak the sugar in water, and when dissolved, bring to the boil. Add cream of tartar and heat. Remove from the flame, stir in the ground almonds and essence, let it cool a little, and add the beaten egg. Turn out the mixture on a slab sprinkled with castor sugar and when cool enough to handle knead it well.

Wrap the marzipan in greased paper and it will keep for a month or two.

THE TEA PARTY

The habit of taking tea in a formal manner, usually from four to five o'clock, with the customs of such an occasion, formed the social round. Aborigines on outback stations, observing the "missus" setting off for a formal At Home at the house of a neighbour, anywhere up to 60 miles distant, caught the idea and asked for tea to be added to their ration of "baccy", flour and sugar.

Advertisements in the columns of country newspapers announced the days in the month various ladies of the town would be At Home - or would not be At Home because of shearing, or a bereavement. It was not acceptable to space one's At Home further than once a month unless the hostess would be out of town on her usual day.

Competition was keen among hostesses and guests. To be At Home and receive no callers was the worst snub one could experience. Only the calling and leaving of a card by a kind and influential lady in the district would set the matter right. The suffering lady could then be included in other tea parties and meet the rest of "the district".

As the guests arrived in their very best afternoon gowns and mantles their visiting cards were placed in the tray on the hall table for that purpose. Before gliding into the drawing-room a quick glance at those cards already in the tray could reveal whom to expect, or a new name with a new At Home day to add to the list.

In the drawing-room the hostess was seated at the tea-table. A white damask or a beautifully embroidered linen cloth covered this. On it stood the tea-tray, large enough to hold in addition to the china, silver teapot, sugar bowl and a silver urn for hot water. A tiered stand holding dishes and plates of hot cakes, an uncut cake, small cakes, tiny sandwiches and thin bread and butter, stood by the tea-table. Small tea plates were placed in a pile upon the tea-tray with afternoon knives and forks.

The hostess or her daughter poured out the tea. A servant in frilly white apron over a black dress, with white cap, after answering the door and ushering in the guests, would depart and bring in the freshly-made tea made according to the rules of the day: Two minutes to warm the teapot which stood on the bricks beside the stove with sufficient tea for the number of guests — one teaspoon per person and one for the pot. One half to three quarters of a pint of boiling water was poured over the leaves, the lid closed, and the teapot stood for five to ten minutes before filling the pot. For a mixture of teas the usual proportion was four spoonfuls of black to one of green. The lady of the house wore a chatelaine around her waist and from it would sometimes use a key to unlock the tea caddy, an elegant rosewood box lined with tin. Tea would be taken in delicate sips. Fingers of the gloves were tucked under at the wrist. The ladies NEVER removed their long kid gloves. The dexterity needed to balance a cup and saucer and a plate and still have a spare hand was considerable. Rings were worn under the gloves. Hats were always worn. The tightness of the corset was reflected in the uplift of the bosom. Veils were lifted to just above the nose. Not a detail would escape the eyes of the guests as they noted everyone's garments and their manners. A cocked little right-hand finger would be noted with disapproval. "I was lately at a tea-table" wrote a lady "where the discourse, from being witty, grew to be malicious". A distressed aunt complained that her nieces "were altogether unmanageable with their preoccupation over their dress, their teas and their visits to the point that the art of needlework had become quite neglected. It grieves my heart to see a couple of proud idle flirts sipping their tea for a whole afternoon in a room hung with the industry of their grandmother".

A particularly hot piece of scandalous news would cause the sudden departure of the guests with various excuses. The real reason was the urge to go quickly to other At Homes with their news.

Twenty minutes was the accepted time for a casual afternoon call. When rising to take leave of the hostess it was not necessary to make an individual adieu to other callers present. It was courteous to bow pleasantly to a particular lady to whom an introduction had been made, or with whom one had been conversing. Visits of congratulation should be short, and made always before dinner. It is extremely rude, on being admitted to a private apartment, to look curiously about as if taking an inventory of all that is to be seen.

Make no remark upon the work in which you find your friend engaged. If she lays it aside, desire her not to leave it because of your presence but propound no questions concerning it. Do not look over her books or ask to borrow them. In short, meddle with nothing.

Married ladies have cards separate from those of their husbands. Both cards and card cases differ in size. The names of grown-up daughters are on the mother's card beneath her name. Cards are left in person. Should the lady of the house not be at home, the lady should leave one of her own cards and two of her husbands. If the lady of the house is at home, only two of one's husband's cards are left. Cards should be left the day after a dinner party or any other form of entertainment and hospitality. The recipient of a card should return the call within a week or ten days.

WHITEWASH

For general use (inside and outside) on farm buildings, sheds, fences, poles, roadside obstructions, either on wood, glass or metal surfaces:

Dissolve 2 lb. of common salt in a 10 quart bucket, three-quarters filled with water. Stir well to hasten solution. When all salt has dissolved, add slowly 10 lbs. of Limil and constant stirring, and continue until the mixture has the consistency of a smooth cream.

Allow the mixture to stand overnight, or for a few days if possible, keeping the bucket well covered, and stir the contents occasionally. When needed again, stir thoroughly and add sufficient water to make a good workable wash.

Alum added to this mixture prevents it rubbing. One ounce to a gallon of wash is sufficient.

For masonry surfaces such as brickwork, concrete, stone, cinder blocks, stucco, etc.:

Make a mixture in the proportion of 50 lbs. of Limil, 25 lbs. of grey or white cement, and 5 lbs. of common salt. Stir mixture in with water until it is of the required consistency and the salt is fully dissolved.

If two coats are to be applied, allow one full day for the first coat to dry.

Do not make up more of this formula than can be used in one hour.

Whitewash must be applied thin. Best results will be obtained if the application is so thin that the surface to which it is applied can be easily seen through the "film" when it is wet. When using a brush, do not attempt to brush out the coating as is done with oil paint. Spread it on as evenly as possible.

If possible, apply whitewash in clear, dry weather and take care in preparing the surface to be treated so that all dirt, grease, scale and other loose material is removed before the whitewash is applied.

Whitewash brushes, after use, should be washed thoroughly in clean water and hung in the air to dry with the brush part downwards. Do not allow brush to come in contact with dry Limil. The makers of Limil say a gallon of whitewash should have the following covering capacity:

On wood, about 225 square feet (10 ft. x 22½ ft.)

On brick, about 180 square feet (10 ft. x 18 ft.)

On plaster, about 270 square feet (about 9 ft. x 30 ft.)

It is estimated that a man using a 4 inch brush should cover in an hour: on rough walls, 22 square yards; on smooth walls, 38 square yards; on flat surfaces, 40 square yards; on ceilings (using a step ladder), 25 square yards.

Remember the old yeast bottle on the kitchen mantelpiece? When baking with compressed yeast the cook should know that half an oz. will leaven any quantity of flour below and up to 1 lb. of flour.

One ounce of compressed yeast will leaven up to 7 lbs. of flour and 2 ozs. up to 14 lbs. Extra yeast is needed for rich mixtures using butter and eggs.

List of wedding anniversaries:

First	.....	Paper	13th	.....	Lace
Second	.....	Cotton	14th	.....	Ivory
Third	.....	Leather	15th	.....	Crystal
Fourth	.....	Flowers	20th	.....	China
Fifth	.....	Wooden	25th	.....	Silver
Sixth	.....	Candy	30th	.....	Pearl
Seventh	.....	Copper	35th	.....	Coral
Eighth	.....	Bronze	40th	.....	Ruby
Ninth	......	Pottery	45th	.....	Sapphire
10th	.....	Tin	50th	.....	Golden
11th	.....	Steel	55th	.....	Emerald
12th	.....	Linen	60th	.....	Diamond

FLOWER GLAZING

You need 1 cup of sugar, a dessertspoon of liquid, ½ cup of water, a little food coloring, and selected fresh flowers such as violets or sweet peas.

Combine sugar and water in a saucepan. Heat slowly until it boils. Keep it boiling until it reaches 230 deg. F. or until a little of the mixture forms a soft ball when tested in cold water. Allow the mixture to stand until it cools to a lukewarm temperature then add a few drops of food coloring to match the color of the flowers on which it is to be used.

Use a small paintbrush to brush it on the individual petals of the flowers. Make sure to cover all the surface. Allow the first coat to dry then cover with another coat. Sprinkle lightly with sugar and let it dry. Store the flowers in a cool dry place.

Dip violets or mint leaves into some thinned down egg white and slightly warmed water. Then sprinkle with finely granulated sugar. Dry on a rack. Use to garnish salads, fruit cups, punches and desserts.

HANDLING OLIVES AT HOME

To pickle olives, they ought to be fully grown but picked before the fruit changes color, and care must be exercised so that the olives are not bruised.

Grade to size and, to remove the bitter taste, put the olives into a solution made from 1 gallon of water, 2 ozs. caustic soda, 1 oz. lime (garden lime will do) and 1 oz. salt. Boil the water and allow it to cool before mixing the lye solution. Then allow it to stand for an hour before using. The olives must be kept submerged to prevent discoloration.

When the bitterness has left the fruit, pour off the lye and cover the olives with water, which should be renewed morning and night so long as the fruit has the peculiar hot taste due to the presence of lye. When the caustic taste has completely left them, the olives are ready for pickling.

For this process, some use brine only, beginning with a strength of 2 ozs. of salt to a gallon of water. Leave the olives in this overnight. Next morning this brine should be replaced with a salt solution containing 4 ozs. of salt to a gallon of water.

Two days later, the strength of the solution is again increased to 6 ozs. salt to a gallon of water; two days later, to 8 ozs. to the gallon; two days later again to 10 ozs. to the gallon, and finally the brine should contain 14 ozs. salt to the gallon.

RHUBARB WINE

6 lbs. of rhubarb, 5 lbs. of sugar, the rind of one lemon and half an ounce of waterglass (silicate of soda).

Wash rhubarb, cut into one-inch lengths, and place in large pan with one gallon of water. Leave for one week, stirring thoroughly at least twice a day. Then strain and add the sugar, stirring until dissolved. Add lemon rind and waterglass and leave for a week to ferment, keeping surface skimmed. Strain into covered pan or barrel. Bottle after two weeks.

If you cannot obtain waterglass from your chemist — it usually comes in 4 oz. bottles — seek his advice on where you may get it.

CHEESE MAKING

Here is one recipe for cheese: Milk into a clean bucket, then strain the milk and stand overnight in a clean, cool place.

In the morning stand the bucket in a tub of warm water in summer (86 deg. F.) in cold weather and stir. Dissolve rennet tablets according to directions in a cup of water of the same temperature, and add to the milk, stirring well. Let the milk stand for three minutes, when it should thicken. Then break up the curd with the hand or a large fork, and it will settle down again.

Press the curd into a lump, and put into a cheese cloth to drain. Having drained off the whey, in 10 minutes break up the curd again with the hand. Drain, and repeat, thus working over three times in 30 minutes. Warm up whey to 100 deg. F. and pour over the curd a few times until it toughens and will squeak when rubbed.

Drain and cut up again into small pieces. Salt at about 1 oz. a lb. put into tins without ends or small boxes without tops and bottoms and place under weight. In 24 hours it should have set. It may then be neatly bandaged and put into the press again for a few hours. Grease all around and stand in a cool place for a few weeks to ripen. Grease daily in warm weather, or twice weekly in colder weather. Before re-bandaging in cold weather plunge cheese into water at 115 to 120 deg. F. Keep cheese for about three months.

It is advisable to buy only small amounts of rennet for thickening as it loses its strength when stored.

BUTTER MAKING

Control of temperature, cleanliness at all stages and thorough working are the chief essentials for successful butter making.

Cream should never be allowed to stand near anything with a strong odor such as apples, soap, kerosene or onions as it will absorb any strong odors with which it comes in contact.

A traditional butter recipe states that to get the best of butter making, cream should be allowed to mature before churning — that is kept for two or three days at a temperature of 60 to 65 deg. F. This allows lactic acid to ripen the cream. Butter made from fresh cream always has a flat, insipid taste, and usually contains too much moisture. Ripened cream is more easily churned.

In hot weather, to keep the cream exact temperature, set the cream can in a vessel of cold water and keep changing it when necessary to lower the temperature. Sufficient acid will have developed in three days. Cool each lot of cream as it is obtained and then thoroughly mix with that already in the cream can, using a properly tinned stirrer. Use ½ to ¾ oz. of fine salt to each 1 lb. of butter.

When churning the butter, just as it begins to break add one cup of hot water. Care should be taken not to make it too soft. If the weather is hot use a large quantity of water. Finish churning, wash and salt the butter and let it stand in a warm room for about an hour, then work it well. Working it well is most important. It is claimed that this will never be hard.

YORKSHIRE PUDDING

On a snowy day scoop us a small amount of soft snow where it has settled — to mix into the batter for a Yorkshire pudding. Also use one egg. The addition of snow is supposed to make the batter much lighter — my grandmother said so many years ago.

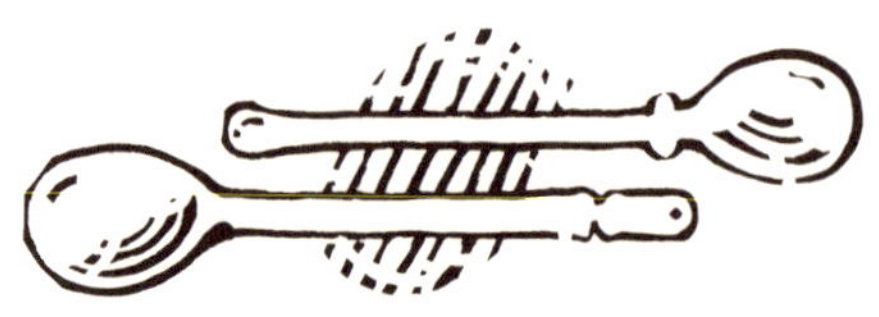

Celandine
Bay
Borage
Basil
Lavender
Elder
Dandelion

LOTIONS, POTIONS, BALMS AND CREAMS

These recipes are mostly to do with nature's bounty, with grasses, flowers and herbs. Many of them involve reducing the plant matter to liquid form. This is called an infusion and is made by adding a pint of boiling water to 1 oz. of the essential ingredient (in a stone jar or jug if possible). Cover with a cloth, leave to cool, stir, strain, use.

To prevent wrinkles: Make an anti-wrinkle lotion with ½ oz. glycerine, ½oz. rosewater, ½oz. witchhazel and 3 tablespoons honey. Massage warm olive oil into the forehead, or make a paste of fine oatmeal and lemon juice and spread thickly all over your face.

For a good complexion: Eat green leafy vegetables and raw carrots, but — best of all — dandelion leaves.

To cleanse your face and stimulate circulation: Rinse it with camomile tea or try a tincture of benzoin in water.

For greasy skins: Use oatmeal instead of soap — half fill a small muslin bag, use it like a sponge with warm water.

For Freckles: Make a lotion from fresh elder flowers: cover them with cold rain or distilled water, allow to stand overnight, then strain.

For Sunburn: Apply a mixture of glycerine, witchhazel and sunflower seed oil.

To tan easily and evenly: Drink rich iron herb teas or add a few drops of iodine to your bath.

The best conditioner: True cold cream made from ½ oz. spermaceti, ½ oz. white wax, 4 oz. almond oil. Shred the waxes, put all ingredients into a stone jar. Place jar in a pan of hot water and simmer until the wax is melted, then add 2 ozs. rosewater carefully, drop by drop, beating the mixture continuously.

For Corns: Soak your feet in salted hot water, and, after drying, squeeze on a drop or two of the juice from the broken stem of a fresh celandine plant. Leave to dry. Use celandine also for warts. A drop of cinnamon oil applied daily is said to remove a wart; or try rubbing it with a radish or the juice of marigold flowers.

To make Hair curl: Try this solution — 1 part gum arabic combined with 4 parts rosewater, a few drops of sesame oil, wheatgerm oil, 1 tablespoon glycerine and a very small amount of pure lanolin.

To clear the blood and strengthen the digestion: Make nettle beer. Into an earthenware pot pour 1½ gallons boiling water and stir in half a peck of malt. Leave to cool, then strain away the malt. Return it again to the liquid, stirring thoroughly. Strain again and throw away the malt. Put the liquid in a preserving pan and add 1 oz. whole well-bruised ginger, 1 lb. Demerara sugar, 1 oz. hops and 4 gallons nettles washed and cut with scissors into small pieces. Bring to the boil, simmer for half an hour, then put back into the earthenware pot. When lukewarm, stir in ½ oz. yeast. Leave for three days, giving a daily stir. Strain and put into cask or stone bottles. You can drink it as soon as all trace of fermentation is over, but it improves if sealed and kept for at least a month.

To stop a cold: In the early stages take a hot infusion of basil. If it is past the early stages, take plenty of alfalfa or peppermint tea, or an elderberry brew. Ordinary tea with a large sprig of mint in it is good, too.

A good gargle for a sore throat: A glass of sage infusion with honey and a pinch of cayenne.

To ease a cough: Cut the leaves of agrimony into inch-long pieces, make an infusion, sweeten with honey. Take a wine-glass a day.

For a tonic: Make an infusion from the bruised root of angelica, and take three times a day after meals. It also serves as a digestive.

Overweight problems: are often caused by retention of water in the tissues. Try this potion: put ½ oz. dandelion root in a pan with a quart of cold water. Bring to the boil and simmer until reduced to a pint. Into a jug put ½ oz. broom tops and over them pour the dandelion brew after bringing it to the boil again. Leave to cool and strain. Drink a glass a day. Fennel seeds, leaves and root, eaten raw, are also said to help you to slim.

To soothe nerves, induce sleep and prevent nightmares: Drink camomile tea.

For sores, burns and swellings: Make a poultice of brooklime. Wash the leaves, bruise them, then put on the offending spots. Comfrey is said to be remarkable for healing sores, too: the root is crushed and securely bound around the sore places.

For bad breath: Take peppermint tea daily. Use it also for hiccoughs (3 drops of peppermint oil on a lump of sugar).

To cure snoring: Take 6 drops of olive oil and a pinch of mustard before getting into bed.

For insomnia: Take a glass of warm milk with 9 drops of oil of cloves.

To prevent insect bites: Sponge your body with an infusion of camomile flowers; or rub on citronella oil or oil of eucalyptus. If bitten, wipe the bites with weak ammonia. For bee stings, remove the sting and apply the bruised leaf of plaintain. For wasp stings, use vinegar or lemon juice.

To refine Skin, Pores: Lightly beat raw egg white and spread on the face. Beaten egg white mixed with milk of magnesia softens rough elbows, heels, knees and ankles.

INSTRUCTIONS ABOUT SMOKING OF FISH

For smoking you need a smoke box, which can be made with a large wooden case by taking the bottom out and standing it on the ground. It should have two doors, a small one at the bottom and the larger one higher up.

To avoid risk of fire, have the sides and back of the smoke-house near the bottom lined with tin. Brown paper pasted inside and outside prevents any undue escape of smoke.

In the top of the smoke house a piece of piping is placed so as to emit any steam arising.

Pieces of wood are nailed on both sides of the smoke-house at various distances and the fish on the spits are hung on wires, the ends of the spits resting on the pieces of wood.

After the fish have been pickled in a brine mixture (this is a separate process), hang them in the smoke-house before lighting the fire. They must be at least 4 ft. from the fire in the bottom. Pine sawdust is considered the best for smoking fish. A small fire of shavings is made on a sheet of iron in the bottom of the smoke-house and sawdust gradually sprinkled on it. When the sawdust catches alight it will smoulder for some time. Fresh sawdust must be added at intervals until the fish are smoked. Do not have a blaze in the smoke-house, as too much heat will spoil the fish. The smoking process usually takes from four to six hours.

That is as far as can be gone here into the question of smoking, which is done after the curing of the fish by the following method of pickling:- First scale and gut the fish; then with a sharp knife remove the backbone with the exception of about 1½ inches near the tail. They should then be washed in clean, cold water and drained, after which they are ready for curing and pickling. Before being pickled, the fish are scored once on each side in the thickest part so that the pickle may easily penetrate.

The pickle is composed of 3 lbs. of salt to 1½ lbs. of brown sugar, and 2 gallons of water. Have the pickle prepared to receive the fish as they are scaled etc. The pickle may be mixed in an ordinary clean washing tub, the fish being laid upside down in the mixture, which is sufficient if it covers them. The fish are allowed to remain in pickle for three hours, but very large-sized fish are given half an hour longer.

On removal from the pickling tub, the fish are drained, hung on spits (rounded sticks) back to back in the open air, holes being made at each side (where the head has been wrenched off) to receive the spits. They should remain until thoroughly dry.

PICKLED BEEF

The kind of wooden barrel used for pickling is not easily come by these days.

The solution is made from 1½ lbs. of bay salt or common salt, 6 to 8 lbs. of brown sugar, 1 oz. of saltpetre and 1 gallon of water. Put all ingredients into a large clean saucepan and bring them to the boil. Allow to boil for 15 to 20 minutes, skimming carefully. Strain and use when cold.

Almost any fleshy piece of beef may be used for pickling, but a piece from the round or flank is generally used. The meat must be very fresh, and is usually boned. Wipe and trim carefully, removing any discolored parts. Then rub the meat well with common salt and let it stand for at least 12 hours. Afterwards, rub off this salt, and then put the meat in the pickling solution. This should be in an earthenware or wooden container. The meat should be left there for 10 days, completely covered with the pickle or else it will require turning every day.

SIMPLE WAY OF TANNING HIDES

Being a perishable commodity, raw hides must be preserved if they are not tanned soon after removal from slaughtered animals. Traditionally, slaughterhouses and hide curers use salting as the method of preservation. However, in some distribution circumstances it may be necessary to preserve hides for only a few days before tanning. In the recommended method the hides are soaked for 16 hours in a solution containing 0.375 per cent sodium chlorite and 0.05 per cent sodium pentachlorophenate — both percentages being calculated on hide weight, using a hide to liquor ratio of 2-1 to 1-1. After this treatment the hides will keep for six days at temperature of about 77 deg. F. The treatment does not affect leather quality or yield and it is believed that the costs compare more than favourably with those of conventional salting.

SOME EARLY ADVERTISEMENTS FROM MAIN ROAD, BALLARAT.

TO THE LADIES OF BALLARAT: Miss Reed's new premises, opposite the Baths, Main Road, Ballarat, are now open with an extensive and splendid stock of Ladies' and Children's Ready-made Dresses and Underclothing, Millinery and Straw Bonnets etc.

Miss R., having recently arrived from the London and Paris markets, feels confident that for style and quality, her stock will exceed anything yet offered to the ladies of Ballarat.

TO SHOEMAKERS: Wanted, Customers for leather and grindery, good and cheap at the Saddlery, Harness and Leather Store, near Eureka Jack's, Ballarat Flat.

LAFAYETTE BAKERY, Main Road, French, English and American loaves, delivered twice a day by J. D. Feraud.

The First Australians used over a thousand food plants growing on the continent. The early settlers also made good use of them. Some of Captain Cook's sailors with scurvy, found on landing at Botany Bay, that this was cured by drinking a kind of tea, made from the leaves of the Manuka tea-tree — hence the name.

It was found that the small leaves of the Sweet Bursaria, (called in some parts of Australia the Christmas tree) contain a substance, which absorbs the rays from the sun, preventing serious sunburn.

Another useful tree, the Rasp Pod tree, provided aborigines with rasps for food preparation from the seed pods. Red fruit from the Quandong tree, have a fleshy layer, which can be used for jam or jelly. The Kernels of this fruit are of good value and flavour. They are full of oil and useful as fuel.

The native cherry tree, a parasitic tree found widely in Australia, has unusual seeds with the appearance of a fleshy stalk, which provided nourishment when eaten. Another common group of trees the Melaleucas, or paperbarks, gave aborigines bark, in which to wrap food being cooked on their camp fires.

To start the fire a fireboard was made from the dry seasoned wood of grass trees, mulga, and some types of hakea. It was cut flat and a cavity bored into it. Into this, went a long round piece of wood as a drill twirled by rubbing it between the palms of the hands. As the drill stick rubbed against the walls of the cavity, friction with the wood dust made it hot enough to smoulder. Put on a pile of dry grass or other light material, it would produce a flame when blown upon.

Eucalyptus oil was first distilled from the leaves of peppermint gums, and exported from Australia in 1788. The name means "well covered", referring to the caps on the buds.

"Here's flowers for you, Hot Lavender, Mints, Savory, Majoram."

Sachets for Chests, Linen press and Bath.

Dry damask rose petals on fire racks before a sunny window or near a fire. When crisp to the touch, dust with powdered cloves and cinnamon, before placing in thin rose satin sachets, edged with coffee coloured lace frills.

Equal parts of dried lavender, sweet geranium leaves and lemon scented verbena enclosed in a book muslin cover.

Herb bags for the bath were of transparent muslin with tape drawer strings. Fill with one part of each of crushed rosemary and thyme leaves mixed with two parts sieved bicarbonate of soda.

Southernwood or lad's love dried and strewn in drawers and cupboards, keeps away clothes moths. The old French name for this plant was garde-robe.

ROSE OIL

Put any quantity of dried rose leaves into earthen pipkin and cover them with olive oil. Keep it hot for some hours. The oil will extract both odour and colour. A little oil of rosemary may be added.

TINCTURE OF ROSES

Put into a bottle the petals of roses. Pour upon them spirits of wine. Cork and allow to stand 2-3 months.

CLOVED POMANDER

Queen Elizabeth I, was wont to carry a pomander in one hand and a sceptre in the other. In the middle ages it was often encased in a frame-work of gold set with jewels. It was regarded as a charm against illness.

The most popular pomander is the humble orange, cloved. Hung in the wardrobe, placed in your linen-press, it will impart its fragrance and keep the moths at bay.

To Dwarf Trees for Table Decoration

Take an orange, and having cut a small hole in the peel, remove all the pulp and juice; fill the skin thus emptied with coco-nut fibre, fine moss, and charcoal, just stiffened with a little loam. In the centre of this put an acorn, date-stone or the seed of any tree that it is proposed to obtain a dwarf from.

Place the orange peel in a tumbler or vase in a window and moisten contents occasionally with a little water through the hole in the peel, and sprinkle the surface with wood ashes. In due time the tree will push up its stem through the compost, and its roots through the orange peel. The roots must then be cut flush with the peel, and the process repeated frequently for some time. The stem of the tree will assume a stunted, gnarled appearance, making it look like an old tree. When the ends of the roots are cut for the last time, the orange peel, which curiously enough, does not rot, may be painted black and varnished.

Wattle is a beautiful house decoration, but needs special treatment to keep it fresh for any length of time. Immediately after cutting, put stems in boiling water and leave until water is quite cold. Then place wattle in vase of fresh water, to which has been added ½ teaspoon alum.

Maiden-hair fern, if pressed with a hot iron soon after being gathered, will retain its color and make a beautiful table decoration.

To destroy Slugs and Snails

Take 1 tablespoonful of Arsenate of Lime, a dipper of Bran. Mix these. Then dissolve 1 tablespoon of Treacle or Golden Syrup in ½ cup of water. Add to dry mash and spread around plants.

Chives grown near roses, keep aphis at bay.

Borage leaves and flowers can be substituted for cucumber, having a similar flavour.

Dried lavender, rosemary, thyme or southernwood, keep moths from clothes and silverfish from books.

GARLIC SPRAY

This spray is said to kill cockchafer larvae, wireworms, snails, ophides, cabbage white butterflies and codling moths.

Take 3 ozs. of garlic cloves and mix with two teaspoons of medicinal liquid paraffin oil. Leave for 48 hours.

Add a pint of water and mix well with ¼ oz. of good oil-based soap.

Filter and store in a plastic container. This spray is used in various dilutions, but a 1 per cent solution is good to start with.

This is made by mixing 1 pint of spray with 99 pints of water. It should cover about 100 sq. yards of foliage.

However, you would have to see how many of the particular pests were killed with this dilution, as some are tougher than others.

CEPHALIC SNUFF

Take half an ounce each of rosemary, sage, lilies of the valley, and the tops of sweet marjoram, with a drachm each of asarabacca root, lavender flowers and nutmeg. Reduce the whole to a fine powder, and take it like common snuff for the relief of the head etc.

JACK — WRINGING

A good way of wringing flannels and light fabrics, is to submit them thus. Get a good strong endless roller towel or "Jack" towel and have ready 2 mop or broom sticks, for the management of which, 2 persons are necessary. Place the "Jack" towel smoothly on a table; put whatever is to be wrung between its 2 sides; pass a stick through either end of the towel, and turn the sticks round in contrary directions.

Cleaning a Kettle: There is a rust which comes from an iron deposit in water, and to guard against it, you should never put the kettle away for any length of time without cleaning it out. Then let it stand in a dry place.

The way to get rid of the coating that is there, is to put a big dessertspoon of powdered borax in the kettle, in warm water, and bring it to the boil. Let it stand to cool, then wash the kettle out thoroughly.

When once moths are in a carpet neither camphor nor tobacco will stop them. The only way is to take a damp towel, spread it out upon the carpet, and iron it dry with a hot iron, repeating this all over the carpet. Less ironing is needed where the chief wear on the carpet shows. The heat and steam will destroy both moths and eggs.

Keep the piano and other highly polished furniture clean and bright by wiping over with a chamois leather wrung out in vinegar and water, then rubbing with a dry soft cloth.

OIL PAINTINGS

Mix 1 oz. spirits of turpentine and 1 oz. of spirits of wine. Wash paintings gently with cotton wool dipped in this.

A little salt and water sprinkled on coals and cinders saves accumulation of soot.

Soak lamp wicks in vinegar overnight and dry before using and the lamps will never smoke.

If a rag with a little turps on it is put in the larder it will keep the blow-flies away from the food.

BOOTS: To make leather boots waterproof, saturate them with castor oil; to stop squeaking, drive a peg into the middle of the sole.

Bitter apples sewn in muslin bags, placed between folds of articles or soap in pockets, keeps away clothes moths from woollens.

CLINKERS: To remove clinkers from stoves or fire-brick, put in about half-a-peck of oyster shells on top of bright fire. Repeat if needful.

Mix soft soap with powdered starch, half as much salt and juice of lemon. Smear on cloth. Let it lie on grass day and night to rid cloth of mildew.

SILVERWARE: Silverware can be kept bright for months if placed with a largish piece of camphor in an air-tight case.

CEMENT for mending Copper articles
Mix powdered lime and ox-blood intimately, and apply while fresh.

The dirtiest frying pan will become clean if soaked five minutes in ammonia and water.

To remove mustiness from a metal teapot, and to clean the inside, fill the pot with boiling water and drop into it a red-hot cinder. Close the lid and let the tea-pot stand for some time, then empty it, and after rinsing it with perfectly clear water, it will be found clean and sweet.

Use tissue paper instead of a brush for cleaning furniture upholstered in plush. It not only removes the dust but cleans the pile.

A small piece of candle may be made to burn all night by putting powdered salt on it until it reaches the blackest part of the wick.

To darken tan shoes, clean them with milk to which a little ammonia is added.

Before wearing new boots rub neatsfoot oil well into the soles, and they will wear nearly as long again.

You may preserve the soles of boots by using equal parts of beeswax, olive-oil and mutton suet melted together. Use often and the soles will be good when the uppers are worn out.

Dogs dislike the taste of soap, so if your pet has a sore leg or foot, wet a cake of soap and rub it over the bandage. This will prevent the animal from tearing off the bandage.

Try the following recipe for washing blankets and all good woollens: 8 ozs. soap flakes, 1 large cup methylated spirit, 3 dessertspoons eucalyptus oil; mix thoroughly until smooth and creamy and store in covered container. Use a generous tablespoon to one gallon of water. Do not rinse. The woollens will be beautifully fresh and soft.

To remove scorch-marks on linen, rub with a piece of freshly cut onion, soak the place in a solution of peroxide of hydrogen and a little cold water. After drying in open air, iron as usual, or put lemon juice on the scorch and place in the sun.

A strip of elastic tacked inside the front of a dressing-table drawer, will form a convenient holder for bottles of perfume or lotions.

If you have trouble keeping small children from pulling out drawers stacked one on top of the other, slip a length of dowel vertically through drawer handles.

Parchment lamp-shades which have become dusty and soiled may be renovated in the following way. A loaf of warm white bread and break off in big chunks. Rub the shade over well with this doughy bread and it will look almost new.

To make Brown Shoes Black: Cut a raw potato in two, and well rub the shoes with it. Then dry well, and polish with any good black shoe polish.

Oil Paint Stains: To remove, apply oil of eucalyptus to stain. After a short time wash with soap.

William Howitt, writing from Ballarat, Victoria, 1855

I had occasion to go into a druggist's here to procure a little opodeldoc for a bruise. It was only 3s. per ounce; being about as many pence at home. Twelve times the English price appears to be the cost of drugs on the diggings; and perhaps from the quantity consumed it could not be less.

I imagine that it is the excessive cost of regular medical treatment which causes the diggers to take Holloway's pills so universally, and in such amazing quantities. They are the digger's established nostrum. He takes them by handfuls; and when his dog is ill, he gives him a few dozen as a dose. Holloway's ointment is in scarcely less repute. If Professor Holloway had only the diggers for purchasers he must make a fortune.

Card playing on the diggings is as universal as the taking of Holloway's pills. Cards are the diggers' grand resource, next to drinking and pills. In the fine weather you see them seated by their holes at all leisure hours, or by their tents, deeply intent on these magical bits of pasteboard.

HAIR

To clean hair, wash well with a mixture of soft water, 1 pint; sal-soda, 1 ounce; cream tartar, ¼ ounce.

BALDNESS

Rub the part morning and evening with onions, till it is red, afterwards with honey — or wash it with a decoction of boxwood.

BITES OF MAD DOGS

Apply caustic potash at once to the wound, and give enough whiskey to cause sleep.

Warts disappear if castor oil is applied regularly.

EMBROCATION FOR HOOPING COUGH

Olive oil eight ounces, oil of amber, four ounces, oil of cloves, sufficient to scent it strongly, croton oil 3 drops; mix, rub on the chest — or oil of amber, and spirits of hartshorn, equal parts. Mix. Apply to the soles of the feet, and the palms of the hands, morning, noon, and night.

HOW TO REMOVE TIGHT FINGER RINGS

Pass the end of a piece of fine twine underneath the ring, and wind it evenly around the finger upward as far as the middle joint. Then take hold of the lower end of the string beneath the ring, and begin to slowly unwind upward, when the ring will gradually move along the twine towards the tip of the finger and come off.

William Howitt from Sydney, June 14, 1854

. . . The most remarkable nettle, however, of this country is the URTICA GIGAS, or rough nettle tree. This tree has a large leaf, something like a sun-flower leaf, hirsute beneath, and every bristle has a most painful sting. Some gentlemen who had been in Illawarra, collecting specimens of trees for the Paris exhibition, told me, that they measured one of these wonderful trees, which was thirty-two feet round, and, I think, one hundred and forty feet high.

Such is the potency of the virus of this tree, that horses which are driven rapidly through the forests where they abound, if they come in contact with their leaves, die in convulsions. I have seen a statement of the actual death in convulsions of his horse by a traveller through these parts; and one of the gentlemen of the exhibition committee told me, that as they were riding in the Illawarra forest, a young man who had lately arrived, and was ignorant of the nature of the tree, breaking off a twig as they rode along, had his hand instantly paralyzed by it. His fingers were pressed firmly together, and were as rigid as stone. Fortunately, a stockman who was near, observing it, came up and said, 'I see what is amiss, and will soon set alright'. He gathered a species of arum, which grew near, for nature has planted the bane and antidote together, in the low grounds, and rubbing the hand with it, it very soon relaxed, and resumed its natural pliancy.

This is precisely the process used by the children in England. When nettled, they rub the place with a bruised dock-leaf, saying all the while, 'Nettle go out, dock go in'.

HOME-MADE TOILET SOAP

5 lbs. mutton fat
1 lb. caustic soda
½ oz. oil lavender
2 tablespoons ammonia
2 tablespoons powdered borax
4 ozs. glycerine
1 quart water

Make sure fat is clean and free from salt. Melt fat at low temperature.

Dissolve soda in cold water, which will become hot; wait till both are same temperature, then pour fat into lye, stirring all the time.

Add oil, borax and ammonia in that order, beating well.

Pour into a flat tin lined with a damp cloth. Do not lose any time pouring into tin after beating and do not disturb till nearly set then cut.

Make sure there are no small children around while you are at work.

CLEANSING CREAM FOR THE FACE

Equal parts of Milk of Magnesia, Paraffin oil and Witchhazel. Shake and bottle.

OUTBACK CURE-ALL

Add two tablespoons of sulphur to one pound of treacle or mollasses. Take a generous teaspoon each Saturday night for general health.

Stye in the Eye: Rub with wedding ring.

SORE THROAT

Cut slices of fat boneless bacon, pepper thickly, and tie around the throat with a flannel cloth.

MANAGEMENT OF INFANTS

A child, when born, should be laid, for the first month, upon a thin mattress, which the nurse may sometimes keep on her knee, that the child may always lie, and only sit up as the nurse slants the mattress. Keep it as dry as possible. At the end of a month, the nurse may set it up, and dance it by degrees.

Do not keep a child too long in the arms, lest the legs should be cramped, and the toes turned inwards. The oftener the posture is changed the better.

It is injurious to be laid always asleep on a person's knee.

Infants should by imperceptible degrees be inured to the cool, and then to the cold bath. If they have been accustomed to an effeminate treatment, and should be suddenly subjected to an opposite extreme, such a change would be attended with danger.

The first milk a baby can draw from its mother's breast is medicine and nourishment for it, and if she is too ill to give it, it is better to let it wait a few hours, than to give it any kind of food.

If a mother cannot suckle the child, get a healthy cheerful woman, with young milk, who is fond of infants. After the first six months, broths and simple food, may do as well as living wholly upon milk.

In laying a child to sleep, place it upon the right side oftener than on the left, but twice in the twenty-four hours it should be changed to the left side. Laying it on its back when it awakes, is enough of that posture, in which alone it can move its legs and arms with freedom.

To awaken children from sleep with a noise, or in an impetuous manner, is unwise and hurtful; also to carry them from a dark room immediately into a glaring light, for the sudden impression of light debilitates the organs of vision, and lays the foundation of weak eyes from infancy.

Infants are sometimes very restless at night, caused by either cramming them with too much food, by tight night clothes, or by being overheated with blankets etc.

All violent impressions on the senses and bodies of children should be avoided. It is injurious to toss them about rapidly and violently in their arms. Loud crying, or shouting in their ears, presenting glittering objects to their view, and sudden and too great a degree of light; such practices are very injurious.

WEATHER LORE

Bright yellow sky at sunset presages wind, pale yellow, wet.

Flowers open with greater freedom in anticipation of fine weather.

Spiders remain quiet or spin with restricted effect, when it is likely to rain.

Birds fly low for rain.

Cocks crow, when rainy weather is likely to clear.

Animals shelter instead of spreading over their usual range, or when pigs carry straw to their sties, bad weather may be expected.

Dew and fog are indications of fine weather.

LEECH BAROMETER

Put into a 2 oz. phial 3 parts filled with pure water, a healthy leech. Cover the mouth of the bottle with a piece of linen rag. Change water in winter once a month; in summer once a fortnight.

1. Leek lies motionless in the bottom if serene weather.
2. Rain either before or after noon, leech creeps to top of its lodgings and there remains until weather settles.
3. If wind is expected it gallops through its limpid habitation with amazing swiftness and seldom rests until the wind begins to blow hard.

4. If a remarkable storm of thunder and rain is due, for some days before the leech lodge almost continually without water and discovers uncommon uneasiness, in violent throes and convulsive motions.
5. In frost, as in summer weather, it lies constantly at the bottom, and in snow as in rainy weather it pitches its dwelling near the mouth of the phial.

William Howitt, writing from Bendigo, Victoria, October 10th, 1853

One of the great nuisances at the diggings, are the mice. These are English mice. They swarm on the diggings; and we find it one of the most difficult things in the world to catch them. I have made a great round amongst the stores, to purchase a few of those old-fashioned traps consisting of a little log of wood with a hole in it, and a spring-bar to hang them, but neither these nor any other traps were to be had. I have, therefore, tried sundry improved traps, and tricks recommended, but without the slightest success. They destroy everything you have. They have torn up 'Uncle Tom's Cabin' and made a mouse-nest of it. The other day I removed everything out of the tent, but in vain. The few mice that I could see scampered up the canvas, and went out at the eaves. At night there they were all again, as merry as ever, running over my hands and face, and waking me! I made up my mind to set up a cat; and cats here are 2L. 10s. a-piece! When, lo! a lucky discovery! — the mention of which may be of service to others on the diggings — removing a bucket from a corner, into which had fallen a woollen jumper, I detected within a whole tribe of mice! The hint was sufficient. Every morning we carried out the bucket, and let the dogs kill the mice as long as there were any left.

RATS

Chloride of lime is an infallible preventive against rats, as they flee from its odour as from a pestilence.

If ants are troublesome, place slices of freshly cut lemon in their path.

FLIES

20 drops of carbolic acid evaporates from a hot shovel, will go far to banish flies from a room, while a bit of camphor gum, the size of a walnut, held over a lamp until consumed, will do the same for the mosquito.

To keep plated silver clean and bright without constant cleaning, which is so injurious to plated articles, dissolve a small handful of borax in a basin with a little hot water and a little soap, put the silver in, and let it stand for 3 or 4 hours; then pour off the suds, rinse with clean cold water, and wipe with a soft cloth.

When sending a trimmed hat by rail or carriage, sew the hat to the bottom of the box by two strand threads, and the hat will not crush the trimming if turned the wrong way up in carrying.

To Prevent Moths getting into a Carpet: A good layer of newspaper underneath a carpet will prevent moths getting into it.

Carpet moths may often be got rid of by scrubbing the floors with hot, strong, salted water before laying the carpet, and a light sprinkling each week or two of salt brushed in.

Sunshine is destructive to mirrors. It causes the glass to assume a milky appearance, and the mirror will never be so clear again in spite of whatever is done to it.

A little egg white rubbed on the toes of children's shoes hides scratches on the leather. Leave them to dry and polish well, and the shoes will look like new.

To remove water marks from furniture, apply mayonnaise and rub it in well. Let stand for one hour then wipe clean with a soft cloth.

If you cannot loosen a rusty screw, dab a little vinegar on it, and after a few minutes it should move easily.

To clean the spout of a teapot, pack it tightly with damp salt, then leave overnight; next morning, empty out salt and scald the spout with boiling water. All stains will be removed and the teapot will be sweet and clean.

A simple way to give a fresh light perfume to clothes, is to place a few (4 or 5) cloves in each drawer. This also acts as a deterrent to silverfish and moths.

A small handful of bicarbonate of soda added to the last rinsing water when washing nappies, will remove all traces of soap and ammonia, and will prevent nappy-rash.

If it is necessary to send china or other fragile articles through the post, try packing in a dampened newspaper. As the paper dries out, it forms a protective layer the same shape as the article.

To remove mould from furniture, sponge with hot water and ammonia. Add one dessertspoon of ammonia to a pint of boiling water. After the treatment, wipe furniture dry, and polish.

Keep mothballs in small screw-top jars with holes punched in lids, so the vapor can escape. You don't have mothballs scattered through your clothes, giving off too strong a smell and can easily see when the jar needs refilling.

In the event of bushfires, place old balls on top of downpipes and fill guttering with water. This helps prevent flying sparks igniting the eaves of the house.

Keep a piece of camphor in your jewellery case during damp weather. Camphor will prevent jewellery from tarnishing and stop gold and silver losing their lustre.

The pioneering bush housewife found a standby for many uses in the Kerosine tin. Clothes were boiled in them on a fire in the open. Water was carried from the creek, lagoon or river in them back to the bark hut or cottage. Meat was boiled in them often followed by a "spotted clager" (boiled pudding) and when these were almost done vegetables were thrown in too. They all tasted very good.

Kitchen cupboards were made of wooden Kerosine-tin cases. Seven of these made a very nice dressing table — three horizontal and two up-ended at each side gave a recessed middle. The two sides had tin drawers. On top of two of these a piece of ply was tacked over the front. With the addition of knobs and paint and a curtain over the middle area and a mirror in the centre of the top, a dressing table of great usefulness.

Ceilings and walls of a bark hut cracked after a time and an end of a Kerosine tin and case went into the rafters to repair. For washing up a dish cut on the diagonal and opened out, in a light wooden frame with the second part for rinsing lasted for a long time.

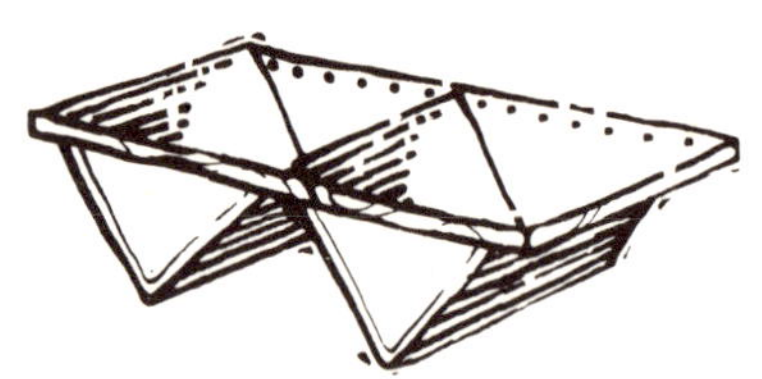

She looketh well to the ways of her household
And eateth not the bread of idleness.
Proverbs 31 — V27

Dressmakers will do well to remember that needles and pins will never rust in a cushion filled with coffee grounds. Rinse the grounds in cold water, spread on a sheet of paper to dry thoroughly and then stuff the cushion.

If scissors do not cut cleanly, and it is not convenient to send them to be ground, take a common glass bottle and make several attempts to cut the neck in two. The hard flint will turn back the edges of the steel, and the scissors will then be found to cut almost as well as if they had been ground.

For a cut or wound, cover with cobwebs. (It is now known that the webs contain penicillin.)

Poultice for boils and other inflamations. Equal parts of melted soap and sugar.

MAKING CANDLES

10 ozs. mutton fat or suet
¼ lb. white wax
¼ oz. camphor brick
2 ozs. alum.

Cut up all ingredients and melt together, stirring well while melting. Wicks should be soaked in vinegar, then dried thoroughly before they are fixed in the mould, which should be wet before pouring in the mixture, slightly cool. Leave to harden for 24 hours or longer.

OLD STYLE FLY-PAPER

Boil linseed oil to which a small amount of ground resin has been added until it forms a stringy paste. Spread this while it is hot on sheets of heavy paper and set aside to cool. It is then ready for use.

A TESTED SOAP RECIPE

Take 12lbs. fat, 2¼lbs. caustic soda, 1 lb. and 14 ozs. resin, 3 gallons and 3 pints of water. Boil all together until stringy, but be careful, when near the boil, take out a little fire or the mixture will boil over.

This polish improves shabby leather-covered chairs wonderfully. Boil ½ pint of linseed oil. Let it stand till nearly cold, then stir in ½ pint of vinegar. Stir till thoroughly mixed and bottle for use. When needed, shake the bottle well, pour a very little on to a soft flannel, rub thoroughly into the leather, turning the flannel when it gets dirty, and rub with soft dusters till the polish on the leather is restored.

To keep Black Walnut Polished: Black walnut or any wood finished in oil may be kept bright by polishing with kerosene.

To Clean Bamboo Furniture: To clean bamboo furniture use a brush dipped in warm water and salt. The salt prevents the bamboo changing color.

To Remove Stains from Mahogany: Stains on mahogany may be removed by rubbing them with a cork dipped into a little oxalic acid and water. When the stains have disappeared, wash the wood thoroughly with pure water, then dry and polish as usual.

To Restore Varnish on Furniture: Mix linseed oil and turpentine in equal quantities. Apply with a soft rag, rubbing in well; then wipe off with another rag; and polish with an old silk handkerchief. Chamois leather should not be used on varnished articles.

FURNITURE, TO CLEAN

First rub with cotton waste, dipped in boiled linseed oil; then rub clean and dry with a soft flannel cloth. Care should be taken that the oil is all removed.

A great help in cleaning is to have a jar of cleansing material made from the following ingredients always at hand. Added to warm water, it is easy to clean with, and does its work quickly:- Any pieces of shredded soap, a spoonful of saltpetre, a good tablespoonful of powdered ammonia, and a quart of boiling water. Mix, place in a bottle or jar, and cork tightly.

TO MEND BROKEN GLASS

Valuable glass, when broken, can be easily and effectually mended by the following means. Melt a little isinglass in spirits of wine, and add a small quantity of water. Warm the mixture gently over a moderate fire. When mixed, by thoroughly melting, it will form a perfectly transparent glue which will unite glass so firmly that the joining will scarcely be seen even by the most critical eye.

FLOOR POLISH

Save all candle ends, and when a sufficient number of pieces are saved, melt them down, removing wicks, then add equal parts of kerosene and turpentine. Stir well and allow to set before using. It will be then a soft wax. Apply in the usual way with cotton cloth and rub over with large cloth. It will be found an excellent polish and most economical.

TO REMOVE SOOT FROM CARPET

If soot should fall on the carpet, cover it thickly with salt. The salt and soot can then be swept up, without damaging the carpet.

WHEN WASHING LINOLEUM

Oilcloth or linoleum will look much brighter if two tablespoons of kerosine be put into the water it is washed with. No soap is necessary with this.

TO REMOVE MARKS CAUSED BY HOT DISHES

Marks on tables caused by hot dishes may be removed by kerosine rubbed in well with a soft cloth, finishing with a little cologne water, rubbed dry with another cloth.

A good cement for a cracked stove is made by mixing wood ashes and salt in equal quantities. Make this into a paste with cold water, and fill the cracks when the stove is cold. It soon hardens, and will last a long time.

A good French Polish for boots is made by mixing together two pints of best vinegar, one pint of soft water. Add to this ¼ lb. best soft glue broken up, ½ lb. logwood chips, ¼ oz. best soft soap, and a ¼ oz. of gelatine. Put the mixture over a fire and let it boil for 10 minutes or more; then strain the liquid and bottle and cork it. Use when cold. It should be applied with a clean sponge.

You will save time, temper and broken eggs, if you add a little vinegar to the water in which they are being poached.

A few drops of lemon juice in the water in which you poach eggs, will keep eggs firm and whole.

It's much easier to cut hard-boiled eggs into slices, if you first dip the knife into boiling water and wipe it dry. Repeat the dipping and wiping after every few cuts.

To find out whether eggs are fresh, fill a basin with water. A fresh egg will lie flat on the bottom; not so fresh will rise slightly; and a bad egg will float on the top.

Cover a left-over egg-yolk with a little cold water to keep.

Soda ruins aluminium articles, but lemon pulp and odd bits of rind clean them beautifully. Drop the pulp and rind inside and fill the vessel with water and boil for a few minutes, and then rub with a dish-cloth.

Stains in tan calf leather boots and shoes should be first washed in soapy water to which has been added a little washing soda. When dry rub the stain with methylated spirits. Finally polish with a tan polish.

If your tan boots or shoes happen to get oil or grease spots on them, mix equal parts of French chalk with Fuller's earth into a paste with milk. Cover the soiled parts, allow to dry, then brush off, when the spots will have vanished.

Before putting on a pair of new kid gloves, warm them by the fire. They will then be more elastic, and it will be easier to fit them on without risk of tearing them.

If you get your light clothes splashed with sea-water, rub powdered starch well into the stain, let it remain on for 24 hours, then brush off, when the marks will have disappeared without injuring the surface of the material.

A good way to revive a bit of black lace is to boil old kid gloves with it. Let the gloves boil a little while, and then dip the lace in the water. Then roll up the lace in a cloth, and iron it while still damp.

Clean celluloid with Pumice-Stone: Put a little powdered pumice-stone in a saucer, and get a piece of flannel, rub a little soap on it, and dip in the powder, rub this well inside and out of a celluloid collar, then rinse with cold water, and your collar will be beautifully clean.

TO MAKE CAMPHORATED OIL

Take 2 pennyworth of lump camphor and shred it finely into about 3 tablespoonsful of sweet oil. Cork the bottle loosely and stand it in a basin of hot water till the camphor is thoroughly dissolved. Splendid for children's colds.

Put scones straight out of the oven on to a wire rack and cover with clean tea-towel.

A little salt and water sprinkled on coals and cinders saves accumulation of soot.

In wiping china dishes do not pile one upon another while still hot. Spread out to cool off, then pack. Piling together while warm is apt to make the glaze crack.

To prevent a lamp from smoking, soak the wick in a strong vinegar and dry thoroughly before using. It will burn both sweetly and pleasantly.

Dampen clothes with warm water — it makes ironing easier.

TO DRY CLEAN WHITE LACE

Lay the lace out quite evenly on clean white paper, cover it with magnesia, then put another paper on the top. Lay it inside the leaves of a book for three days, and it will look as fresh as new. After being cleaned, if the lace is not in use, keep it in blue paper, as this preserves its whiteness.

TO RAISE THE PILE OF VELVET

Warm an ordinary iron, cover it with a wet cloth, and hold it under the velvet, the vapour arising will raise the pile, and give it quite a new look.

CLEANING SUEDE SHOES

Suede shoes that have become shiny can be cleaned by rubbing gently with fine emery paper.

OIL PAINT STAINS

To remove, apply oil of eucalyptus to stain. After a short time wash with soap.

TO CLEANSE WATER BOTTLES

To cleanse water bottles cut a potato into small dice and cover it with vinegar. Put some of this mixture into each bottle and shake till clean; then rinse in clean water and drain dry.

A little borax in the suds in which silver is washed adds to the lustre.

TO RESTORE GILT FRAMES

Rub with a sponge moistened with turpentine.

FASTENING KNIFE-BLADES INTO HANDLES

Clean out the holes of the handles, then fill lightly with a mixture of equal parts of resin and brickdust, taking care that the latter is dry. Make the tangs or spikes of the blades hot enough to melt the resin, and push into place in the handle. When cold the handles will be firmly fixed, and any of the cement that has been forced out may be chipped off. A little practice to get the right heat of the spike and the amount of filling will soon make the process satisfactory.

TO WASH GLASS

To bring out the brilliancy of cut-glass, ammonia should be placed in the rinsing water. All glass should be dried immediately, not drained.

To prevent steel brooches and ornaments going rusty, keep them, when not in use, in a box with some powdered starch.

If silver must be stored away for some time, it will keep perfectly bright if kept in tins or boxes full of powdered starch.

NOTES

A stitch in time saves nine.

POULTRY AND GAME

COOKING WILD DUCK

The ducks are improved by being hung for a few days before cooking. The birds should be plucked dry, and care should be taken not to break the skin when plucking. Remove the oil glands on each side of the tail to get rid of the strong taste. Clean out the inside of the birds and wipe out with a damp cloth, wrung out in vinegar.

Season inside with salt and pepper, and place a small sliced onion, a piece of celery or parsley, and ½ a peeled cooking apple inside each bird. Fasten openings with small skewers or sew with thread. Place in a baking dish with a few strips of fat bacon over breasts of birds, pour 1 cup of claret over the top and bake in a hot oven for 20 minutes, basting once or twice. The birds should be rare when served, but if you like your ducks better done, bake a little longer, basting well to keep them moist. Buttered paper placed over the top during the latter part of cooking is advisable.

Remove birds to a heated serving plate and keep hot while you make the gravy, using the juices which have accumulated inside the birds while cooking. Add this to the gravy in the baking dish, add 2 tablespoons of either red currant or apple jelly, juice of a lemon and 1 teaspoon Worcestershire sauce, and a little more claret if desired. Heat all together, then strain over the duck.

When carving wild ducks, be sure to slice the breast, and pour over the cuts a few spoonsful of sauce composed of port wine, or claret (warmed), lemon-juice, salt, and cayenne pepper. The manner in which this is done is said to be the criteria of gentlemanly habits and practice.

WILD DUCK CASSEROLE

Prepare the duck as given above, but stuff with a mixture of breadcrumbs, grated onion, chopped celery and a chopped whole orange, binding mixture with orange juice and seasoning with salt and pepper. Melt some bacon fat in a thick pan and brown the bird on all sides, turning to brown evenly. Place the duck in a casserole, cover breast with orange slices and add either claret or orange juice to the juices left in the pan in which bird was browned, thickening with a little flour. Pour this gravy over the duck in the casserole, cover and cook in a moderate oven for about 45 minutes or until duck is tender.

Serve with halved baked tomatoes and oven-baked potatoes in jackets. A green salad of lettuce tossed in French dressing, is excellent served with duck.

And wilful waste, depend upon 't,
Brings, almost always, woeful want!
Ann Taylor

HUNTER'S DUCK
with Apricot Sauce

In Victoria the season for ducks is from the last Saturday in February to the last Saturday in April.

Do not spoil your ducks by leaving the birds in a pile on return to camp. Clean the ducks and fill the body cavity with dry grass or twists of paper to soak up any blood.

Then hang the birds, batches of six or eight, to cool in the shade of a tree.

Wrap in sacking for transport home, after dividing the birds into small batches, separated with dry grass.

Take three plump wild ducks, some celery leaves, a cup of melted butter, and half-cup of claret.

Rub the prepared ducks, inside and out, with salt and some freshly ground black pepper.

Then fill the body cavities with fresh washed celery leaves, and brush the skin well with half of the butter.

Now place the birds, breasts up, in a roasting dish, and cook in a very hot oven for 30 minutes.

While the birds are cooking baste every five minutes with the wine and the remainder of the butter.

Carve into medium slices and set aside to keep warm, pouring off the liquid for use in the Apricot Sauce.

Sieve 2½ cups of stewed apricots through a coarse sieve.

Mix into this one teaspoon of grated orange rind, two cups of dry claret, six tablespoons of butter, and some freshly ground black pepper. Cook for five minutes.

Cut up three duck livers, or press them through a coarse sieve, and add to the first mixture with the duck juices from the roasting pan.

Simmer over hot water for five or six minutes, stirring while it thickens slightly. Pour over the duck and serve immediately.

SALMI OF WILD DUCK

This is a very old dish. Red wine can be used instead of white if preferred.

One or two wild ducks, one gill of white or red wine, one gill of Spanish sauce, 3 or 4 shallots, ¼ lb. mushrooms, one liqueur glass of brandy, one bay leaf, a sprig of thyme, salt, pepper.

Roast the birds, and whilst they are being roasted, put the chopped shallots, herbs, etc., in a small saucepan with the wine, and simmer gently till reduced to about one third. When the birds are nearly done, carve them carefully, removing all the flesh from the carcase; place the pieces of duck in a saucepan with the brandy and set alight. When the brandy is burnt out, add a little Spanish sauce, cover with a lid and keep warm. Chop up the bones or pound them in a mortar, and add to the wine and shallots, mixing well.

Add the remaining Spanish sauce, stir well, simmer gently and skin carefully. Cook for about 20 minutes. 5 minutes before serving, strain half the sauce over the pieces of duck and place the saucepan over a slow fire, but on no account should the sauce be allowed to boil. Remove the remainder of the sauce from the fire, add a few small pieces of butter, not quite 1 oz. altogether, and strain over the birds. Garnish with the cooked mushrooms and croutons of fried bread.

WILD DUCK

Pluck, draw and wash the bird. Stuff with one whole cored apple and one whole peeled onion. Have frying pan very hot indeed. Place in one tablespoon oil and quickly brown bird Pour 2 tablespoons of sherry over bird and reduce heat and cook until tender. Thicken juices and add orange juice to make gravy.

WILD DUCK AND CHERRIES

1 wild duck, quartered
1 clove garlic, crushed
1 tablespoon cooking oil
2 tablespoons dry sherry
1 lb. cherries, stewed
1 teaspoon tomato puree
2 ozs. butter — ½ oz. cornflour
¼ pint stock — 1 orange, sliced
1 bay leaf — ½ bunch watercress

Heat the butter and oil in a large frying pan. Add the pieces of duck and brown them on all sides. Pour the sherry over. Remove duck from pan and place on hot dish. Put the garlic and half the drained cherries into the frying pan. Allow to cook for a few minutes.

Blend the cornflour with a little of the drained cherry juice and tomato puree. Add to the sherry mixture in the pan with the rest of the cherry juice and the stock. Cook over a moderate heat, stirring well until the sauce is thickened.

Put the duck back into the pan and add the bay leaf. Cover with a lid and simmer over a low heat for 40 minutes.

Arrange duck on dish, pour over sauce and garnish with rest of the cherries, orange slices and watercress.

SHEARWATER BIRDS (Mutton Birds)

(Protected in Victoria but obtainable sometimes from Tasmania.)

Use only very young birds fried in their own fat.

Remove the envelope of fat by sliding the fingers beneath it and levering it gently away, leaving flecks of it on the flesh for grilling. Season with a stuffing made of breadcrumbs, grated apple, grated onion, and a little grated lemon peel, pepper, salt and marjoram. Rub a generous amount of lemon juice into the bird and bake in the oven for ¾ hour. The bird is good either hot or cold.

Tiger Country — Patsy Adam Smith

"Many are the ways, and many the recipes,
For dressing hares; but this is best of all:
To place before a hungry set of guests,
A slice of roasted meat fresh from the spit,
Hot, season'd only with plain, simple salt,
Not too much done. And do not you be vexed
At seeing blood fresh trickling from the meat,
But eat it eagerly. All otherways
Are quite superfluous; such as when cooks pour
A lot of sticky, clammy sauce upon it,
Parings of cheese, and lees, and dregs of oil,
As if they were preparing cats' meat."

"Atheneus"

HUNTERS' HARE

Take the meat from the bones while raw. Boil the bones for 20 minutes in 1½ pints of water, 1 dozen cloves, 1 onion, bay leaves, a few sprigs of thyme, carrots and peppercorns. Strain the stock from the bones and into this put the pieces of hare and minced hare-liver. Cook for 20 minutes. Fry shredded carrots and onions until brown, add 1 large tablespoon of flour, fry until golden. Add hare stock. Bring to the boil. Drop in pieces of hare.

HARE STEW

Dice and brown 6 ozs. of cheap fat bacon in 3 ozs. butter. Add 3 medium-sized chopped onions, and when they too have browned, remove them with the bacon fat. Throw into the hot fat the pieces of hare, and when they begin to brown sprinkle them with flour. Bring all to boil in weak stock and then pour the contents of the pan into a casserole to which add some red wine. Cook covered in very slow oven for 2 to 3 hours.

Vegetables — hot beetroot or cauliflower.

Fillets of hare saddle — serve with red jelly and garnish with cooked or raw celery.

SAUTEED QUAIL

6 quail — ½ bay leaf
2 whole cloves — 1 cup cream
Salt — 6 peppercorns
1 small onion, chopped fine
½ cup butter or ½ butter and ½ bacon fat
1 cup dry white wine
1 cup stock or water
Few grains cayenne

Have the quail dressed, cleaned and trussed. Heat the butter in a thick pan with a lid, add chopped onion, peppercorns, cloves and bay leaf and cook for 8 minutes, stirring frequently. Push the onions and other ingredients to one side of the pan and saute the quail on all sides until evenly browned. Add the wine and stock, cover and simmer for 30 minutes, or until tender. Remove the quail to a casserole and keep hot while you strain the sauce from the pan into a saucepan. Slowly add the cream, season to taste and heat until nearly boiling but do not allow to boil. Pour sauce over the quail and serve at once. Some people like to serve each quail on a square of crisp fried bread and pour the sauce over them.

STUFFED QUAIL (to be eaten cold)

Few cooks know the secret of roasting quail and keeping it tender and moist to eat cold. Squab and other small birds could be cooked in similar fashion.

Prepare birds as if for roasting. Mince a little cold cooked veal. Season it with minced celery, parsley and a very little onion or chives. Add a pat of pate-de-fois-gras, salt and pepper. Stuff birds with this. Put them in a baking tin. Cover with thin slices of bacon. Add a little stock. Cover with another pan to steam them and cook 1 hour. When about half done sprinkle with fine soft breadcrumbs and dust with salt and pepper.

ROAST SNIPE

(Open season in Victoria)

A great daintly here, they are plentiful in Tasmania. Snipe, toast, bacon, good gravy, lard or dripping for basting. These birds are dressed without being "drawn" because they only "feed" by suction. They are trussed in the same way as other birds for roasting, but the head is skinned and left on, the long beaks of the birds being passed through the legs and body instead of a skewer. Brush them over with warm butter, tie a thin slice of fat bacon over each breast. Keep basting them well and serve on hot buttered toast with bread sauce.

PIGEON SOVEREIGN

(Now protected in Victoria)

Select two young dressed pigeons. Lard the birds and roast for 15 minutes in a hot oven. Remove and place in a casserole with some demiglace, pate-de-fois and brandy. Return to the oven for a further 15 minutes at reduced heat or until cooked.

Serve in the casserole garnished with chopped parsley.

STUFFED PHEASANT

1½ lb. pheasant or chicken
¾ lb. mushrooms
6 ducks livers
½ bottle port wine

Bone bird and stuff with ducks liver and ½ lb. mushrooms previously cooked in port wine. Marinate the bird for 3 days in port wine, taking care that it is well covered. Cook in a casserole for ½ hour at barely moderate heat. Remove bird from casserole, reduce marinade to 1/3 volume, add 12 medium-sized mushrooms. Set pheasant or chicken on these and heat for a further 10 minutes. Serve reduced marinade as sauce.

STEAMER PHEASANT

4lb. pheasant, ½ lb. raisins, 1 large glass of cream, parsley, thyme, ½ glass whisky, chopped onions.

Have the pheasant cut in about 8 pieces and cook in hot butter and let it take a nice roasted colour. Add the whisky to the pheasant and ignite. Add chopped onion, parsley and other herbs, and salt and pepper. Cover very tightly, let it cook very slowly for 15 minutes, then add the raisins, washed but dried. Cook for another ¾ hour. Just before serving add the cream without letting it boil. Serve hot with chestnut puree.

FARMERS JUGGED HARE

Soak jointed pieces for several hours in red wine. Then flour the pieces and fry them a rich brown, packing them into a casserole with a covering of good bacon rind and some onion. Cook slowly sealed in a very slow oven for about 3 hours. Just before the dish is ready to be served, make the gravy with some blood and a glass of good port. Mix into the casserole.

HARE HASELET

1 hare	¼ small loaf bread
½ lb. bacon	1 onion
1 cup flour	Dried herbs
Pepper and salt	

Cut the meat off the bones and mince. Add bread, bacon, onion, all minced, flour and season with herbs, pepper and salt. Mix well together and form into two big rolls. Put into greased dish with a slice of bacon on each roll, and cover with another dish. Bake in moderate oven for two hours.

ROAST HARE

1 hare	2 ozs. larding bacon
½ pint sour cream	Salt
Butter for roasting	Freshly ground pepper

Skin hare if it was not done before, then, if it is freshly killed, keep on ice for about six days. Use only the saddle and the two hind legs, the rest can be made into a stew or pate. Scald with boiling water, carefully remove the hard skin, and lard with the aid of a larding needle and strips of smoked bacon (obtainable from Continental butchers as Speck). Rub with salt, lightly pepper and place in a well-buttered dish. Begin to roast in a low oven — adding a little water and a few tablespoons of sour cream to the pan whenever necessary. Baste frequently, and gradually, after an hour, increasing the temperature of the oven to hot. A medium-sized hare should require about an hour or an hour and a half to be roasted. Serve with crab-apples and potato croquettes.

BRAISED QUAIL
(Open season in Victoria)

A little port wine or sherry
1 dessertspoon of breadcrumbs
Some beef or mutton bones

1 quail	A slice of tongue
Chopped parsley	Stock
Pepper and Salt	

Fill the body of the quail with a seasoning made with a little finely chopped parsley, finely chopped tongue and a dessertspoon of breadcrumbs, salt and pepper moistened with a little port wine, sherry or stock. Sew up the opening (being careful not to put a knot in the cotton and to leave an end sufficiently long to draw it out when the bird is cooked). Bake in a brisk oven, basting frequently for about 15 minutes, then lift out and place in a stewpan with the bones and enough stock to come to about halfway up the pan. Place the quail on top of the bones, cover tightly and cook till tender. Strain the gravy, remove any fat, season and thicken with a little well-blended flour and water. Brown with caramel if necessary. Thoroughly reheat and pour a little around the bird. Use same recipe for young chicken.

TO COOK VENISON

About four pounds of haunch (rump). This should hang for some days in a cool place. Make deep incisions in haunch and stuff with a good bread stuffing. Roll in flour and braise till nicely brown. Combine ½ pint vinegar (or red wine), 1 pint water, 6 cloves, 2 bay leaves, 2 teaspoons salt, 1 tablespoon brown sugar, 2 cups diced carrots, 2 cups diced onion, pepper. Place all in heavy saucepan with a tight lid. Cook slowly until tender, about 3 hours. Make gravy with liquid.

RABBIT CASSEROLE

Soak rabbit in salt and water all night. Next day, cut into pieces, put in casserole, cover with layer of onion, then layer of peeled, sliced cooking apples and about ½ cup water, then breadcrumbs well seasoned with pepper and salt, herbs and mace. Put dabs of butter on top. Simmer on low gas, lid tightly on. Time according to size of rabbit.

BUSHMAN'S MINCE

First catch your hare and use it fresh. Take all solid flesh and put it uncooked through a mincer. Add to this mince one cup of breadcrumbs, one small onion, three slices of bacon, and a sprinkle of mixed herbs, plus salt and pepper. Blend together with an egg.

HARVEST RABBIT

Allow 1 small rabbit to every two persons
Dripping
3 prunes to each rabbit
A bunch of fresh herbs to each rabbit
Seasoned flour
Onions (large, or salad onions)
1 thin slice of fat bacon to each rabbit
Stock

Forcemeat Balls

Chopped bacon (or suet)
Chives (or young onion tops)
Sweet majoram Parsley
Seasoning Breadcrumbs
1 or 2 eggs

Skin, draw and cut off the heads, scuts and feet of the rabbits. Wash well, leave in salt water for 15 minutes, then dry and fry whole in dripping until a pale golden-brown all over. Drain, and stuff under the ribs of each 3 well-soaked prunes and a bunch of fresh herbs. Coat thickly with well-seasoned flour. Cover the bottom of a large deep baking-dish with thinly sliced onions, or the bulbs of salad onions, lay the floured rabbits on them, with a thin slice of fat bacon over each, and just cover with stock. Bake slowly for 2 hours.

Serve on a hot dish, garnished with the onions and plenty of large force-meat balls, made of the ingredients above bound with egg, or 2 eggs if as many as 3 rabbits are cooked.

Fry a deep brown, and be sure that plenty of fresh herb is used, as they must cut a bright green. Strain the gravy, and serve separately.

KANGAROO TAIL STEW

(Kangaroos are now protected in Victoria unless a license is obtained.)

1 tail from about half grown kangaroo
1 parsnip 2 onions
1 carrot 3 or 4 potatoes
salt and pepper

After carefully removing skin, joint tail disregarding sinews. Slice onions and lightly brown meat and onions by frying. Cut carrot and parsnip into fine rings and potatoes into fairly small pieces. Place in pressure cooker with 1 to 1½ cups water and seasonings. Bring up to pressure and hold for about 1 hour. Remove bone from top joint before serving.

KANGAROO STEAMER

Cut the meat off the hind-quarters, take away the skin and mince, pound or grind the meat in a sausage mill, not set finely. Set it aside until the next day and prepare the gravy meanwhile.

For this you can use the bones, skin, tail or part of the fore-quarter, well bruised and hacked up and slowly simmered with three pints of water and a small onion, until reduced to little more than one pint. Do this the day before you want to serve the steamer and strain off the gravy to be cold.

Next day take a pound (or more, if liked) of nice fat bacon, free from rust, cut it into dice, add it to the minced meat. Stir all well into the cold gravy (which should be a jelly, if good). Let the whole warm gradually, simmer slowly until cooked. Season to your palate, being careful not to add much salt, if any, as the bacon salts it. A spoonful or two of mushroom ketchup and a dredge of flour will improve the flavour and consistency of the steamer. Serve with sippets of toasted bread.

O, yet we trust that somehow good
Will be the final goal of ill,
To pangs of nature, sins of will,
Defects of doubt, and taints of blood.
Tennyson

BRAISED DUCK WITH CHERRIES

1 duck, of approximately 4 lbs.
1 tablespoon salt 1 lb. cherries
1 small glass brandy 4 ozs. butter

For the Spanish Sauce:

1 oz. butter 1 oz. flour
2 cups brown stock ½ oz. bacon, diced
bay leaf, parsley, thyme, pepper
1 dessertspoon worcestershire sauce

Prepare the sauce first by browning flour and butter together, then adding the other ingredients. Let simmer for 15 minutes and pass through sieve.

Roast the duck on all sides in the butter. When brown, remove duck and add to the butter the brown sauce and the cherries. Let simmer for 10 minutes and remove cherries. Place duck back in gravy and braise with lid on the pan for 1½ hours or until tender. Turn duck from time to time. Five minutes before serving, add cherries again. Place duck and cherries on a plate, pour brandy over it and light. For a good effect this can be done at the table. Serve sauce separately. For extra flavour, one glass of Madeira may be added to sauce before the braising.

ROAST DUCKLING WITH MARINATED FIGS

4½-5 lb. duck — 1 lb. dried figs
Port wine

Place figs in dish and port wine on top of dish. Allow to stand for 36 hours. Place duck in roasting pan and cook until half done. Remove juices from roasting pan and replace with port wine used to marinate figs. Allow port wine to reduce to half, basting duck with a little water from time to time. When duck is cooked take half the sauce from roasting pan, add figs, then simmer until figs have a glazed appearance. Divide duck into four serving portions and garnish with figs. Pour remaining sauce over duck.

Serve with new potatoes and green salad.

VINEYARD DUCK WITH ORANGE

A duck about 4-5 lbs. — ½ cup sugar
Juice of 2 oranges — Grated rind of 1 orange
Salt and pepper
1 tablespoon wine vinegar
¼ cup Grand Marnier Liqueur
Orange slices to garnish

Clean the duck well and sprinkle inside and out with salt and pepper, then rub over with butter. Roast in a hot oven for about 35 to 40 minutes, as the duck should be slightly rare. If desired, it can be baked rather longer. Remove the duck from the baking dish and keep hot. Skim excess fat from pan. In a heavy frying pan combine the sugar and vinegar and allow sugar to melt and just start to caramelise. Add the orange juice, Grand Marnier and grated orange rind and blend well together, then add to the juices in the baking dish and bring to the boil. Taste for seasoning and pour over the duck. Garnish the platter with orange slices.

DUCKLING WITH RAISIN FLAVOUR

Cut 8 or 9 raisins into pieces and crush slightly. Soak for an hour or two in two tablespoons of muscat — the sweet dessert wine.

Prepare a special basting mixture with the juices of half an orange, half a lemon, one-third cup muscat and a big tablespoon butter. Put in a little saucepan until required.

Bring bird to room temperature and wash inside and out in running water. Rub inside with salt and rinse again. Pat dry with a cloth. Now rub all over the inside cavity with the wine-soaked raisins. Leave these in and also add a sprig of washed parsley and a small peeled onion slashed in one or two places. No other stuffing is used. When celery is in season, substitute it for the onion. Rub the outside of the bird with the merest trifle of salt, and brush all over with salad oil or a little soft butter. Stand on a rack (right side up) in a dry baking pan. Put in a moderate oven on coolest shelf. If you have a bit of bacon to spare, lay it over the bird. Heat your basting mixture and have it ready on top of the stove.

Cook gently, basting every 20 minutes. After a little time fat will begin to drip into the pan and bird will begin to colour. Turn it upside down on the rack and baste well. In the last hour remove rack and lower duck into the pan, turning it right side up again. It is done when you can pierce the leg meat easily with a skewer. Adjust oven heat as required to get perfect colour and tenderness.

Garnish dish with orange circles and raisins.

GEORGIAN DUCK

1 large duck or drake
Freshly ground black pepper
Cup sour cream (or fresh cream)
4 ozs. walnuts — 2 tablespoons lard
4 onions — Salt
3 ripe tomatoes — 1 lemon

Clean and wash the duck and cut into approximately twelve pieces. Do not remove from bones. Finely chop the onion and similarly chop up the walnut pieces.

In a saucepan melt the lard and fry the onions until golden brown. Add the duck pieces, salt and black pepper, cover and let simmer first in its own juice, then add a very little water to prevent it from sticking to the pan. After three quarters of an hour add the quartered tomatoes and continue stewing until the meat is tender. When it is ready for serving add the juice of a lemon and the chopped walnut, cook for five more minutes, stirring frequently, then pour on the cream. Heat, but do not boil, and serve immediately. Rice is the appropriate garnishing with this dish.

DUCK IN WINE JELLY

48 pitted black cherries
3 tablespoons cognac
4 cups wine flavoured meat jelly
1 tablespoon lemon juice
2 tablespoons sugar
5½ to 6lb. roast duck, chilled
and carved into pieces.

Marinade cherries with lemon juice, cognac and sugar for one hour. Heat meat jelly in a saucepan and add cherries and marinade.

On a serving platter pour a thin layer of jelly and chill to set. Skin duck and arrange pieces on serving platter. Spoon chilled jelly over duck, chill 10 minutes and repeat until duck is well coated.

Place cherries around duck and add a final layer of jelly. Chill well until ready to serve.

DUCK WITH BROWN RICE

1 good-sized duck   Salt and black pepper
1 flat teaspoon cinnamon
2 tablespoons thin honey
5 small tart apples (little cider apples are perfect if available)
2 slices of crustless bread cut ½ inch thick

Place duck on ordinary rack. Prick all over with a fork and do this really vigourously. Season with salt and pepper and rub honey all over the upper part of the bird. Take a standard meat baking tin, and peel, core and halve the little apples. Place them cut side downwards on the baking tin and sprinkle them lightly with salt and pepper. Now lift the pan over the top of the meat baking tin. Put in the oven on the middle shelf at moderate heat and roast until fat runs freely down the sides as a result of the fork proddings.

When the fat runs really freely and a little has dripped into the pan, sprinkle the cinnamon over the upper part of the bird and return to the oven and continue roasting with the oven a little hotter. The total baking time is 75 minutes, so at half-time spoon up a little of the pan fat and baste the pieces of apple. When the bird is cooked the skin will be very crisp and the colour of horse-chestnuts.

Remove duck and carve it into neat portions in the kitchen. Lift out the now soft duck-juice-impregnated apples and arrange these alternately with the carved duck pieces on a heated serving dish.

Finally, place the baking tin of duck fat over a medium heat, and when sizzling, slip in the quartered bread slices. Fry them until they are fairly crisp and arrange around the dish. Hand a bowl of sweated brown rice.

BROWN RICE

8 ozs. brown rice   2 ozs. butter
1 quart stock   Salt and pepper
1 finely chopped shallot or small onion

Dissolve butter in a frying pan and when it sweats toss in both rice and onion and stir and turn with a wooden spoon or slice until the rice grains take up the colour of the butter. Scrape into a medium casserole. Pour all the stock over and cover with a lid. Cook in moderate oven 40 to 45 minutes. Season rice with salt and pepper, stir well and heap into a heated dish.

CARVING POULTRY

In carving a goose, cut off the apron, or part directly under the neck and outside the merry-thought; then turn the neck end towards you and cut the breast in slices. Take off the leg by putting the fork into the small end of the bone, pressing it close to the body while the knife is dividing the joint. Take off the wing by putting the fork in the small end of the pinion, and pressing it close to the body, while the knife is dividing the joint. The wing side-bones and back and lower side-bones should then be cut off. The best pieces are the breast and thighs.

A fowl or chicken is carved by first detaching the legs. Next take off the wings by dividing the joint; lift up the pinion with your fork, and draw the wing towards the leg, and the muscles will separate better than if cut. Remove the merry-thought from neck-bones, and divide breast from the body by cutting through the tender ribs. Lay the back upwards and cut it across half-way between neck and rump. The breast and thighs are considered the choicest bits.

Nearly all kinds of small game birds are carved by simply cutting them in two, from the neck to the tail, unless they are given whole. Never pour gravy over white meat, as it would destroy its delicate appearance.

CHICKEN MARSALA

1 2½-3lb. cooked chicken
4 ozs. grated cheddar cheese
½ clove crushed garlic
½ teaspoon mixed mustard
½ cup marsala   ½ teaspoon paprika
2 ozs. butter   ½ cup cream

Cut chicken into serving pieces. Saute in butter in frying pan until golden brown, turning once. Pour marsala over chicken. Cover, simmer 30 minutes or until tender. Combine remaining ingredients. Blend well. Transfer chicken to casserole. Spoon cheese mixture over. Grill or place in moderately hot oven until cheese is slightly browned and bubbling. Serve with a salad.

CHICKEN with MUSHROOM DRESSING

2 small roasting chickens (or 1 large)
¼ pint strong jellied stock
Salt and pepper 2-3 ozs. butter
Parsley

Mushroom Dressing

6 ozs. button mushrooms
2 glasses port or burgundy
1 tablespoon lemon juice
2 tablespoons olive oil
2 tablespoons French dressing
Chopped herbs

Rub the chicken well with butter, place a small nut of butter inside each bird with the parsley and seasonings; place in a roasting dish, with the stock and cook in a moderate oven until brown and tender, basting frequently. Allow to cool before cutting into neat joints.

Cut the mushrooms into quarters and saute quickly in the oil for a few minutes. Reduce the wine by half and pour on to the mushrooms. When cold, add the French dressing, lemon juice and chopped herbs. Arrange the chicken in the serving dish, spoon over the mushroom dressing and garnish with a tomato salad.

FAST CHICKEN

Put 4 silver (not plated) forks into a chicken. Place in cold water in a cooking pot. Add salt, pepper, 1 tablespoon vinegar, 1 teaspoon ginger. With lid on, bring to the boil. Simmer for 5 minutes and leave overnight in lidded pot. Useful for chicken based dishes.

CHICKEN SOUFFLE

Use basic sauce and three eggs. Take four ounces of cooked - or better still, uncooked chicken meat, and pass twice through a fine mincer. Pound well, as it may be very smooth. Season with pepper, salt and squeeze of lemon juice and work into the sauce. Add the yolks of the eggs, one at a time, beating well between each. Last of all fold in whisked whites of the eggs.

This recipe can be used with white fish, lobster, rabbit, veal or any kind of poultry or game.

CHICKEN WITH LEMON SAUCE

Remove all the fat from the inside of the chicken and render it by putting in a pan over low heat until it is melted, then strain through a fine strainer or muslin. Put the bird on to boil in a saucepan, with enough water to come half-way up the side of the chicken, add salt and simmer until tender. Wash two cups of rice well in running water and add to two cups of boiling water, with a little salt and one tablespoon clarified chicken fat. Lower the heat so that water is just simmering, cover with lid and cook for 15 minutes, stirring occasionally with a fork. Cook until all liquid has disappeared, then remove lid and allow rice to steam for 10 minutes, being careful it does not burn. If necessary, keep hot in oven until chicken is ready.

Make lemon sauce with two cups cooled broth strained from chicken, two eggs, juice of two lemons, salt and pepper to taste. Beat eggs lightly and add with lemon juice to cooled broth, then stir over low heat until thickened, but do not boil. Place rice in serving dish and arrange carved chicken round it, then either pour the sauce over it or serve separately in a sauce-boat.

CHICKEN PORTLAND

1 roasting chicken 3-3½ lbs.
(alternatively the chicken may be jointed before cooking thus reducing cooking time)
1 small head celery 2 tablespoons flour
2½ ozs. cream Butter for browning
Chopped parsley 1 medium-sized onion
Butter 3 glasses port
Bouquet garni ½ pint good stock
1 doz. or so large soft prunes
(if using dried prunes, soak in a little tea, stone, then cook in tea until tender)

Brown the chicken all over in the hot butter. Then cook the finely chopped onion and, after a minute or two, add two glasses or port. Shake the pan, then take out the chicken, draw aside and stir in the flour and the stock. Bring to the boil, replace the bird, add the bouquet garni and stalk of celery, cover tightly and cook gently on the stove top or in the oven for about 30-40 minutes, turning the bird occasionally. Add 1 glass of port, a spoonful of sugar to the stoned prunes, and continue to cook until the prunes are well glazed — keep warm.

Meanwhile, shred the celery and cook in an ounce or two of butter in a shallow pan until barely tender, shaking the pan frequently. Season well and finish with a good shaking of chopped parsley. Take up the chicken, carve and dish. Keep warm.

Reduce the sauce a little and add the cream. Reheat without boiling and spoon over the dish. Garnish with the prunes and celery.

THE WATERZOI

1 tender, plump spring chicken (allow ½ a small chicken per person)
1 leek (the white part only)
1 tablespoon plain flour
Small piece of parsley root (if available)

1 small onion	1 young carrot
2 small celery stalks	½ lemon
1 egg yolk	2-3 ozs. butter
Salt	Black pepper

Dice vegetables and gently fry in butter. Place on top the whole chicken and pour on sufficient hot water to cover the meat. Add salt, pepper, bring to the boil then very slowly simmer for half to three-quarters of an hour, depending on the size of the chicken. (If larger birds are used allow a quarter per person and cook, naturally, longer).

When meat is tender, carefully cut into halves. Keep warm. In a separate saucepan, heat one ounce of butter, stir in the flour and let cook for a short time. Strain on the liquid from the chicken (it should be exactly three-quarters of a pint to each chicken), stir until it thickens. Now add the egg yolk, but do not boil, or else it curdles. The sauce should have the consistency of very thin, light cream. Lastly, squeeze in the juice of the lemon.

Pour this sauce over the chicken and the diced vegetables, and serve at once either in a soup tureen or in individual deep plates.

Eat with a spoon and fork.

CHICKEN CASSEROLE

This is a most delicious and rich tasting dish.
1 young roasting bird and divided into 4 or 5 portions. Remove skin. Put chicken pieces aside until required.
2 level tablespoons each of oil and butter,
10 small onions (or five of medium sized, peeled and cut in half across the centre,
six very small whole carrots (or three of medium size, cut into strips or quarters),
12 small fresh mushrooms,
half an 8 oz. cup each of tomato puree, water, dry sherry or chablis,
Flour as required,
Pepper and salt,
Parsley and fried bread croutons for garnishing.

Melt oil and butter in a roomy saucepan and gently fry onions and carrots until a pale brown tint begins to show. At once, lift the vegetables on a draining spoon onto a plate.

Toss the chicken joints in dry flour seasoned with a little salt and pepper. Fry them slowly and carefully two pieces at a time until delicately gold, turning them two or three times. When all are cooked, there should be a generous tablespoonful of fat in the pan. Add a tablespoon of flour (or enough to absorb the fat). Stir until it is pale gold. Then add the mixed liquids and stir until mixture boils and slightly thickens. Remove from heat and add chicken pieces and the vegetables. Spoon the liquid over all. Cover saucepan and simmer over low heat until the chicken is tender enough to pierce with a skewer (1-1¼ hours). Cook the peeled mushrooms in a little butter until tender, thicken with flour, and add to the pan. Stir and cook another 10 minutes.

Lift chicken on to a hot dish or into a casserole. Arrange vegetables on top and pour sauce over all. Sprinkle with parsley and garnish with croutons.

CHICKEN MOUSSE

1 steamed chicken	1 slice onion
1 cup cream	1 cup dry white wine
2 cloves	1 pint chicken stock
Nutmeg	2 tablespoons gelatine
Salt	1 slice lemon
1 bay leaf	grated rind 1 lemon

Cayenne pepper
1 tablespoon lemon juice
2 tablespoons chopped onion

Add lemon and onion slices, cloves and bay leaf to chicken stock. Simmer 15 minutes. Strain, reserving 2 cups stock. Soften gelatine in wine. Add reserved stock, stir over low heat until gelatine is dissolved. Remove from heat. Take meat from chicken bones. Chop fairly finely. Put with chopped onion, lemon rind and juice to wine mixture. Season well with nutmeg, pepper and salt. Fold in whipped cream. Pour into wet 3 pint mould. Chill overnight. Next day take mould out and put on to serving dish. Serves 6 persons.

Sauce

1 teaspoon lemon juice

½ cup cream	¾ cup mayonnaise

Lightly whip cream and stir in mayonnaise and lemon juice. Blend until smooth.

BUTTER BASTED TURKEY

One 8 lb. turkey 2 ozs. butter
Stuffing (see below)

Prepare and stuff turkey. Melt butter, add a squeeze of lemon juice. Brush turkey well with the melted butter. Cover breast bone with a piece of buttered paper. Place turkey in baking dish, with 1 cup of water. Place in a moderate oven and cook at same temperature. Allow 20 minutes for each 1 lb. + 20 minutes over. Baste frequently after the first 40 minutes.

Stuffing

½ lb. mince steak Salt and pepper
1 chopped onion Pinch of thyme
½ lb. white breadcrumbs
½ lb. grated strong cheddar cheese
1 tablespoon tomato paste or
2 tablespoons tomato puree

Mix all ingredients together and stuff turkey.

VEAL FORCEMEAT FOR ROAST TURKEY

Mince 8 ozs. fillet of veal and 4 ozs. of raw ham or gammon very fine. Add 1 teacupful of fine white breadcrumbs, a little chopped truffle and salt and pepper. Mix this with a raw egg. Press it all through a sieve.

THE MAJOR'S RECIPE FOR COOKING TURKEY

Blanch a hen turkey for 30 minutes in water or mutton barley broth. The bird being wet out of the pot, rub it well over with fresh butter, then breadcrumbs all over. Roast, or cook it in a pan in the oven. Baste it now and again. Very tender and juicy.

ROAST TURKEY

Turkey, like sucking-pig, requires great attention in roasting, and after having been properly trussed and stuffed with veal stuffing. The time of roasting will depend on the size of the turkey. Pork sausages, ham, pork or bacon, are generally served with roast turkey, and sometimes forcemeat balls; and egg, bread, oyster, celery, or gravy sauce. Turkey may be stuffed with forcemeat of veal mixed with sausage meat, liver, parsley and chives, chopped fine.

A turkey is improved by roasting it covered with bacon and paper; to be taken off a short time before it is done, to brown. Chestnuts, roasted, grated or sliced, and truffles or mushrooms, stewed and sliced, are both an addition and improvement to forcemeat for turkeys. Chestnuts, stewed in brown gravy, are the correct thing to be served with this dish.

The turkey did not arrive in England till A.D. 1524, about the fifteenth year of the reign of Henry VIII according to 'Baker's Chronicle'.

From the low peasant to the Lord,
The Turkey smokes on every board.
John Gay

TURKEY ROLL

One 12-14 lb. turkey
4 cups cooked rice (approx. 1¼ cups raw)
1 cup turkey broth (from turkey bones) or chicken broth
2 to 3 tablespoons water
¼ teaspoon cayenne pepper
1 dessertspoon cinnamon
4 tablespoons butter or margarine
1 chopped turkey liver
½ teaspoon black pepper
½ cup broken pecans or walnuts
1 cup currants 2 teaspoons salt
2 onions

To bone the turkey

Remove end joints of wings and legs, lay bird breast down and with small, very sharp knife cut flesh through to the bone straight down the back. Working first to the left, insert knife under flesh and cut away flesh as close to the bone as possible. Break wing and leg joints, and cut flesh carefully down one side, lay open flesh, pull away disjointed bones. Continue cutting flesh around to centre breast section, then turn bird around and cut other side in similar fashion. Flatten bird out and arrange any cut pieces of flesh over thin patches.

To prepare stuffing

Add slightly warmed broth to rice and stand aside. Melt butter, add finely chopped onions and saute until lightly browned. Add a little water and chopped liver. Remove from heat, add seasonings and spices (more or less as desired), currants and nuts. Mix well and cook 10 minutes longer over low heat. Pour over rice and blend well.

Spread stuffing thickly on to flattened turkey, fold in any uneven edges, and roll up as for Swiss roll. Steep a piece of cheese cloth in cooking oil, then wrap it around the turkey roll. Tie, not too tightly, at 2 in. intervals along the roll with string or strong cotton. Place in well-greased baking dish and bake in a moderate oven, allowing 20 minutes per pound of turkey. For a crisp brown skin, cut away cheese cloth about 20 minutes before turkey finishes cooking.

Lift out turkey and keep hot while making a rich brown gravy from remaining fat and juices and extra turkey or chicken broth.

"Turkey boiled
Is turkey spoiled,
And turkey roast
Is turkey lost;
But turkey braised
The Lord be praised!"
Anon.

RICE AND PICKLED WALNUT SEASONING

1 dessertspoon chopped onion
1 dessertspoon chopped parsley
2 teaspoon pepper — 2 cups cooked rice
¼ lb. butter — 1 cup pickled walnuts

Melt butter, saute onion — mix in rest of ingredients.

LIVER STUFFING FOR GAME

The liver of wild ducks or wild turkeys, or half a pound of sheep's liver, 1 slice of bacon, 1 egg, 1 tablespoon of butter, juice of a lemon, 1 cup of breadcrumbs, cayenne and salt.

Mince the liver and bacon, then add the juice of the lemon, cayenne, and a cupful of fine breadcrumbs; mix these well together with the butter and egg. If the mixture appears too dry, add a little milk or stock.

NUT STUFFING FOR DUCK

2 tablespoons chopped herbs and parsley mixed
4 ozs. nuts — 1 small onion
1 oz. butter — grated rind 1 lemon
1 beaten egg — 3-4 ozs. breadcrumbs
Salt and pepper — ½ teaspoon cinnamon

Chop the nuts finely. Chop the onion and saute in butter, add the nuts and cook 3-4 minutes. Cool slightly, then add the lemon rind, breadcrumbs, chopped herbs and cinnamon. Season with salt and pepper. Bind together with the beaten egg.

SEASONING

Melt good tablespoon of butter in pan, add small onion chopped fine, then add crumbs (large cup) and seasoning, then 1 dessertspoon lemon juice. Stuff while warm.

STUFFING FOR ROAST CHICKEN

1 cup of cooked rice, a handful of raisins, ½ cup of blanched and pounded almonds, ¼ cup of finely chopped raw onion, ½ cup of chopped parsley, liver of chicken, 2 ozs. butter, a sprig of basil, 1 egg.

Mash the liver and mix all the ingredients together, working the butter well into the mixture, adding the beaten egg last.

APRICOT STUFFING
(Turkey or Chicken)

6 ozs. dried apricots
6 ozs. fresh breadcrumbs
¼ teaspoon mixed spice
1 oz. butter, melted
¼ teaspoon salt — ¼ teaspoon pepper
Juice ½ lemon — 1 egg

Soak the apricots in cold water (approximately 2 hours), drain off the liquid and chop. Stir in the crumbs, spice, salt, pepper, lemon juice and melted butter, and bind with lightly beaten egg.

RAISIN AND NUT STUFFING
(Birds or Pork)

3 ozs. chopped raisins
3 ozs. chopped walnuts
1 rounded tablespoon chopped parsley
6 ozs. breadcrumbs — 2 ozs. butter
Salt and pepper — 1 egg

Mix all the ingredients binding with melted butter and beaten egg.

APPLE AND PRUNE STUFFING
(Turkey or Chicken)

Approximately 12 prunes
6 ozs. fresh breadcrumbs
Grated rind and juice of ½ lemon
2 ozs. melted butter
2 large apples — 2 ozs. nut kernels
Seasoning — 1 egg, beaten

Steam, stone and split the dried prunes in two; peel, core and chop the apples finely and chop the nut kernels. Combine prunes, apples and nuts, add breadcrumbs, seasoning and lemon rind and juice. Bind together with melted butter and egg.

SAGE AND ONION STUFFING
(Pork, Duck, Goose)

4 ozs. fresh breadcrumbs
1 large apple, peeled, cored and diced
8 ozs. onion — 3 teaspoon sage
Salt and pepper — ½ lemon rind
Squeeze lemon juice — 1½ oz. butter
1 egg

Chop the onion, place in pan and cover with cold water. Bring to the boil and simmer 4-5 minutes. Drain the onions thoroughly. Place breadcrumbs in a basin, add onions, sage, apple and seasoning. Add lemon juice and rind and the egg, which has been added to the melted butter. If mixture is too dry — bind with a spoonful of cider or stock.

NOTES

Avoid luxuries, plain living is best for bodily health, and mental comfort.

VEGETABLES

Last evening you were drinking deep,
So now your head aches. Go to sleep;
Take some boil'd cabbage when you awake,
And there's an end of your headache.

BRUSSEL SPROUTS or CABBAGE ENTREE

1½ lbs. sprouts, which are small and young
4 ozs. ham, or lean bacon
1 teaspoon chopped parsley
½ cup breadcrumbs
2 ozs. butter
Salt and pepper

Clean sprouts and steam in ¾ cup of water for 10 minutes. Dice ham. If bacon is used, it should be fried for a few minutes after dicing.

Drain sprouts thoroughly, season, mix with diced ham or bacon; sprinkle with parsley. Heat the butter separately. In it fry breadcrumbs until golden. Pour these over the sprouts and serve.

Another way

Saute the sprouts in the butter with ham or bacon pieces (12 minutes), with a few spoonsful of water if necessary, then put in buttered casserole. Sprinkle with crumbs. Put dabs of butter on top and bake in hot oven for 10 minutes.

BRUSSEL SPROUTS

Small sprouts are the best. Make two cross-cuts at the stalk base. Put into fast boiling water. Cook for a short time and remove while still firm. Strain, shake in melted butter to which can be added chopped toasted almonds or hot boiled chestnuts.

BRUSSEL SPROUTS

If properly cooked, brussel sprouts are delicious and can look very attractive. Always buy the smallest possible size, which are the most appetizing. Allow ½ lb. of sprouts for each serving. Wash, drain and leave in bowl of salted water about 20 minutes. Bring pan of salted water to boil — just enough water to cover sprouts. Drop strained sprouts into boiling water, cook quickly with lid off 15 to 20 minutes. Drain well without mashing.

Put 2 ozs. melted butter into sprouts saucepan, put sprouts back in. Heat over flame 2 or 3 minutes, shaking occasionally, until butter is absorbed. Remove from saucepan with holed vegetable spoon so no liquid goes into vegetable dish, which should be hot and ready to take to table.

PUMPKIN TOPS

Pumpkin tops
Carbonate of soda
Buttered toast
Salt
Pepper
Butter and poached eggs

Pluck a large quantity of the shoots of a pumpkin vine; wash well and boil in salted water, to which a pinch of soda has been added; when soft, strain thoroughly and press in a colander, then return it to the saucepan and add a little piece of butter and seasoning of pepper; have ready some buttered toast cut in squares, and place in a vegetable dish. Just before the pumpkin tops are ready to strain, poach some eggs nicely; and when the greens are placed neatly on the buttered toast, arrange the poached eggs on top and serve.

FRIED CELERY

Cut tender celery into pieces the size of an old fashioned match. Cook over steam for a few minutes, until they have lost their initial crispness. Turn on to paper. Pat until quite dry. Dust with flour and shake off any excess.

STUFFED PUMPKIN

1 butternut pumpkin
1 crushed sweet biscuit (stale)
1 heaped tablespoon chopped onion
1 rounded dessertspoon seasoned breadcrumbs
1½ thick rashers of chopped bacon
1/3rd tomato, chopped
Pinch each of sage, thyme, marjoram, pepper and salt

Mix all ingredients together and lightly stuff into hollowed out butternut pumpkin portions. Place a knob of butter on top, and bake in moderate oven for approximately one hour.

Serve with seasoned rump steak baked with half a cup of beef stock and a little butter.

FIDGET PIE

1 lb. potatoes, peeled and cut into thick rounds
½ lb. bacon diced
1 lb. apples, peeled, cored and sliced,
salt, pepper and sugar as required
some light stock, cold
short paste for top.

Fill a dish with layers of potato, bacon and apples in that order, adding seasonings. If apples are sour, dip slices in sugar. Add enough stock to come about three parts up the dish. Cover with a rather thick short crust and bake in a fairly hot oven at first, and finish off at a reduced heat. Test with skewer to see if contents are cooked before removing pie. Serve hot.

Chips first made their appearance in Dundee, in the old Green Market at a stall run by Edward de Guernsey, selling hot boiled peas and fried chipped potatoes.

POTATOES BUCKINGHAM

Bake some large potatoes in the oven. When done, cut off slice from each side and carefully scoop out the centre. Mash it with some butter, milk, pepper, salt and a little grated cheese. Add a little minced ham and mix thoroughly. Now line shells of the potatoes with this mixture and in the centre of each, drop in an egg carefully. Cover with more of the potato mixture, add a small dab of butter on top, then return to the oven until well browned.

Sprinkle mixed chopped Mint with the Parsley scattered on new Potatoes or Carrots when cooked.

CLAPSHOT

Equal parts of well drained potatoes and white turnips mashed very well, adding a generous piece of butter, salt and pepper to a nice consistency. Finely chopped mint in small amount, can be added if desired.

Serve piping hot, with mutton as the meat.

COLCANNON

6 medium sized potatoes, peeled and quartered
⅜ pint lukewarm milk
1 teaspoon ground black pepper
1 tablespoon finely chopped parsley (fresh)
1 lb. finely shredded cabbage
6 medium sized spring onions, including 2″ of green tops cut lengthwise in half and crosswise in ⅛″ slices
2 ozs. butter

Cook potatoes until tender, but not falling apart. Place cabbage in saucepan and cover with cold water. Boil rapidly for 10 minutes. Drain. Melt 1 oz. butter and add cabbage and cook, stirring for 2 minutes. Cover the pan and set aside. Drain potatoes and return them to the pan. Shake over a low heat until dry and mealy, then mash to smooth puree. Beat into this 6 tablespoons of milk, 2 tablespoons at a time. Puree at the end of this should hold it's shape in a spoon. Stir in cooked cabbage and spring onions, add salt and few grindings of pepper. Sprinkle with parsley, when in serving dish. Serve at once.

The young leaves of dandelions are excellent in a salad. Use leaves also as spinach.

Common **chickweed** cooked is a tasty green vegetable.

ROSTI (SWISS POTATOES)

2 lbs. potatoes 1 onion
Lard or Butter Salt and Pepper

Wash potatoes, boil in their skins until almost tender, peel and cut into thin slices. Heat lard in frying pan, saute chopped onion a few minutes. Add potato slices, season with salt and pepper. Cook quickly turning frequently until golden brown adding more lard if necessary. Reduce heat, press potatoes down well with spatula, leave until golden crust forms underneath.

LEMON POTATOES

2 pounds new small potatoes
¼ pound butter
3 strips lemon peel
6 tablespoons lemon juice

Wash and scrub potatoes. Cook with lemon peel in slightly salted water until tender. Drain. Heat butter and lemon juice in frying pan. Toss the potatoes in the butter for 5 minutes. Serve garnished with lemon mint chopped finely.

POTATOES WITH MINTED BUTTER

Just give these pinky skinned potatoes a quick scrub and boil in their jackets until tender. Drain and lift carefully into a hot deep casserole lined with a table-napkin. Fold napkin back over the potatoes so that they steam cosily beneath. Serve with a little dish of butter balls with enough finely chopped mint to give them a green look. Use a little lemon juice to blend.

17TH CENTURY "BOILED SALADS"

In the 17th century "boiled salads" were popular and might well be revived as hors d'oeuvres. For instance, Spinach boiled in its own juice and rubbed through a sieve, currants and butter added, and flavoured with just a little ginger and cinnamon and served boiling hot or ice cold on thin buttered toast is delicious.

Cooked vegetables of all sorts — peas, beans, carrots, celeriac, onion, Jerusalem artichokes, kohl-rabi, etc. — rubbed through a sieve and flavoured with tomato juice, or chopped herbs, lemon, nutmeg or cinnamon, make a good salad served either hot or cold on thin buttered toast or biscuits. Cooked Jerusalem artichokes cut in slices and served cold with mayonnaise sauce make an excellent winter salad.

VEGETABLE SOUFFLE

The following is a good recipe for making a souffle with any vegetable.

Rub the cooked vegetable through a fine wire sieve, also a very little cooked onion or shallot. To 4 ozs. of this mixture allow a gill of water, 1 oz. of butter, 1 oz. flour, and a pinch of salt. Make a smooth paste with these ingredients and then add the sieved vegetables. When almost but not quite boiling remove from the fire and whilst stirring well add the yolks of two eggs one at a time, then a whole egg, and then fold in the whipped whites of the two eggs. Fill a greased souffle dish half full of the mixture and bake for ten minutes in a hot oven. The souffle rises high and must be served immediately. Broccoli, broad beans, carrots, cauliflowers, celery, onions, spinach, tomatoes all make excellent souffles.

SAVOURY BEET

Slice cooked beet and put the slices in a shallow pan with a tablespoonful of vegetable stock, a pinch of flour, some finely grated shallot or onion, a handful of sweet herbs such as sweet marjoram, chervil, parsley, chives, thyme, etc., all very finely shredded and let them boil 15 minutes. After removing from the fire add a dessertspoonful of cream. Serve immediately.

BEETROOT FROM BENDIGO

Cook beetroots in usual salted water until tender, then peel and slice while still hot. Keep warm while sauce is made.

Sauce

¾ cup honey	½ cup vinegar
1 dessertspoon butter	a few whole cloves
1 dessertspoon cornflour	

Blend cornflour with vinegar. Heat honey with cloves. Stir cornflour and vinegar to slow boil. Boil for 5 minutes, then add butter and pour sauce over the beetroots. Keep hot for 15 minutes to allow flavours to go through the beetroots.

SAUCY CARROTS

Cut up 2 lbs. carrots. Cook in boiling water until just tender. Drain. Mix in a small saucepan ¼ cup of butter, seasonings, ¼ cup prepared mustard, ½ cup honey, 2 tablespoons chopped parsley. Cook for about 3 minutes, stirring all the time, until well blended. Mix in carrots gently. Heat for several minutes. Serve immediately.

RHINELAND CARROTS

1 lb. carrots	salt, sugar
2 sliced onions	pepper
½ lb. peeled sliced apples	

Slice carrots lengthwise. Cook in boiling water and sugar till tender. Fry onions, add carrots and carrot water, then add apples and cook till ingredients are soft. Season. Just before serving, squeeze lemon juice over all.

CARROTS

Slice carrots (as young as possible). Cook for 5 minutes in salted water. Drain. Heat butter and put in carrots with tightly fitting lid. Cook gently till tender, about 25 minutes. Remove lid; sprinkle with good teaspoonful of powdered sugar. Cook, shaking them until they are full of light brown bits like fried onions. Sprinkle with chopped parsley.

Sprinkle finely chopped mint with parsley to garnish carrots when cooked.

TOMATO SOUFFLE

4 tomatoes	Butter
Yolk of 1 egg	Cayenne
Whites of 2 eggs	Salt to taste

Pour boiling water over the tomatoes so that you can peel them easily; put them into a sieve and rub through as much as you can, then beat this up with the yolk of one egg; cayenne and salt to taste; then beat up the whites to a stiff froth, and mix all well together. If you have souffle cases fill each and sprinkle over them some breadcrumbs; put a piece of butter on top of each and bake for twenty minutes.

A little minced ham or tongue is very nice mixed with this.

DRESSED TOMATOES

Thickly slice tomatoes. Pour over them a dressing made from a small jar of cream and French mustard. Stir in a teaspoon at a time. Scatter over finely chopped mint and some freshly grated pepper.

TOMATO FARNI

6-8 medium sized ripe tomatoes
1 dessertspoon chopped parsley
1 dessertspoon chopped ham
1 dessertspoon grated Parmesan cheese
2 dessertspoons button mushrooms finely chopped
Few drops of lemon juice
Brown and white breadcrumbs
1 oz. butter ½ oz. flour
2 tablespoons milk pepper and salt

Melt the butter in a saucepan. Mix in the flour, add milk, stir and cook well. Then mix in enough white breadcrumbs to make the mixture stiff. Add parsley, mushrooms, cheese, ham, lemon juice, seasoning. Scoop out the top of each tomato. Pile the stuffing into each. Sprinkle a few brown breadcrumbs over. Put the tomatoes on a greased baking sheet and cook in a moderate oven for 15-20 minutes.

PARSNIP BALLS

6 parsnips a little flour and salt
2 eggs lard to fry

Parboil the parsnips and let them become thoroughly cold. Peel and grate them upon a grater. Beat the eggs till light and mix well with the grated parsnips, adding sufficient flour to bind the mixture together. Make into balls with floured hands. Have lard boiling hot in a deep pan. Fry quickly until a goodly brown. Serve very hot.

I eat my peas with honey
I've done it all my life
It makes the peas taste funny
But it keeps 'em on the knife!
Anon.

Little peas cooked in stock with baby onions, ham, herbs and lettuce . . . and long fresh French beans cooked in butter, and nutmeg.

With 1 lb. of thin, stringless beans, 1 oz. of butter, salt and black peppercorns to season, ½ lemon, 1 tablespoon parsley, and a dusting of nutmeg.

If the beans are thin, young and tender, leave whole, if larger, then cut into three-inch lengths. Squeeze half the lemon, chop the parsley and measure butter. Place the butter in a pan, then beans. Season, cover, and cook approximately ten minutes on medium heat or until tender. Toss from time to time with lid on. Just before serving, add the juice of half lemon, parsley, and a light dusting of nutmeg.

STRING BEANS WITH SOUR CREAM AND CHIVES

Wash and cut off the strings of 3 lbs. of green string beans, leaving them whole. Tie them securely in 6 or 8 bundles. Lay them in a large enamel pan and sprinkle them with salt. Pour over them sufficient actively boiling water to cover. Add a tiny pinch of soda. Cover the pan and bring to a boil. Remove cover, skim carefully and cook until tender, but not floppy. Drain and place the bundles on a hot dish and remove the strings, being careful not to disturb the symmetry of the beans. Pour over them the following well seasoned sour cream sauce, sprinkle with a tablespoon or more of cut chives and serve at once.

MUSHROOMS

Sprinkle with little salt and a lot of lemon juice. Leave 10 minutes. Place on baking dish, face up. Dab each with piece of butter. Cook gently. Serve on toast.

CREAMED SPINACH WITH NUTMEG

8 cups spinach 1½ teaspoons salt
½ cup butter ½ teaspoon pepper
¼ cup flour 1 cup cream
½ to 1 teaspoon nutmeg

Wash the spinach, changing the water several times. Cook for a few minutes with just the water than clings to the leaves until the spinach is thoroughly wilted. Drain well, saving ½ cup of liquid. Press through a coarse sieve. Melt the butter and blend in the flour. Add the seasonings and spinach juice. Stir in the cream and cook, stirring constantly, until thickened.

Add the pureed spinach, mix and heat thoroughly.

SPINACH

When cooked, chop. Mix with chopped hard boiled egg and grated onion. Make into balls. Dip in beaten egg. Roll in fine breadcrumbs and fry in deep fat — a delicious dish.

OR

Put a layer of cooked spinach in a shallow dish. Cover with grated cheese. Add a little cream. Repeat with another layer. Toast until cheese melts and bubbles.

VEGETABLE ENTREE

1 lb. spinach	2 large tomatoes
2 eggs	4 ozs. cheese
½ pint stock or milk	

Steam spinach and chop fine. Mince onion. Skin tomatoes and cut them up. Mix with breadcrumbs and cheese. Add stock, then egg yolks — finally stiffly beaten whites. Bake in oven until set.

Wilful waste brings woeful want.
Thomas Fuller

TURNIP BROSE

Wash and pare 6 Swedish turnips. Cut into small dice. Place in a pot with enough water just to cover, a marrow bone, and a little salt. Boil gently until the turnips are soft and richly yellow.

Put 3 tablespoons oatmeal in a bowl. Add a knob of margarine and a little salt and pepper. Strain the liquid from the turnips into a small saucepan, and bring to the boil. Pour a little of the liquid into the prepared oatmeal and stir until the brose forms into small knots. Add a little more liquid and serve piping hot.

Mash the turnips well. Add a little creamy milk, a knob of butter and salt and pepper to taste. Stir over the fire until boiling; then serve at once in a hot dish.

TURNIPS BUTTERED

Some roast turnips in a Paper under the Embers and eat them with Sugar and Butter.

GLAZED TURNIPS

Choose turnips of equal size. Parboil them, drain. Put in a buttered casserole that can hold them in a single layer. Brown them lightly with a little sugar. Add a good bouillon and more sugar, a little salt, and a stick of cinnamon. Bring to the boil, cover, bake. Uncover, let the juice reduce to a glaze. Arrange turnips on a platter. Add a little bouillon to the pan to melt the glaze. Take out the cinnamon. Pour glaze over the turnips.

TOMATO ROYAL

Chop 4 large tomatoes into quarters. Heat in a saucepan until soft. Season. Take off the stove and add 3 beaten eggs. Stir together. Serve on or with toast.

Under this sod
And under these trees
Lieth the bod-
y of Solomon Pease,
He's not in this hole,
But only his pod;
He shelled out his soul
And went up to his God.
J.R. Kippax

CAULIFLOWER NUT PIE

One small cauliflower
1 tablespoon grated tasty cheese
1 cup self-raising flour
1 tablespoon butter or substitute

Milk	½ cup chopped nuts
1 cup white sauce	½ lb. mashed potato
Salt and pepper	Extra cheese

Wash cauliflower, cut into small flowerettes. Drop into boiling salted water, cook until tender, about 8 or 10 minutes; drain. Arrange cauliflower pieces in greased casserole, pour over combined cheese, nuts, and white sauce. Sift flour, salt and pepper into basin, rub in butter. Add mashed potato and a little milk to bind. Roll out on floured board, cover mixture in dish, trim edges. Sprinkle top with a little extra cheese, bake in a moderate oven 30 minutes or until topping is cooked and golden brown. Serve piping hot.

CAULIFLOWER MOUNTAIN

1 large cauliflower	1 cup sour cream
Salted water	Salt and pepper
2 ozs. butter	Pinch nutmeg

1½ cups diced cooked ham
1 large onion, finely chopped
2 egg yolks (beaten lightly)
1 cup grated tasty cheese

Trim off outer leaves from cauliflower, cut into flowerettes. Cook in salted water until nearly tender. Drain and cool. Grease casserole and fill alternate layers of ham and cauliflower into it. Dot with butter. Combine onion, sour cream, paprika, salt, pepper, nutmeg and egg yolks; pour over casserole. Bake covered in moderate oven 30 minutes. Remove cover, top with grated cheese. Bake further 15 minutes.

CAULIFLOWER

Cauliflower sprigs boiled until tender but not mushy and served in hot boiled mayonnaise, are wonderful with fried fillets of fish and fried potatoes.

With fried sausages — crisp and brown — there is nothing much nicer, however, than cooked cauliflower sprigs crushed into a thick creamy white sauce and then baked with crumbs and grated cheese until golden. Little bacon rolls complete an appetising dish.

SPINACH TART

8 ozs. plain flour — 4 ozs. butter
pinch salt — cold water
1 egg white
good squeeze lemon juice

Chop up cold butter and rub into flour and salt with both hands. Add lemon juice and water (just enough to mix to a firm dough), mixing with a knife. Roll into ball and keep very cool. Leave 1 hour if possible. Roll out on to floured board, and line round pie plate neatly. Cut edges, use fork to make clean edge. Beat egg-white just a little, brush over pastry. Chill.

Filling

3 tablespoons plain flour
3 bacon rashers (chopped)
2 cups cooked spinach
1 cup chopped cheese
½ cup cream — salt and pepper
2 eggs

SPINACH CROQUETTES

Brown a small onion in a tablespoon of butter; remove the onion and put in a pint of spinach which has been cooked and chopped very fine, stirring constantly. Add gradually 2 tablespoons of breadcrumbs, ½ cup of grated cheese, ¼ cup of milk, yolks of 2 well-beaten eggs, and a scant teaspoonful of salt. Mould into croquettes, roll in bread or biscuit crumbs, fry in hot fat, and after draining, dust with grated cheese.

SUGARED MARROW

1 medium-sized marrow
3 level tablespoons brown sugar
1 teaspoon cayenne pepper
6 tablespoons water
¼ pount butter — Salt to taste

Peel the marrow. Cut into ½ inch slices. Remove seeds. Melt butter in large frying pan. Brown the slices on both sides, then add the sugar, water, salt and cayenne pepper. Cover tightly and simmer slowly, turning over once, until tender. Serve hot. Pour juices over all, adding water if necessary.

SQUASH SOUFFLE

Half a pound of peeled apples and the same quantity of squash, boiling them separately with a little vanilla. Mash them. Dry out the puree and mix the two together. Stir in the yolks of two eggs with some sugar and cook a little more than a minute, stirring all the time. When mixture is almost cold, add the beaten egg whites of 4 eggs and a teaspoonful of Kirsch. Put in a souffle dish standing in a pan of water. Cook in a moderate oven about 10 minutes.

CUCUMBERS ON TOAST

Blanch, slice, saute in butter with a pinch of flour. Add water, salt, pepper. Cook to reduce water. Add chopped parsley and a little nutmeg. Thicken with egg yolks and cream. Continue to cook, but do not boil, until thickened.

Any port in a storm.

CHINESE CHOW

William Howitt, writing from Ballarat, May 16, 1854
. . . Near Ballarat we met a company of Chinese removing to Creswick's Creek. It was quite a picture, and a curious one. The Chinese here, who have come lately in crowds still continue their national costume in a great measure, and their national custom of carrying everything on their necks on a long pole. This, to us, is apparently a most uncomfortable plan, they adhere to pertinaciously, as the only easy one. At each end of a pole of some two inches thick, and six or eight feet long, they suspend weights, astonishing considering their slight physical structure. You would think the pole would cut their bare necks, if not their heads off. But, only now and then shifting the pole a little, more or less inclined to one shoulder or the other, they go for scores of miles with ponderous burthens, keeping up a shuffling kind of trot, their very legs seeming to stagger and their bodies to waver under their loads.

The number of Chinese miners during the height of the gold rush is given as 4,238 alluvial; 196 quartz. Many were smuggled into the country. They were itinerant, so the exact numbers were difficult to decide. In Ballarat most of the Chinese lived in Main Road. There was a Joss House there. Large numbers were employed after the gold rush, digging the underground cellars at the Great Western vineyards west of Ballarat, famous now for champagne.

These recipes were used by the early Chinese miners at the Ballarat Gold Fields and are still used by their descendants one of whom wrote the following five recipes.

PEAS AND EGGS AND PORK

Parboil ½ cup of peas about 2 minutes, strain and keep a little of the water. 2 or 3 pork chops minced, add a little ginger and gin, and see-you sauce, and cook for about ten minutes, add a little water, then peas. Have about 5 eggs beaten up with green onions and a little milk and stir into meat. Keep stirring until set. (Green onions = green part of spring onions).

SYPOON

Soak sypoon in boiling water for a few hours, enough to cover, strain in a colander and cut with scissors.

Same amount of pork as for peas (minced) and ginger, and Cheong Toy, gin or whisky, sprinkle with a little sugar and See-You. When meat is cooked, about 10 minutes, add sypoon (armies that have been soaked in boiling water), and omelette (made of 2 eggs beaten up and green onions and little milk). Fry in a little oil, slice, and add to sypoon.

POTATO AND BACON

2 Pork Chops
Few slices of bacon, scalded
Cheong Toy, Ginger

Cut pork in thin pieces, add ginger and Cheong Toy, a little sugar sprinkled over it, and See-You, also Whisky or Gin, a dry onion cut in slices. Cut potatoes in cubes and sprinkle with a little See-You Sauce.

Cover the pan with oil, about 3 tablespoons, let it boil, add salt (about a dessertspoon), put in meat and brown, keep stirring, then add potatoes and keep stirring, also add a little boiling water to keep from burning. Put on side of stove for about ¾ hour. Keep turning. Put pan lid on after they are browned and you put them on stove.

CELERY STEAK

About ¾ lb. thick skirt steak, cut in thin pieces
Ginger and Chung Toy
A little sugar sprinkled over it
Gin or whisky and See-You Sauce

Have celery cut up and add to meat, then water to cover, and thicken with about ½ tablespoon of cornflour, a little See-You and water to a thin paste. Add to boiling mixture.

RICE

To cook rice - wash 5 times in cold water prior to placing in water to boil. When placing in saucepan place enough water in bottom of saucepan to cover the flat hand and cook until water boils over.

FRIED RICE

(1 teacup uncooked rice for 2 people.) Wash rice thoroughly, until water is clear. Cover with fresh water, having water 1 inch above level of rice. Cover - quickly bring to boil for 5 minutes without removing lid. Reduce heat, simmer approximately 20 minutes.

2 tablespoons butter or lard   4 eggs
1 cup chopped prawns or meat
Cooked rice   3 spring onions
2 teaspoons salt   Soya bean sauce

Add beaten eggs, onions and salt to melted butter. Stir well until half cooked or consistency of cream. Add meat etc.

CANTONESE SCHNAPPER AND PEA IN THE POD

1 lb. Schnapper fresh or dried
2 tablespoons plain flour
1 cup sliced fresh Mushrooms
1 teaspoon Soya Bean Sauce if possible
Roasted Almonds cut lengthwise
½ lb. Pea Pods which must be young
1 tablespoon Stock or Water
½ cup sliced Spring Onions
1 cup oil   1 egg
Salt and Pepper   Pinch Sugar

Slice the fish fillets lengthwise into halves, and then each into two pieces. Make a creamy batter with the flour, egg (and perhaps a little milk or water), salt and pepper. Coat the fish pieces in the batter. In a large frying pan heat the cooking oil, and when it is very hot, quickly fry the fish pieces on all sides until the batter is golden. Remove and keep warm by the stove. Fry now the tender pea pods, having first strung them along with the fresh sliced mushrooms, turning frequently, for a maximum of 5 minutes - the less time the better. Season at the last minute with soya bean sauce mixed with water and the sugar. Fry for another few seconds. Garnish the fried schnapper with mushrooms and pea pods. Sprinkle sprig onions and roast almonds on top. Serve with fried rice.

CHINESE STEAMED CHICKEN

1 chicken cut in small pieces
1 oz. thinly sliced mushrooms
1 thinly sliced spring onion
½ oz. thinly sliced salt cabbage
Chinese wine
4 pieces red dates, sliced,
A few slices of ginger root
Peaflour   Peanut oil
Parsley   Mustard
Chinese sauce

Mix all the ingredients, adding a little peaflour and peanut oil and the wine; put on a dish and steam for ten minutes. Garnish with parsley and serve with mustard and Chinese sauce.

God's jolly cafeteria is the cow with four legs and a tail — *E.M. Root*

PUDDINGS

William Howitt, writing from White Hills, Bendigo, Victoria, October 10, 1853

. . . Amongst the placards which attracted our eyes on this walk was one with immense letters, "EGGS! EGGS! EGGS! Immense reduction in Eggs! EGGS now only ONE SHILLING EACH!" They were a few days ago two shillings each; and as I was walking with a gentleman in front of his tent lately, he suddenly exclaimed, "There! I have lost two shillings!" and he showed me that one of his hens had just laid an egg without a shell; a very common thing here, because they cannot procure lime, the whole neighbourhood being pulverized quartz and slate.

The following are the prices of things at the diggings, as quoted today:- Flour, from 9L. to 10L. per bag; butter, 5s. per pound; sugar 2s.; carting store for three or four hours, from 8L. to 10L. It is said that a man with a horse and cart at the diggings might make 1000L. a year by merely doing job cart work.

TRANSPARENT PUDDING

Beat 8 eggs very well, and put them in a pan with half a pound of sugar. Beat very fine, add a little grated nutmeg; set it on the fire, stirring till it thickens like buttered eggs, then put it in a basin to cool. Roll a rich puff paste very thin, lay it around the edge of a china dish, then pour in the pudding and bake it in a moderate oven half an hour. It will cut clean and light.

QUEEN PUDDING

Mix ¾ pint, or 6 ozs. soft white breadcrumbs with 1 tablespoon of softened butter, pour 1 pint of very hot milk on it. Cover it, and let it stand until the bread is well soaked, then stir in 2 whole beaten eggs, and 3 egg yolks together with 3 ozs. sugar. Add 2 ozs. mixed peel and a little grated nutmeg. Have ready a buttered fireproof dish and when the mixture is barely cold, pour it in.

Then, having whipped 3 egg whites so stiffly that the basin can be turned upside down without them falling out, fold 3 tablespoons sifted icing sugar into them. Pile this meringue mixture on top of your pudding and bake it for ½ an hour in a pre-heated moderate oven.

Sometimes raspberry jam is spread thickly over the pudding before the meringue is piled on top.

CARAMEL CUSTARD

The secret is to put custard on to steam over cold water and once the first wisp of steam shows, reduce heat so that the water never boils again. Leave until custard is firm to touch in the centre. Never hurry it. Put aside to cool until next day. Then turn out carefully. Texture should be velvet smooth.

For the caramel put 3 tablespoons sugar into a small strong saucepan with one tablespoon water. Cook over very moderate heat shaking pan constantly until syrup is a lovely golden brown. Pour at once into an earthenware basin, coating sides and bottom and cool.

For the custard heat one pint of milk. Add two tablespoons of sugar stirring until dissolved. Whisk three eggs until yolks and whites are nicely blended. Add a little lemon essence. Pour warm milk slowly into the eggs stirring all the time. Strain into the caramel lined basin. (For a very rich custard add an extra yolk.) Cover basin with a plate and place in a steamer over a saucepan of cold water. Cover saucepan, stand over strictly moderate heat until you see the first wisp of steam. Then draw pan to back or side of stove. Leave until custard is set.

My more-having would be a sauce
To make me hunger more.
Shakespeare

TIPSY CAKE

Pour over a sponge cake as much white wine as will be absorbed and stick with blanched almonds cut thin in spikes. Pour a rich cold custard around it.

PARTY CUSTARD

Make a really delicious special sweet by preparing an ordinary stirred custard. Flavour with your favourite liqueur, and when custard is cooled whip ½ pint cream and fold through it.

ZABAGLIONE

You need a saucepan of water, heated (but not to boiling point), a basin to fit over it. Into the basin you place 1 egg-yolk per person (plus 1 extra for every 4 yolks), 1 teaspoon of castor sugar per person, a pinch of salt, and 1 glass of marsala (small) per person.

Beat the mixture steadily to a stiff consistency. Remove the basin from the water as you continue to beat, pour the mixture into glasses and serve immediately with a sponge finger per head. The secret is only that it must be brought nearly to boiling point but must under no circumstances actually boil. Otherwise it will curdle.

You can make cold zabaglione, too. After preparing as above carry on mixing over ice until it becomes quite cold. Then fold in half the quantity of whipped cream.

They dined on mince, and slices of quince
Which they ate with a runcible spoon.
Edward Lear

QUINCE ROLY-POLY

1½ cups flour — Pinch of salt
1 large teaspoon baking powder

Rub in one large tablespoon dripping. Mix to a light dough with cold water. Roll out and cover with sliced quinces and sprinkle thickly with sugar. Roll up in a cloth and boil for 1½ hours.

Place pudding into a pot of boiling water and keep boiling for the entire cooking period. This will prevent pudding from sticking to the cloth.

When making a roly-poly pudding, grease the cloth instead of flouring it and the pudding will not stick.

Omit the quinces and add 1 cup of currants. This becomes a Spotted Dog.

ROLY-POLY

Instead of boiling it in a cloth, curl it round like a snail in a well buttered basin and steam it at least two hours under a well-fitting, greased saucepan lid (to keep out drips or steam).

A "Roly" made with four ounces of self-raising flour and two ounces very finely shredded suet is a nice size. Remember to use really thick jam in the filling and to leave a nice bit of margin. Have extra jam (hot as a sauce).

BREAD AND BUTTER PUDDING

Grate the rind of half a lemon into ½ pint of milk, with a pinch of grated nutmeg, or ground cinnamon. Stir in 2 well-beaten eggs. Butter a fireproof dish, sprinkle the bottom generously with sugar, raisins, currants and mixed peel. Take 4 thickly buttered slices of bread, without the crusts, make a layer of 2 slices, sprinkling them with more fruit and sugar before laying on the rest. Pour the egg mixture into the fireproof dish gently, and if possible, leave the pudding for 2 hours to soak before sprinkling the top with sugar and nutmeg. Bake it for 30 minutes in a pre-heated moderate oven. The pudding is much improved by the addition of 2 tablespoonsful of brandy before baking.

MINCE PIES

½ lb. apples — 6 ozs. sugar
6 ozs. sultanas — 6 ozs. currants
6 ozs. raisins — ½ oz. mixed spice
Juice and rind 1 lemon
2 teaspoons rum or brandy
¼ lb. finely shredded suet.

Peel, core and grate the apples. Put dried fruits through the mincer, then mix with all other ingredients. Stir well and keep in screw top jar until required. It is best made one month before using.

Lemon rind should be finely grated, using only the yellow portion.

BUTTERMILK CUSTARD

3 eggs (separated) — 4 tablespoons butter
1 cup raw sugar — 1 teaspoon each of rind
2 cups buttermilk — Pinch Salt
3 tablespoons wholemeal flour
1 tablespoon lemon juice
2 tablespoons orange juice

Cream butter and sugar. Stir in flour, salt, juices and rind. Add well beaten egg yolk mixed with buttermilk. Beat until smooth. Fold in egg whites, stiffly beaten.

Bake as a baked custard until set.

The Governor of the colonies, government officers and those of the services, brought with them the etiquette of the polite society in England. Food became plentiful and fruit and vegetables grew, superbly, tended by men trained in these things in "the old country". As large homesteads were established with their attendant cottages and storehouses, living was often luxurious for the pioneers with large holdings, not too far from the major settlements.

MISS MUFFET'S CURDS

Put a pan of milk at the cool end of the stove overnight. In the morning the cream will be on the surface. Remove this and the thickened milk curd will be underneath. If chilled it is a good accompaniment to stewed fruits. Very soothing to the stomach.

CUSTARD WITH CINNAMON

Mix by degrees a pint of good milk with a large spoonful of flour and some sugar to taste; boil them together for 10 minutes, then add the yolks of five eggs and a little pounded cinnamon. Butter a basin that will exactly hold it, pour the batter in, and tie a floured cloth over Put it in boiling water over the fire, and turn it about for a few minutes to prevent the eggs going to one side. Put currant jelly on it, and throw with sweet sauce.

SETTLERS' CHRISTMAS PUDDING

Pudding

1 lb. raisins — 1 lb. sultanas
¼ lb. currants — ½ lb. dates
½ lb. mixed peel — ¾ lb. butter
½ lb. brown sugar — 4 eggs
8 ozs. breadcrumbs (white)
8 ozs. (2 cups) plain flour
¼ level teaspoon salt
4 level teaspoons mixed spice
2 level teaspoons nutmeg
½ level teaspoon bicarbonate of soda
½ cup brandy

Wash, dry and chop fruits. Cream butter and brown sugar together. Add eggs one at a time beating well after each addition. Stir in breadcrumbs, prepared fruits and sifted dry ingredients. Lastly, stir in spirits. Mix well, place in a scalded and flavoured pudding cloth; tie securely with string. Place in a large vessel of fast boiling water, or in a steamer over boiling water. Steam for 7 hours. Hang to store. On day of serving steam another 2 hours.

Rum Butter

1 lb. butter — 1 teaspoon cinnamon
2 lbs. sugar (castor) — 1 teaspoon nutmeg
2 glasses rum

Cream butter and add sugar gradually. Add rum, cinnamon, nutmeg. Make a smooth round and chill. Cut into slices and serve with piping hot pudding.

TREACLE PUDDING

2 cups flour — 3 ozs. butter
2 tablespoons treacle — a little milk
1 teaspoon ground ginger
½ teaspoon bicarbonate of soda
2 tablespoons moist sugar
1 teaspoon cream of tartar

Rub butter into flour with rising and other ingredients. Mix into thick batter with milk. Beat together for 10 minutes, tie in cloth. Boil 1½ hours.

DUMPLINGS IN GOLDEN SYRUP

1½ cups self raising flour
Pinch salt — 1 egg (beaten)
Butter size of walnut
Enough milk to make a scone dough

Sift flour and salt, rub in butter, add egg, then milk. Roll into dumplings.

Syrup

1½ cups water — ½ cup sugar (small)
1 tablespoon golden syrup
1 tablespoon butter (optional)

Put all in saucepan and when boiling add dumplings.

YULE LOG

Make a vanilla flavoured jam roll. When cold, slice a slanting piece off one end, like a sawn log. Mould a thick piece of almond paste over this end, using a film of jam to attach it. Rub powdered chocolate or cocoa over the almond paste, but don't darken too much, and groove circles in it like the life circles of a tree.

Cover the entire cake, except the slanting end, with coffee or chocolate butter icing, grooving it like bark, and scatter grated or shredded pistachio nut in the grooves to look like moss or lichen. Put a little bird or any suitable decoration on top.

HALWA PUDDING

¾ lb. carrots — 1 tablespoon sultanas
¼ lb. butter — 1 oz. almonds
1 cup sugar — 2 pints milk
1 tablespoon golden syrup

Grate carrots. Add milk to grated carrots and boil until they are really soft. Put aside in dish. Heat sugar and butter until brown, mix with the boiled carrots; add syrup and sultanas, mix in well. Stir frequently for 1 hour until carrots are red or until butter absorbed and carrot floats on top. Scatter sliced almonds on dish. Serve with cream.

DELICIOUS PUDDING

1 tablespoon butter — 1¼ cups milk
¾ cup sugar — 2 lemons
2 eggs
2 tablespoons self raising flour

Cream butter and sugar, add flour then milk, then juice of 2 lemons and rind of one (grated), then beaten egg yolks. Fold in stiffly beaten egg whites. Cook in dish, standing in another dish of warm water.

HONEY MERINGUE

¼ cup of honey, 1 egg white, beaten, one large pinch of salt

Heat honey over hot water. Pour over egg white; add salt. Beat until thick enough to spread.

CHRISTMAS PUDDING - Using Carrots and Old Ale.

7 ozs. flour, 14 ozs. beef suet, 14 ozs. currants, ½ lb. brown loaf sugar, ½ lemon, 3 eggs, 1 gill Old Ale, ½ lb. stoned raisins, ⅛ oz. baking powder, 7 ozs. breadcrumbs, ½ oz. mixed peel, 10 ozs. sultanas, 1 oz. ground almonds, ⅛ teaspoonful grated nutmeg, ¼ lb. carrots, ¼ teaspoonful ground cinnamon, ⅛ teaspoonful mixed spice, silver pudding favours.

Prepare the suet, currants, peel, raisins and sultanas as for mincemeat. Sift the flour with salt, spices and baking powder into a large mixing bowl. Rub the crumbs through a wire sieve, scrape, wash and dry the carrots and then grate them. Turn into basin containing fruit and suet. Stir crumbs and sugar into flour mixture. Add suet and fruit and mix well. Stir in washed dried and grated lemon rind. Cover basin with a clean cloth and stand overnight in a cool but dry place. Next day stir in the Ale and strained lemon juice with your hand, and keep mixing well until well incorporated.

Beat eggs well together in a basin, and stir in with your hand. If eggs are small you may need two more or add a little more ale. Beat well, then bury the pudding favours in the mixture.

Fill buttered basins or moulds with the mixture, but only to within an inch of the top to allow for swelling. Cover with buttered paper, tie securely, then tie up with pudding cloths. Steam for 7 hours. Store in a dry but airy cupboard until required, then steam for another two hours. This will make two large puddings.

PORK AND APPLE SUET PUDDING

Filling

1 level tablespoon flour
1 stick of celery, chopped
1 teaspoon dried sage
2 apples, peeled, cored and sliced
1 large onion, sliced
½ oz. butter — salt and pepper
1 lb. pork — 1 lb. tomatoes

Pastry

1 lb. self raising flour
1 teaspoon baking powder
¼ pint cold water — ½ teaspoon salt
½ lb. shredded suet

Toss pork in flour until evenly coated. Fry in melted butter until meat changes colour. Add salt and pepper, apples, onions and celery and fry gently for a few minutes. Stir in tomatoes and sage. Simmer gently for about 15 minutes.

Meanwhile, sift the flour, salt and baking powder into a bowl. Add the suet, toss ingredients lightly together and mix to a soft paste with water. Turn out on to a floured board, knead until smooth, then roll out to ½ inch thickness and use to line a 1½ pint pudding basin. Place pork filling into lined basin.

Moisten edges of lining with water, cover with "lid" rolled from the remainder of pastry. Press edges well together to seal. Cover with a double thickness of buttered grease proof paper and steam steadily for 3-3½ hours. Serves four.

SOVEREIGN HILL PUDDING

2 cups flour, 1 cup sugar, 1 lb. raisins, dates and lemon peel, pinch of salt, 1 tablespoon butter, 1 teaspoon carbonate soda.

Put the soda in 1 small cup of boiling water, and the butter in another small cup of boiling water, and mix all the other ingredients with it; stir all well together. Tie in a floured cloth, and boil for 2½ hours. Re-fill saucepan now and then with boiling water.

Substitute cider for any recipe which calls for white wine.

DARK CHRISTMAS PUDDING

(Keeps for 4 months. Enough for one 3 pint basin and two 1 pint basins)

8 ozs. best quality beef suet (prepared weight)
6 ozs. fine stale breadcrumbs
6 ozs. flour (4 plain and 2 self-raising)
6 ozs. light brown sugar
1 level teaspoon salt
8 ozs. each of currants, sultanas and seeded raisins (cut in halves)
4 ozs. chopped mixed candied peel
Half a little pack of cake spice
½ teaspoon powdered cinnamon
6 eggs, well beaten
Grated rind and juice of a large lemon
1 brimming breakfast cup of beer

Buy 12 ounces of suet as there is always a definite amount of wastage.

Remove all discoloured parts and skin. Then shave and chop to finest crumbs. Use a sharp knife and spend time over doing this well. There is nothing worse than having nobbly little bits of undissolved suet in your pudding. (You may prefer to put it through the mincer.)

Get a small sandwich loaf three or four days before pudding mixing time so that it will be stale enough to sieve the crumbs finely.

Prepare the fruit and peel. Mix well together and dust with the spice and cinnamon. Sieve the flours with the salt. Sieve the sugar to eliminate lumps. Now mix the suet, crumbs, flour, sugar, fruit and peel. Grate lemon rind on top and mix it in. Your hands do this better than a spoon. Beat the eggs until nice and frothy. Add lemon juice. Pour over the dry ingredients and blend with a big wooden spoon.

Open the bottle of beer. Pour out a generous breakfast cupful. Pour over the pudding and mix very well. it will fall heavily from the spoon but be nice and moist.

This quantity will make two nice sized puddings each to serve six - eight. Be sure to butter the basins well. Steam the large size six hours and the small ones for four hours. Stand basins on a rack in the boiler with gently bubbling water to come nearly half way up the sides of the basin.

Slip a circle of buttered lunchwrap paper in each basin over the pudding mixture, which must never fill the basin above three quarter level. Cover each basin with a saucepan lid lightly greased on the underside and big enough to come well down over the basin rim.

Remember to keep the water in the pot boiling steadily all the time or your pudding could be heavy.

If after half time you feel you should add extra water, be sure to use a really boiling kettle and pour it in at the side of your basin. Always raise the heat under the boiler before lifting the lid to do this, then recover boiler and leave heat high until you see a wisp of steam, then lower heat to a simmer.

When cooking is over, dry the saucepan lid well before removing it from the basin. Leave pudding uncovered until quite cold. Then replace greased paper and tie a muslin loosely over the top to keep out dust.

Store in a cool airy place, never in a closed cupboard. Re-steam on Christmas Day - up to 3 hours for a big pudding and 2 hours for a small one.

MOTHER EVE'S PUDDING

If you would have a good pudding, observe what you are taught:
Take two penny worth of eggs, when twelve for a groat,
And one of the same fruit, that Eve had once chosen,
Well pared and well chopped, at least half a dozen,
Six ounces of bread, (let your maid eat the crust),
The crumbs must be grated, as small as the dust;
Six ounces of currants, from the stones you must sort,
Lest they break out your teeth, and spoil all your sport,
Five ounces of sugar, won't make it too sweet,
Some salt and some nutmeg, will make it complete,
Three hours let it boil, without hurry or flutter
And thus serve it up, without sugar or butter.

PLUMB DUFF

One half-cup of breadcrumbs, half-cup plain flour, half-cup self-raising flour, one tablespoon of sugar, one cup of shredded suet, one tablespoon of treacle, one heaped teaspoon of mixed spice, half-cup each of currants and sultanas, one egg, a little water, half teaspoon carb. soda. Mix in the usual way. Ring out a piece of unbleached calico in hot water, lightly dust it with flour and tip on to it the mixture. Gather up tightly, leaving room for pudding to expand, and tie securely. Have a large saucepan with boiling water about one-third full and put into it the Plumb Duff. Keep boiling gently but steadily for 3 hours — more boiling water may be added as required.

TREACLE PUDDING

½ lb. flour, ½ lb. finely minced suet, ¼ lb. seedless raisins cut up, ¼ lb. currants, 3 tablespoons treacle, ½ pint water. Mix all well together. Boil in cloth for 4 hours.

Serve with sweet sauce or brandy or sherry sauce.

SWEET RICE

2 ozs. butter — 4 bay leaves
4 cloves — 6 ozs. rice
4 almonds — ¼ pint milk
6 ozs. sugar — Juice of 1 orange
2 inch stick of cinnamon
1-2 ozs. sultanas and currants
½ pint water (good measure) coloured with a few drops of cochineal or saffron
½ level teaspoonful ground ginger
4 tablespoons water

Melt butter in a 6 inch saucepan. Add bay leaves, cloves, stick of cinnamon, and heat gently for one minute. Add rice, chopped almonds, sultanas and currants, and cook for three minutes, stirring all the time. Add milk and coloured water and bring to boiling point. Place the saucepan in the oven, which is fairly hot. Cook for 15 minutes.

Melt sugar and ginger in the warmed four tablespoonfuls of water. Add the orange juice and stir into the rice mixture. Continue cooking for a further 25 minutes in the oven. When ready, the rice should have absorbed all the liquid but the grains should be separate and fluffy. Serve either hot or cold, decorated with cream and slices of fresh orange.

SEVEN CUP PUDDING

1 cup each of the following;
Dry breadcrumbs (from stale bread); flour; sugar; grated suet; milk; raisins and currants.
1 teaspoon bi-carbonate of soda
1 teaspoon cinnamon — 1 egg

Mix dry ingredients together. Beat egg, add milk and stir into dry ingredients. Mix well. Put into cloth and boil for two hours. May be eaten hot or cold.

OLD FASHIONED HONEY DUMPLINGS

The Dumplings

2 cups self-raising flour
1 teaspoon baking powder
1 cup finely grated cheddar cheese
2 tablespoons butter
1 cup water — Pinch salt

Sift flour, baking powder and salt into a bowl. Rub in butter till mixture resembles fine breadcrumbs. Add grated cheese. Mix in water to make soft dough.

The Syrup

Place in a large saucepan:
3 tablespoons butter
1 cup honey — 1 cup water

Bring syrup to the boil. Place tablespoons of dumpling mixture in the syrup. Cover and simmer for 20 minutes. Serve hot with whipped cream. Makes 12 dumplings.

SAGO PLUM PUDDING

4 tablespoons sago
1 tablespoon butter
2 teaspoons carbonate of soda
1 cup raisins or dates or figs
1 cup breadcrumbs
1 cup sugar — 1 egg

Soak sago in cup of milk (or more). Mix all dry ingredients, then add butter and beaten egg. Steam for 2½ hours.

BROWN MOUNTAIN

½ cup sour cream or fresh cream with squeeze lemon juice
¾ cup self-raising flour with ¼ teaspoon salt
1 tablespoon golden syrup
½ cup sugar — 1 egg

Place golden syrup in bottom of basin in which pudding is to be steamed. In another basin beat together sugar, egg and sour cream. Sift in flour and salt. Mix well and pour over golden syrup. Cover and steam 1 hour. Serves 3 to 4.

BUSY-DAY PUDDING

No need to sift flour or grease basin — mix in basin to be used. Cover and steam.

2 tablespoons golden syrup
½ teaspoon bicarbonate of soda
2 tablespoons butter
1½ cups self-raising flour
¾ cup milk

Put golden syrup and butter in steamer and melt on top of stove over gentle heat. Add milk in which soda has been dissolved and mix in flour. Cover and steam for 1 to 1¼ hours. Serve with cream or custard.

JIFFY JAM ROLL

2 tablespoons castor sugar
2 tablespoons plain flour
2 teaspoons baking powder
2 eggs

Beat eggs then beat in sugar. Sift in flour and baking powder. Put in greased shallow tin. Cook 5-10 minutes. Spread with jam while hot and roll.

BAKED INDIAN PUDDING

½ cup yellow cornflour
4 cups milk ½ teaspoon ginger
1/3 cup sugar 2/3 cup light molasses
1 teaspoon salt ¾ teaspoon cinnamon
½ teaspoon nutmeg ¼ cup butter
raisins if desired

Scald the milk; add the remaining ingredients; cook over hot water 20 minutes, stirring constantly. Turn into a large baking dish, 12 or 14 inches long. Add 1 cup of cold milk, **do not stir.** Bake in a slow oven for 3 hours, without stirring. Serve warm with cream.

The pudding usually has a curdled consistency.

FRUIT WEDGES

2 cups self-raising flour
1 dessertspoon honey
½ teaspoon cinnamon 1/3rd cup sugar
¼ teaspoon salt 3 tablespoons milk
3 ozs. butter 1 egg

Sift together in basin the flour, cinnamon, and salt. Rub in butter until mixture resembles fine breadcrumbs; add sugar. Combine honey, milk and egg, beat well. Make well in centre of dry ingredients; add milk mixture. Mix to a soft dough, turn on to a lightly floured surface; knead lightly. Divide dough in half, knead until smooth. Press one half into well-greased 8 inch sandwich tin. Spread with filling (see below). Press remaining dough evenly over filling. Bake in moderate oven 40 to 45 minutes.Sprinkle with icing sugar, cut into wedges. Serve warm with cream or custard.

Filling

3 ozs. mixed fruit (saltanas, raisins) soaked 30 minutes in ½ cup boiling water, drained, then combined with 1 dessertspoon honey and ½ teaspoon grated lemon rind.

Cooked apple slices combined with halved glace cherries and sultanas is also a delightful filling.

BAKED CARAMEL DATE PUDDING

½ cup sugar 1 cup chopped dates
½ cup milk 3 tablespoons butter
1 cup self-raising flour

Sauce:

1 cup brown sugar 1½ cups hot water
½ cup sherry 2 tablespoons butter

Sift flour into basin, rub in butter, add dates, sugar and milk. Mix well. Spread mixture evenly in greased 9 inch square tin, pour sauce over carefully. Bake in moderately hot oven 40 minutes. Serve hot with whipped cream. Serves 4 heartily.

Sauce:

Combine all ingredients in saucepan over low heat. Stir until sugar dissolves. Bring to boil, reduce heat, simmer 3 minutes.

GOOSEBERRY FOOL

1 quart gooseberries (or other berries)
A little grated nutmeg
1 pint water Sugar to taste
1 quart milk Yolks of 2 eggs

Put the gooseberries in stewpan with water. When they turn yellow and swell, drain them and press through a colander with the back of spoon, sweeten to taste and set to cool. Put milk over the fire with beaten egg yolks and nutmeg and stir till it begins to simmer. Take off and stir gradually into cold gooseberries. Stand aside until cold and serve.

EUREKA PUDDING

1 teaspoon mixed spice
½ teaspoon cinnamon
1 cup milk 2 ozs. butter
½ cup sugar 1 cup mixed fruit

Put all ingredients in saucepan and bring slowly to almost boiling. Take away from stove, put in 1 teaspoon carbonate of soda dissolved in a little water. Add cup of sifted self-raising flour. Put in basin. Steam 1½-2 hours.

SPICED GOOSEBERRY CREAM

Top and tail 1 lb. gooseberries. Simmer until berries are soft with half a cup water and a cupful of sugar. Sift two level tablespoons of plain flour with half a teaspoon each of powdered cinnamon and cloves, and a pinch of salt. Add half a cup of sugar. Turn all this queer mixture straight on top of the hot gooseberries. Stir hard until it is all mixed in and evenly thickened. Turn into a bowl to cool.

Just before serving time whisk up two or three egg whites really stiff and beat them into the gooseberries. It should look like a snowy mountain. Serve with crisp sweet biscuits.

BLACKCURRANT LEAF CREAM

Blackcurrant leaves are most delicately scented in the spring and then is the time to use them for flavouring sweets and all kinds of creams and puddings.

Boil 1 lb. white sugar with ½ pint water and a cupful of **young** blackcurrant leaves. Boil, without stirring, for 15 minutes; then strain and pour the hot syrup very gently on to 2 beaten egg whites. Beat all the time, until the mixture begins to thicken; then stir in the juice of a lemon and a gill of whipped cream.

Serve in individual glasses — it is the most delicate sweet.

OLD ENGLISH GOOSEBERRY PUDDING

Mix together four ounces plain flour with half a teaspoon baking powder, two ounces very finely chopped beef suet, one generous tablespoon sugar and three ounces of really **small green** gooseberries which have been carefully "topped and tailed". Blend to a stiff sticky paste with a beaten egg and a little milk.

Steam 2½ hours in a well buttered 1½ pint basin covered with a saucepan lid greased on the underside. Serve in fairly thick slices and hand pots of butter and castor sugar so that everyone can butter and sugar their own slices.

One egg will be enough for double the mixture.

APPLE BETTY

3 cups sliced apples
1½ cups stale cake or breadcrumbs
1/3 cup brown sugar
¾ cup water, hot or cold
4 tablespoons melted butter
1 teaspoon cinnamon

Mix apples with 1 cup crumbs, brown sugar and cinnamon. Place in buttered dish and pour over melted butter and water over all. Mix rest of crumbs with a little extra melted butter. Add also chopped walnuts, if desired. Bake in moderate oven 30-45 minutes.

APPLE DUMPLINGS

Use really small quick-cooking apples and quarter inch thick shortcake pastry.

For 4 dumplings

6 ozs. self raising flour
a saltspoon of salt 1 tablespoon sugar
2½ ozs. butter rubbed into the dry ingredients until like fine breadcrumbs, and just enough cold water to mix to a firm but supple pastry. Roll out and cut into four.

Stand each peeled and cored apple on a pastry square. Fill centre cavity in each apple with a spoonful of sugar. Add a pinch of cinnamon and press a bit of butter on top. Fold pastry over apples damping edges with milk or water.

Melt a rounded tablespoon of butter in a cake pan of convenient size. Stir two tablespoons sugar into the butter and add quarter cup boiling water. Lift the dumplings into this. Bake 40-50 minutes in a moderately hot oven basting occasionally once pastry tints. Test with a skewer before removing. Serve at once.

PLUM DUMPLINGS

8 ozs. potatoes 1 dessertspoon butter
2 eggs 2½ to 3 lb. plums
1½ cups plain flour

Peel potatoes, cook in boiling salted water, drain, cool and grate. Sift flour, add grated potatoes, rub in butter. Make well in centre of flour mixture, add well-beaten eggs; mix to a soft dough, adding a little milk if necessary. Knead lightly, roll into a sausage shape. Wash and dry plums. Mould sufficient dough over each plum to cover thinly. Lower into rapidly boiling salted water; boil 5 minutes. Drain; sprinkle with sugar and, if desired, poppy seeds; top each with a little butter. (Apricots can be substituted for plums if desired.)

APPLE HEDGEHOG

9 medium cooking apples
1 tablespoon castor sugar
grating of lemon rind
1 oz. blanched almonds
3 ozs. brown sugar
2½ gills of water
1 egg white

Core and peel 6 of the apples. Put in pan with brown sugar and water and gently cook till tender. Do not overcook. Carefully lift out from pan. Peel, core and slice rest of apples and add with grated rind to the syrup in pan. Cook to pulp. Beat this well and spread a thin layer in a serving dish. On this foundation, build up the six whole apples, making a slight hump in middle to look like a hedgehog's back.

Fill in spaces with some pulped apple and cover rest with it. Stiffly beat white of egg and castor sugar and spread over whole. Lastly, split almonds lengthwise and stick uniformly into the sweet. Set in cool place 2 hours before serving with cream.

"Let me introduce the topic by mentioning that in London it is not the custom to put the knife in the mouth - for fear of accidents; and that while the fork is reserved for that use, it is not put further in than is necessary. It is scarcely worth mentioning, only it is as well to do as other people do. Also, the spoon is not generally used overhand, but under. This has two advantages. You get at your mouth better (which, after all, is the object), and you save a good deal of the attitude of opening oysters on the part of the right elbow. And excuse my mentioning, that society as a body does not expect one to be so strictly conscientious in emptying one's glass as to turn it bottom upwards with the rim on one's nose."

(Charles Dickens in "Great Expectations".)

APRICOT MADEIRA PUDDING

1½ cups plain flour ½ cup sugar
½ cup milk ½ cup grated beef suet
½ teaspoon carbonate of soda
2 tablespoons apricot jam

Sift flour into bowl. Stir in the suet and sugar, and add apricot jam. Dissolve soda in milk and stir into other ingredients. Mix well together and steam in a greased pudding basin for two hours. Serve with a sweet white sauce flavoured with almond essence, or serve with boiled custard.

APRICOT SHORTCAKE

½ cup sugar ½ cup good shortening
Pinch salt 1 egg
½ teaspoon grated lemon rind
1½ cups self-raising flour
1 to 1¼ cups cooked dried apricots well drained of syrup and sweetened to taste

Topping:
1 egg, ½ cup sugar, 1 cup coconut, few drops almond essence

Cream shortening, sugar and lemon rind. Add egg, mix well. Work in sifted flour and salt. Spread over greased slab-tin, cover with apricot pulp. Prepare topping. Mix beaten egg, sugar, coconut and almond essence. Spread over apricot pulp. Bake in moderate oven approximately ½ hour. Cut into squares, serve hot or cold with custard or cream.

RHUBARB MERINGUE TART

One 8 or 9 inch cooked and cooled short-crust or biscuit pastry flan
3 cups diced fresh rhubarb
1 cup stewed apple pieces
1 to 2 tablespoons honey
1 dessertspoon arrowroot blended with a little extra water
½ cup sugar for meringue
2 tablespoons water Squeeze lemon juice
2 egg whites

Place water and honey in saucepan, stir over low heat until mixed. Add rhubarb and lemon juice, cover with a tightly fitting lid, and simmer 8 to 10 minutes or until soft but not broken; strain liquid. Add blended arrowroot to liquid in saucepan, stir over heat until mixture boils and thickens. Fold in cooked rhubarb and apple. Fill into flan. Beat egg-whites stiffly, gradually add the ½ cup of sugar, and continue beating until meringue stands in peaks. Pile around edge of fruit filling; return to slow oven until meringue is set and lightly browned. Serve in wedges with whipped cream or boiled egg custard.

Note: If rhubarb is not a good red colour, a few drops of red food colouring may be added while it is cooking.

RHUBARB

Rhubarb takes all flavours but gives none, so most economical to use for tarts or jam with expensive fruits.

Mince rhubarb very small and wash well. Boil with blackcurrants till juice is extracted from both. Then strain through two sieves of different fineness. Boil it with weight in sugar, and you have blackcurrant jelly.

RHUBARB PUDDING

Stew 1 lb. of rhubarb with a little lemon peel and plenty of sugar. Rub it through a sieve, then mix with 1 oz. of butter (melted), 2 tablespoons of breadcrumbs, and 3 beaten eggs. Line the edge of the pie-dish with good pastry, pour the mixture into the dish, cover with pastry, and bake until done.

OF SYLLABUB

Entertaining during the Christmas and New Year period in the 17th century in England required the mistress of the manor to be an expert in preparing syllabub. Every house had its particular favourite, but basically there were three distinct types.

One was mixed in a punch bowl on a basis of cider or ale (sometimes both), sweetened with sugar and spiced with cinnamon or nutmeg. Into the bowl the milkmaid milked the cow, so that the new warm milk fell in a foam and froth on to the cider. The contents of the bowl were left undisturbed for an hour or two, by which time a kind of honey-combed curd had formed on the top, leaving alcoholic whey underneath. Sometimes a layer of thick fresh cream was poured on top of the milk curd. This syllabub was more a drink than a whip, a diversion for country parties and rustic festivals.

Then there was a syllabub made with wine and spirits instead of cider and ale, and with cream instead of milk. This mixture was a more solid one. It was about four-fifths sweetened whipped cream, to be spooned rather than drunk out of the glass in which it was served, and one-fifth of wine and whey which had separated from the whip, and which you then drank when you reached the end of the cream.

By the 18th century, many recipes were available. For lemon syllabub you took a pint of cream, added a pound of fine sugar, the juice of seven lemons, the grated rind of two lemons, a pint of white wine, a half pint of sherry. You poured it all into a deep pot, whisked it for half an hour, and poured it into glasses the night before you wanted it. At a later stage it was discovered that by reducing the proportions of wine and sugar to cream the whip would remain thick and light without separating. This version was called everlasting syllabub and could be kept for several days.

Not all syllabubs were necessarily made with wine. Sir Kenelm Digby, whose book of recipes collected from his contemporaries and friends provided posterity with a graphic account of Stuart cookery, noted that he made a fine syllabub with syrup left over from the home-drying of plums; being "very quick of the fruit and very weak of the sugar", this syrup "makes the syllabub exceedingly well-tasted".

OLD ENGLISH SYLLABUB

1 orange — ¼ pint white wine
1 oz. castor sugar — ½ pint dairy cream
3 tablespoons Old English Marmalade
5-6 individual glasses

Grate rind of orange and squeeze out the juice, place in a bowl with the wine and sugar. Stir to dissolve sugar. Add the cream, whisk mixture until it forms peaks when the whisk is lifted out. Fold in marmalade, divide between 5 or 6 individual glasses and leave in cool place until required. Decorate each glass with a twist of orange before serving. This dessert can be kept in a cool place for several hours.

MASQUERADE PUDDING

3½ cups scalded milk — ½ cup sugar
1/3 cup tapioca — 1 egg

Put milk in the top of a double boiler and add tapioca, sugar and a pinch of salt. Cook, stirring frequently, for 15 minutes or until tapioca is clear. Then pour a small amount of the tapioca on the beaten egg-yolk and stir vigorously. Return to top of double boiler and cook until thickened. Remove from fire, add dash of vanilla, fold in the stiffly-beaten egg-white and turn into serving bowl.

BAKEWELL PUDDING

To the yolks of 3 eggs add the white of one, 4 ozs. sugar, 4 ozs. of butter and grated rind of 1 lemon. Beat butter and sugar to a cream, then add eggs and lemon. Spread a layer of pastry on a plate, then layer of blackcurrant jam, and cover with the mixture. Bake in a quick oven. Best cold.

STEAMED LEMON PUDDING

4 ozs. self-raising flour
3 tablespoons brown sugar
2 ozs. shredded suet
1 tablespoon sugar Pinch salt
1 lemon 3 tablespoons water

Sift flour and salt and rub in the suet. Add 1 tablespoon sugar and mix to a dough with the water. Roll out and cut off one-third of the pastry, then use other two-thirds to line a small well-greased basin. Grate the yellow rind of the lemon and mix with the brown sugar. Cut away all the white pith from the lemon, prick it well with a fork and place the lemon in the pastry-lined basin. Sprinkle with the mixed brown sugar and lemon rind, then cover the whole pudding with the remaining pastry cut to fit like a lid, pinching the edges together. Tie a piece of thick, well-greased paper over the top of the pudding basin, stand on a rack in a saucepan with boiling water coming 2/3rds up to the top. Steam for 1¼ hours. Serve with custard sauce flavoured with a twist of lemon rind.

GRANNY'S APPLE FRITTERS

3 to 4 green apples ½ cup sugar
¾ cup plain flour Pinch salt
1 egg separated ½ cup milk
2 tablespoons brandy ½ oz. butter
Melted oil for deep frying

Peel apples, leave whole and remove core, cut into half inch slices. Put in bowl, sprinkle with sugar, cover and let stand for 1 hour.

Sift flour and salt into bowl. Make well in centre, add egg yolk and milk. Beat thoroughly until batter is smooth. Add brandy and melted butter, beat well. Let stand 30 minutes. Fold in stiffly beaten egg white. Coat apple slices with batter. Deep fry in hot oil until golden brown on both sides, lift on to a kitchen paper. Sprinkle with sugar, serve hot with cream. Serves 4.

HENRY VIII's FAVOURITE PUDDING

(This pudding - it is really an open tart) is usually baked in the King of England's kitchen in winter time. The recipe has been handed down from the days of Henry VIII.

Take ½ lb. of almonds and beat them fine with a few drops of sweet (distilled) water, add orange-flower water to taste, and 1 pint rich cream. Warm cream and melt in ½ lb. fresh butter, add to the almonds, stir in a pinch of salt, powdered sugar and grated nutmeg to taste. Add the beaten yolks of 6 eggs. Beat all together and pour into a dish lined with fine puff pastry. Dust fine sugar upon it before serving.

Bake pastry case in a hot oven before filling, then fill and bake in moderate oven till filling is set. Take half the given quantities for the tart. Decorate with whipped cream and glace cherries.

WINTER BREAD PUDDING

Children love it hot and most adults prefer it cold, when it is heavy and juicy, like a cold plum pudding.

Start with 2 cups of white breadcrumbs from a stale loaf and 8 ozs. of rye bread crumbled into tiny pieces. Keep a few white crumbs aside to sprinkle on the greased mould. Fry the other crumbs slightly in ½ cup butter. Remove from heat, then mix in ½ cup water, 1 teaspoon lemon juice, ½ cup sugar, 1 teaspoon grated orange rind, a teaspoon of vanilla and a pinch of salt.

Mince or chop fine six to eight apples. Then, starting and ending with the bread mixture, fill your ovenproof dish (tall rather than shallow) with layers of apples and bread, sprinkling cinnamon over each layer of apples. Bake in a slow oven for an hour or a little less. This quantity is ample for eight. Serve with a fruit sauce or cream or just as it is.

GRANDMA'S APPLE DUMPLING

4 cups self-raising flour
pinch of salt 1 cup butter
apples 1½ cups milk
nutmeg as needed

Pare and quarter apples. Sift flour and salt into basin. Rub in butter. Mix to a stiff paste with milk. Roll out a quarter inch thick. Cut into rounds. Place an apple on each, add a little sugar and nutmeg. Form into a ball and bake in following syrup.

3 cups water, 1 tablespoon butter, 1 cup sugar. Bake about 45 minutes till apples are tender.

FIGGY OGGEN

Although the name of this recipe implies the use of Figs, in reality "Figs" is Cornish for Raisins.

For the Pastry

Take 8 ozs. plain flour, a pinch of salt, 2 ozs. butter and 2 ozs. Lard, cold water to mix. Make into a stiff dough on a lightly floured board. Roll out the pastry into a 12 inch square. Then sprinkle over it 8 ozs. of cleaned seeded raisins with the rind of one lemon and one heaped tablespoon of sugar to within ½ inch of the edges. Moisten one side with a little cold water, then roll the pastry up tightly like a Swiss Roll toward the moistened edge. Seal the edge, and with the sealed edge underneath, place the roll on a lightly greased slide, and with the back of a knife mark a criss-cross design over the top. Mix one tablespoon of castor sugar and one tablespoon of water together for a glaze and brush it over the surface of the Roll. Bake in a moderate oven for 30 to 35 minutes until the pastry is golden-brown.

BATTER PUDDING

Make a batter by beating 4 egg yolks into 6 tablespoonsful of flour, adding a pinch of salt, then beating in enough milk and water, about 1 pint, to make it into a thin creamy batter. Let it stand for about 1 hour, reserving the whites of the eggs. Peel 6 good apples, remove the cores, being sure to leave the apples whole, beat 1½ tablespoonsful of butter with an equal amount of sugar, add a pinch of ground nutmeg and a teaspoonful of ground cinnamon. Stuff this into the middle of the apples. Place them in a buttered pie dish.

At the last moment beat the egg whites stiff enough to stand in peaks. Stir them gently into the batter, which pour over the apples. Bake in a moderate oven for about 1 hour, until the apples are soft and the batter is well risen and crusty. The pudding is eaten hot, sprinkled with sugar.

Sauce for Batter Pudding

A small teacupful of cream, a glass of port wine and sugar to taste well mixed up together, and put round the pudding when hot.

APPLE JALOUSIE

Make 12 ozs. of puff pastry

Have ready:

2 cups stewed apple	¼ teaspoon nutmeg
3 ozs. sultanas	½ teaspoon cinnamon
3 ozs. brown sugar.	

Mix all together.

Cut pastry into two portions. Roll each on a floured board, lightly floured to a 12 x 5 inch rectangle, one slightly larger than the other. Place prepared filling down the centre of smaller piece of pastry, leaving 1 inch margin all round. Fold remaining piece of pastry into half down it's length. Using a sharp knife, make cuts through fold of top pastry, ½ inch apart and to within 1 inch of edge. Leave piece 1 inch wide at the end. Open out pastry, place on top of filling. Press edges together to seal. Brush with egg glaze. Bake in hot oven for approximately 20 minutes - until golden. Sprinkle with sifted icing sugar, when cooled. cut into slices.

Instead of apple, mincemeat filling, raspberry jam, can be used. After baking, brush with heated sieved apricot jam and sprinkle edges with chopped almonds, or finely chopped apricot kernels.

APPLE SNOW

Cook the apples until they become a puree, with sugar and cloves. Beat two egg whites until stiff. Fold in hot apple. Chill. Serve with cream. Brown sugar and a small amount of cinnamon can be added to the apples.

APPLE CAKE ROYAL

1 egg	½ teaspoon nutmeg
4 ozs. butter	Squeeze lemon juice
1 cup castor sugar	1 cup chopped raisins
2½ cups plain flour	½ cup chopped walnuts

½ teaspoon salt
1 teaspoon bicarbonate of soda
½ teaspoon mixed spice
1½ cups drained apple pulp

Topping

2 tablespoons thin cream
2 tablespoons butter
½ cup brown sugar ½ cup coconut

Sift dry ingredients three times. Mix together apple pulp, lemon juice, raisins and walnuts. Cream together butter and sugar until light and creamy. Add egg and beat well. Gently fold in dry ingredients alternately with fruit mixture. Turn mixture into 8 inch tin lightly greased.

Preheat oven to hot, and reduce to moderate heat when ready to bake cake. Bake in moderate oven approximately 1 hour 15 minutes. At the end of this time, cover cake with combined topping ingredients, return to slow oven, and cook until topping bubbles and browns slightly.

Turn out onto wire rack, topping side up, when cooled.

CAMP FIRE EGGS

Cut off the top of an orange, so that the lid has a small amount of orange pulp on it.

Scoop out the rest of the pulp, and shell an egg into the cavity, adding salt and pepper. Set it in the hot ashes to cook.

The pulp inside the lid, drips gently on to the egg as it cooks, giving an enchanting flavour.

A little flaked fish and butter can be added with butter, stirred with the egg in the orange.

APPLE STRUDEL

2 cups plain flour 2 ozs. butter
½ teaspoon salt
approximately ¼ pint warm water

Sift flour and salt into bowl, rub in softened butter. Add little warm water gradually, kneading to soft dough. Turn out on lightly floured surface, continue kneading and adding water until mixture is smooth and shiny. This should take about 15 minutes. Hit dough a few times with a heavy wooden spoon during kneading. Form dough into a ball, place in heated bowl or saucepan. Cover and stand in warm place 1 hour. Meanwhile, prepare filling.

Filling

4 or 5 green apples extra sugar
4 tablespoons sugar extra cinnamon
½ pint sour cream 2 teaspoons cinnamon
1/3rd cup sultanas melted butter
icing sugar
finely grated rind 1 small lemon

Peel, core and slice apples very thinly, stir in sugar, lemon rind, and cinnamon, mix well. Place sultanas in small bowl, add enough hot water to cover, set aside.

Divide pastry into thirds; roll each piece out very thinly on floured surface. Spread 1/3rd apple mixture in centre of dough, sprinkle over a little extra sugar and cinnamon. Drain sultanas, pat dry; sprinkle a few over apples. Lightly spread 1/3rd of the sour cream over mixture. Roll up pastry into a long shape and seal edges.

Prepare remaining two rolls in the same way. Grease a deep 8 inch round tin. Place rolls side by side in tin, curving them carefully to fit. Bake in moderately slow oven approximately 1¾ hours. Brush a little melted butter over strudel several times during baking. When golden brown and crisp, remove from oven, glaze again with melted butter. Leave in tin 15 minutes before turning out on to serving plate. Sift over a little icing sugar. Serve warm with whipped cream.

APPLE PANDOWDY

1¼ lb. good short pastry, 8 medium sized cooking apples, ½ cup sugar, ¼ teaspoon each salt, grated nutmeg and cinnamon, 4 tablespoons water, ½ cup treacle or golden syrup, 2 ozs. butter.

Line a deep pan with pastry, leaving enough to cover apple mixture. Place apples sliced finely, layer on layer over the pastry. Mix sugar with salt and spices and sprinkle over apples.

Mix water with treacle or syrup and pour over apples, dot with butter. Cover with remaining pastry, seal edges. Bake in a hot oven for 40 minutes. Lower heat to medium cool until apples are cooked. Take out of oven and thoroughly chop apples and pastry, adding more water and syrup if dry. Return to oven and bake another hour. Serve hot with whipped cream.

APPLE CRISP

4-5 cooking apples 3 ozs. plain flour
1 oz. castor sugar Pinch salt
2 ozs. butter ½ teaspoon cinnamon
3 ozs. castor sugar Whipped cream
¼ teaspoon ground cloves
2 teaspoons lemon juice
1 ozs. chopped almonds

Peel, core and slice the apples into a basin. Add 1 oz. castor sugar, the spices and lemon juice. Mix lightly and put in a buttered pie-dish or tin (about 2¼ pint capacity). Blend the castor sugar with the sifted flour and salt, and rub in the butter to a crumbly consistency. Spoon over the apple mixture and sprinkle with the nuts. Bake about 40 minutes in a moderately slow oven, or until the apples are tender and the crust is crisp. Serve with whipped cream.

APPLES IN HONEY

Boil two cups of honey with one cup of water. Wash the required number of apples and remove cores, but not peel. Place the fruit in the boiling honey syrup and cover the pan. Cook until tender. Serve with only just enough of the honey syrup to flavour the fruit nicely. Use the rest of the syrup another time. Serve hot or cold.

APPLE-DATE CAKE PUDDING

1 cup plain flour — 4 ozs. butter
½ teaspoon salt — 1 egg
½ teaspoon cinnamon — 1 tablespoon milk
½ teaspoon nutmeg — ½ cup chopped dates
2/3rd cup sugar — ½ cup chopped raisins
¼ teaspoon bicarbonate of soda
1½ cups coarsely grated apple

Butterscotch Sauce

1 cup firmly packed brown sugar
1 cup liquid sugar syrup
2 ozs. butter — 2/3 cup cream

Sift together flour, bicarbonate of soda, salt, cinnamon and nutmeg. Cream butter and sugar together until light and fluffy. Add egg and milk gradually, beat well. Add dry ingredients to creamed mixture gradually, beat well. Stir in prepared dates, apple and raisins. Turn into well-greased 8 inch tin. Bake in a moderate oven 45 to 50 minutes or until cooked when tested. Serve with cream and butterscotch sauce.

Butterscotch sauce

Combine in saucepan brown sugar, sugar syrup, and butter. Stir over low heat until all ingredients are melted and smooth. Bring to boil and boil gently until a little dropped in cold water forms a soft ball. Remove from heat, add the cream gradually, stirring until smooth. Serve hot or cold.

SPICED APPLE CAKE

1 heaped cup self-raising flour
½ teaspoon mixed spice
¼ lb. butter (or less)
½ teaspoon ginger — ¼ lb. sugar — 1 egg

Cream butter and sugar. Add egg, then flour sifted with spices. Have plenty of hot stewed apple ready. Roll out mixture lightly, using some extra flour to stop mixture from sticking to board. Grease a sponge sandwich tin well and line the tin bottom and sides with the pastry. Pour in the hot apple, then cover the top with more pastry. Bake in medium oven for 15 to 20 minutes. Turn out while hot by holding a plate over top of tin and turning upside down, then back on to another plate. Sprinkle top with icing sugar. Serve hot or cold with cream.

APPLE BUTTERSCOTCH

4 green apples — 2 tablespoons sugar
2 tablespoons butter — ½ cup extra sugar
Grated rind of 1 lemon and ½ orange
½ cup soft breadcrumbs
½ teaspoon grated nutmeg
½ teaspoon ground cinnamon
3 ozs. butterscotch

Peel apples, slice thinly; place on flat plate, sprinkle with sugar, grated lemon and orange rinds. Melt butter, add crumbs. Stir over low heat until crumbs absorb butter. Place half the crumbs in greased dish, add ¼ of the apples. Sprinkle with half the extra sugar mixed with the nutmeg and cinnamon. Add half the remaining crumbs, then another layer of apples. Pour over the lemon and orange juices, cover with balance of crumbs. Cover and bake 45 minutes in moderate oven. Sprinkle top with finely crushed butterscotch, place in hot oven until butterscotch is slightly melted. Serve hot or cold, with or without cream.

GOOSEBERRY FOOL AND TANSY

1 lb. gooseberries topped and tailed
1 egg white stiffly whipped — A little water
½ cup heavy cream — ½ cup sugar to taste

Stew the gooseberries gently with the sugar and just enough water to protect the saucepan. When they are soft and mushy, add the egg white stirring over gentle heat until fluffy and set. When cold, stir in the cream. Serve very cold in individual dishes or parfait glasses.

For gooseberry tansy omit the cream. Make a thin custard. When cold mix with stewed gooseberries. Serve cold with whipped cream if desired.

From the greengrocer tree you get grapes and green peas,
Cauliflower, red apple, and raspberries,
While the pastrycook plant cherry brandy will grant,
Apple puffs and three corners and Bantings.
Gilbert

ORANGE COBBLER

3 slightly rounded dessertspoons Cornflour
¼ cup sugar — 2 cups orange juice
1 tablespoon Butter — ¼ cup orange marmalade

Combine the sugar, cornflour and marmalade. Gradually stir in the orange juice. Stir over a medium heat until the mixture boils and thickens. Cook 2 minutes. Remove from the heat and stir in the butter.

Make Topping

Sift 1 cup self-raising flour and ¼ teaspoon nutmeg. Rub in 1½ tablespoons butter until crumbly. Add 1 oz. of sugar and then a tablespoon of orange juice and one beaten egg. Stir until moistened. Reheat the orange mixture and pour into greased shallow casserole. Place a spoonful of the topping.

Bake in a moderate oven for about 30 minutes.

LEMON WATER ICE IN ORANGE CASES

4 oranges ¾ cup lemon juice
2 cups sugar 4 cups boiling water
1 dessertspoon grated lemon rind

Boil sugar and water together for 10 minutes. Cool. Add lemon juice and rind. Place in shallow dish. Cut off lids of oranges and remove pulp. Fill with water ice and replace lid with a piece of fresh mint in stem hole. Place on green leaf on plate. Use drained orange pulp for orange juice.

ORANGES AND LEMONS

3 large oranges 3 large lemons
A little whipped cream. Some leaves to garnish
1 pint of lemon water ice (sorbet)
4 lbs. grapes for decorative setting

Cut off the tops of the fruit and put on one side. Level the base of the fruit, taking care not to cut the flesh. Scoop out the flesh with a sharp knife. Fill the fruit with scoops of lemon ice, top with a dollop of cream and replace the tops. Put a circle of grapes around the border of the serving dish and one cluster in the centre. Place the fruit between the grapes which act as a support. Garnish with leaves and serve immediately.

PEAR SURPRISE

3 firm pears 1 cup diced orange pulp
2/3 cup orange juice ½ cup sugar
1 dessertspoon brown sugar
1 dessertspoon lemon juice
1 dessertspoon grated orange rind

Wash pears, remove cores carefully but do not peel. Fill cavities with orange pulp and brown sugar. Place in baking dish. Mix together orange and lemon juice and add grated rind and sugar. Pour over pears and bake in slow oven until pears are tender but not broken. Baste during cooking two or three times with liquid in the dish. Chill and serve with the liquid.

GARDEN PUDDING

Bread and butter, stewed fruit, a breakfast cup of milk, 1 heaped teaspoon flour, 1 egg.

Line a basin with slices of bread and butter fitted neatly together, fill with stewed fruit, put a saucer with a weight on it on the top, and leave for some hours or till next day. Make a custard with the egg, milk and flour, stirring smoothly till perfectly cooked. Sweeten and flavour, and leave till cold. Pour round the pudding. Fresh uncooked raspberries, or loganberries or blackberries, well sprinkled with sugar, are delicious instead of stewed fruit. Serve with cream.

PEAR ROYAL

To serve six, take a 12 inch enamelled saucepan, or anything wide that does not give off a metallic flavour, and in it put 2 cups dry red wine, 2 tablespoons lemon juice, 1 cup sugar, one 2 inch stick of cinnamon or ½ teaspoon ground cinnamon (stick is better) and bring to boil over a moderate heat.

Add 6 small or 3 large ripe but firm fresh pears, peeled, cored and halved. Partly cover pan, reduce heat to low. Simmer slowly for 15 to 20 minutes until pears are soft but not mushy. Cool in syrup until lukewarm. Discard cinnamon stick.

To serve warm, transfer pears with a slotted spoon to dessert dishes, small bowls or champagne glasses. Spoon a little syrup over them. To serve cold, chill in syrup in bowl or baking dish until thoroughly chilled.

PEARS IN WINE

1 lemon 4 large cooking pears
1 cup water 1 cup sugar
½ cup sweet sherry (or cooking Marsala)
1 dessertspoon gelatine (optional)

Allow one pear per person. Peel carefully, then leave whole and preserve the stem. Blanch with the juice of a lemon. Meanwhile make a syrup by boiling the water with the sugar for 20 minutes. Add the sherry or sweet cooking wine and poach the pears in this liquid, very slowly, for another 20 minutes. Serve chilled.

Another method is to boil sugar and water for only five minutes, then proceed as above. When pears are cooked, have ready the gelatine in a deep bowl dissolved in a little cold water — pour over it the boiling liquid strained off the pears and let set. When serving, cut this wine-and-fruit-flavoured jelly into small cubes and garnish around the chilled whole pears.

SWEET APPLE CRUMBLE

Stewed apple, covered with mixture of 1 cup self-raising flour, ½ cup sugar, ½ cup shortening. Rub these ingredients together and sprinkle over stewed fruit. Add sprinkling of cinnamon and chopped nuts. Bake 20 minutes in moderate oven.

SWEET FRUIT SPONGE

Stewed rhubarb, apples or any fruit in season, topped with sponge made as follows; 1 egg, ½ cup sugar, ¾ cup (small) self-raising flour, 1 tablespoon hot water. Pour on to hot fruit and bake for 20 minutes.

DRIED FIGS AND PEARS IN HONEY

Soak figs overnight. If using dried pears, soak also, otherwise use cooking pears; peel cut in halves and core. Place a fig in hollow of each pear half, place in rows in a flat dish and run honey over. Add ½ cup hot water and bake slowly until fruit is cooked.

FRUIT CRUMBLE

Apples or pears are suitable for this pudding which can be served hot with custard or cream.

You need 1½ to 2 lb. apples or pears, which should be peeled, cored, sliced and stewed with a very little water, lemon juice and sugar to taste. Allow fruit to cool, drain off any surplus juice and arrange in shallow oven-proof dish.

Make the topping with 1 cup coarse biscuit crumbs, 2 tablespoons wholemeal flour, 2 tablespoons brown sugar, 1½ ozs. butter melted, 1 dessertspoon cocoa, 1 teaspoon cinnamon.

Mix dry ingredients together. Melt shortening and blend with dry ingredients until mixture resembles coarse breadcrumbs. Sprinkle thickly and evenly over the fruit, sprinkle a little more brown sugar over the top and put into a hot oven for 20 to 25 minutes until fruit is bubbling and the topping is crisp.

"Give me a women as soft and as delicate, and as velvet as my peaches."

Ouida

THE GOVERNOR'S PEACHES

Mash enough of the flesh of ripe peaches to half fill your drinking glass. Crack open two peach stones and add the well-crushed kernels before filling the glass with sherry. After the mixture has reposed covered for a day in as cold a place as can be found, strain and pour juices over a bowl of sliced and sugared peaches.

A DISH OF POMEGRANATES

Take all the inside from 6 pomegranates and mash them into a silver bowl. Sprinkle with rose-water, lime juice, and sugar and serve very cold.

HEAVENLY STRAWBERRIES

Stem, wash and drain well one pint of ripe strawberries. Place them in a serving bowl, sprinkle over them four tablespoons of powdered sugar, the juice of half an orange, the grated rind of one orange and about 3 tablespoons of Curacao liqueur. Cover and chill for several hours.

In the meantime make one cup of liquid custard in the usual way, using 2 egg yolks, 1 cup of milk, 2 tablespoons of sugar and one teaspoon of vanilla. Cool and chill. When ready to serve the strawberries beat ½ cup of heavy cream until stiff and fold into it five tablespoons of the chilled custard. Pour over the strawberries so as to completely hide them. Serve at once with meringues baked in finger-length strips.

NAVAL APRICOTS

Put ½ lb. dried apricots, a wineglass of rum, a heaped tablespoon of soft brown sugar into a dish. Add enough water to barely cover the apricots, and leave overnight. Bake in a low oven until the apricots are tender. Serve hot or cold with cream.

Stir some finely chopped Mint into a bowl of cream and put large blobs of it on crushed strawberries sometimes.

FRUITS IN MARSALA

1 cup sugar	4-6 small peaches
¼ pint water	Strawberries
juice of 1 lemon	¼ pint marsala

Dissolve sugar in the water and lemon juice, boil to form a heavy syrup. Allow to cool. Stir in marsala, leave to become quite cold. Blanch peaches by plunging quickly into boiling water, and remove skins. Immerse in the syrup. Wash strawberries, but do not remove stems and leaves. Stir into the syrup. Chill thoroughly before serving. Serves 4 to 6.

LEMON GELATO WITH BRANDIED STRAWBERRIES

1¼ cups sugar	rind 2 lemons
½ cup lemon juice	½ pint sour cream
4¾ cups water	

In large saucepan place sugar, lemon juice, water and lemon rind. Bring slowly to boil, stirring until sugar has dissolved. Boil 15 minutes, strain; cool. When quite cold, stir in sour cream; chill.

To serve, wash 1 or 2 punnets strawberries lightly, pat dry, hull. Place about 6 strawberries in each serving glass or dish, pour over little brandy. Top with spoonfuls of Gelato just before serving.

Cook prunes in weak China tea with a strip of orange peel and brown sugar to sweeten.

ORANGE SNOW

Peel a large sweet orange. Remove pith and pips and cut the fruit into small pieces with the kitchen scissors. Put in a breakfastcup and fill to brim with sliced bananas and passionfruit pulp. Sweeten to taste and steep 30 minutes.

Separate the yolks and whites of 4 eggs. Dissolve one brimful dessertspoon of gelatine in a quarter cup of water. (Soften the gelatine first in the cold water and then stand the cup in hot water until the gelatine is dissolved.)

Measure out 6 ounces of castor sugar. Beat egg whites very stiff. Then gradually beat in half the sugar. Beat egg yolks to a creamy consistency and whisk in the remaining sugar. When the egg yolk mixture is thick and smooth, add the dissolved gelatine slowly, and then stir in the sweetened fruit. Blend well. Leave a few minutes and then add the stiffly whisked egg whites. Beat all together until like snow. Turn into a serving dish and chill.

Dining is the privilege of civilisation. The rank which people occupy in the grand scale may be measured by their way of taking their meals, as well as by their way of treating women. The nation which knows how to dine has learnt the leading lesson of progress.

These sentences were written in 1861 by a woman whose name was destined to become a household word, Mrs. Beeton.

What she was trying to drum into the heads of the newly rich is how to dine if they wish to be accepted by society and how to give a dinner — if accepted.

. . . The first course began with soups and fish, with a few little light dishes such as oyster or lobster patties on the side. This preceded the entree which was followed by roasts. Then came lighter game birds and fowls and wonderfully elaborate sweets. Finally all was cleared away for the dessert.

It will be noticed that all dishes are given in the plural, that is because they were usually in the plural. The smallest dinner for six people might have but one soup and one fish but two entrees were the absolute minimum permitted.

. . . At grand dinners, 30 or 40 dishes were quite usual, and at a dinner given by Queen Victoria somewhere about 1840, there were no fewer than 70 dishes, although Queen Victoria preferred plain food.

. . . The dinner did not end with the pudding. The table was cleared to make room for the dessert and ices.

. . . The epergne, well known to the 18th century as a dispenser of sweets or pickles, was transformed by the Victorians into a magnificent dispenser of fruits and an eye-catching ornament. Epergnes came in a bewildering variety of shapes and sizes and the more contorted, ornamented and involved the better.

The epergne with its tree-like branches or arms, often detachable, supported as a crest a curved dish, where a variety of fruits rioted in nests of real or artificial leaves — silver pepper leaves — were tasteful.

Its branches held at the tips glass dishes filled with individual fruits and often glass baskets swung gently below. Pottery or china pine stands shaped like pineapples held this fruit when in season.

Tall stemmed tazze and ornamented baskets held other fresh fruits, low ornate glass or silver dishes and baskets offered dried fruits and nuts as well as delicately flavoured sweet biscuits and cakes to accompany the ices which were handed around separately. Coffee in small cups and liqueurs ended the dinner.

The ladies, after a short interval, left the dining-room to be followed at a longer interval by the gentlemen. During the evening, tea and coffee were served. Guests were often invited to join the party after dinner and could arrive in succession from nine o'clock until midnight and light refreshments were provided.

. . . Gargling at the table had been a common English habit not 50 years before, and guests had been warned not to use the tablecloth as a napkin.

By the late 1850's, even wetting the mouth with a napkin was manners, although some gentlemen still followed this custom, but the ladies were to set a good example here and wet only the tips of the fingers.

During the early part of the reign, a transition in table manners seems to have been taking place, and it was just as well to be au fait with what was being done.

One should not eat food with a knife as forks and spoons were provided — the broad round-ended knife so useful for eating peas was definitely out in good society. Nor should one eat largely or toss off a glass of wine in one gulp.

Fish should be eaten with a fork only, assisted with a piece of bread, but in first-rate society silver fish-knives were replacing bread.

Nothing was so vulgar as to make a clatter with a knife and fork, and it was also vulgar for a hostess to festoon herself with jewels or to be more richly dressed than her guests.

Ladies now stayed longer at table, while gentlemen no longer became inebriated so quickly. All these were pleasing and sure steps in the progress of refinement.

GOVERNOR PHILLIP'S RUM PIE

Pastry

6 ozs. flour, 3 ozs. butter, 2 tablespoons water, 1 tablespoon sugar.

Sift flour and rub in butter. Dissolve sugar in hot water, before adding to flour mixture. Mix to a soft dough and chill for 15 to 20 minutes. Roll out and line an 8 inch pie dish with pastry and cook in hot oven for 15 minutes. Allow to cool before filling.

Rum Cream Filling

3 egg yolks, 1 tablespoon soft butter, ¼ cup water, ½ cup sugar, 1 dessertspoon gelatine, ½ pint cream, ¼ cup rum.

Beat yolks, butter, gradually adding sugar, and beat until frothy. In saucepan soften gelatine in water and bring to boil over low heat. Slowly pour this into egg mixture, beating well. Whip cream until stiff and fold into egg mixture, then fold in rum.

Chill until stiff enough to form peaks when dropped from a spoon, then heap into crust and chill 3 to 4 hours before serving. Decorate with grated chocolate.

LEMON WATER ICE

½ pint lemon juice, ½ pint water, 1 pint strong syrup. Grated rind of 3 lemons with sugar added. Mix the whole. Strain after letting it stand an hour. Chill. Beat with a little sugar, 3 egg whites. Fold in as mixture begins to set.

SORBET

26 oz. bottle of sweet cider
26 oz. bottle of champagne
juice 1 lemon 2 egg whites sugar

Pour the cider and champagne and lemon juice into trays, freeze until almost frozen.

Beat egg whites stiffly and fold into the frozen champagne. Pour back into the trays and refreeze.

Dip edges of stemmed glasses in a little extra egg white, then into sugar coloured pale yellow. Fill glasses with sorbet and serve before or after the main course. Serves 14.

CHOCOLATE MOUSSE

4 egg yolks ¼ cup castor sugar
2 tablespoons cognac 4 egg whites
6 ozs. semi-sweet chocolate cut in small pieces
3 tablespoons strong coffee
¼ lb. soft unsalted butter
½ cup cream, whipped

Brush inside of a quart mould with a film of oil. Invert to drain.

In an oven-proof mixing bowl, beat egg yolks and sugar for two to three minutes, or until they are pale yellow and thick enough to form a ribbon when whisk is lifted from bowl. Beat in cognac. Set mixing bowl over a pan of barely simmering water, continue beating for 3 to 4 minutes or until mixture is foamy and hot. Then set bowl over a pan of iced water, and beat for 3 to 4 minutes longer, or until mixture is cool again and as thick and creamy as mayonnaise.

In a heavy four-to-six-cup saucepan set over hot water, melt chocolate with coffee, stirring constantly. When dissolved, beat in butter, one piece at a time, to make a smooth cream. Beat chocolate mixture into egg yolks and sugar.

In a separate bowl, with clean whisk, beat egg whites until they are stiff enough to form stiff peaks. Stir about one-quarter of egg whites into chocolate mixture to lighten it then very gently fold in remaining egg whites. Spoon the mousse into oiled mould and chill for at least four hours or until set.

To unmould, run a long sharp knife around sides of mould and dip bottom of mould in hot water for a few seconds. Wipe outside of mould dry, place a chilled serving plate upside down over mould, and, grasping both sides firmly, quickly turn plate and mould over. Rap plate on a table and the mousse should slide easily out of mould. If mousse doesn't unmould at once, repeat the whole process.

Whip chilled cream in a large chilled bowl until it is firm enough to hold its shape softly. Garnish mousse with whipped cream. Serves 6 to 8.

TUTTI FRUTTI

1 pint cream 6 ozs. icing sugar
2 ozs. almonds 2 ozs. cherries
2 ozs. candied peel ½ cup raisins
½ cup sultanas 4 egg whites
1 dessertspoon, rum, brandy or vanilla
1 dessertspoon mixed spice
1 teaspoon cinnamon
1 teaspoon nutmeg
1 dessertspoon hot water
1 dessertspoon cocoa

Slice almonds, chop fruit and mix with spice. Pour brandy over fruit and allow to stand overnight. Whip cream stiffly. Add half the sugar in one basin. In another basin beat egg whites stiffly, add remaining sugar. Blend both together by folding gently. Add fruit and nuts and dissolved cocoa. Pour into lined mould. Freeze.

ALMOND AND COFFEE SWEET

A creamy boiled custard flavoured with almond and served on coffee jelly.

BAKERY HILL MARMALADE CREAM

Take 2 tablespoonfuls of orange marmalade; add to it a quart of cream; a little, at first, for mincing the marmalade, a wine-glassful of brandy; 8 ozs. of ground loaf sugar, and the juice of a lemon; whisk it for half an hour; and drain. Serve in custard glasses.

ALMOND ICE

¾ pint milk 4 ozs. castor sugar
5 fluid ozs. cream 4 ozs. ground almonds
1 separated egg 1 level teaspoon gelatine
Few drops almond essence
6 blanched, chopped and roasted almonds

Soften gelatine in a little cold water; add to warmed milk; cook gently until gelatine has dissolved. Add sugar. Stir in. Add slightly-beaten egg yolk; cook gently for 1 to 2 minutes stirring all the time. Cool. Beat thoroughly. Fold in stiffly beaten egg white and cream, whipped. Stir in ground almonds and add almond essence. Chill. Serve sprinkled with chopped almonds, heated in oven until golden.

DOTTY SAGO

3 cups water ½ cup port wine
¾ cup sugar ¼ cup currants
½ cup sago (washed)
½ teaspoon (bare) cinnamon
½ teaspoon (bare) ground cloves

Boil together until sago dissolves and is clear. Chill, and serve in a glass dish.

ALMONDA

Line a bowl with stale sponge fingers, covering bottom of vessel also. Mix together 4 ozs. softened butter, 4 or 6 ozs. castor sugar, 4 or 6 ozs. almond meal, ¼ cup of whisky. Fill into bowl. Chill. Before serving top with whipped cream and decorate with cherries.

APPLE MOUSSE

2½-3 lb. firm cooking apples
(2 for decoration)
1 dessertspoon gelatine
a little castor sugar
crushed walnuts for decoration

1 oz. butter	3 tablespoons water
1 teaspoon vanilla	½ pint cream
3 tablespoons water	3 tablespoons honey

Peel, core and chop the apples. Melt the butter in a shallow pan, put in the apples with the vanilla and three tablespoons of water, cover and set on a low heat until soft.

Draw aside, add the honey and leave on a low heat until melted. Soak and dissolve the gelatine in three tablespoons of water and add to the mixture. Turn out and allow to get cold. Whip the cream and add to the puree with a little castor sugar if necessary.

Pile the mixture in a bowl or in individual dishes and chill.

Before serving, if liked, surround with quarters of apple and sprinkle over crushed walnuts.

PUMPKIN CHIFFON

2 level dessertspoons gelatine
2 or 3 tablespoons cold water
1½ cups of pumpkin (steamed in its skin and then mashed)
¾ cup light brown sugar
1/3 cup castor sugar
Brimming teaspoon powdered cinnamon
½ level teaspoon powdered ginger
¼ level teaspoon allspice
Level dessertspoon grated orange rind

3 eggs (separated)	Big pinch salt
1/3 cup milk	¼ pint cream

Remove seeds and pithy centre from a good-sized piece of pumpkin. Cut it in 2 or 3 chunks and boil it until tender, but not wet and mushy. Drain. Scoop out pulp and mash or sieve it very smoothly. Measure out 1½ cups (8 oz. cup).

Put gelatine in a cup and cover with the cold water. Combine pumpkin, brown sugar, milk, salt and spices in a saucepan. Cook over low heat, stirring constantly until mixture really reaches boiling point — not just bubbles at the edges. Stir in the slightly beaten egg yolks and blend quickly and evenly. Then add the softened gelatine and go on stirring for two minutes or until gelatine dissolves. (Keep heat very low.) Then stand saucepan in cold water until mixture cools and shows signs of setting. Have the cream whipped until fluffy in one bowl, grate the orange rind on to a saucer.

Whisk the egg whites until stiff but not dry. Beat the castor sugar in slowly. Blend egg whites, whipped cream and orange rind into the mixture. See that it is evenly blended so that you don't get dark streaks of pumpkin through the cream. Turn into dish and chill.

RED FRUIT SALAD

4 ozs. castor sugar; 8 ozs. each of red cherries, red currants, strawberries and raspberries.

Dissolve sugar in ½ pint water over a gentle heat. Leave to cool. Cut cherries in half. Stone. Pour cold syrup over the strawberries, raspberries and red currants. Serve very cold.

BRANDIED ORANGES

2 teaspoons finely grated lemon rind;
1 oz. ground almonds; 1½ tablespoons castor sugar; 2 tablespoons lemon juice;
1¼ cups cream; 3 or 4 oranges;
2-3 tablespoons brandy.

Peel oranges, divide into segments, marinate in brandy for one hour. Whip cream until stiff, beat in lemon juice, grated rind and ground almonds. Lastly beat in the sugar, whip well once more; chill. Place marinated orange segments in individual glasses, top with the almond cream.

ORCHARD DELIGHT

3 rounded teaspoons gelatine
¼ pint each of orange and lemon juice
¼ lb. sugar or more to taste
¼ cup hot water   3 eggs

Separate yolks and whites of eggs. Beat yolks and sugar together until white and creamy. Dissolve gelatine in hot water and add to yolk mixture with fruit juices.

Beat egg whites until stiff, but not dry and blend with fruit mixture. Spoon into a mould or basin to set.

Silence is the wall that surrounds wisdom.

SAUCES AND DRESSINGS

A SALAD DRESSING

by the Rev. Sydney Smith

'To make this condiment your poet begs
The pounded yellow of two hard-boil'd eggs,
Two boiled potatoes, passed through kitchen sieve,
Smoothness and softness to the salad give.
Let onion atoms lurk within the bowl,
And, half-suspected, animate the whole.
Of mordant mustard add a single spoon.
Distrust the condiment that bites too soon;
But deem it not, though man of herbs, a fault,
To add a double quantity of salt;
Four times the spoon with oil from Lucca Brown,
And twice with vinegar procured from town;
And, lastly o'er the flavoured compound toss
A magic soupcon of anchovy sauce.
Oh, green and glorious! Oh, herbaceous treat!
'Twould tempt the dying anchorite to eat:
Back to the world he'd turn his fleeting soul
And plunge his fingers in the salad bowl!
Serenely full, the epicure would say,
Fate cannot harm me, I have dined today.'

Napoleon's chef first made his renowned "mahonaise" when the garrison had run out of flour and the Emperor ordered a thick sauce. Rather than lose his job (or his head), the fellow thickened the sauce with the yolk of an egg.

How would he have known that the egg-yolk and not the white would thicken the sauce? How did he guess that by adding the oil drip by drip and beating furiously he would achieve such a superlative result? How did he guess that salt would thicken it, vinegar make it thinner and lemon juice not alter the consistency?

When the whole thing does curdle (often because the ingredients are too cold), rather than throw it down the drain, put a drop of hot water into a new receptacle and spoon the mess into it, little by little, beating constantly.

MAYONNAISE

2 raw egg yolks	2 tablespoons vinegar
1 gill olive oil	½ teaspoon mustard
1 teaspoon sugar	½ teaspoon salt

pinch of cayenne pepper

Put egg yolks in basin and beat lightly with sugar, salt, mustard and cayenne. Add oil a drop at a time. Stir well, one way until mixture is thick and creamy. Add vinegar, drop at a time. This mayonnaise must be made in a cool place. Best to stand basin in cold water. Store in cool place. Before using, whipped cream may be added.

SOUR CREAM MAYONNAISE

Combine 3 egg yolks and 1 cup sour cream in top of double boiler beating with a fork. Place over bubbling hot water and give frequent stirrings with wooden spoon until well thickened. Cool. Then stir in 1 dessertspoon of fine-chopped white onion, 1 dessertspoon lemon juice and 1 dessertspoon mustard. Check for salt and pepper.

SOUR CREAM DRESSING (another way)

1½ cups sour cream	2 tablespoons capers
½ cup white vinegar	1 teaspoon dill seeds
¾ cup oil	1 teaspoon salt

2 tablespoons grated onion
2 tablespoons horseradish
Freshly ground black pepper

Combine all ingredients in a jar and shake well before using. Makes about 3 cups.

HONEY DRESSING

2 tablespoons of run honey
Grated rind of half a lemon
2½ tablespoons lemon juice
½ breakfast cup olive oil
3 ozs. cream (cottage) cheese
dash of pepper and salt

Gradually beat the honey and lemon juice into the cheese until smooth. Add the lemon rind and then, very gradually, the olive oil, beating well after each addition. Season. Serve separately.

According to the Spanish proverb, four persons are wanted to make a good salad; a spendthrift for oil, a miser for vinegar, a counsellor for salt, and a madman to stir all up.

OX KIDNEY AND MUSTARD SAUCE

½ ox kidney or 3 sheeps' kidneys, 1 teaspoon chopped parsley, ¾ teaspoon mustard, 1 oz. butter, 1 teaspoon flour, 1 teaspoon vinegar, 1 onion, salt, pepper, 1 gill tomato puree, puree of spinach or green peas.

Wash kidney; remove core; cut up (not too small). Heat butter, fry onion, then kidney, add mustard, salt and flour; stir well; add vinegar, pinch cayenne, tomato or brown sauce. Cook very gently ¾ to 1 hour; stir now and then. Cook spinach or green peas. Dish in the centre. Garnish with puree of green peas or spinach.

KELLY'S SAUCE

Put a tablespoon each of capers and parsley in a bowl. Pound them. Add a tablespoon of French Mustard and 3 hard yolks of eggs. Mix well. Add 6 anchovies, boned and sieved, a tablespoon of vinegar, 2 tablespoons of oil, and a finely-chopped shallot, and mix with the rest. Put in a jar. When it is to be used stir into ½ pint of melted butter or strong gravy.

LETHE LORY (Milk with things added)

From a 15th Century Cookry Boke. To show that cooking has not changed very much.

Take mylke, and cast it in a potte, and case there-to salt and saffron; and pen take and hewe faire (clean) buttes (buttocks) of calves or porke al smalle and caste there-to. And take the white and yolkes of eyren (eggs), and draw them thorough streynor; and when the licour is at boyle caste there-to the eyren. And a litull Ale, And styrre till hit crudde (curdles); And if wilt have hit farced (stuffed), take mylke, and make hit scalding hote, and caste there-to rawe yolkes of eyren, sugur, powder of gyngere, peper, clowes and maces, and lete hit not fully boyle; And then take a faire lynnen clothe, and presse the cruddes there-on, and then leche it; And lay ye leches (slices), ij, or iij, in a dissh, and cast saffron there-on in the dissh, and so serve hit forth al hote (hot).

And when the jug is empty quite,
I shall not mew in vain,
The Friendly Cow, all red and white,
Will fill her up again.

Oliver Herford

CLOTTED CREAM

Pour 3 pints of rich creamy milk into a large pan and leave it for 24 hours in winter and 12 hours or less in summer, in the larder for the cream to rise. Then set the pan of milk on the stove on a low heat. Let it heat slowly and remain there till the cream begins to show a raised ring around the edge. When sufficiently done the undulations on the surface look thick and sometimes small rings appear. The pan should now be lifted very carefully into the larder or other cool place for it is important that the cream should not be broken either in putting it on the fire or taking it off. Next day the clotted cream may be skimmed off in layers into a serving dish, care being taken to have a good crust on top. At no time must it boil or there will be a thick skin on the surface. The time required for scalding cream depends upon the size of the pan and the heat of the cooker — but the slower it is done the better.

Before factory butter was made and the dairy cow was not in milk, in place of butter, good home made clarified beef or mutton dripping was used. It made excellent biscuits and essence of lemon made a nice flavouring.

CUMBERLAND SAUCE

Heat ½ pint of red currant jelly with the juice of an orange and of half a lemon, a dash of cayenne pepper and ½ teaspoonful of Worcestershire sauce. Bring it to the boil, stir it well, and add ½ tumbler of port, a few glace cherries and the rind of the orange and lemon (cut in thin strips and previously boiled in water for 5 minutes, then strained).

Sometimes a teaspoonful of mustard and a dash of powdered ginger are added instead of the Worcestershire sauce and the cherries are omitted. Served with hot or cold ham, cold venison, roast goose or duck and with meat pies and pâtés. Keeps for weeks in a cool dry place.

WORCESTERSHIRE SAUCE

One ounce of ground pepper, one pint treacle, half ounce bruised cloves, half ounce powdered mace, half ounce cayenne pepper, half ounce garlic, half pound onions, two quarts of vinegar. Put mixture into jar and let it stand two weeks, closely covered; stir daily. At the end of two weeks boil for twenty minutes and strain through muslin. When cold bottle and cork.

AUTUMN SAUCE for Game and Meats

1 lb. cooked prunes with gill of liquid
3 ozs. brown sugar
4 ozs. chopped onions
1-2 chopped cloves garlic
Pinch cayenne pepper
6 whole allspice
1 teaspoon salt
3 tablespoons tomato puree
¼ teaspoon cayenne
½ pint malt vinegar
1 teaspoon malt vinegar
1 teaspoon mustard
1 teaspoon spice
12 crushed peppercorns

Simmer prunes gently, while other ingredients are thoroughly mashed and mixed. Add to prunes and simmer until thickened and of creamy consistency. Rub through sieve. Bottle. Keep few weeks before using.

CURRY SAUCE

Chop four good-sized lemons, with peel left on, into small pieces. Save the juice, discard the pips. Put them in a bowl and add 2 tablespoons brown sugar, 2 teaspoons salt, 1 teaspoon chilli powder, 1 teaspoon curry powder, ½ teaspoon tumeric. Mix everything well, put it into a preserving jar, and keep it a week in a warm place. Good with curried chicken or fish.

CUCUMBER SAUCE FOR SALMON

½ teaspoon salt   1 cucumber
1 teaspoon grated onion
1 teaspoon Worcestershire sauce
2 tablespoons vinegar
¼ pint whipped cream

Mix the onion with the vinegar, salt and Worcestershire sauce. Fold lightly into the cream. Peel and grate cucumber. Drain thoroughly. Fold into sauce, chill. Serve with cold salmon.

1. SAUCE FOR FISH

Mayonnaise, mixed tomato ketchup, Worcestershire sauce (a dash), few dashes of brandy, salt and pepper. Mix with egg yolk. Lemon on glass.

2. SAUCE FOR FISH

Blend a cup of sour cream with 1 tablespoon tomato ketchup and a dash of Worcestershire sauce, salt and pepper.

WALNUT SAUCE

Put ½ lb. of peeled walnuts through a mincer then pound them in a mortar with a little salt, adding gradually a cup of water and a little vinegar, stirring all the time as for mayonnaise. Serve the sauce with a cold trout which has been simply poached in a court bouillon.

SHERRIED APPLE SAUCE

4 green apples   3 dessertspoons sugar
3 tablespoons water   3 dessertspoons sherry
½ oz. butter   Pinch salt.

Peel, core, and slice apples, put in pan with sugar, water, salt and butter. Cook until soft. Beat until smooth and add sherry. Serve hot.

RAISIN SAUCE - to serve with ham.

Take 1 cup seedless raisins, 1 cup cold water, ½ cup sugar, 2 tablespoons lemon juice, ½ cup orange juice.

Simmer the raisins in water until they are soft, then add the sugar and boil gently for 15 minutes. Lastly add the juices and heat.

1. SOUR CREAM SAUCE - for chicken, fish or vegetables.

Beat two egg yolks, blend in ¼ pint soured cream, cook in double saucepan until thick and smooth. Stir in teaspoonful of made mustard, juice of half a lemon, a little chopped parsley and seasoning to taste.

2. SOUR CREAM SAUCE

Prepare one tablespoon of cut chives and a heaping tablespoon of grated onions. Make a cream sauce in the top of a small enamel double boiler in the usual way using 2 tablespoons of butter, 2 tablespoons of flour and one cup of hot milk. Cook until well thickened and season highly to taste with salt and coarsely ground black pepper. Add the grated onion, stir and cover and continue cooking over hot water for fifteen minutes. Just before serving add one cup of sour cream and stir constantly until heated through. Be careful not to overheat. Pour over the string beans, sprinkle with chives.

RAISIN SAUCE

Brown 1 teaspoon granulated or brown sugar in a dry pan and add 1 teaspoon vinegar. Stir in 1 cup brown sauce. Boil up twice, stirring constantly, and remove the sauce from the fire. Add ¼ cup seedless raisins, plumped in boiling water and thoroughly drained. Suitable for smoked meats, pork, marinated dark meat and game.

APPLE SAUCE

Use tart green cooking apples, peeled, cored and thinly sliced. Put in a saucepan with only just enough water to start them cooking and keep them from "catching" on the pan. Keep heat low once the fruit begins to cook. Add a little sugar — not more than ¼ cup to four good-sized apples. Remove saucepan lid once fruit is soft. Simmer a few minutes to evaporate surplus moisture. Beat apple smooth. Serve warm or cold.

PLAIN CARAMEL SAUCE

1 cup sugar ¾ cup water

Brown, but do not burn, the sugar in a heavy saucepan; add water gradually, stirring until syrupy. Serve hot or cold.

HOLLANDAISE SAUCE

¾ cup butter
3 egg yolks (well beaten)
1½ tablespoons lemon juice
Dash of salt and cayenne pepper

Divide butter into three pieces. Put one into top of double boiler over hot - not boiling water and add eggs and lemon juice. Stir all the time with wooden spoon or wire whisk. As butter melts add extra butter slowly. Keep stirring and remove from fire when mixture thickens. If mixture curdles, add hot water by the teaspoon and beat well.

RICH SAUCE for use with roasted sheep

Put 1 oz. sugar into a saucepan and melt brown over the fire, then add a claret glass of wine or vinegar and bring to the boil. Now add the above strained liquor together with a bare ounce of roasted pine nuts, 2/3 of an ounce each of raisins, candied citron peel and currants (chopped), (the currants have been soaked previously in water) and 3 ozs. of chocolate (powdered). Stir well over the fire. If not thick enough, thicken a little. Serve hot. Pour immediately over hot slices of the roasted sheep. Serve with a rough red wine and pureed chestnuts.

CAPER SAUCE

A small bottle of capers will make several cookings of delicate caper sauce — to transform the humble mutton or the most ordinary fish.

Melt two tablespoons butter in a stout saucepan. When melted stir in 2 tablespoons plain flour and continue stirring until cooked and forming tiny balls. Now remove from fire and add 1 cup fish or mutton stock (depending on which dish you will use) and ½ cup top milk. Cook over medium heat, stirring constantly, until the sauce thickens and comes to boil. Remove from heat.

Now stir in 1 tablespoon lemon juice. Beat the yolk of one egg and a little cream in a cup together, stir in a little of hot sauce, return mixture to pan and cook gently, stirring all the time, until sauce is cooked, thick and creamy. Last, add 2 tablespoons capers. Makes a large breakfast cup of rich, delicous sauce. Add salt and pepper to taste.

A SUBSTITUTE FOR CAPER SAUCE

½ pint of melted butter, 2 tablespoonfuls of cut parsley, ½ teaspoonful of salt, 1 tablespoonful of vinegar.

Boil the parsley slowly to let it become a bad colour; cut, but do not chop it fine. Add it to ½ pint of melted butter, with salt and vinegar in the above proportions. Simmer for a few minutes.

HORSERADISH BUTTER

excellent with cold roast or corned beef.

Cream 2 tablespoons butter with 1 tablespoon horseradish, then add 1 tablespoon finely chopped parsley and a little grated onion, if liked.

SAUCE FOR ROAST BEEF

instead of horseradish.

Mix 1 tablespoonful of mustard, 1 tablespoonful of vinegar with 2 tablespoonsful of cream, 1 tablespoonful of grated parsnip and a little salt. Dish in a sauce-boat, no sugar is required as the parsnip is sweet.

SAUCE FOR PICKLED MEATS

Put into ¼ cup of liquor in which meat cooked, ¼ cup vinegar, 1 tablespoon sugar, 1 teaspoon mustard blended in little vinegar. Beat yolk of egg and add to mixture. Stir until thickened — but do not boil. Serve plain for corned beef or with gherkin for tongue.

ORANGE MINT SAUCE for Roast Lamb.

Take ½ cup finely chopped mint, ¼ cup orange juice, ¼ cup of lemon juice, 1 tablespoon powdered sugar. Add sugar and juices to the mint and allow to stand in a warm place for 30 minutes.

HONEY SAUCE

Heat ¼ cup water with 2 tablespoons vinegar then add 1 cup honey and stir until honey is melted. Add ¼ cup freshly chopped mint and heat slowly for 5 minutes, but do not allow to boil. Serve hot with lamb chops or roast lamb.

BREAD SAUCE

Peel an onion. Stick 6 cloves in it. Place in a small saucepan and cover with milk. Bring gently to boil and then stand at back of stove for 20 minutes. Lift out onion. Add a generous bit of butter and crumble in enough soft stale breadcrumbs to give a thick, soft creamy texture. Beat smooth. Season with salt and pepper. Bring to boil again. If possible, add a little cream.

ONION PUREE SAUCE

Served with roasts, grills and fried meats

1 oz. lard — 1½ ozs. flour
1 oz. butter — 1 tablespoon vinegar
1 lb. chopped onions — 3 tablespoons hot water

Melt butter and lard in a heavy pan. Gently simmer the chopped onions until soft but not coloured. Add flour, blend well, then add vinegar and hot water. Blend well, season to taste with salt and pepper and allow to cook slowly for a further 10 minutes. This sauce should have the consistency of a thick puree.

Mint sauce is made by chopping a big handful of Mint leaves as fine as possible. Do not chop it on a board. Use a non -absorbing plate instead. When the Mint is pulverised, place 4 tablespoons of it in a china jug or cup, and over this pour 2 tablespoons of boiling water. Stir well and add sugar to taste, 2 level tablespoons is usual. Stir again and then pour on a quarter of a pint of best wine vinegar.

It is best not to chop herbs on a board.

HARD SAUCE

1 cup castor sugar — 1/3 cup butter
2 tablespoons grated orange rind
2 tablespoons orange juice, or
half orange juice and half rum.

Put the butter in a warm place until it is softened, but do not allow it to melt, then cream it with sugar and orange rind. Very slowly blend in the orange juice, beating very well until light and creamy. Put into a square tin or plate and chill until very firm, then cut into squares. Serve one square on each serve of hot pudding. A beaten white of egg may be added before chilling.

VIKING SAUCE

2 cups home-made mayonnaise
2 teaspoons grated onion
Cayenne pepper (to taste)
1 teaspoon lemon juice
Salt and pepper

Combine ingredients in a bowl, making any additions according to taste.

HONEY-BUTTER SAUCE

to serve with pancakes

1 cup honey — ¼ cup butter
¼ teaspoon cinnamon — little nutmeg

Place honey in top of a double saucepan. Stand over gently boiling water and when warm add other ingredients, stirring until thoroughly blended. Serve warm.

BUTTERSCOTCH SAUCE

1 egg yolk, beaten — 4 tablespoons butter
1 cup brown sugar — 1 cup water
Pinch of salt

Mix all ingredients and cook in double boiler, stirring until thick and syrupy. Beat before using, hot or cold.

HEAVENLY SAUCE

Equal parts of honey and creme de menthe.

CHOCOLATE SAUCE

1 ounce cocoa — 2 cups sugar
1 cup water
1 teaspoon, vanilla essence

Make paste of cocoa with part of water, add remainder of water and boil 4 to 5 minutes. Add sugar, and when thoroughly dissolved remove from heat, let cool, and add vanilla.

MINCEMEAT SAUCE

A delicious sauce to serve with vanilla steamed pudding - just stir a little sherry into fruit mincemeat and heat until bubbling in a saucepan.

SAUCE FOR BOILED PUDDINGS

2 ozs. butter — 4 ozs. icing sugar
2 tablespoons orange juice or stewed fruit juice.

This is made in the same way as Hard Sauce, but instead of the brandy or sherry use fruit juice. A tart fruit juice such as stewed plum or red currant is better than a very sweet one. Cream the butter until soft and white. Sift the icing sugar and add it a spoonful at a time, beating each lot well in. Stir in the juice gradually till the right consistency.

SPICED SAUCE

Take some orange marmalade, thin it with a little ginger syrup from preserved ginger, and fresh orange juice. When heated it may be served as it is or strained to leave orange chips behind. This is a suitable sauce for batter or fruitless bread puddings.

MAPLE SYRUP

6 ozs. brown sugar — ½ pint water
1 ozs. butter — 3 ozs. granulated sugar
1 teaspoon vanilla essence

Boil together brown sugar and water. Cook granulated sugar on a low flame until it melts and begins to colour. Add the brown sugar mixture, stirring until smooth and thick. Mix in butter and vanilla. This will keep in a screw top jar for a week, if chilled. It can also be served hot or cold and is especially good with pancakes.

APRICOT SAUCE

Crush apricot kernels and add to apricot jam or stewed apricots with water added if necessary to get suitable consistency.

BRANDY SAUCE

1¼ pints milk
2½ tablespoons sugar
2 tablespoons cornflour
2½ tablespoons brandy

Boil milk. Mix cornflour and sugar to a thin paste with a little cold milk; add this to hot milk, and cook over slow flame till thickened. Add brandy just before serving, or if you prefer use vanilla essence to taste.

BRANDY BUTTER

3 ozs. butter — 3 ozs. castor sugar
2-3 tablespoons brandy

Cream the butter until white. Beat in the sugar gradually. When thoroughly mixed, add the brandy, a few drops at a time, beating continuously. Add enough to flavour well, taking care towards the end that the mixture does not curdle. It should now look white and foamy. Pile up in a glass dish and leave to harden.

RUM BUTTER

3 ozs. butter
2½ ozs. rum approximately
Squeeze of lemon juice
3 ozs. soft brown sugar
Little grated lemon or orange rind

Cream the butter thoroughly. Beat the sugar in by degrees with the grated rind and lemon juice. Then add the rum to flavour well. Chill.

RUM SAUCE

1/3 cup sugar — ½ teaspoon cinnamon
Pinch salt — 1 cup boiling water
1 tablespoon butter
1 level tablespoon cornflour
1 tablespoon orange juice
1 tablespoon rum (or use all orange juice if preferred)

Mix sugar, cinnamon and cornflour in a saucepan then gradually stir in the boiling water, stirring all the time until blended. Cook over low heat for 5 minutes, still stirring, then add the butter, orange juice, rum and salt, and stir until butter is melted and well blended.

ORANGE BUTTER

¾ cup butter, softened; finely grated rind of 2 oranges; ¼ teaspoon of prepared French mustard; 2 teaspoons orange juice; ½ teaspoon salt; ½ teaspoon black pepper.

In a small bowl, cream the butter with a wooden spoon until it is soft. Beat in the orange rind, mustard, orange juice, salt and pepper. When the mixture is smooth and thoroughly combined, spoon it into a small earthenware pot or basin. Place the butter in the refrigerator and chill it for 30 minutes before serving. This savory orange butter may be served with fish or grilled meat, especially pork and lamb chops. Alternatively you can omit the mustard, salt and pepper and serve the butter spread on hot cinnamon toast for a snack treat.

WHISKY SAUCE

6 ozs. castor sugar; ¼ lb. melted butter; 2½ ozs. whisky; 3 tablespoons water; ¼ of well-beaten egg.

In a saucepan, cook sugar and water over moderately high heat, washing down undissolved sugar clinging to the sides with a brush dipped in cold water until sugar is completely dissolved. Stir in melted butter, quickly beat in egg and cook sauce over low heat stirring for 4 minutes or until slightly thickened. Stir in whisky.

Whipped cream sweetened with golden syrup and mixed with chopped toasted walnuts and a little ground ginger added goes well with apple or pumpkin pie.

PASTRIES AND PIES

William Howitt, writing from Melbourne, September 29, 1852
That which now requires twelve thousand sovereigns then was purchaseable for three thousand. The prices of all things are in proportion. Flour is now 36L. per ton, and is expected shortly to be 40L. Bread, the four pound loaf, is now 2s.; hay is 40L. per ton, actually more than sugar! Oats, 15s. per bushel; we have ten bushels in our cart, which cost us 4L. in London. All tools and the like, which we brought out with us, are 100L. per cent. higher, whilst long mining boots, for which we paid 1L. 15s., are here worth 9L. per pair. A. could sell his minie rifle for 30L.

Butter is 3s. per lb.; cabbages, 1s. each; cauliflowers, 2s.6d.; onions, 8d., per lb. B. Could sell his house and garden — a good house, it is true, with stables and green houses — for 12,000L.

SHORT CRUST

6 ozs. plain flour, salt,
6 ozs. cream cheese or 6 ozs. butter
2 ozs. bicarb. soda & cream of tartar
1 egg yolk, beaten
2 tablespoons cold water
squeeze lemon juice or teaspoon vinegar

Sift flour and salt. Rub in shortening, etc. Roll out. Cream cheese made from sour milk, gives a continental flavour.

HOW MUCH TO USE

When a recipe calls for 8 ozs. of pastry, this means the amount of pastry made with 8 ozs. of flour among the ingredients. The list below will help you assess the quantity of pastry you will need. The basic pastry recipe can be reduced or increased if necessary to suit the size of the pie you want to make. Be sure to reduce or increase all other ingredients in proportion.

Tart Plates:
- For 7 inch tart-plate use 6 ozs. of pastry
- For 8 inch or 9 inch tart-plate use 8 to 10 ozs. of pastry.

Double Crust Pies and Tarts:
- For 7 inch size, use 10 ozs. pastry
- For 8 inch or 9 inch size, use 12 to 14 ozs. pastry.

Small Tartlets.
- For 2 to 2½ dozen small tartlet-cases, use 10 to 12 ozs. pastry.

CREAM CHEESE APPLE PIE

4 ozs. plain flour — 4 ozs. butter
3 ozs. sugar — 2 lbs. apples (or less)
2 ozs. sultanas — 1 oz. currants
4 ozs. cottage cheese (made by setting sour milk and pouring off liquid when set)
2 tablespoons brandy (or any white wine, or water)
Juice and grated rind of ½ lemon
1 egg yolk beaten with 1 tablespoon water

Sift flour into bowl, chop in butter with a knife, then stir in cottage cheese. Press into a ball shape, but do not knead. Cover and chill for 3-4 hours.

Peel, core and quarter apples. Halve quarters if very large. Mix with wine, sugar, fruits and juice and rind of ½ lemon. Simmer very gently until apples are soft. Cool.

Roll pastry out on a floured board. Put in filling lengthwise. The filling must be cold. Moisten edge and fold over into roll. Pinch edges and put roll on a greased oven tray, join side down. Brush surface with egg and water and cook in a hot oven for 30 minutes. When cold cut in slices and serve with cream.

GOLDEN RABBIT PIE

Take a pair of rabbits, cut them into neat pieces and soak in salt and water for 1 hour. (Be sure to remove the tail bone to avoid the strong taste.)

Put in a saucepan with 2 onions, 1 or 2 carrots cut up, and a bunch of herbs; also a few rough pieces of bacon or any bacon rind you may have. Cover well with water and cook till tender, then take meat off the bones and put into a pie dish, removing the herbs and bacon rind if used. Keep hot.

Cover with the following: Cream 2 tablespoons of beef dripping with a pinch of salt, beat in 1 egg and add a cup of flour sifted with ½ teaspoon carbonate soda and 1 teaspoon cream of tartar. Use enough milk or water to make a batter that will spread easily over the hot rabbit. Bake 20 to 30 minutes in a moderate oven till the top is golden brown.

RABBIT AND PORK PIE

3 lbs. rabbit 1 lb. belly pork
1 dessertspoon salt ¼ teaspoon pepper
1¼ pints stock ½ cup gravy or stock
3 tablespoons chopped parsley

Cut and joint fresh rabbit. Soak ¾ hour in cold salted water. Cut rabbit into smaller pieces. Remove rind and cut up pork. Combine rabbit, pork, stock, salt and pepper. Simmer 1½ hours or until tender. Bring to boil. Thicken if necessary, check seasoning. Put meat into dishes, allow to cool. Roll out pastry a little larger than the dish. Cover meat with pastry and glaze. Bake in a hot oven ½-¾ hour until golden brown. Serve garnished with parsley. 10 persons.

If you are using lard or dripping instead of butter, remember you will need a little more salt than required in the recipe, to replace the salt contained in the butter.

COLONIAL CURD CAKE

Pastry

3 ozs. (3 tablespoons) soft butter
5 ozs. (1¼ cups) plain flour
2 ozs. sugar 1 egg yolk

Cream the butter and sugar. Mix in the egg yolk, then the flour. Butter the sides of an 8 inch tin. Line the base and sides with pastry.

Filling:

1 lb. cottage cheese 2 ozs. soft butter
2/3rd cup sugar 2 tablespoons milk
½ teaspoon vanilla essence
Grated rind of a lemon
3 large (or 4 medium) eggs
1½ tablespoons cornflour
3½ ozs. cream

Force the cheese through a sieve. Cream the butter with some of the sugar, the vanilla and the lemon rind. Add the remaining sugar and the milk and mix well. Beat in the yolks of the eggs with the cornflour, then the sieved cheese in alternate lots with the cream. Fold in the stiffly-beaten egg whites. Turn into pastry-lined tin.

Have oven hot. Bake curd cake until the top edge of pastry begins to brown (about 8 minutes). Immediately reduce heat to very moderate. Cook 40-50 minutes longer, or until nearly (but not quite) set in centre. Reduce heat. Leave in oven at least 15 minutes. Cool before removing from tin. Cover with whipped cream and sprinkle with nutmeg. Chill several hours (better still till next day) before serving.

CHERRY CUSTARD PIE

This is one of the loveliest custard pies. Overnight, steep 4 ozs. of glace cherries with 1 or 2 tablespoons of cherry brandy (you can also use plain brandy or rum). Only use plain flour for pastry and be sure the pie goes into a hot oven.

Take a tart plate with a 7 inch base and 8-9 inch diameter top. Line with shortcrust pastry rolled one-eighth inch thick. Allow enough margin for an upstanding fluted rim. Brush over base with a little unbeaten egg-white. Chill for 1½ hours. Then stand on an oven tray on the kitchen bench.

Drain cherries. Cut each in half. Lay them all over the "floor" of your pastry case. Make a custard by scalding one 8 ounce cup of milk and pouring it quickly into two eggs whisked up with one tablespoon of castor sugar and a pinch of salt. Stir well.

Pour over the cherries in case, letting the custard splash down gently over the bowl of a tablespoon to avoid disturbing the cherries. Lift tray with pie deftly into the oven.

Pastry:

6 ozs. of sifted plain flour and 3 ozs. of butter cut on a floured board to the size of green peas. Mix flour and fat. Add 4 tablespoons of cold water (approximately) sprinkling it in a spoonful at a time. Blend with a fork or knife. As soon as possible, gather dough together, form it into a "bolster" with gentle pressure. Fold in greased paper. Chill one hour. Roll out on lightly floured board with quick, springy touch.

Never stretch pastry when fitting into plate. Never prick the bottom of a custard pie shell. Use left-over pastry bits for patty shells.

ALMOND MERINGUE

4 ozs.ground almonds 2 ozs. flaked almonds
a little sugar egg yolk
vanilla

Make a paste of these. Roll out and bake in a flan case for 20 to 30 minutes. Let it cool, then fill it with fruit, or puree of fruit, so long as it is not too wet. Top with stiffly beaten egg white and cook in a cooler oven for another 10 minutes.

EGGNOG TART

4 tablespoons flour ½ cup sugar
2 cups milk 2 eggs (separated)
¼ teaspoon nutmeg Tart case
2 dessertspoons brandy or sherry

ALMOND DELIGHT

5 ozs. self raising flour
½ teaspoon lemon juice
The yolk of 1 egg
1 ozs. lard 2 ozs. butter

For the filling:

2 ozs. ground almonds
Almonds for decoration
4 tablespoonfuls mincemeat
2 eggs 2 ozs. castor sugar
2 ozs. butter Almond essence

Sieve the flour into a basin, add a pinch of salt, then lightly rub in the lard and butter. Beat the egg yolk, add the lemon juice and 1 tablespoonful of cold water; add gradually to the flour. Mix to a stiff paste, adding more water if required.

For the filling:

Cream the butter and sugar together, stir in the beaten eggs, ground almonds, almond essence: mix well.

Line a pie dish with the pastry; almost fill it with alternate layers of mincemeat, then spread the almond mixture on the top. Decorate with the almonds (blanched and halved), bake in a quick oven for ½ hour.

MANCHESTER TART

½ cup raspberry or strawberry jam
2 ozs. fine white breadcrumbs
Rind of a small lemon
4 ozs. puff pastry ½ pint milk
2 eggs 2 ozs. butter
1 oz. castor sugar 1 tablespoon brandy

Place breadcrumbs in a basin. Add lemon rind to cold milk and bring milk to boil. Pour milk and rind over crumbs and let stand for five minutes. Remove rind. Add butter, beaten yolks of eggs, sugar and brandy to crumb mixture. Line a fireproof pie dish with pastry and cover pastry with jam. Pour mixture over pastry and bake gently in moderate oven for about 45 minutes. Make a meringue with egg white and 2 ozs. castor sugar, pile on tart and brown in oven. Serve cold with cream.

YORKSHIRE CURD TART

8 ozs. shortcrust pastry
4 pints milk 4 junket tablets
½ cup sugar ¼ cup currants
2 eggs nutmeg

Roll pastry out thinly and line greased 8 inch pie plate. Pour milk into saucepan, heat until lukewarm, add junket tablets, which have been dissolved in a little cold water. Stir gently until curd forms, remove from heat, allow to cool. Strain to separate curds from whey. Combine curds, sugar, currants, and beaten eggs, mix well. Pour into pie shell, sprinkle with nutmeg. Bake in a moderately hot oven approximately 25 minutes.

THE SQUIRE'S CUSTARD TART

Pastry:

4 ozs. plain flour, ½ teaspoon baking powder, pinch salt, 2 ozs. butter, 1 tablespoon sugar, 1 egg yolk, 1 dessertspoon milk, vanilla essence.

Beat butter and sugar, add egg yolk, essence to taste, and milk, beating well. Stir in sifted dry ingredients, making a dry dough. Roll out on floured board, to fit a tart plate. Pinch frill around edge, brush base with little egg white.

Filling:

Beat together 1 cup of sugar, 1 tablespoon melted butter, ½ teaspoon lemon essence, 1 egg, and 2 tablespoons plain flour. Lastly, stir in 1 cup boiling water. Half a cup of currants may be added if desired. Pour into pastry case, bake in moderate oven for about half an hour, or until set and the base cooked. Dust top with nutmeg.

TREACLE (OR GOLDEN SYRUP) TART

Line a greased fireproof plate with shortcrust pastry, an old tart tin or enamel picnic plate is very suitable for this purpose. Crimp the pastry edges with a fork or with the fingers. Fill it to within an inch of the edge with a mixture in the proportion of 4 tablespoons of treacle (or golden syrup) to 1 teaspoon of lemon juice and 1 heaped tablespoon of fresh white breadcrumbs. A pinch of ground ginger or cinnamon may be added if liked. Arrange strips of pastry about ½ inch wide in a pattern across the top. Bake it for about 15 minutes in a fairly hot oven. It is sometimes served with whipped cream spiced with rum.

GOLDEN TART

Into a short crust flan, pour warmed golden syrup, to which dissolved butter, cream, grated lemon rind and beaten egg have been added. Cook in a moderate oven for half an hour.

ALMOND TART

4 ozs. butter 2 ozs. castor sugar

Cream, add beaten egg, then 1 oz. flour. Put aside for ½ hour. Cut 9 inch round.

Cream 4 ozs. butter with 4 ozs. sugar. Add 3 beaten eggs, then 3 ozs. ground almonds, 1 oz. plain flour and essence. Bake 45 minutes in moderate oven. When cool, if needed, add a topping of 2 ozs. icing sugar mixed with 2-3 tablespoons water. Top with browned almonds.

ANNIVERSARY MINCE PIE

Pastry:

1 cup butter, 2½ cups plain flour, 1/3rd cup water, 1 tablespoon white vinegar, sugar and water to glaze.

Rub butter into flour until mixture looks like breadcrumbs. Stir in water and vinegar. Knead lightly. Divide into two balls and chill for 20 minutes. Roll one ball to fit 8 inch pie plate or pie dish. Place cold mince filling in shell and roll out second ball to cover pie. Moisten the edge of crust and press well together. Glaze with water and sprinkle well with sugar. Bake in moderate oven for 30 minutes.

Colonial Mince:

½ lb. raisins ½ teaspoon cinnamon
½ lb. apples ½ cup white wine
¼ lb. currants ½ lb. brown sugar
½ teaspoon nutmeg ½ cup butter
2 ozs. of citron peel
½ teaspoon mixed spice
½ cup orange juice

Cut all fruit roughly. Combine with spices, wine, sugar and orange juice. Bring to a boil. Allow to simmer for half an hour. Stir occasionally and let get cold before using. Best made a few days before use.

MATRIMONY TART

Line a tin with short pastry. Partly stew 6 cooking apples with 1 teaspoon cinnamon, ½ cup brown sugar and 1/3 cup currants. Put into the lined tin. Cook for 20 minutes in fairly hot oven.

STRAWBERRY TART

9 inch tin 1 dessertspoon sugar
7 ozs. flour 1 teaspoon vanilla
4 ozs. butter 1 teaspoon lemon juice
1 egg yolk 3 teaspoons iced water

Sift flour and salt into bowl. Add butter and rub in until the mixture has the consistency of breadcrumbs. Mix yolk and water and blend into the flour with a round bladed knife until the mixture just holds together. Allow to rest for 10 minutes if possible. Roll out thinly and fit into tin. Prick bottom of tart. Trim edge and line inside with a layer of greased paper and sprinkle with dried peas. Cook in moderate oven for 1½-1¾ hours, reducing heat if necessary.

Filling:

1 pound strawberries
½ pint cream
1 tablespoon Kirsch
3 tablespoons red currant jelly
Squeeze lemon juice
1 dessertspoon sugar
1 tablespoon potato flour

Whip the cream and flavour with sugar and Kirsch. Cover bottom of cold tart case with whipped cream and arrange strawberries. Boil jelly adding a little lemon juice. Stir in the potato flour slaked in a little cold water. Boil for a minute and glaze with a brush while hot.

The friendly cow, all red and white
I love with all my heart
She gives me cream with all her might
To eat with apple tart.

R.L. Stevenson

YORKSHIRE PORK PIE

Pastry:

Melt 2 ozs. lard and 2 ozs. butter in about ¼ pint hot water. Boil it and remove the pan from the heat. Pour liquid into ¾ lb. of sifted flour. Mix it quickly in a warm place, adding an egg well beaten.

Mince 2 lbs. pork, adding salt and pepper and ½ teaspoonful of chopped sage (or grated nutmeg).

Line a greased 1 lb. cake tin with the pastry, leaving some for the lid. Fill it, cover as usual. Bake 2 hours in a pre-heated moderate oven. Have ready some good jellying stock, made if possible by boiling a pig's trotter with herbs and seasoning. Pour stock through the hole in the pie, when it is cooked. Leave it until quite cold, before turning it out of the tin.

SQUAB PIE

Take a pie dish and put at the bottom a layer of sliced apples. Strew over them a little sugar, then a layer of fresh mutton (well seasoned with salt and pepper). Then put another layer of apples. Peel some onions and slice them. Lay them on the apples, then a later of mutton, then apples and onions. Pour in a quantity of water. Cover all with a good crust and bake.

COLONIAL COTTAGE PIE

Place in a pie dish four to five cups of minced cold lamb or beef with 2 cups of minced assorted vegetables, such as carrots, onion and parsnip. Pour over gravy or stock to make a moist mixture.

Make a pancake batter by beating 1 egg slightly, add half a cup of milk, 1 tablespoon of melted butter and mix well.

Now add ¾ cup of sifted self-raising flour with a pinch of salt, beat till smooth. Pour batter over hash and bake in a hot oven about 25 minutes. You can tone up the hash if desired with a dash of your favourite sauce.

"A good dinner sharpens wit and softens the heart."

STANDING GAME PIE

Use a boiled pastry for the crust of this pie and work quickly while the paste is still warm. But first prepare the filling. As this is a way to use old birds I find it more satisfactory to cook the filling beforehand.

This time pluck and clean the birds and joint them. For a pie approximately 8 by 3 inches high, you will need three old grouse, 1 lb. of steak, and either a piece of bacon about half-an-inch thick, or three rashers. There is no hard and fast rule about what you use. After March you could substitute a partridge for ½ lb. of the steak, or a small rabbit at any time. At least ½ lb. of steak should be used to help the gravy and ¼ lb. of beast's kidney could be used for this purpose, too. But presuming that it is Summer and your rabbits have not been allowed to return, the quantities above are correct.

Cut the steak and bacon into pieces, dust them and the joints of grouse with a little flour and brown them lightly in butter in an enamelled cast-iron pan or casserole. Add a chopped shallot or two, the cleaned gizzards, the livers and the hearts, and a bouquet garni, using rosemary instead of thyme if you have it. Season with salt and black pepper and cover with water. Cook very slowly for two hours or more, depending on the toughness of the birds.

Lift the meats out of the gravy and take the grouse meat off the bones. Put the bones back into the stock and add a sherry glass of red wine. Boil briskly until it is reduced to half a pint. Sieve the stock into a basin and leave to set. If the stock jellies firmly, use it as it is; if it is a feeble jelly melt it down again and add ½ oz. of gelatine, previously soaked, then leave it to set once more.

Now make your boiled pastry and boil an egg hard at the same time.

¾ lb. plain flour, 6 ozs. lard, teacupful of water, salt.

Boil the lard and water together and mix into the flour and salt. You may think at first that you need more liquid, but you don't. Squeeze and work the paste together with the hands into a ball and roll out while still warm. This pastry is tricky to handle; it breaks easily, but is just as easily patched up, even after it is in the tin. Use plenty of flour on both pastry board and roller. Keep a third of pastry for a lid and line your tin with the rest. Make it as thin as possible and, I must repeat, don't worry about patching up any holes you make, for make some you surely will, but they will hardly show when the pie is baked. Leave the lining hanging half to three-quarters of an inch over the tin's edge.

Half fill the pie with the mixed meats (excluding the gizzard), put the hard boiled egg in the middle, then fill up with the rest of the meat. Cut the lid from the remaining pastry rather larger than the tin, damp the overhanging edge of pastry, press the two pastries together, and turn this double edge over on to the top of the pie, making a decorative surround. I use the thumb and forefinger of both hands, pushing outwards with the left hand and inwards with the right, making a form of fluting. Make two pastry leaves and a pastry rose; cut a hole in the centre of the pie and lay the rose lightly on top with a leaf at each side. Bake in a brisk oven for about 1½ hours. This pastry takes some time to colour and it is almost impossible to burn it. Put it on the floor of the oven for the last quarter of an hour to be sure that the bottom is well cooked. Allow the pie to become quite cold before pouring in the jelly.

Warm your jelly stock only enough to melt it. Leave it until it is just beginning to set again and then pour it through a small funnel into the hole under the rose. Tilt the pie gently from side to side and even press the meat down with a knife to make sure the jelly gets right through. Replace the rose and leave in a cold place. Take the pie from it's tin only after several hours. Decorate with any remaining jelly chopped up.

HAM AND APRICOT PIE

1 ham rasher 1 inch thick
½ lb. dried apricots
Pepper — 1 oz. sultanas
6 potatoes — A little gravy

Lightly brown the rasher on both sides in a frying-pan. Lay in a large pie-dish. Place apricots - which have been in water 12 hours previously - on top. Sprinkle a little pepper over, add the sultanas, pour a little gravy over, cover with sliced potatoes. Put a piece of greaseproof paper over all and bake in a moderate oven for 1 hour. Serve hot.

MUTTON PIE

Chop 8 mutton chops, put the meat in the dish in layers with 8 ozs. currants, 8 ozs. seedless raisins, 8 ozs. sultanas, 6 ozs. sugar, 3 ozs. chopped mixed peel, the juice of a large lemon. Add a seasoning of grated nutmeg, cinnamon, white pepper and a little salt to your taste. Add 1, 2 or more glasses of rum. Cover the top with puff pastry and bake the pie for an hour, in a hot oven for the first fifteen minutes to raise the pastry. Then reduce the heat to moderate for the remainder of the cooking time. Cover the pie with paper if it is getting too brown.

APPLE PIE KINGSLEY

Puff Paste — an 8 inch pie dish
Stewed apple — 4 ozs. creamed cheese
3 whole cloves — 3 slices of lemon peel
3 slices of orange peel

Roll out the paste to cover your pie dish, and let it stand 5 or 10 minutes till it shrinks. Spread it with a layer of stewed apple, then a layer of four ounces of creamed cheese, then another layer of apple, and finally top with puff paste rolled thinly. Crimp around the edge, make a hole in the centre and glaze with milk and sugar. Bake for 30-35 minutes in moderate oven.

GOLDEN MERINGUE PIE

One 8 inch crumb pastry case
grated rind of 2 lemons
1 cup sugar — 1 cup water
½ cup lemon juice — 2 egg yolks
4 tablespoons milk — 1 tablespoon butter
½ teaspoon nutmeg — ½ teaspoon cinnamon
¾ cup mashed cooked pumpkin
½ teaspoon ground cloves
2 tablespoons flour)
2 tablespoons cornflour)
both blended smoothly with a little extra water.

Meringue topping:
2 egg whites, pinch salt, ¾ tablespoons sugar, ½ teaspoon vanilla.

Place sugar, water, lemon juice and rind in saucepan. When nearly boiling, stir in blended cornflour and flour. Continue stirring while mixture simmers 2 or 3 minutes. Remove from heat. Fold in butter and then the egg-yolks beaten with milk. Add pumpkin and spices, fill into crumb case, allow to become quite cold. Prepare meringue: Beat egg-whites stiffly with salt, gradually add sugar, beat until sugar is dissolved. Add vanilla. Pile around top of tart. Place in slow oven to set and lightly brown meringue.

Crumb Pastry-case:

Crush ½ lb. plain sweet biscuit finely and mix with 3 tablespoons melted butter. Press into a greased 8 inch pie plate and chill until firm.

He that keeps nor crust nor crum,
Weary of all, shall want some.
Shakespeare

BA-TA-CLAN (ALMOND RUM TART)

Serves 12.

½ lb. blanched almonds
1 teaspoon vanilla essence
8 eggs — 1 cup rum
8 ozs. sugar — 4 ozs. butter
1 cup vanilla icing

Grate almonds finely and mix eggs in, one by one, kneading firmly to start with, later stirring with a wooden spoon. Add the sugar, vanilla essence, rum, butter and flour, stir till the batter is very smooth.

Butter a flat round cake tin, pour batter in and bake in a moderate oven for one hour. Ice after cooling with vanilla icing.

BUTTERSCOTCH PIE

1 baked pastry case of short or biscuit pastry
3 slightly rounded tablespoons cornflour
2 teaspoons caramelised sugar
Nuts or whipped cream for topping
1½ cups milk — ¾ cup brown sugar
1 oz. butter — ½ teaspoon vanilla

Blend the cornflour with a little milk. Combine the remaining milk with the sugar and bring to the boil. Pour on to the blended mixture and stir until smooth. Return to the saucepan and stir until boiling. Cook 2 minutes. Add the butter, caramel, and vanilla. Pour in to the cooked pastry case. Top with chopped nuts or nuts and cream.

PUFF PUMPKIN PIE

2 cups cooked and strained pumpkin
1¼ teaspoons ground ginger
¼ teaspoon ground cloves
¼ teaspoon ground nutmeg
1 cup milk 1 teaspoon vanilla
1 cup sugar 1 teaspoon salt
1¼ teaspoons cinnamon
3 egg whites, beaten
3 egg yolks, beaten
1 teaspoon vanilla

Mix the pumpkin and the milk, add the egg yolks. Mix the sugar, salt and spices and add to the above. Beat well. Add the vanilla, and fold in the egg whites. Pour into a previously prepared crust. Bake at 350° for 45 minutes. Serve immediately, while hot, like a souffle.

RHUBARB MERINGUE TART

One 8 or 9 inch cooked and cooled short-crust flan
3 cups diced fresh rhubarb
1 cup stewed apple pieces
1 to 2 tablespoons honey
1 dessertspoon arrowroot blended with a little extra water
½ cup sugar for meringue
2 tablespoons water
Squeeze lemon juice
2 egg whites

Place water and honey in saucepan, stir over low heat until mixed. Add rhubarb and lemon juice, cover with a tightly fitting lid, and simmer 8 to 10 minutes or until soft but not broken; strain liquid. Add blended arrowroot to liquid in saucepan, stir over heat until mixture boils and thickens. Fold in cooked rhubarb and apple. Fill into flan. Beat egg-whites stiffly, gradually add the ½ cup of sugar, and continue beating until meringue stands in peaks. Pile around edge of fruit filling; return to slow oven urtil meringue is set and lightly browned. Serve in wedges with whipped cream or boiled egg custard.

CHEESE AND RAISIN TARTS

4 ozs. pastry - either rough puff pastry or short pastry
2 ozs. grated cheese
1½ ozs. raisins or sultanas
2 ozs. diced cheddar cheese
¼ level teaspoon mixed spice
2 teaspoons golden syrup.

Roll out the pastry, sprinkle with the grated cheese, and lightly roll to press the cheese into the pastry. Cut into 8 circles to fit small pie tins, and cut 8 more circles for the tops of the tartlets. Line the tins, having the cheese-sprinkled part of the pastry uppermost. Prepare the filling by mixing all ingredients together, then divide between the eight tarts. Brush edges round with milk and seal the tops in place. Bake in a hot oven for 20 to 30 minutes. Serve hot with cream or custard as a pudding.

POTATO TART

4 ozs. cooked sieved potatoes
4 ozs. self-raising flour
1 oz. melted butter 1 tablespoon milk
½ lb. tomatoes, sliced 1 finely chopped onion
4 ozs. grated cheese
2 ozs. mushroom, sliced and cooked

Beat together potatoes, flour, salt and butter. Add flour and milk to form a stiff dough. Cut into an 8 inch round. Cook on greased frying pan.

Place on tart, grated cheese, sliced tomatoes, chopped onion, then arrange sliced mushrooms on top. Brown in hot oven. Serves four.

BREAD PUDDING

1 day-old pound loaf of bread, broken in pieces
1½ pints of milk 2 eggs lightly beaten
9 ozs. sugar 2½ ozs. raisins
1½ teaspoons vanilla 1½ tablespoons butter

In a bowl, soak the bread in milk until softened. Mix until smooth. Stir in eggs, sugar and raisins, butter and vanilla. Pour the mixture into a buttered baking tray (12 inches by 9 inches). Bake in a moderately slow oven for 2 hours or until well browned.

NOTES

You cannot make a silk purse out of a sow's ear.

SMALL CAKES AND BISCUITS

In 1841, one of the nameless heroines of Australia's pioneer days recounted her experiences on one of the first Victorian dairy farms (in the Buninyong territory, near the present site of Ballarat) for a London magazine. In her story, which was signed modestly "By a Lady", she recounts how the lack of butter was one of her greatest deprivations. But later, she was able to comment, "our dairy was a great comfort and saving to us, as we could use milk, prepared in many ways, instead of meat. The shepherds were very fond of it. We gave them no butter except on churning days, on which occasion I sent them some for tea, which was a great treat . . . "

As the herds increased, women throughout the settlement churned their own butter, made their own cheeses and prepared the soft white 'curd' which was identical with the commercially prepared cottage cheese we buy today. With this curd, and fresh butter and cream from their dairies, they baked tarts and pies — and magnificent cheesecakes.

BUNINYONG CHEESECAKES

Strain the whey from the curd of 2 quarts of milk; when rather dry, crumble it through a coarse sieve, and mix with 6 ozs. of butter, 1 oz. of pounded blanched almonds, a little orange-flower water, half a glass of raisin wine, a grated biscuit, 4 ozs. of currants, some nutmeg, powdered fine, and beat all with 3 eggs, and half a pint of cream till quite light; then fill the tins three parts full.

ALMOND TARTLETS

Pastry:

Cream of tartar and Bicarbonate of soda
2 tablespoons icing sugar
3 ozs. butter 1 egg yolk

Sift dry ingredients together. Rub in butter and mix to a soft dough with egg yolk. Roll out to ⅛ inch thickness and cut into small shells. Add ½ teaspoon jam to each and 1 teaspoon of filling. Top with half blanched almond or cherry and bake in moderate oven for 25-30 minutes.

Filling:

1 egg white, 1 cup finely chopped almonds, ½ cup sugar. Beat egg white slightly, add almonds and sugar, mix well.

SAND TARTS

Take one cupful of breadcrumbs, two tablespoonfuls of sugar, one tablespoonful of butter, juice and rind of two lemons, three eggs. Put butter in bottom of pie-dish, put breadcrumbs in and put a little water over them, add yolks beaten, the grated rind and juice of the lemons, sugar, and stir well together and bake until set. Then add the whites of eggs well beaten with two tablespoonfuls of sugar, and brown.

Evil minds Change good to their own nature.
Shelley

CLOVE CAKES

Beat 6 eggs with 2 teaspoons of rose-water, ½ oz. of cloves, ¼ lb. sugar, 1 lb. sifted flour. Make into thin paste, divide into cakes. Bake them in white paper.

ANISE ROLLS

Cream three whole eggs with the weight of 3 eggs of sugar with lemon flavour until fluffy. Add the weight of two eggs of ordinary flour. Prepare your trays with beeswax and put the mixture with a teaspoon thinly in the shape of a circle, about 2½ inches diameter on the tray. Sprinkle a few aniseeds on each. Bake in a low oven until slightly golden, remove from tray and roll while still hot over the handle of a thick wooden spoon. You have to work pretty fast because they break as soon as they get cold and cannot be twisted any longer.

MINERS CRACKNELS

6 tablespoons flour 1 oz. butter
1 dessertspoon castor sugar 2 eggs

Cream butter and sugar, work in flour and beaten eggs. Work into balls, flatten slightly and drop into cold water for a few minutes.

Drain off water carefully, and when dry prick them, then bake in a moderate oven until golden brown.

WASH DAY BUNS

1 lb. flour, 3 ozs. clarified fat, 6 ozs. sugar, 2 to 4 ozs. currants, pinch of salt, 1 teaspoon baking powder.

Sift flour, salt and rising, add dry ingredients and mix into a limp dough with water. Put in pieces on to a greased tray and bake in a moderate oven 10-15 minutes. These must be eaten fresh.

JOHNNY CAKES

3 lbs. of flour   1 teaspoon salt
3 teaspoons cream of tartar
½ oz. bicarbonate soda
water.

Mix all together into a light dough. Knead for a few minutes. Make rounds and pat thinly. Sprinkle with flour to prevent sticking. Cook on top of hot coals. Turn after 2 minutes. When cooked, eat with butter or honey or a slice of meat.

BUSHMAN'S BROWNIE

4 cups plain flour   ½ teaspoon cinnamon
8 ozs. butter   1 cup raisins
1 cup sugar   1 cup currants
½ teaspoon cream of tartar
½ teaspoon bicarbonate of soda
½ teaspoon mixed spice
1 cup milk

Sift flour, spice and cinnamon and rub in the butter. Add the fruit, sugar and milk alternately. Bake in a 9 inch cake tin in moderate oven for 1½ hours.

TUCKER BOX BISCUITS

1 cup rolled oats, 1 cup plain flour, 1 cup sugar, ¾ cup coconut, 2 tablespoons powdered milk, 1 tablespoon golden syrup, 4 ozs. butter, 1½ teaspoons bicarbonate soda, 2 tablespoons of boiling water.

Combine rolled oats, sifted flour, sugar, coconut, and powdered milk. In saucepan melt butter and golden syrup, and combined bicarbonate of soda and boiling water. Pour over dry ingredients; mix well. Place heaped teaspoonfuls of mixture on greased oven trays. Bake in moderate oven for 12 to 15 minutes. Makes approximately 2½ dozen.

We may live without poetry, music and art
We may live without conscience, and live without heart
We may live without friends, we may live without books;
But civilized man cannot live without cooks.
Meredith

VANILLA SLICES

¼ lb. rough puff pastry, ½ pint milk, 3 tablespoons of cornflour, 2 tablespoons sugar, 1 teaspoon butter, 1 egg, vanilla, soft icing, chopped nuts.

To make the filling: Blend cornflour and sugar with the milk. Bring to the boil and boil 2 minutes. Cool, add beaten egg. Re-heat but do not boil. When cold add vanilla essence. Roll pastry into a square about ½ inch thick. Trim edges, mark top into squares with the knife. Bake in a hot oven 15 minutes. Separate the squares and split each one into half. Spread one half with slightly warm custard mixture. Cover with second piece of pastry. When quite cold, ice with soft icing and sprinkle with nuts.

DATE SLICES

2¾ cups self-raising flour
½ cup castor sugar
4 ozs. butter   1 tablespoon milk
1 egg   Pinch salt

Filling:

1 dessertspoon lemon juice
1 lb. chopped dates   2 tablespoons water
4 ozs. butter

Cream butter and sugar together, add egg and milk and beat well. Sift together flour and salt, stir into creamed mixture. Turn out on to lightly floured board, knead lightly, and divide dough into two. Roll out half to fit 11 in. x 7 in. lamington tin, cover with filling; roll out remaining half of pastry and place on top. Prick lightly with a fork. Bake in moderate oven 30 to 35 minutes. Allow to cool, then ice with lemon flavoured icing, sprinkle with coconut. Cut into slices.

Filling:

Place all ingredients in saucepan over medium heat; cook, stirring, until ingredients are well blended and dates are soft. Allow to cool slightly before using.

DATE AND NUT SQUARES

2 eggs   ½ cup sugar
½ teaspoon vanilla   ¾ cup self-raising flour
½ teaspoon salt   ½ teaspoon cinnamon
1 cup walnuts, chopped
2 cups finely chopped dates or raisins

Beat eggs until foamy. Beat in sugar and vanilla. Stir dry ingredients together and stir into egg-sugar mixture. Mix in dates and nuts. Spread in well-greased biscuit slice tray. Bake until top has a dull crust. Cut into squares while still warm. Bake in a slow oven for 25 to 30 minutes. Makes about 16 two-inch squares.

PARKIN

4 level tablespoons golden syrup
4 level tablespoons black treacle
3 ozs. soft brown sugar (dark)
8 ozs. butter
8 ozs. fine or medium oatmeal
8 ozs. plain flour
2 level teaspoons bicarbonate soda
¼ pint milk
2 level teaspoons ground ginger
1 level teaspoon salt

Prepare a cool oven. Brush an 11" x 7" and 1½ inches deep cake tin with melted fat or oil. Line base and sides with greased paper.

Measure golden syrup and treacle carefully, levelling off spoon with a knife and making sure there is none on underside of spoon. Place in a medium sized saucepan with sugar, butter and milk. Heat gently until butter has melted, stirring occasionally. Remove from heat.

Sift flour, ginger, bicarbonate of soda and salt in a bowl. Add oatmeal and melted mixture and mix together with a wooden spoon. Beat until smooth.

Pour mixture into tin, bake in centre of oven for 40-45 minutes. Test by pressing with fingers. If cooked cake should spring back and have begun to shrink from sides of tin; cake will have a shrunken appearance. Leave to cool in tin for 10 minutes. Turn out, remove paper, and leave to cool completely on a wire rack. When Parkin is cold, cut into squares. Parkin improves with keeping; store in a tin for up to 4 weeks.

HOMEMADE BAKING POWDER

Take ½ lb. ground rice, ¼ lb. carbonate of soda, 2 ozs. tartaric acid, 1 oz. cream of tartar. Mix all thoroughly, then rub through wire sieve twice. Three teaspoonfuls of this are required to 1 lb. of flour.

Buttermilk was a much used ingredient in early settler's cookery.

ANCHOVY BISCUITS

2 ozs. self-raising flour
2 tablespoon butter
1 egg yolk
1 dessertspoon anchovy sauce
1 dessertspoon cold water
Squeeze lemon juice, cayenne, and egg yolk for glazing.

Sift flour with a pinch of cayenne into a bowl. Rub in butter lightly. Mix egg yolk with lemon juice, anchovy and water. Add just enough of this liquid to the flour mixture to form a firm paste. Roll out thinly on a lightly floured board and stamp out small rounds. Glaze with egg yolk, and bake on a greased slide in a moderate oven for 8 to 10 minutes.

CARAMEL BISCUITS

1 lb. butter — ¼ cup milk
1¼ lbs. sugar — 2 lbs. flour
2 tablespoons golden syrup
¾ teaspoon salt
½ teaspoon bicarbonate of soda

Melt butter in double saucepan. Add milk, sugar, golden syrup and bring to boiling point. Add soda, then salt and lastly sifted flour. Place 1½ ozs. of mixture on cold greased tray and flatten. Bake in moderate oven 15-20 minutes. 4 dozen.

WALNUT BISCUITS

½ lb. butter, ½ lb. sugar, 1 egg,
Cream of tartar and bicarbonate of soda
½ teaspoon almond essence.

Cream butter and sugar, add egg and essence, then flour. Drop per teaspoon on cold buttered slide and flatten with half walnut (or almond). Bake in moderate oven. These will keep for weeks in an airtight tin.

HOMEMADE SELF-RAISING FLOUR
as used in colonial kitchens

Take 10 lbs. of flour, 4 ozs. cream of tartar, 2 ozs. of carbonate of soda, one teaspoonful of tartaric acid. Mix all thoroughly and pass through a sieve twice.

MELTING MOMENTS

6 ozs. butter — 3 ozs. icing sugar
6 ozs. plain flour — 2 ozs. cornflour

Cream butter and sugar. Add sifted flour and work into firm paste. Force through star or desired shape. Bake in moderate oven about 20 minutes or until light brown.

Evil minds change good to their own nature.
Shelley

GINGER FAIRLINGS

4 ozs. butter, 2 level tablespoons Golden Syrup, a pinch of salt and a pinch of carbonate of soda, 1 heaped teaspoon Ground Ginger, 3 ozs. Castor Sugar.

Melt the butter and golden syrup in a saucepan over a gentle heat. Sieve the dry ingredients and add these to the melted mixture and mix well. Put rounded teaspoonfuls on greased trays, leaving a good space between each as the mixture will spread during cooking. Bake the fairlings on the shelf above the centre of a moderately hot oven for 12 to 15 minutes. When the biscuits are cooked, leave them on the trays to cool slightly before transferring to a rack to get cold. This recipe makes 25 Fairlings.

GINGER CREAMS

¼ lb. butter ½ cup sugar
1 egg 1 teaspoon treacle
1½ teaspoons ginger ½ teaspoon spice
½ teaspoon carbonate of soda

Cream butter and sugar. Add egg, treacle and then dry ingredients. Teaspoonful on greased slide and cook in moderate oven. Join together with butter icing.

OATMEAL CRUNCHIES

¾ cup butter ½ teaspoon salt
1½ cups sugar 2 eggs
1½ teaspoons vanilla
1¼ cups plain flour sifted
1 teaspoon bicarbonate of soda
1/3 cup evaporated milk
2 cups rolled oats
1 cup chopped nuts
Quartered glace cherries

Cream butter with sugar until light and fluffy. Beat in egg and vanilla. Sift dry ingredients together. Add the dry ingredients alternately with milk. Add oats, coconut and nuts. Mix well. Chill at least two hours. Place in teaspoonfuls on greased trays, top with a piece of cherry. Bake in a moderate oven for 8-10 minutes or until golden brown. Remove from the trays immediately. Cool.

DOG BISCUITS

To make dog biscuits, take equal parts bran and pollard, ten per cent each meatmeal, bone meal and milk, mix 2 eggs with each batch and add a small quantity of molasses to the water used for mixing the bran. Keep the mixture light and porous, divide into squares and bake in shallow trays. Raw meat may be used instead of meatmeal if desired.

SPICY ROCK CAKES

½ lb. butter 4 eggs
½ teaspoon salt 2 ozs. peel
14 ozs. sugar
14 ozs. approximately milk
½ lb. sultanas and currants mixed
¾ teaspoon lemon essence
2½ teaspoons cinnamon
1½ teaspoons mixed spice
1 lb. self-raising flour

Cream butter and sugar. Add beaten eggs and essence. Add sifted dry ingredients and fruit alternately with milk to form a stiff dough. Put into 1½ oz. portions on to greased trays. Bake in hot oven 10 to 15 minutes or until golden brown.

For wilful waste makes woeful want,
And I may live to say,
Oh! how I wish I had the bread
That once I threw away!
Unknown, The Crust of Bread

MISTLETOE MINCIES

Orange Pastry:

3 ozs. butter 2 ozs. sugar
Pinch salt 1 egg yolk
3 ozs. plain flour 1 oz. cornflour
1 dessertspoon water
1 teaspoon grated orange rind
½ teaspoon vanilla essence
2 ozs. self-raising flour
1½ cups prepared fruit mince, flavoured with 4 teaspoons brandy.

Cream together butter and sugar until light and fluffy. Add the orange rind, egg yolk, water and vanilla, and beat well. Sift together the dry ingredients and blend into the mixture, making a firm dough. Knead lightly and chill for about an hour. This pastry may be made the day before required.

Roll out the pastry thinly to line tartlet or patty tin trays. Trim the edges. Fill with a quantity of fruit mince. Roll out any remaining pastry and cut into shapes such as stars, bells, Christmas trees. Arrange over fruit mince. Place in a hot oven and bake for 10 minutes, reduce the heat to moderate, and bake a further 20 minutes until the pastry is golden and cooked through. If liked, dust lightly with sifted icing sugar.

APPLE GINGERBREAD

½ lb. butter — ½ cup brown sugar
2 eggs — ½ cup treacle
1½ cups plain flour — Pinch salt
½ cup grated apple — ½ cup water
½ cup self-raising flour
1½ teaspoons bicarbonate of soda
1½ tablespoons ground ginger
3 teaspoons cinnamon

Cream together butter and sugar, add eggs one at a time, beating well after each addition. Stir in treacle. Sift together dry ingredients 3 times, fold into creamed mixture. Fold in grated apple and lastly, the hot water. Turn mixture into greased 7 x 11 inch tin. Bake in moderate oven 35 to 40 minutes or until cooked when tested.

Ice with lemon icing when cold.

FEATHERY SHORTBREADS

Beat ½ lb. unsalted butter until white, then gradually add 4 ozs. castor sugar, beating constantly for about 5 minutes or until the mixture becomes a smooth cream. Stir in slowly 10 ozs. plain flour, sifted, and knead by hand. No liquid is added. Add more flour if the dough is too soft.

Divide into walnut-sized balls, flatten one side to put on baking tray, a little distance apart, because they will spread. Put blanched almond on top of each. Bake in slow oven for 20 or more minutes.

Another way is to use a clove instead of an almond. Sprinkle with icing sugar and rosewater while still hot after removing from the oven, then repeating when cold. Leave the cakes plain or add vanilla before cooking.

ABERDEEN SHORTBREAD

Cream 4 ozs. sugar and 8 ozs. butter, then gradually work in 12 ozs. plain flour. Roll the dough out about ⅛ inch thick. Cut it in circles with the aid of a wineglass. Prick the discs and bake them on a buttered tray in a moderate oven for about 15 minutes.

ECONOMICAL SHORTBREAD

4 ozs. plain flour — 2 or 3 ozs. butter
1 oz. castor sugar — Squeeze of lemon juice
Scrape of lemon peel.

Sift flour, add sugar, lemon juice and peel. Work in butter till all in one lump. Turn on to board, flatten out to 1 inch thickness. Form into circle and shape edge with fork. Prick all over with fork, cut across in triangular pieces, place on cold oven slide and cook in cool oven ¼ hour.

BROWNIES

3 ozs. plain flour — 2 ozs. cocoa
Pinch salt — 2½ ozs. butter
6 ozs. castor sugar — ½ teaspoon vanilla
½ teaspoon baking powder
2 eggs (not too large)
about 1¼ ozs. nuts (almonds and walnuts)

Sift the flour, salt, baking powder, sugar and cocoa into a bowl. Melt the butter and add to the mixture. Add the vanilla, eggs and chopped nuts and mix well. Spoon into a greased lined tin (7½ x 7½ x 1¼ inches) and bake in a moderate oven for 30 minutes.

When cool, spread with peppermint icing and when set, cut into squares.

HOKEY POKEY BISCUITS

4 ozs. butter — 1 small cup sugar
1 dessertspoon milk — 1 large cup plain flour
1 dessertspoon golden syrup
1 teaspoon bicarbonate of soda

Cream butter and sugar together. Warm milk and golden syrup, then add the bicarbonate of soda. Add this to the creamed mixture, then add flour. Spoon into balls and place on oven tray, then bake for 30 minutes in a slow oven.

One may not doubt that, somehow Good
Shall come of Water and of Mud;
And sure, the reverent eye must see
A purpose in Liquidity.

Rupert Brooke

ECONOMY MIXTURE FOR THREE ITEMS

2 tablespoons butter — ½ cup sugar
1 egg — 1 tablespoon milk
½ cup self-raising flour

Cream the butter and sugar, break in the egg, add milk and mix well. Sift the flour into the mixture and stir lightly. Flavour portion of the mixture and make 8 small cakes in patty tins.

To the rest of the mixture, add a tablespoon of cornflour and 3 tablespoons of plain flour. Take half, roll thinly on a well floured board.

Cut out 16 little tarts, pricking the centres with a fork to stop bulging.

To the remainder of the mixture add a few drops of vanilla and a tablespoon of finely chopped walnuts. After mixing, roll thinly and cut into fingers. This makes 16 biscuits. Bake in a moderate oven.

MOLASSES CRINKLES

A biscuit with a crackled sugar topping.

¾ cup soft shortening 1 egg
2¼ cups sifted flour ¼ teaspoon salt
1 teaspoon cinnamon ¼ cup molasses
½ teaspoon cloves
1 teaspoon ginger
1 cup brown sugar (packed)
2 teaspoons bicarbonate of soda

Mix shortening, sugar, egg and molasses thoroughly. Sift together remaining ingredients and stir in. Chill dough, then roll into balls the size of a large walnut. Dip tops in sugar. Place sugared side up, a little apart on greased baking tray. Sprinkle each with 2 or 3 drops of water to produce a crackled surface. Bake for 10-12 minutes or until set but not hard. Makes 4 dozen.

OLD ENGLISH EASTER CAKES

¼ lb. plain flour 6 ozs. currants
1 egg 8 ozs. sugar
1 tablespoon milk Nutmeg and cinnamon
8 ozs. shortening Lemon essence
Cream of tartar and bicarbonate of soda

Cream the shortening and sugar, add sifted flour and spices. Knead well. Roll out to ¼ inch thickness and cut with 2 inch fluted cutter. Glaze with milk and sprinkle with sugar. Bake in hot oven until golden brown. The cakes may be piped with a cross when cold.

QUEEN OF HEARTS TARTS

½ lb. sweet shortcrust pastry
½ cup chopped walnuts
1 cup chopped raisins
½ teaspoon vanilla essence
1/3 cup of butter ½ cup brown sugar
1 egg Pinch salt

Roll out the pastry and cut into rounds to fit shallow patty moulds. Dissolve butter, sugar, over gentle heat, and remove to cool. Beat the egg and add to sugar mixture. Add walnuts, raisins, salt, vanilla essence. Spoon a quantity of the mixture into pastry shells and bake in moderate oven for about 15 minutes. When cold, decorate centre of tarts with a little icing and a piece of cherry.

SOVEREIGNS

2 egg whites ½ lb. icing sugar
½ lb. chopped walnuts
1 teaspoon vanilla essence
Rum-moistened icing sugar

Beat egg whites until stiff. Lightly fold in sugar, walnuts and vanilla essence. Divide into 4 or 5 equal portions. Shape each into a roll about ¾ inch across. Chill thoroughly until stiff enough to slice without breaking. With a very sharp knife cut into slices about ½ inch thick. Bake a little apart on a greased tray in a moderate oven for about ¼ hour. Spread with icing sugar, moistened with rum. Sprinkle with chopped blanched nuts.

WELSH CAKES

6 ozs. flour 2 ozs. fat
1 oz. sugar 1 egg
Pinch salt
1 tablespoon golden syrup
A few currants or sultanas
1 tablespoon marmalade
½ teaspoon bicarbonate of soda
Milk, or milk and water, to mix

Beat fat, sugar, syrup, marmalade and egg until light and frothy, then gradually add flour and liquid until mixture is stiff enough to roll out. Roll out to ¼ inch in thickness, stamp into rounds and cook on a griddle over any heat. When one side is delicate brown, turn over and brown other side. Make the griddle moderately hot before cooking cakes, or put on a greased tray and cook as little cakes in oven.

CREAM PUFFS

Take ¼ lb. flour, ½ lb. butter, four egs, and one cup of water. Put water and butter in saucepan and bring to the boil. Stir in the flour and boil two minutes, turn into dish and leave to cool; add eggs one at a time. Beat well. Put teaspoonfuls on buttered paper and bake 30 minutes in hot oven.

HONEY DROPS

¼ cup shortening (butter, dripping, lard)
6 tablespoons sugar
½ cup strained honey
½ teaspoon baking soda
⅜ teaspoon cinnamon
½ teaspoon vanilla extract
2 cups sifted flour 1 egg
¼ cup blanched almonds, split
⅛ teaspoon nutmeg
1 teaspoon baking powder

Cream shortening, then add 4 tablespoons of sugar and blend: beat the egg with the honey and vanilla and add to the sugar mixture. Mix well.

Sift the flour, salt, soda, nutmeg, baking powder and ⅛ teaspoon cinnamon together and add to the sugar mixture. Mix well. Drop by level teaspoons on to greased slide and sprinkle with remaining 2 tablespoons of sugar mixed with remaining ¼ teaspoon of cinnamon. Bake in moderately hot oven 10 to 12 minutes.

WALNUT SHORTIES

1 egg — Chopped walnuts
4 ozs. butter — 8 ozs. plain flour
4 ozs. sugar — Lemon essence

Sift flour and 1 teaspoon baking powder. Make hole in centre and add rest of ingredients. Mix together with rest of ingredients to form a stiff dough. Knead on a floured board. Roll out thinly. Press walnut pieces on top of each biscuit. Bake in moderate oven for 10-15 minutes.

COME AGAIN BISCUITS

1 tablespoon butter, ½ cup sugar, 1 egg
Cream of tartar and bicarbonate of soda
vanilla

Cream the butter and sugar, add beaten egg, then sifted flour and vanilla. Roll out on floured board and cut in shapes. Decorate each with a chopped nut. Bake in a moderate oven.

ALMOND APRICOT BISCUITS

2 ozs. butter or substitute
¼ cup icing sugar
4 ozs. ground almonds
1½ cups plain flour
¼ cup apricot jam
extra icing sugar
1 egg

Cream butter, add sifted icing sugar, beat well until mixture is light and creamy. Add egg, beat well. Fold in sifted flour alternately with ground almonds to form a firm dough.

Roll out between 2 sheets of greaseproof paper to ¼ inch thickness. Cut into fingers 1 x 3 inches. Put on lightly greased baking tray.

Bake in moderate oven 10 to 12 minutes or until pale golden brown. Cool on trays. Join together with apricot jam and dust tops with sifted icing sugar.

LACY ROLLS

½ cup molasses — ½ cup dripping
1 teaspoon ginger — 1 cup sifted flour
⅛ teaspoon salt
2/3 cup granulated sugar

Heat molasses to boiling point. Add the margarine and stir well. Mix and sift the dry ingredients and add slowly to the first mixture, stirring constantly. Drop by ½ teaspoonfuls about 3 inches apart on a greased baking sheet. Bake in a moderate oven until golden brown (about 8 to 10 minutes). Allow the biscuits to cool slightly, then remove with a spatulate knife and wrap each biscuit quickly around the handle of a wooden spoon into a roll, then remove. If biscuits cool too much for rolling, return to oven for a minute to soften.

BUSTERS

12 ozs. plain flour — 4 ozs. soft butter
10 ozs. grated cheese — A little very cold water
½ teaspoon Cayenne Pepper
2 teaspoon Baking Powder

Sift flour and baking powder into a bowl. Rub butter into it. Add cheese and cayenne pepper. Add approximately 2 tablespoons water to bind the mixture. Place on a floury board. Roll until ¼ inch thick and cut into 2 inch squares. Place on a well-buttered baking sheet. Prick all over. Cook in a hot oven for 15 to 18 minutes until lightly coloured.

BEES IN AMBER

1 cup self raising flour
½ cup sugar — 1 tablespoon butter
3 eggs — 1 tablespoon honey
Small teaspoon salt — 2 tablespoons milk

Line two sandwich tins with paper. Combine butter, honey and milk in small saucepan and heat gently on stove. Sift flour and salt. Beat eggs well, gradually add sugar, and beat till light and creamy. Fold in flour and lightly stir in hot mixture. Pour into tins and bake in moderate oven about 25 to 30 minutes. Cool. Fill centre with unsweetened whipped cream.

Amber topping:

¾ cup honey — 10 almonds
1 oz. butter — Cherry
3 or 4 walnuts

Bring butter and honey to boil and cook slowly about 8 minutes, or until reaches very soft ball stage when dropped into cold water. Partly cool and pour half of above mixture over cake. Decorate top of cake with flower made with cherry centre and split almond petals. Arrange flight of bees in formation over the top of the cake heading for the flower. Use ¼ walnut for each. Use ¼ walnut for each bee body and a split almond for wings. Then pour over the bees the remainder of the amber topping. Cut with hot knife. (Note: better if eaten on day it is made.)

DATE AND GINGER STICKS

3 tablespoons chopped crystallised ginger
½ cup chopped dates
3 ozs. melted chocolate

Put ginger and dates through fine mincer. Shape into sticks approximately 2 inches in length and ¼ inch wide; coat each in melted chocolate. Place on wire rack or oiled baking sheet and leave in cool place to set. Makes approximately 1½ dozen.

PETTICOAT TAILS

Make up a batch of shortbread mixture and roll out into a square block, quite ¾ inch thick. Roll out another block same size, only about 1/3rd inch thick.

Prepare the following mixture:

2 tablespoons raisins (cut up), 2 tablespoons currants, 1 piece of candied peel (shredded very finely), 1 dessertspoon lemon juice, 3 dessertspoons sugar, 1 dessertspoon flour, 1 teaspoon cinnamon, ½ teaspoon spice, ½ teaspoon nutmeg (grated), all blended together.

Now spread on top of thick block, damp it round the edge, place thinner piece on top. Roll it lightly over with rolling-pin to joint it, and bake rather slowly in moderately hot oven for 15 minutes, then very slowly for another 30 minutes. Ten minutes after it leaves the oven (when still warm) cut into small block or finger lengths.

MAIDS OF HONOUR

Beat 1 lb. sugar with yolks of 12 eggs, 1 oz. sweet almond meal, 12 bitter almonds, 4 tablespoons orange, flour and water. Add almonds last. Bake in moderate oven.

ALMOND SHORTBREAD

8 ozs. butter — ¼ cup icing sugar
1 egg yolk — Whole cloves
3 cups self-raising flour
½ teaspoon baking powder
½ cup chopped almonds
1 tablespoon whisky
Extra icing sugar

Soften butter, beat well, add sifted icing sugar, beat until fluffy and light in colour. Add egg yolk, beat thoroughly. Sift flour and baking powder, mix into butter mixture. Add chopped almonds. Sprinkle dough lightly with whisky, knead thoroughly. Roll out dough to ¼ inch thickness, cut into diamond shapes or roll into balls and centre each with a whole clove.

Place on oven trays, bake in a moderate oven approximately 20 minutes. Sprinkle generously with icing sugar while still hot. Makes approximately 4 dozen.

FRUIT SLICE

Pastry:

½ lb. self-raising flour, ¼ lb. butter, 1 teaspoon sugar, a little water to mix.

Filling:

½ lb. currants, 2 large apples, ½ cup sugar, little water.

Rub butter into flour until it looks like breadcrumbs, add sugar and mix with water to a stiff dough. Roll out three times. Put filling ingredients into saucepan and cook until apples are soft. Cool. Cover slide with butter paper. Roll out half pastry to fit slide, add filling. Roll out second half of pastry, prick with fork. Brush over with egg. Cook in moderate oven 30 minutes. While cake is still warm, sprinkle with castor sugar. When cold cut into squares.

CLOUD BIKKIES

1 lb. butter — 1 egg yolk
½ cup sugar — 1 teaspoon vanilla
Whole cloves — 4¾ cups sifted flour

Cream butter until soft and fluffy, beat in egg yolk well, add sugar and vanilla, then flour. Dough should be heavy and slightly moist, but not sticky. Shape dough into balls about the size of a walnut, decorate with clove. Bake on ungreased slide in slow oven for 15-20 minutes. When cool, roll in icing sugar. Makes 7 to 8 dozen.

Animals feed, man eats,
There is no one who does not eat and drink,
But few there are who can appreciate flavour.
Confucious

SHERRY DROPS

¼ lb. castor sugar — ½ lb. butter
1 grated lemon rind — ½ lb. flour
2 egg yolks — Pinch of salt
½ teaspoon baking powder
3 dessertspoons sherry

Beat butter to a cream. Gradually beat in sugar and beat till fluffy. Stir in lemon rind, then the egg yolks, one at a time. Very slowly stir in the sherry. Sift flour with baking powder and salt, and stir into egg mixture. Drop the mixture in small mounds on to a well-greased baking sheet and bake in a moderate oven for 15 to 20 minutes. Leave on baking sheet until cold, then remove and pair with jam or whipped cream. Place a glace cherry or a walnut on the centre of each.

BANBURY CAKES

(Recipe 140 years old)

1 cup currants — 1 tablespoon sugar
½ teaspoon spice or ground ginger
1 teaspoon butter melted

Mix all together. Cut out rounds of puff pastry. Place mixture on each round. Fold over. Pinch together, turn over and roll out flat. Cut with pointed knife across. Sift icing sugar over and bake on hot slide until a nice brown.

LEMON CREAM BISCUITS

4 ozs. butter — 2 cups flour
½ cup castor sugar — Pinch salt
1 egg
1 teaspoon baking powder
Finely grated rind 1 lemon

Lemon filling:
1½ cups icing sugar
1 dessertspoon butter
2 tablespoons lemon juice

Cream butter, add sugar, beat until creamy; add egg and lemon rind, beat well. Sift flour with salt and baking powder, add to creamed mixture, mixing well. Take small teaspoonfuls, roll into balls and place on greased baking slide a small distance apart. Flatten biscuits with the end of a glass dipped in flour. Bake in moderate oven until pale golden. When cool, sandwich together in pairs with filling.

Filling:

Melt butter over gentle heat. Add to sifted icing sugar, together with lemon juice. Add few drops boiling water, if necessary, to give fairly firm mixture. If desired, add a few drops yellow food colouring to tint filling pale yellow.

LEMON BISCUIT RING

4 ozs. flour — Pinch salt
3 ozs. butter — 1 egg yolk
2 ozs. castor sugar — 1 teaspoon lemon juice

Rub butter into flour with fingertips until mixture is like fine breadcrumbs; add beaten egg yolk, sugar, salt, lemon juice. Mix well; knead lightly with the fingers until smooth. With piping bag and ½ inch star tube pipe mixture on to greased baking tray in small rings. Bake in moderate oven approximately 12 minutes or until biscuits just begin to tinge with gold.

GOLDEN APRICOT BARS

Base:
¾ cup flour — 1/3 cup sugar
½ cup cornflour — ½ cup rolled oats
Pinch salt — ½ cup butter

Topping:
1 cup dried apricots — 1 cup brown sugar
½ cup sifted flour — ¼ teaspoon salt
2 eggs (well beaten) — 1¼ cups coconut
1 tablespoon maize cornflour
1 teaspoon baking powder
½ teaspoon almond extract
Extra ½ cup each of blanched almonds and coconut

Combine flour, salt, cornflour, sugar and rolled oats. Cut in butter until mixture is crumbly. Press this mixture evenly into a greased shallow tin. Bake for 20 minutes in a moderate oven. Cover apricots with water, bring to the boil, and allow to simmer for 10 minutes. Drain well and cool. Cut apricots into small pieces. Sift flour, cornflour, baking powder, and salt together. Gradually blend together the brown sugar, almond essence and beaten eggs. Stir in flour mixture, apricots and coconut. Spread this mixture carefully over hot baked layer. Sprinkle with coconut and coarsely chopped almonds. Bake in moderate oven further 30 minutes. Cut into bars.

OATMEAL BISCUITS

4 ozs. plain flour — 4 ozs. oatmeal
3 ozs. butter — 2 ozs. sugar
½ small teaspoon cream of tartar
¼ small teaspoon baking soda
Pinch of salt (good pinch)
1/3rd cup milk and water mixed

Rub margarine into dry ingredients, then mix liquid to form a stiffish mixture. Roll out on board sprinkled with oatmeal. Cut out in rounds, prick with fork, bake until faintly coloured in medium oven.

NOTES

CAKES

TIN KETTLING

It is the custom, as a form of welcome in country areas, for the neighbours of a newly married couple to gather together, at a pre-arranged hour of the night, armed with tin kettles, pots and pans, with striking instruments. The marauding party creeps up to the house, just after the last light is extinguished. At a given signal, all the "instruments" are clanged and beaten in a rising crescendo, with demanding shouts for the newly marrieds to appear. The Tin Kettling ceases, on a promise of supper and refreshments.

BILLY SPONGE

4 eggs — 1 cup plain flour
1 cup castor sugar — ½ teaspoon salt
Extra castor sugar — 1 cup plain flour
1 teaspoon vanilla essence

Grease 3 pint billycan, line base with round of greased greaseproof paper. Dust inside of can with castor sugar, shake off excess; grease inside of lid.

Beat eggs until thick and creamy, gradually add the 1 cup sugar, beat until sugar is dissolved; add vanilla. Sift flour and salt, lightly fold into egg mixture. Pour into prepared billycan; place lid on can. Bake in moderate oven 40 minutes or until cooked when tested with a skewer.

SPICED FRUIT BILLY BREAD

3 heaped cups plain flour
3 teaspoons cream of tartar
1½ teaspoons bicarbonate of soda
1 small teaspoon of salt
1 dessertspoon ground cinnamon
1 teaspoon mixed spice
2 tablespoons sugar
1 cup bran

Sift all the dry ingredients together and add the bran. Mix in with the tips of the fingers 1 tablespoon of butter. Mix 1 tablespoon golden syrup or honey in sufficient milk to make a soft dough. Add 1 cup of mixed fruit. Mix thoroughly, then put in a well greased 3 pint billy. Put lid on and bake for 1½ hours in a steady oven. Containers greased with dripping ensures a cake won't stick.

FARMER'S CAKE

1 lb. cooking apples
1 teacup of golden syrup
2 teaspoons cinnamon
1 teaspoon ground cloves
1 lb. flour or enough to make these ingredients into a smooth paste
¼ lb. butter — 1 teaspoon soda
1 teacup sugar — ½ teacup sour milk
1 egg

Peel and chop the apples. Let them simmer in the golden syrup until tender. Work butter into flour, then add sugar and spices, mixing well. Blend in milk and egg, add syrup and apples before they are cold. Beat all well together. Bake in moderate oven.

BUTTERMILK CAKE

¼ lb. butter — 1 cup sugar
2 cups plain flour — ¼ teaspoon nutmeg
1 cup buttermilk or
1 cup milk with 1 dessertspoon vinegar
2 good teaspoons mixed spices
½ teaspoon cinnamon
1 teaspoon bicarbonate of soda
1 cup sultanas

Cream together butter and sugar. Add buttermilk, sifted flour, spices, cinnamon, nutmeg, soda and sultanas. Mix thoroughly and bake for 1 hour in moderate oven.

WRONG WAY CAKE

Prepare moderately hot oven and put baking tin in with 2½ ozs. butter in it.

Measure out a brimming cup of sultanas and sprinkle them with flour, and roll them around until well coated. Take baking tin out of the oven and tip it in all directions so that the sides are washed with melted butter, then drain all the butter out into mixing bowl. Add a cup of brown sugar and mix it with a wooden spoon. Break in 2 eggs, mix well. Add a teaspoon of vanilla essence and ¼ teaspoon of salt. Add to this 1¾ cups of self-raising flour, a teaspoon of baking powder, and half a cup of milk and mix. Add the sultanas, mix, put the mixture in the buttered tin, and put it in the oven for 35 minutes. Eaten on second day is best.

KEEPING EGGS

A freshly laid egg if kept at 12.5 deg.C (about 55 deg.F.) will keep for two to three weeks and it will keep longer at lower temperatures, providing it is not contaminated with bacteria caused by faulty washing.

During storage, providing no rots develop, the white of an egg gradually becomes thin and watery. This is a good guide to the age of an egg.

BRANDY BEAUTY

3 cups chopped walnuts
1½ cups chopped raisins, dates
1 cup chopped glace cherries
¾ cup self-raising flour
¾ cup sugar — Pinch salt
3 eggs — ½ cup brandy

Mix together all fruits and nuts. Mix flour, salt and sugar together and add to fruit mixture. Beat eggs thoroughly and add half the brandy. Pour over other mixture and mix well. Put into well greased loaf tin. Bake in a moderate oven for 1 hour, then wrap cooked cake in a cloth soaked in remainder of the brandy. Store for several days before eating.

GRAND CHOCOLATE CAKE

Make filling first:

½ cup lightly packed brown sugar
1 cup well drained sliced stewed apple
2 ozs. chopped glace cherries
2 ozs. blanched chopped almonds
2 ozs. chopped raisins
1 oz. butter — 3 tablespoons sherry
2 ozs. currants — ½ teaspoon cinnamon

Heat brown sugar and butter until butter melts. Add remaining ingredients. Cook gently for 3 minutes. Allow to become cold.

The Cake:

2 ozs. dark sweetened chocolate
7 rounded tablespoons fine breadcrumbs (sieve)
Small piece of vanilla bean
12 flat tablespoons sugar
5 ozs. butter — 5 large eggs

Cream butter very well with sugar. Beat with egg yolks and vanilla bean. Soften the chocolate in the oven. When cool add to the egg-butter-sugar-cream. Beat egg whites until they stand stiffly, then carefully add alternate spoonfuls of fine breadcrumbs and the stiff whites, folding into the mixture. Butter well and sprinkle with flour, an eight inch, deep cake tin. Put in mixture.

Bake in a moderately hot oven for 45 minutes. When cool, cut in half and put in the filling.

Before icing, spread with apricot jam, rather thinly.

To Ice:

Scald 2 tablespoons of milk in a tiny saucepan. Draw off heat and slice 4 ozs. butter into the saucepan. Stir over a very low heat until the butter melts. It must not be really hot, just lukewarm. Have 16 ozs. carefully sieved icing sugar ready in a basin. Be sure it is without a lump. Stir 2 teaspoons rum into the lukewarm butter mixture. Mix and pour over the fine icing sugar. Blend and stir to a thick creamy consistency. Spread evenly over the top and sides of the cake, with knife dipped in boiling water to ensure smoothness.

Do not eat before the cake is 24 hours old.

CHOCOLATE CUSTARD CAKE

Custard:

3 ozs. cocoa — ½ cup milk
6 ozs. brown sugar — 1 egg yolk
1 teaspoon vanilla

Heat in saucepan until thick.

Cake:

6 ozs. brown sugar — 4 ozs. butter
2 eggs (separated) — ½ cup milk
8 ozs. self-raising flour

Cream butter and sugar, add egg yolks and milk, add cooled custard mixture.

Now add sifted self-raising flour, then stiffly beaten egg whites. Bake in moderate oven for one hour, in 7 inch square cake tin. Ice when cold with vanilla icing.

CRUSTY CAKE

2 ozs. butter, ¾ cup sugar, 1 large egg, ½ cup milk, 2 cups self-raising flour, pinch salt, teaspoon vanilla.

Mix first in a basin ½ cup brown sugar lightly packed, ½ cup chopped walnuts, 2 teaspoons cinnamon, 1/3 cup plain flour and 2 ozs. melted butter.

Sift flour and salt together. Rub in butter until mixture resembles breadcrumbs. Add sugar then beaten egg. Stir in milk and vanilla.

Put half the mixture in well greased 8 inch tin, then lightly flour. Add half the filling, followed by the remaining cake mixture. Lastly add the rest of the filling.

Bake in moderate oven for 40 minutes. Test.

BOILED FRUIT CAKE

1 cup brown sugar — 1 cup seeded raisins
1 cup currants — ½ cup sultanas
1/3 cup chopped peel — ½ lb. butter
2 eggs — 1 cup cold water
1 cup plain flour — 1 teaspoon mixed spice
1 teaspoon bicarbonate of soda
2 cups self-raising flour

Put all ingredients except eggs and flour, into a saucepan and bring to the boil. Take from the heat and cool for 5 minutes. Beat the eggs well and sift the flour, then mix with boiled ingredients, blending well. Turn into an 8 inch cake tin, which has been lined with paper and bake for 1 hour in a moderate oven.

PLUMB CAKE

"Plumb Cake", which was given pride of place on every Christmas table, great or small, was the fore-runner of our modern Christmas Cake, rich with butter and "plumbs" (raisins) and laced with spirits.

Ingredients for a nice sized cake weighing approximately 3¼ lbs. when baked:

Six ounces **each** of butter, sugar, seeded raisins, currants, sultanas and plain flour,
Four ounces mixed candied peel,
2 ounces blanched almonds,
¾ teaspoon (level) of both powdered cinnamon and ginger, and ¼ teaspoon mixed spice.
Grated rind one orange, four eggs,
½ teaspoon of baking powder,
One extra ounce of flour to "coat" the fruit, and one tablespoon of either brandy or orange juice.

A seven inch tin with three inch depth. Grease tin evenly with lard. Put two circles of greased brown paper in the bottom. Have ready a double strip of brown paper greased on the inner side to pin around the **outside** of the tin when mixture is in place. Paper should extend at least an inch above rim of tin.

Sift flour with spices and baking powder. Prepare fruit — cutting the seeded raisins in halves, chopping candied peel in small lengths, shredding almonds and mixing with the currants and sultanas, which should be "picked over" for any stray bits of stem. Then dust all evenly with the extra ounce of flour.

Cream butter and sugar with the grated orange rind. Use a wooden spoon or your hand. The action must be a creaming one. Whisk the four eggs well, (taking care to break each one separately in a cup before putting them in the bowl). Add flour and beaten eggs alternately to the butter mixture. See that everything is smooth.

Now add the floured fruit and brandy. Mix carefully. Test for correct consistency by standing the wooden spoon in the mixture. If it does not remain upright, mixture is too thin. Place mixture in the prepared tin. Pin paper band in position. See that the oven is pre-heated enough to withstand the sudden contact with a cold thick mixture but be very careful to keep the temperature strictly moderate once the cake is in position. Cook for 2¾ hours in gentle heat.

Always remember to leave a rich fruit cake in its tin for at least 15 minutes after it comes from the oven to prevent cracking. Cool on a wire rack. Wrap in greased paper when cold and put in a tin to mature for at least 10 days.

UNCOOKED FRUIT CAKE

¾ cup chopped prunes
¾ cup chopped raisins
¾ cup chopped peel
½ cup chopped cherries
½ cup chopped walnuts
Nearly ½ cup butter
2 brimming tablespoons honey
4 cups fine biscuit crumbs
¾ teaspoon vanilla essence
½ teaspoon nutmeg
¾ teaspoon cinnamon
¼ teaspoon spice

Cream butter and honey till soft and creamy. Mix in fruit and spices. Let mixture stand 1½ hours to plump the fruit. Stir in crumbs, mix thoroughly. Press into a tin lined with waxed paper and leave in cool place 24 hours before cutting.

What has happened to treacle, used so often for cooking in the old days by our pioneering ancestors? Did the richness of treacle give extra flavour to the cakes and puddings made in the early days?

All we know is that treacle and golden syrup appear constantly as ingredients in old-time recipes, dating back to the days of the large kitchen with a huge open fireplace to accommodate a cauldron of broth and a spit for roasting, with a bake oven alongside.

DARK CAKE

4 ozs. lard	3 ozs. sugar
10 ozs. flour	1 egg
Spice	Ginger
1 tablespoon treacle	1 cup of milk

½ teaspoon carbonate of soda
4 ozs. sultanas or currants

Cream lard and sugar well. Stir in egg and beat. Add treacle to flour and salt. Dissolve carbonate of soda in the milk and beat all together thoroughly. Bake 40-45 minutes in a moderate oven.

LARGE FAMILY BLACK CAKE

2 lbs. flour	4 lbs. fruit
1 lb. sugar	1 lb. butter or lard

¾ lb. mixed peel
2 small teaspoons bicarbonate of soda
3 tablespoons black treacle
2 teaspoons mixed spice

Dissolve soda in a little warm milk. Put butter and sugar in a bowl, and beat with the hand to a smooth cream. Then gradually add the other ingredients. Bake for 3 or 4 hours. Leave in the tin to get cold.

ALICE'S FRUIT CAKE

Beat ½ lb. butter and ½ lb. sugar to a cream, add 2 eggs, one at a time.

1 lb. sultanas
¼ lb. currants
½ lb. seeded raisins
2 tablespoons dark plum jam or any dark jam
1 teaspoon bicarbonate of soda, dissolved in a little hot milk
1 egg cup brandy or sherry
Lastly add 1 lb. of plain flour.

Bake about 1½ hours, unless all in one large tin, which would need 2½ hours.

Two eggs make just as good a cake as 10.

TWELFTH NIGHT CAKE

January 6th is Twelfth Night, 12 days after Christmas, commemorating the visit of the Magi to the Christ Child.

10 ozs. plain flour and a pinch of salt; 1 teaspoon grated nutmeg; ½ teaspoon mixed spice; ½ teaspoon powdered cinnamon; 10 ozs. butter; 10 ozs. castor sugar; 6 eggs; 10 ozs. each of sultanas and currants; 8 ozs. stoned and chopped raisins; 4 ozs. each of candied peel, glace cherries and blanched and shredded almonds; the finely grated rind of a lemon; a dessertspoon of rum.

Extras:
Almond paste for middle of cake and for covering the top; candied fruits; 1 haricot bean; china figures of the Three Kings.

For the Almond Paste:
5 ozs. each of castor sugar and icing sugar; 10 ozs. ground almonds; 4 drops of almond essence; ½ teaspoon vanilla essence; 1 teaspoon lemon juice; 2 whole eggs and the yolk of a third.

With a rolling pin roll the icing sugar to free it of lumps, sieve it twice and mix with castor sugar and ground almonds. Add essence and lemon juice, then the beaten eggs. Mix well and knead till smooth. Cover with a damp cloth until wanted.

To make the cake:
Prepare a 9 inch tin by greasing and lining with greased greaseproof paper. Sieve flour, salt and spices into mixing bowl. Cream together fat and sugar till light and fluffy, then beat in eggs, one at a time with a little of the flour mixture. Fold in remainder of flour. Add fruit, chopped peel, quartered cherries and shredded almonds, grated lemon rind and rum. The mixture should be of a rather stiff "dropping consistency", so a little more liquid (milk) may be necessary, depending on the size of the eggs. Put half of mixture in prepared tin. Divide almond paste in half, roll one half out to a round to fit size of cake. Lay this on cake mixture and push in the bean wrapped in greaseproof paper. Put remaining cake mixture on top. Smooth this over and make a tiny dent in centre. (This helps cake to rise evenly.) Place on middle shelf of pre-heated oven, bake for one hour in moderate oven, then reduce heat and bake for a further 2-2½ hours at lowered heat. Test at end of 2 hours by inserting a warmed knitting needle in centre of cake; if it comes out clean the cake is done.

Leave in tin for 10 minutes before turning out to cool. Strip off paper. Next day, roll out remainder of almond paste. Make a round to cover top, and with trimmings make small balls to go around edge. Brush cake with a little warmed jam before placing almond paste in position. Set the balls around the edge, close together. Brush with beaten egg and set in oven to brown slightly. When cold, heap with candied fruits and set the figures of the Magi among these.

Some maids are gifted with the art
Of painting like the Masters
While others with the ready pen
Find hours of busy pleasure
In polished prose, and then again
In light poetic measure.

But there's a maid and there's an art
To which the world is looking
The nearest art unto the heart
The good old art of cooking.

MADEIRA CAKE

5 ozs. butter — ¾ cup sugar (6 ozs.)
2 tablespoons milk — 3 eggs
½ teaspoon vanilla essence
2 cups plain flour (8 ozs.)
1 teaspoon baking powder
Pinch salt.

Sift flour, baking powder and salt together. Cream the butter and sugar until fluffy. Add eggs one at a time, beating well after each addition. Mix in vanilla, then the sifted dry ingredients alternately with the milk. Spoon mixture into a greased and paper lined eight inch cake tin. Bake in a moderate oven for 30 to 35 minutes, or until cooked.

PORK FRUIT CAKE

½ lb. salt pork, finely ground
3 teaspoons baking powder
½ cup lemon finely sliced

1 cup sugar	1 cup boiling water
1 cup light syrup	2 eggs
½ teaspoon cloves	½ teaspoon soda
3 cups plain flour	1 teaspoon cinnamon
1 cup nuts	½ teaspoon nutmeg
1 lb. raisins	1 cup currants

Pour boiling water over pork, and when cool add sugar, then slightly beaten eggs and beat well. Sift soda, baking powder and spices with two cups of flour, dredge the raisins and nuts, etc., with the remaining cup of flour. Add syrup and flour mixture, beat well. Pour into greased paper lined loaf pan or cake tin and bake in moderate oven 1½ hours.

Basic rules for a cake can be the weight of 2 eggs in butter, sugar and flour. Mix with orange juice, or milk, depending on the flavour required.

A rich soup; a small turbot; a saddle of venison; an apricot tart: this is dinner fit for a king.

Brillat-Savarin

FRUIT CENTRE CAKE

Put half a pound of plain sweet biscuits through the mincer. Chop half a breakfastcup each of figs, dates and seeded raisins to small pieces with the kitchen scissors. Put half a cup of preserved ginger through the mincer. Chop half a breakfastcup of walnuts to fine shreds, eliminating all shell and fibre. Mix fruit and nuts. Dust with a generous tablespoon of cocoa and blend with the biscuit crumbs.

Now stir quarter of a pound each of butter and sugar over low heat until butter is melted. Then stand saucepan in simmering water until sugar has lost much of its grain. Bring to boiling point, stirring hard. Cool one or two minutes. Then stir in one well whisked egg. Blend over low heat just enough to cook the egg. Pour while almost boiling over all the dry ingredients. Work to a stiff paste with a strong fork, adding two tablespoons of brandy, rum or sherry to give a real festival flavour. Good blending is essential.

Turn mixture into a greased 7 inch cake pan. Smooth surface and press mixture really hard into tin until level and compact. Cover tin with a plate and leave two days in a cool place. Then ease out of the tin with a knife. Stand on a flat board. Apply a coat of well-kneaded and velvety smooth almond paste, using lightly beaten egg-white to hide any joins.

ALMOND PASTE

Mix half a pound of almond meal with quarter pound each of castor and icing sugars (well sieved). Flavour with a few drops of almond essence, 2 or 3 drops of vanilla, and saltspoon of brandy (lemon juice can be substituted). Add sufficient raw egg to bind ingredients to a beautiful smooth paste (one whole egg or two yolks or two whites as required). Knead on a board well dusted with sieved icing sugar or cornflour.

Roll out, cut and fit, pressing and moulding it closely to the cake. Dust your hands with cornflour before kneading and moulding this paste. Should it seem a little damp when on the cake rub the entire surface all over with a little cornflour.

No decorations are required. Simply prick the top in a pattern with a small metal skewer and mark a crisscross design around the side of it to hide any joins. Leave in the air to dry for 2 or 3 days. Do not shut up in a tin while the paste is still moist. The flavour of this cake improves with keeping, so try not to cut it for a week from the day it is mixed. If you have any almond paste left over, roll it into tiny balls and slip a bit of candied cherry in the centres. Roll each ball in ordinary granulated sugar and leave in the air to dry for a day or two.

Do not increase the depth of this cake. If you want a larger quantity, prepare two mixtures and set in two seven inch tins.

RAISIN ROCK CAKE

2 tablespoons butter	1 cup flour
½ lb. seeded raisins	½ cup sugar
1 egg	

Cream butter and sugar, add egg then sifted flour and raisins. Put in tin. Cover top with almonds. Cook in a slow oven.

HALLOWE'EN DEVIL'S CAKE

8 ozs. plain flour 4 ozs. butter
2 eggs 8 ozs. soft brown sugar
1½ oz. cocoa ¼ pint milk
3 tablespoons of water
1 teaspoonful lemon juice or vinegar
1 level teaspoonful bicarbonate of soda
Two sandwich tins eight inches diameter

For the filling and chocolate icing:

2 tablespoons of apricot jam
10 ozs. castor sugar
1 level tablespoonful of golden syrup
½ teaspoonful of vanilla essence
A sprinkle of icing sugar
2 ozs. of cocoa 1 ozs. of butter
¼ pint of water Pinch of salt

Brush the cake tins with melted fat then line the base of each with a round of greaseproof paper cut to fit.

Sift the flour and bicarbonate of soda. Put the cocoa into a small pan with the water. Stir it over a gentle heat until it is quite smooth, then bring it to the boil. Take the pan off the heat.

Put the sugar and butter into another saucepan and melt them very slowly. When they have melted, take the pan off the heat and stir in the cocoa mixture.

Break the eggs into a bowl and beat them well, then add the milk and vinegar or lemon juice. Stir this liquid into the pan containing the melted ingredients, and stir the whole mixture thoroughly into the sifted flour. Divide the mixture between the prepared sandwich tins and smooth over the surface with a palette knife.

Bake the sandwich cakes in a moderately hot oven for about half an hour. As the tins are fairly large, one will have to be baked on the shelf below the other — it is a good idea to change over their positions after about 15 minutes. When they are ready, turn the cakes out on to a wire tray to cool and remove the greased paper.

The filling and icing:

When the cakes are cold, sandwich them together with apricot jam.

Put the cocoa, water, syrup, sugar, and a pinch of salt into a fairly large, strong saucepan and stir them together over a very gentle heat. Do not allow the mixture to come to the boil until every grain of sugar has dissolved. Bring the mixture to the boil and boil it steadily, stirring occasionally until it thickens. This will take between five and ten minutes, but as the time varies greatly depending on the size of the saucepan and the amount of heat, it is best to test the mixture occasionally. To do this, drop a small teaspoonful into a cup of cold water, and if, after a few seconds, it can be rolled between the fingers into a soft ball, take it off the heat, otherwise cook it for a little longer. Stir in the vanilla essence, then beat the icing until it thickens. Spread it quickly over the cake. When the icing has set, dust the cake lightly with icing sugar sprinkled through a sieve.

SPINNING SUGAR SPONGE

6 ozs. sugar 3 eggs
6 tablespoons water Few drops lemon juice
Pinch of salt Sprinkle of cinnamon
3½ ozs. self-raising flour

Put sugar, water and lemon juice into saucepan and boil rapidly for 3 minutes. Allow sugar to cool a little. Meanwhile, sift flour with pinch of salt and cinnamon and beat eggs till very fluffy. Now pour the cooled syrup over the eggs in a thin stream, beating well till the mixture is thicker and fluffy. Fold in the twice sifted flour very lightly and turn into two 9 inch layer tins which have been lined with well greased rounds of paper cut to fit the base. Bake slowly and longer than the ordinary sponge in moderate oven about 30 minutes. This recipe makes a delicious sponge loaf in a deep tin, but give a longer cooking — about 1½ hours.

Butter Cream Filling:

1 cup milk
1 dessertspoon cornflour
2 tablespoons sugar (preferably castor)
1 tablespoon butter
Few drops vanilla essence or rum.

Blend cornflour with a little milk, then add to the rest of the hot milk. Stir till thickened. Cook 2 minutes stirring. Allow to cool. Meanwhile cream butter and sugar; add cold blancmange in small pieces, beating well till smooth and creamy. Flavour to taste with rum, vanilla or brandy.

Boiled Icing:

2 egg whites 1½ cups sugar
1/3 cupful water 1 teaspoon lemon juice
Extra lemon juice and less water may be used for good flavour.

Combine unbeaten egg whites, sugar, water and lemon juice in top of double boiler, or in a basin standing in a saucepan with 1" of boiling water. Beat enough to blend ingredients. Now set over heat and beat for 10 minutes or till the mixture is light, fluffy and thick enough to hold its shape. Remove from heat, add essence desired for flavour and continue beating until the icing is stiff enough to stand in peaks. Swirl over cake at once.

Decorate with crystallised fruits.

EMERGENCY CAKE

Which will use all manner of bits and pieces from a candied cherry or a "knob" of sugary ginger, to a spoonful of wine or the last scrap of a "nice" jam.

Ingredients:

8 ozs. self-raising flour, 3 ozs. sandy brown sugar, 1½ ozs. butter, 8 ozs. of mixed fruit (the more varied the better), a level teaspoon mixed spice, a tablespoonful of any well-flavoured thick jam, a teaspoon of coffee essence (preferably unsweetened), a small half-teaspoon of bicarbonate of soda, a teaspoon of vinegar or sherry or rum or brandy, and approximately half a cup of milk.

Method:

Well butter a 7 inch cake tin with 3 inch depth (or use a loaf tin). Put a circle of greased brown paper in the bottom. Sift flour into mixing bowl. Add sugar and rub in the butter. Then add the fruit dusted with the spice.

Blend coffee essence with the milk. Stir in the soda. Drop the brimming tablespoon of jam into the mixing bowl and proceed to add the coffee mixture. Blend all very well. Lastly add the teaspoon of vinegar (rum gives the best flavour). Mix again and stand 15 minutes, or even longer, before turning into the tin.

Bake in strictly moderate oven until golden brown and firm to touch in the centre (1½ to 1¾ hours). Do not hurry it out of the tin. Ice the top when cold with a simple icing flavoured with almond essence and sprinkled with nuts.

JEWISH CAKE

1½ cups flour — 3 eggs
2 teaspoons cinnamon — 6 tablespoons milk
½ cup sugar — ¼ lb. butter
1 teaspoon cream of tartar
½ teaspoon carbonate of soda

Cream butter and sugar well, add beaten eggs, then milk, lastly flour and rising. Bake in sandwich tins 20 minutes in moderate oven.

Icing:

Melt about a dessertspoon butter in saucepan, preferably enamel, or a crockery basin. Add lemon juice to taste. Beat in icing sugar to right consistency.

Before creaming butter and sugar together for cakes, add one tablespoon of boiling water. It dissolves the sugar, helps to melt the butter and makes the cakes much lighter.

EASTER HALVA (SEMOLINA) CAKE

6 ozs. butter — 6 ozs. castor sugar
4 eggs — 2 cups semolina
4 ozs. chopped blanched almonds
1 teaspoon ground cinnamon
Extra slivered almonds

Syrup:

1 lb. sugar — 1 teaspoon lemon juice
2 pints water (or 1¾ pints water and ¼ pint brandy)
1 or 2 inch cinnamon stick

Cream butter. Gradually add sugar while continuing to cream. Add eggs one at a time, beating until mixture is very creamy. Add semolina, still beating, then nuts and ground cinnamon.

Pour mixture into 8 inch or 9 inch greased cake tin which must be deep. Bake in a moderate oven about 40 minutes or until knife cutting into the centre comes out clean.

While cake is cooking, prepare syrup by putting sugar, water (not brandy), cinnamon stick and lemon juice in a heavy bottomed saucepan, and bring slowly to boil. Cook fairly slowly until mixture becomes sticky and syrupy. Remove cinnamon stick and pour in brandy. Cook a further few minutes if desired to dissipate the alcohol. Remove cake from oven, leaving in tin, and scattering over it some slivered blanched almonds. Gently pour syrup over cake. Cool.

When mixtures were creamed by hand, or with a wooden spoon, and eggs plus a little baking powder for the "rising" were used, lovely firm, smooth textures, were the result.

DOLLY VARDEN CAKE

Take one cup of sugar, half a cup of milk, 4 eggs, 2 cups flour, 1 tablespoon cocoa, 2 teaspoonfuls of cream of tartar, one teaspoonful of carbonate of soda. Beat the butter and sugar to a cream, add the eggs, one at a time, beat well, add the milk, then the flour with the baking powder in it. Have ready two sandwich tins, pour in one plain cake, one chocolate cake, keeping enough back for a third, thickening with currants the third mixture, and bake; when all are baked, join with icing placing the currant cake in the centre.

HONEY ROLL

3 eggs, separated — ½ cup sugar
1/3rd cup cornflour — 1 tablespoon plain flour
1 teaspoon ginger — 1 teaspoon cinnamon
1 tablespoon honey
1 teaspoon baking powder

Beat egg whites until soft peaks form, gradually add sugar; beat until dissolved. Add egg-yolks, beat until combined. Sift dry ingredients, fold into egg mixture; lightly fold in warmed honey. Spread mixture into greased and lined 10 x 12 inch swiss roll tin. Bake in moderate oven 12 to 15 minutes or until sponge feels elastic to touch. Quickly trim sides from roll, turn on to greaseproof paper sprinkled with sugar. Roll up cake and greaseproof paper, stand 1 minute; unroll, then reroll without paper; cool.

SCRIPTURE CAKE

½ lb. butter	Judges 5.25
1 cup sugar	Jeremiah 6.20
1 cup warm pumpkin	Psalms 63.5
1½ cups plain flour	1 Kings 4.22
1½ cups S.R. Flour	1 Kings 4.22
3 eggs	Isaiah 10.14
2 cups figs	1 Samuel 30.12
2 cups raisins	1 Samuel 30.12
Pinch Salt	Leviticus 2.13
Spices to taste	1 Kings 10.10

Follow Solomon's rule for making good boys (Proverbs 23.14) and you will have an excellent cake.

(Sultanas can be substituted for figs.)

HARVEST LUNCH-BOX GINGER CAKE

2 cups plain flour — Pinch salt
1 egg — 4 ozs. butter
1 cup sugar — 1 cup warm milk
Grated rind from 2 lemons
2 tablespoons golden syrup
2 teaspoons ground ginger
1 teaspoon bicarbonate of soda

Beat butter and sugar to a light fluffy cream. Add egg, beat well. Add lemon rind. Sift flour with salt and ginger. Combine warm milk, bicarbonate of soda and golden syrup and add alternately with flour and ginger. Beat vigorously. Bake in moderate oven about one hour. Test after 45 minutes.

BUTTER SPICE CAKE

6 ozs. (¾ cup) butter — 1 cup mixed fruit
8 ozs. brown sugar — 1 teaspoon cinnamon
3 eggs — 1 cup milk
½ teaspoon mixed spice
½ teaspoon lemon essence
12 ozs. (3 cups) self-raising flour.

Cream butter and sugar until light and fluffy. Add eggs one at a time, beating well after each addition. Add lemon essence and stir in fruit. Sift dry ingredients and stir in half flour and milk — beat well. Stir in remaining flour and milk. Place in greased and lined 13 × 8 inch tin. Sprinkle liberally with chopped peel and cherries. Bake in a moderate oven for 35-40 minutes. Allow to cool before removing paper.

There were cakes and apples in all the chapels,
With fine polonies, and rich mellow pears.
Rev. Barham

VINEGAR CAKE

Half pound flour — Pinch salt
3 ozs. sugar — 2 ozs. butter
1 gill milk — 1 tablespoon vinegar
½ teaspoon baking powder
½ teaspoon mixed spice
4 ozs. chopped mixed fruits
2 ozs. candied peel (finely chopped)
½ teaspoon bicarbonate of soda

Sift flour, salt, baking powder, and spice into a basin; rub in butter and add chopped fruits. Mix soda into milk and while it is still fizzing add vinegar. Make well in centre of flour and pour milk mixture in. Mix all quickly and lightly together and pour into greased loaf tin which has been lined on base with greased paper. Bake in moderate oven 50 to 60 minutes or until it is risen and firm to the touch. Remove from oven and allow to cool 10 minutes. Turn out on to cake cooler. When completely cold top with lemon icing.

BURNT SUGAR CAKE

½ cup white sugar
½ cup boiling water

For batter:

1½ cups sugar — ½ cup butter
1 cup cold water — 2 eggs
2½ cups flour — ½ teaspoon sugar syrup
2 teaspoons baking powder
1 teaspoon vanilla essence

Cream butter and sugar, add egg yolks. Add flour and water alternately, then the syrup. Beat for five minutes. Stir in the beaten egg whites and add vanilla. Bake in layers. Join with a boiled icing added to half the burnt sugar syrup. The syrup is made by browning in a heavy pan, half a cup of white sugar, to which when browned half a cup of boiling water has been added. It is then cooked until it turns to syrup.

APPLE CREAM COFFEE CAKE

2 tablespoons sugar ½ cup chopped walnuts
2 teaspoons cinnamon ½ cup extra sugar
4 ozs. butter 2 eggs
½ teaspoon salt 1 cup sour cream
1 teaspoon vanilla essence
2 cups self-raising flour
1 teaspoon bicarbonate of soda
1 medium cooking apple

Mix 2 tablespoons sugar, walnuts and cinnamon in small bowl. Peel, core and slice apple thinly.

Cream butter and sugar until light and fluffy. Add eggs one at a time, beating well after each addition. Add vanilla. Sift flour and salt. Stir bicarbonate of soda into cream. Fold flour into creamed mixture alternately with sour cream. Spread half cake mixture evenly over base of lightly greased 8 inch cake tin with greased paper at base. Cover with sliced apple, then sprinkle half walnut mixture over. Cover with remaining cake mixture and top with walnut mixture.

Bake in moderate oven approximately 1 hour. Test with skewer, which should come out clean. Leave in tin 10 minutes to cool before turning out on to cooling rack.

CHOCOLATE CAKE without eggs

¼ lb. butter 1 cup sugar
4 teaspoons cocoa ½ teaspoon spice
1¾ cups plain flour 1 teaspoon cinnamon
1 cup sultanas
1 cup stewed apple, fairly dry
1 teaspoon sugar dissolved in hot water mixed with apple.

Cream butter and sugar, add apple then dry ingredients. Bake in moderate oven 1¼ hours.

ALMOND FILLING

2 tablespoons ground almonds (often called almond meal), 2 tablespoons stiff apricot jam, good squeeze lemon or orange juice (1 dessertspoon). Mix well together.
(1) Some whipped cream may be added, if liked.
(2) This is delicious spread over a pastry tart with custard poured over it, and baked in a brisk oven for 10 minutes, and then very slowly till the custard is set.

DATE FILLING

¾ cup dates (stoned and cut up). Put in saucepan, just cover with milk. Stand on the hob or very low heat till all the milk is absorbed (stir now and then); add a little grated lemon rind and juice after it leaves the fire. Use when cool. Decorate the top of cake with pieces of date or chopped dates and nuts. Orange juice (and rind) makes a change from the milk. It may be made in large quantity and will keep well. This is also good to put into tartlets, one-third fill them, then pour over it some sweetened custard made with 1 egg, ½ cup milk, 1 dessertspoon sugar. It is also a nice filling, thickened with cake crumbs, or crumbled sweet biscuits.

NOUGAT CAKE

1 butter sponge, 6 ozs. sugar, lemon juice, 1 gill water, 2 ozs. blanched almonds.

Dissolve sugar in water, add lemon juice and chopped almonds. Bring to the boil and allow to become a pale toffee colour. Pour into a greased tin or enamel plate. When cold break up in a mortar or with the rolling pin. Whip cream, add some of the powdered nougat and some vanilla essence. Put layer of cream mixture between cake. Cover the top roughly with the remainder and sprinkle with the rest of the nougat.

DATE SANDWICH (Large)

¼ lb. butter, 1¾ cups flour, 2 teaspoons baking powder, ¼ teaspoon salt, ½ teaspoon cinnamon, ½ nutmeg, grated, all rubbed in like pastry till it resembles breadcrumbs; 1 cup brown sugar, 2 eggs (well beaten), and ½ cup sweet milk, put together in a basin, 1 cup dates, cut up fine.

Add the sugar and dates to the flour, etc., and butter. Mix with the eggs and milk, and beat for 3 minutes. Bake in sandwich tins in moderate oven 20 minutes.

It may be baked as a cake in the meat dish.

Filling:

One cup sliced dates, ¼ cup of sugar, juice of ½ a lemon, and the juice of 1 orange, 2 tablespoons of hot water. Boil over gentle heat till it thickens. Spread between the cake when both are cool.

Icing:

One dessertspoon butter, 1 dessertspoon boiling water, ¼ teaspoon vanilla and sufficient rolled icing sugar to make it thick enough to spread. Decorate the top with dates or nuts, or both. This is an uncommon and toothsome cake. Useful to make when eggs are dear.

THREE MINUTE CAKE (large)

3 cups self-raising flour
10 dessertspoons melted butter
2 cups castor sugar small teaspoon salt
1 cup milk 4 eggs

Sift dry ingredients three times. Beat all together for three minutes. Bake in 2 tins about 25 minutes.

SWEET MINCE CAKE

1 four egg sponge made in 2 tins
1 cup crushed biscuit crumbs
½ cup chopped walnuts
1 tablespoon apricot jam
½ cup chopped raisins
1 tablespoon chopped peel
1 tablespoon cocoa 2 tablespoons sherry

Mix all ingredients together and spread thickly between the layers of sponge cake. Ice with chocolate butter cream flavoured with sherry, coating top and sides. Sprinkle with grated chocolate and leave 24 hours before cutting.

NEVER FAIL SPONGE

Beat four eggs, toss in ½ teaspoon bicarbonate of soda and beat well again. Add a small cup sugar, beat 3 minutes. Sift in 1 cup plain flour with 1 teaspoon cream of tartar. Mix and bake in a well greased tin 15 to 20 minutes in moderate oven. The success of this sponge depends on the order of adding ingredients.

ORANGE CRUSTY CAKE

Pulp and ¼ cup juice of 1 orange, 1 cup raisins, 2 cups flour, 1 teaspoon baking powder, pinch salt, 1 cup sugar, ¼ lb. butter, ¾ cup milk, 3 eggs.

Topping:

¼ cup sugar, ½ teaspoon mixed spice, ¼ cup finely chopped walnuts.

Mince together walnuts, raisins and pulp of orange after squeezing the required ¼ cup juice. Cream butter and sugar and add the eggs, well beaten, and mix well. Sift baking powder, flour and salt, and stir gradually into mixture alternately with milk, adding only a little at a time. Stir in minced ingredients and mix to smooth consistency. Transfer to a well-greased 8 inch square or 8 inch round, deep-sided cake tin. Bake in moderate oven for 1 hour, and while cake is still warm pour gradually over the ¼ cup orange juice.

Topping:

Mix the ingredients and sprinkle over cake.

SCOTTISH SEED CAKE

4 ozs. butter 4 ozs. castor sugar
7 ozs. flour 3 eggs
4 ozs. lemon peel Rind of 1 lemon
2 ozs. almonds (blanched and chopped)
1½ teaspoons baking powder
2 tablespoons caraway seeds

Cut peel into shreds and mix with 1 tablespoon of the flour and the chopped almonds. Cream butter and sugar until light and fluffy, and add eggs one at a time, beating well after each addition. Add the peel, almonds, lemon rind, and lastly the sifted flour and baking powder. Place into 2 well greased bar tins and sprinkle caraway seeds on top. Bake in a moderate oven for 1 hour to 1¼ hours.

To Blanch Almonds:

Place almonds into boiling water for a few seconds, then immediately into cold water. The skins will then be easy to remove.

ORANGE AND ALMOND CAKE

The juice of 3 oranges, grated rind of 1 orange, 4 ozs. ground almonds, 2 ozs. fine bread-crumbs, 4 ozs. sugar, 4 eggs, ½ teaspoon salt, cream, orange flower water.

Mix together the breadcrumbs, orange juice and grated orange rind, add the ground almonds, and, if available, a tablespoon of orange flower water. Beat the egg yolks with the sugar and salt until almost white. Add to the first mixture. Fold in the stiffly beaten egg whites. Pour into a square cake tin buttered and sprinkled with breadcrumbs, and bake in a moderate oven for about 40 minutes. When cold, turn the cake out and cover with whipped cream (¼ pint).

SAFFRON YEAST CAKE

8 cups plain flour, 1 lb. sultanas, pinch of salt, ½ lb. currants, 2 large cup sugar, 8 ozs. chopped lemon peel, ¼ lb. butter, 3 eggs, ¼ lb. saffron.

Steep the saffron with a pinch of salt in one large cup of water, bring to the boil and simmer gently for ½ to 1 hour. Push to back of stove where it will keep warm until required.

In a large basin set a sponge as follows:

2 large cups of plain flour, a pinch of salt mixed with one large cup of Potato and Hop Yeast. Mix well and place in a warm spot to rise. In a large mixing bowl put the 8 cups of flour (with salt), rub the butter into this and then add the sugar and fruit. Make a well in the centre and add the well risen sponge and lastly the lightly beaten eggs. With the hands mix well then pour over this the warm saffron, mix well, once again, place on oven door or in a warm place, cover with a large sheet of greaseproof and several thicknesses of warm coverings. Next day place into greased patty tins and a greased cake tin or two and allow to stand for a half hour.

Bake in a hot oven — in patty tins 20 to 30 minutes — cake tins approximately 1 to 1¼ hours depending on size and depth of tins.

QUIGLEY CAKE

1 lb. brown flour — Pinch salt
2 eggs — 8 ozs. soft brown sugar
Milk — 8 ozs. butter
½ lb. sultanas — ¼ lb. currants
2 teaspoons baking powder

Mix together flour, baking powder and salt. Rub in butter, add sugar and fruits alternately with flour mixture. Mix with beaten eggs and milk. Bake in a moderate oven in greased tin for 2 hours.

WALNUT CAKE

¼ lb. butter, ½ lb. soft sugar, ½ lb. flour, 3 eggs, ½ teaspoon carbonate soda, 1 teaspoon cream of tartar, ½ lb. walnuts.

Cream butter and sugar, break in eggs one by one. Sift flour, carbonate soda, and cream of tartar, and add to mixture. Then add half the chopped walnuts, and put the others in the filling and on the icing.

WALNUT COFFEE CAKE

¼ lb. butter — Pinch of salt
1 cup sugar — 2 eggs (separated)
1½ cups plain flour — ½ cup milk
4 level teaspoons baking powder
1 teaspoon vanilla essence

Cream butter and sugar, add egg yolks, sifted flour and baking powder, milk and vanilla. Lastly add the stiffly beaten whites of 2 eggs. Put half this mixture in either a round or square tin and cover with the following filling:
½ cup soft brown sugar, 2 teaspoons cinnamon, 2 tablespoons plain flour (level), 1 cup chopped walnuts, 2 ozs. softened butter. Mix well together.

Put remaining half of mixture on top and bake in moderate oven for 45 to 60 minutes.

YUM-YUM CAKE

Base:
2 ozs. brown sugar, 6 ozs. self-raising flour, 2 egg yolks, 1 teaspoon essence of vanilla, 3 ozs. butter.

Cream butter and sugar, add beaten egg yolks, flour and lastly vanilla. Spread over base of greased swiss roll tin.

Topping:
4 ozs. castor sugar, 1 oz. chopped walnuts, 2 egg whites, 1 oz. cherries.

Beat egg whites until stiff, fold in fruit, nuts and sugar. Cover base mixture.

Bake in moderate oven for 20-30 minutes. Lightly brown top only.

Dost thou think, because thou art virtuous, there shalt be no more cakes and ale?
"Twelfth Night" — Shakespeare

ASH CAKE

Scald the meal, and put it in little heaps to cool, then mix with more water (warm) into dough, and mould it into flat cakes rather larger than a breakfast saucer. These are baked as follows:-

Open a place in the side of a wood fire on the hearth, and having put in the cakes, each between two cabbage leaves, lay them on the hot hearth, sprinkle some ashes lightly over first, then put hot coals on the top, and if these appear to cool fast, remove them from time to time, and replace them with hotter coals from the fire.

NOTES

Do unto others you would they should do unto you

SCONES, BUNS AND BREAD

It used to be argued that a cart was necessary if the drover's cook wanted to make yeast bread on the road. This argument is right. If the sponge is mixed in a deep container in the morning, put in the cart and well covered, it can be rolled out and put in the camp ovens when camp is reached in the afternoon. By the time the ashes are ready, it has risen enough to cook. Something of the same sort can be done with pack horses, but the trouble is that the container, a four gallon tin at most, does not hold enough for more than two or three men. It is also a bit of a nuisance to strap on top of a pack horse. Incidentally, yeast bread made on the road is always of the very best, due to the shaking it gets when in the sponge stage. The whole of the time it is trying to rise it is being knocked back by the constant shaking of the cart. "Droving Days"— H.M. BARKER

BUSH DAMPER

Buttered damper made with flour and a pinch of salt, and enough water to mix. Bake on a griddle hung over the open fire, for 12 to 15 minutes. A green stick in the centre of damper can be removed when cooked and meat inserted with butter and seasoning.

Home-baked bread — now nearly as rare as its alternative, damper — appeared on every table.

COTTAGE LOAVES

1 lb. self-raising flour, ¼ lb. butter, 2 teaspoons sugar, 1 saltspoon salt, 2 eggs, milk.

Sift the self-raising flour, sugar and salt and rub in the butter. Beat the eggs and add enough milk to make one cupful of fluid. Mix into the flour, etc. Roll out and cut out with a tumbler and an egg cup. Lay the small round on the large, press a small depression in top.

Glaze with milk and bake in a quick oven. When risen they resemble miniature cottage loaves.

MAKING YEAST

3 unpeeled potatoes, a good handful of hops, a little over a pint of water, a heaped tablespoon of flour and the same of sugar, a teaspoon of salt, and hop water.

Boil potatoes and hops with water for ½ an hour, then strain off the water, blend flour, sugar and hop water until quite smooth. Stir into the strained hops and potatoes, then add the salt.

Bottle (in a stone bottle for preference) and tie down securely. If the bottle is a well-seasoned one the yeast will be ready for use in 7 or 8 hours.

PUFTALOONS

½ lb. self-raising flour 8 ozs. milk pinch salt.

Make into a light dough and cut into rounds ¼ inch thick. Fry in oil to golden brown — not too quickly to avoid soggy centre. Turn with knife while cooking. Drain and serve hot with syrup, jam or honey. Tasty with bacon for breakfast. Popular served with brown gravy for children.

OUT-BACK BUNS

2 cups self-raising flour
2 tablespoons good dripping
A little grated nutmeg ¾ cup brown sugar
1 egg ¾ cup milk

Beat sugar and dripping to a cream. Add the egg, then a little flour, then part of the milk, add more flour till all is used. Grate in nutmeg, put on greased tin in lumps and bake in a brisk oven for about 15 minutes.

SOUTHERN POPOVER

Take 1½ cups of sifted flour, ½ teaspoon of salt, 3 eggs and 1½ cups buttermilk or scalded milk. Put flour and salt into a bowl. Beat eggs and milk and stir gradually into flour until a smooth batter. Beat thoroughly. Fill greased custard cups or sizzling hot heavy metal gem scone containers 2/3 full. Bake in very hot oven for 15 minutes, then reduce to moderate heat and continue baking 20 minutes until firm. They can be used instead of pastry shells, or eaten with butter as a hot bread.

BUSHMAN'S LUNCH CAN

About the size of a 3 quart billy, made in two parts which fit together in the middle. The bottom section holds the meat and vegetables hot, the top the pudding. The bottom can be used to toast a slice of cheese. At the very bottom of the tin there was a hollow for a red hot iron. This was what caused the cheese to sizzle.

Boxty on the griddle
Boxty on the pan,
The wee one in the middle
It is for Mary Ann:
If you don't eat boxty
You'll never get your man.

To be eaten hot with butter and brown sugar rather like a pancake. Having washed, peeled and grated some large potatoes, add half a cup of flour and 1 teaspoonful of salt to each cupful of grated potato, with enough milk to make a batter of a fairly stiff dropping consistency. Let it stand for an hour. Grease frying pan well with bacon. When very hot, fry mixture as you would pancakes. When set and brown, serve it straight from the pan with butter, melted, and brown sugar.

BRIOCH DOUGH (Easy Style)

Put ¼ pint of milk and ¼ pint of water in a small saucepan. Bring to the boil. Cool to lukewarm. Serve one pound of plain flour on to a dish. Cream two ounces of lard and butter with one pinch of sugar and a good pinch of salt.

Crumble one ounce of compressed yeast into a cup with one teaspoon of sugar and mix to a smooth thin consistency with quarter a cup of tepid milk and water. Sprinkle ¼ teaspoon of flour on top and stir. Cover cup and stand aside for five minutes in a bowl of luke warm water. It will then be frothing nicely.

Now beat one egg into the creamed fat adding a little of the flour to make it smooth. Then pour in the yeast and put in enough of the flour to beat it to a batter with some of the milk.

The beating distributes the yeast well. Now add the remaining flour and enough of the milk to make soft dough. Beat with your wooden spoon or knead with your hands until it leaves the basin clean.

Lift into a greased straight sided bowl or billy twice as deep as the ball of dough. Stand bowl in a larger pan containing comfortably warm (NOT HOT) water. Cover bowl with a folded cloth. Leave 40-60 minutes when it should have come to the top of the bowl. With a knife turn the light dough onto a board sprinkled with flour.

Do not be frightened by its softness. Pull off small pieces. Mould lightly. Drop into well greased patty tins. (Enough dough for 36.) Stand the tins on trays over warm water. Cover with a hood of greased brown paper. Now set aside to rise for about 15 minutes. When they have risen, brush them over lightly with beaten egg.

Bake in a quick oven for about 20 minutes.

Brioches may be served with honey or apricot jam.

ORIGINS OF BREAD MAKING

The origins of bread making date back to neolithic times when the seeds of wild grasses were gathered and baked on hot stones. Baking made the separation of the grain from the husk easier.

Flour was the next development. It was made by pounding the grain. This was then mixed with water or milk to give a mash. When this mash was baked on hot stones the first bread was made. Bronze age "cakes" of this sort have been found by archaelogists.

The final step in the process was the leavening or rising of the dough. This was discovered by the Egyptians, who left their dough out in the sun to "go bad". This caused fermentation and so bread reached the final form we know today after thousands of years.

Now almost all bread is leavened and the most usual agent is yeast. There are two types of yeast — cakes of compressed yeast and dry powder form. The compressed type does not keep well and must be made into a liquid before use.

TREACLE SCONES

1 cup self-raising flour, 3 ozs. dripping (beaten up with a few drops of lemon juice to disguise its taste), 1 oz. sultanas, 2 ozs. sugar, 1 tablespoon treacle, milk to mix (about 1/3 cup).

Rub dripping into flour, add sugar and sultanas, and mix with the blended treacle and milk. Make fairly moist. Roll out, bake 10 minutes very hot oven, reduce the heat, bake 8 to 10 minutes more (slowly). These are delicious eaten with butter and quince jelly.

PUMPKIN SCONES

Take 1 cup cold mashed pumpkin, 3 cups self-raising flour, 1 egg, and ½ cup of sugar. Mix butter and sugar to a cream, add egg and pumpkin, then flour. If too stiff, add a little milk. Cook as ordinary scones, in a hot oven for 8-10 minutes.

COLONIAL DAMPER

This bush fare is simply composed of flour and water, with a little salt, made into flat round pieces on bark, and baked in the ashes. All old colonists are experts in making damper. "Tea, damper, and mutton", is a colonial institution, as the weary bushman is fully aware.

POTATO YEAST

Boil 6 moderate sized potatoes in plenty of water. When soft take them from the water, which must be saved. Mash them smoothly and mix with them 1 cup of flour and the same of sugar. Then gradually stir in the potato water. Put all in a jug and add ½-1 cup of old yeast — or beer. Stir all together and let stand for a few hours. It will probably rise to the top of the jug and must be stirred down or bottled. This yeast makes the quickest bread.

OLD TIME GINGER BREAD

½ lb. flour	1 tablespoon syrup
¾ teaspoon ginger	1 tablespoon treacle
½ teaspoon cinnamon	2 tablespoons hot water
2 ozs. butter	2 ozs. sugar
1 egg	Pinch of salt

½ teaspoon carbonate of soda

Rub butter into flour, add all dry ingredients; beat up egg and mix with heated treacle and syrup; also add hot water. Pour into flat tin, and bake in moderate oven for 20 minutes.

CHEESE SCONES

½ lb. self-raising flour
2 level dessertspoons butter
4 rounded tablespoons grated cheese
1 level teaspoon mustard

¼ teaspoon salt	Good pinch cayenne
7 tablespoons milk	1 egg

Rub butter into flour which has been sifted. Add mustard, salt, cayenne and grated cheese. Beat egg, add milk, then add to dry ingredients. Mix lightly. Press into shape. Cook 10 to 15 minutes in moderate oven.

PLAIN WHOLEMEAL BREAD

2 lbs. wholemeal flour 1 tablespoon honey
1 teaspoon salt
1 pkt. (1 tablespoon) dry yeast
1 pint warm water (approximately)

Mix dry ingredients.

Add the water and honey, slowly beating all the time until the dough is well mixed and leaves the side of the bowl. Put it on a lightly floured board and knead until smooth and elastic, about 10 minutes.

Cover and leave to rise until it has doubled in bulk. Punch down and divide into two loaves. Place in the pans and let rise again until double the size.

Bake for 35 to 40 minutes in hot oven.

When making your bread, remember the old Scottish saying:
"The whiter your bread — The sooner you're dead."

He that keeps nor crust nor crumb,
Weary of all, shall want some.
Shakespeare

GREAT-GRANDMA'S SCONES

Next time you set the heat control of your modern oven and pop in a batch of scones, spare a thought for great-grandma.

Her scones were cooked in a baker's oven, which had to be heated with hot coals for two hours beforehand. When ready, the coals were scraped out and the tray of scones was then lifted inside on a peel — a long, flat wooden carrier with a handle.

Take four cups of self-raising flour, a pinch of salt, 1 teaspoon sugar, 2 ozs. butter, melted, and two cups of milk to mix.

Sift flour, salt and sugar. Melt the butter, add milk and mix into flour lightly. Mould scones into shape, glaze with milk, and bake in a hot oven for 8-10 minutes.

DATE SCONES

2 cups self-raising flour
2 tablespoons sugar
½ to ¾ cup milk (depending on size of egg)

¼ teaspoon salt	1 tablespoon butter
½ cup chopped dates	1 egg

Sift flour and salt into basin, rub in butter well; add sugar and dates. Beat egg, add milk; pour into dry ingredients gradually. Mix to a soft dough, turn on to floured board and knead lightly. Roll out to ½ inch thickness, cut out with floured scone cutter. Place on greased oven tray, glaze with a little milk, bake in hot oven 12 to 15 minutes. Makes 1 dozen.

CHEESE AND DATE RING

Sift 3 cups of self-raising flour and salt into a bowl. Rub in 2 ozs. butter. Add ¼ cup sugar and 1 teaspoon grated lemon rind. Mix to a soft dough with 2 beaten eggs and ½ cup milk. Turn on to floured board. Knead lightly. Roll dough out to an oblong approximately 30 x 10 inches and ¼ inch thick. Combine 1 cup chopped dates, ½ cup grated cheese and ¼ cup nuts. Sprinkle over dough. Moisten edges. Roll into long thin roll. Form into a ring on oven tray. With clean scissors, cut nearly through to centre at 1½ inch intervals, turning each snipped section slightly sideways to show filling. Brush top with a little extra milk and sprinkle with some extra chopped nuts. Bake in hot oven approximately 25 minutes or until brown on top. Serve in slices, plain or buttered.

APRICOT NUT BREAD

½ cup honey	¾ cup milk
1 lb. apricots	2 tablespoons butter
1 egg	½ cup chopped nuts

3 cups self-raising flour
½ teaspoon bicarbonate of soda

Cook apricots in ½ cup water until tender. Rub through sieve and boil until there is 1 cup pulp. Sift dry ingredients, rub in butter. Beat egg well. Add with milk and apricot pulp, mix into a light dough. Pour into a well greased loaf tin and bake for 45 minutes in a hot oven.

A loaf of bread, the walrus said,
Is what we chiefly need
Pepper and vinegar besides
Are very good indeed —
Now if you're ready, Oysters dear,
We can begin to feed.
Lewis Carroll

KITTY'S BROWN LOAF

3 cups flour	1 tablespoon treacle
1 cup bran	1 cup boiling water
1 cup milk	Salt

4 teaspoons cream of tartar
2 teaspoons bicarbonate of soda

Sift flour and rising — add bran. Mix treacle and water together first, then milk and lastly all dry ingredients. Bake in loaf tin ¾ to 1 hour in hot oven.

RYE AND TREACLE BREAD

1 quart of Ale, 2 lbs. coarse rye flour, 2 quarts of milk, 3½ ozs. yeast, 6 lbs. white flour, 1 quart treacle, 2 tablespoons fennel, 3 tablespoons chopped orange peel, 7 ozs. butter.

Warm the Ale. Put the rye flour in a basin, and add the ale. Work for 15 minutes and let stand for 12 hours. Then add the lukewarm milk with the dissolved yeast and the white flour. Set aside till the dough has risen to double the original volume. Then work in the treacle, the chopped fennel and orange peel, and more white flour to make a very stiff dough. Let it rise once more. Shape into oblong loaves, put these on a cloth to rise.

When well risen, brush them over with cold water and bake in a warm oven. They should be brushed over with cold water twice during the process of baking and again on being taken out of the oven. They take about 40 minutes to bake.

DROP SCONES

1 scant teaspoon cream of tartar
½ scant teaspoon soda bicarbonate
1 tablespoon sugar

½ cup milk	4 ozs. flour
1 egg	Pinch of salt

Sift dry ingredients, add sugar, then make a batter by stirring the egg and milk in gradually. Have ready a greased griddle pan or iron baking slide. Heat this on top of the stove, then put the mixture on, using about a dessertspoon for each pikelet. Turn once with a knife directly they are set and lightly browned underneath.

CURRANTY BUNS

6 ozs. butter, 2 large cups sugar, 3 large cups self-raising flour with a pinch of salt added, 4 eggs, 1 large cup of milk, 2 cups currants and a dash of essence of lemon.

Cream butter and sugar, add eggs and sifted flour alternately. Beat well, gradually adding the milk, and lastly the currants sprinkled with lemon essence. Put into greased patty tins and cook in a moderate oven for 15 to 20 minutes.

TEACAKE

1 egg	½ cup sugar
½ cup milk	1 level cup self-raising flour

½ teaspoon vanilla essence
1 rounded tablespoon butter

Separate the white from the yolk of the egg. Place the egg white in warm dry basin and add pinch of salt. Beat until mixture stands in peaks. Gradually add the sugar, beating until the mixture is stiff and shiny. Add egg yolk and mix well. Add milk and vanilla. Sift flour and add lightly. Finally add melted butter. Bake 20-25 minutes. Cut and butter hot.

SPICED FRUIT BILLY BREAD

3 heaped cups plain flour
3 teaspoons cream of tartar
1½ teaspoons bicarbonate of soda
1 small teaspoon of salt
1 dessertspoon ground cinnamon
1 teaspoon mixed spice
2 tablespoons sugar 1 cup bran

Sift all the dry ingredients together and add the bran. Mix in with the tips of the fingers 1 tablespoon of butter. Mix 1 tablespoon golden syrup or honey in sufficient milk to make a soft dough. Add 1 cup of mixed fruit. Mix thoroughly, then put in a well greased 3 pint billy. Put lid on, and bake for 1½ hours in a steady oven.

BUBBLE BREAD

8 tablespoons plain flour, 3 teaspoons butter, 1 teaspoon salt, pepper, water to mix.

Rub butter into flour. Add water to make a firm dough. Roll out very thinly. Prick well, cut into squares and bake in a cool oven 12 minutes. Serve with butter, 2 tablespoons of finely grated cheese can be added for extra flavour.

If you wish to grow thinner, diminish your dinner,
And take to light claret instead of pale ale;
Look down with an utter contempt upon butter
And never touch bread till it's toasted - or stale.
H.S. Leigh

BOILED DROUGHT LOAF

2 cups bran 2 cups plain flour
1 cup sugar 1 cup sultanas
2 tablespoons treacle
2 teaspoons bicarbonate of soda
2 cups milk

Mix together bran, flour, sugar and sultanas. Add treacle, then bicarbonate of soda dissolved in milk. Mix well. Put into tins with lids on and boil for two hours. When cold, slice and butter.

(NOTE: Soup tins covered can be used. Boil for an hour. Half this recipe makes three soup tins.

CRUMPETS

2 eggs ¼ cup milk
2 teaspoons sugar ½ teaspoon salt
8 ozs. self-raising flour

Beat eggs with sugar lightly, add milk. Sift flour and salt in a basin, stir in beaten eggs and milk. Mix lightly, adding a little more milk if needed. Turn on to floured board, knead lightly. Roll or pat to ½ inch thickness, cut into rounds, prick tops with fork. Bake in hot oven for 10-12 minutes. Tear open and serve hot with butter and honey.

BUSH SCONES

1 lb. self-raising flour
1 cup of sour milk

Put flour in bowl, add milk and mix quickly with knife blade. Turn on to floured board, knead quickly and cut shapes as required. Place on warm floured tray into hot oven 10 to 15 minutes. Wonderful made in a camp oven and eaten with lemon butter — home-made — and scalded cream.

AUNT BESSIE'S BUNS

1 cup mashed potatoes
1 cup dried fruits
2 cups self-raising flour
1 cup sugar 1 cup milk

Mix potatoes and sugar to a cream, add the fruit, mix well, then add the milk and the flour gradually. Put into well greased sandwich tins and bake in a moderate oven for half an hour. When cool, ice lightly and sprinkle with coconut.

POTATO SCONES

½ lb. potatoes, peeled and cooked, ½ lb. butter, pinch of salt, 2 ozs. plain flour.

Mash the potatoes with butter, while still hot. Add salt and gradually mix in flour. Knead well. Roll out to the size of a large dinner plate and cut into four.

Place pieces in a piping hot frying pan or on a hot ungreased griddle. Prick with a fork and cook for 3 minutes on each side.

Serve at once or roll in a cloth to keep soft and tender.

IRISH SODA BREAD

Grease and flour a cold slide. Now in a bowl mix together 3 cups of wholemeal plain flour, 1 cup white flour, a good teaspoon of salt and a generous teaspoon of bicarbonate of soda.

Rub in ¼ lb. of butter and mix to a soft dough with half a pint of milk. With floured hands, shape into an oval loaf and place on prepared tray. Flour a knife and make a cross on top. Cook for 50 minutes in a moderate oven.

RYE BREAD

1 lb. rye flour — 1 teaspoon honey
1½ teaspoons salt — ½ cup sour cream
1 oz. yeast (not brewers)

Dissolve honey and yeast in ¼ cup warm water. Let it rise for 15 minutes, less in warm weather. Put unsieved flour and salt in basin, add yeast mixture, then ½ cup sour cream. Knead it and add at least ½ pint of warm water. Allow to double in size in warm spot, with tea towel over it. Bake for 40 minutes in moderately hot oven, in warm greased loaf tin.

BARA BRITH BREAD

½ lb. raisins, seeded
1 teaspoon baking powder
½ pint cold tea — ½ lb. sultanas
½ lb. flour — 6 ozs. brown sugar

Soak the fruit and sugar in cold tea. Beat in the flour and baking soda until well mixed. Bake in a medium oven for approximately 1½ hours or until done, tested by a straw or skewer. Leave to cool.

WALNUT BREAD

2½ cups self-raising flour, 1 egg beaten, 1 cup milk, ½ cup sugar, ½ teaspoon salt, 1 cup chopped walnuts.

Sift flour and mix with salt and sugar. Combine well beaten egg and milk and add all at once to dry ingredients, stirring quickly until flour is all dampened, but not until smooth. Quickly fold in the nuts, just enough to distribute. Turn into greased loaf pan (8 x 4 x 2½ inches) pushing well into corners. To prevent a crack from forming on loaf, cover with a second pan of the same size and bake in a slow oven for 20 minutes. Then remove top pan and increase heat and bake 25-30 minutes or until browned. Sultanas may be used instead of walnuts.

DROUGHT BUNS

1 lb. flour, 3 ozs. clarified dripping, 6 ozs. sugar, 1 teaspoon baking powder, a few currants, a little spice or nutmeg, 1 teaspoon salt, cup cold water.

Mix everything together except water, then add it and make a limp dough. Put in pieces on to a greased tin and bake in moderate oven. Very nice if eaten fresh.

It is very nice to think
The world is full of meat and drink,
With little children saying grace
In every Christian kind of place.
R.L. Stevenson

POTATO BREAD

Cook potatoes in their skins, peel and mash. Add as much flour as potato pulp and some yeast. Knead well, maybe adding water. Make into loaf or loaves. Put in oven, not as hot as for ordinary bread. Cook more slowly also. Do not close oven door as soon as usual.

CRACKLING BREAD

¾ cup corn flour — 1 cup plain flour
½ teaspoon salt — 2 eggs, beaten
¼ cup melted butter — 1 cup milk
1 small white onion, grated
½ cup crumbled, fried or grilled bacon
1½ teaspoons baking powder

Mix together flour, salt, baking powder and the corn flour. Stir milk and melted butter into the beaten eggs, add to dry ingredients with the onion and bacon. Beat until smooth. Turn into a greased 9 inch sandwich tin and bake in a hot oven about 20 minutes. Serve warm with grills, soups, salads, stews or casseroles.

AUNT DAPHNE'S SCONE BREAD

4 ozs. butter — 2 eggs
4 ozs. sugar
2 tablespoons boiling water

Cream butter and sugar with two tablespoons boiling water, add 2 eggs and beat well. Add enough flour and rising to roll out 1 inch thick. Cut as for scones. After being in oven 10 minutes and brown, take out and cut in half. Leave rough side up. Return to oven and brown. Cook in all about 20 minutes. Leave enough room on tray for this operation.

APRICOT SCONES

3 or 4 ozs. very finely shred dried apricots
8 ozs. self-raising flour sifted with a pinch of salt
1 teaspoon of grated lemon rind
1 dessertspoon lemon juice
1 dessertspoon sugar — 1 tablespoon butter
1 egg — 3 tablespoons milk
Some loaf sugar broken into quarters and moistened at the last moment with a squeeze of orange juice.

Sift flour into mixing bowl. Stir in the sugar. Rub in the butter. Add grated lemon rind and the very finely cut apricots (which are not soaked for this recipe). Beat the egg with the lemon juice. Add the milk and use to make a stiff scone dough. Mould with floured hands. Pat or roll ½ inch thick. Cut in 2 inch rounds. Place on greased oven tray. Press a sugar cube on each. Bake hot oven 12-14 minutes. Serve well buttered.

APRICOT LOAF

4 ozs. dried apricots
2 ozs. finely chopped walnuts
8 ozs. self-raising flour sifted with a pinch of salt
¼ cup each of orange juice and water mixed (use an 8 oz. cup)
1 egg, ¾ cup sugar, 1 oz. butter

Cut the apricots into shreds. Soak for an hour in cold water to cover. Then drain well through a wire strainer pressing out surplus liquid.

Beat up the egg, gradually beating in the sugar until it is creamy. Add the warm melted butter and then the drained apricots and nuts. Blend together, turn this queer mixture into the sifted flour, and use the orange juice and water to blend it to a smooth thick cake texture. Turn into a generously buttered cake tin. Bake in a moderate oven approximately 60 minutes or until golden brown and firm to touch. Cool on wire rack. Don't cut until next day. Spread slices with creamed butter.

GINGERBREAD

Boil together for 5 minutes, ¾ lb. treacle, ½ lb. butter, 6 ozs. sugar. Whilst boiling, pour on to 12 ozs. flour, 1 teaspoon ginger and allspice, with peel of 1 lemon grated. When cold bake in tins.

Another Way:

2lbs. honey, 1¾ lbs. sugar, 2¾ lbs. flour, ½ lb. almonds chopped fine, ½ lb. each orange or lemon peel, 1 oz. cinnamon, ¼ oz. mace, ¼ oz. cardamom, ¾ oz. each of cloves and grated nutmeg.

Melt honey and sugar with 1 glass of water. Add rest of ingredients until a stiff paste. Roll out thin. Cut into small squares or gingerbread men.

HONEY DATE LOAF

1 cup boiling water
1 egg
1 tablespoon butter
2 cups plain flour
½ cup honey
½ cup walnuts
1 teaspoon salt
1 teaspoon vanilla
1½ cups chopped dates
2/3 cup brown sugar
1 teaspoon bicarbonate of soda

Pour boiling water over dates, add butter, sugar, honey and salt, stir to blend, cool a little. When mixture is lukewarm, add beaten egg and soda. Sift flour, add to date mixture, mix well; stir in walnuts and vanilla. Turn into well-greased 9 x 5 inch loaf tin; bake in moderately slow oven about 1 hour 15 minutes or until the cake is cooked when tested with a skewer. Serve sliced and buttered.

NORMANDY LOAF

¼ lb. bacon
One egg
1 medium size onion
½ pint milk
4 ozs. butter
Egg glazing
1 lb. self-raising flour
1 tablespoon minced parsley
1½ ozs. grated cheddar cheese

Remove rind from the bacon and cut into small dice. Peel and dice the onion. Place both in a frying pan and saute for five minutes. Drain well and cool. Sift the flour, rub in butter until the mixture resembles fine breadcrumbs. Add the bacon and onion mixture, parsley, beaten egg and milk. Mix to a smooth dough and turn into a well greased orange loaf tin. Brush the top with a little egg glazing before sprinkling with grated cheese. Bake in moderately hot oven for about one hour or until well risen and golden brown. Remove from the tin and allow to cool slightly. Serve warm, sliced. Garnish with parsley. Butter well.

BACON AND ONION ROLL

3 ozs. butter
2 teaspoons sugar
1 egg
½ cup milk
2 tablespoons finely chopped onion
8 ozs. self-raising flour
2 ozs. grated tasty cheese
2 rashers bacon, finely chopped

Place the chopped bacon in a pan, heat until fat melts, add chopped onion and cook in the bacon fat until transparent but not browned.

Cream butter and sugar, add egg. Mix in sifted flour alternately with the milk. Add grated cheese, onion and bacon.

Place in a greased nut loaf tin and bake in a moderate oven for 50 minutes to 1 hour. Serve sliced, buttered and sprinkled with a little chopped parsley, then cut into quarters.

CHEESE ROLL

2 ozs. butter
2 ozs. castor sugar
1 egg
Salt
½ cup milk
Pinch cayenne
8 ozs. self-raising flour
3 ozs. grated tasty cheese
Grated rind 1 lemon
2 tablespoons chopped chives

Cream butter and sugar, add egg. Add sifted flour, salt and cayenne, alternately with the milk, blend grated cheese, and lemon rind.

Place into a greased nut loaf tin and bake in a moderate oven for 50 minutes to 1 hour. Serve cut in slices, buttered and sprinkled with chopped chives.

WHEN FATHER SHOOK THE STOVE

I never heard him quit his bed
Or his alarm bell ring;
I never heard his gentle tread ,
Or his attempts to sing;
To human voice I never stirred,
But deeper down I dove
Beneath the covers, when I heard
My father shake the stove.

He flung the noisy dampers back,
Then rattled steel on steel,
Until the force of his attack
The building seemed to feel.
Though I'd a youngster's heavy eyes
All sleep from them he drove;
It seemed to me the dead must rise
When father shook the stove.

WHOLEMEAL ONION ROLLS

8 ozs. wholemeal self-raising flour
8 ozs. white self-raising flour
1 level teaspoon salt
Pinch cayenne pepper
1 tablespoon finely chopped onion
1 cup grated tasty cheese
2 ozs. butter — 1 egg
1¼ cup milk — Extra 2 ozs. butter

Sift flours, salt and cayenne together into a basin. Rub in the butter with the finger-tips. Make a well in centre of mixture and add egg beaten with the milk, stirring quickly and lightly to a soft dough. Turn out on a lightly floured board and knead just enough to make a smooth surface. Roll into an oblong about ¼ inch thick. Melt extra butter and brush over the dough, then sprinkle with the mixed cheese and onion. Roll up lengthwise, pressing lightly to make a firm roll, then cut into 1 inch slices. Place slices on a greased oven tray and bake in hot oven for 15 to 20 minutes.

CHEESE LOAF

2 cups self-raising flour, ¾ cup of grated cheese, pinch of salt and cayenne. Mix together with a beaten egg and a little milk. Bake in moderate oven 30 minutes.

ORANGE BREAD

Peel from 1 large orange, finely sliced;
2 cups self-raising flour;
extra ½ cup sugar;
2 cups cold water — ½ cup sugar;
1 tablespoon butter — 1 egg
1 cup milk — pinch salt

Put the sliced peel in a saucepan, cover with the cold water, bring slowly to boil and cook until tender. Add the sugar and boil until the syrup is nearly absorbed and the peel has a candied appearance. Set aside. Cream butter with the extra sugar, add the well beaten egg.

Stir in the sifted flour and salt, alternately with the milk. Add the orange peel and mix well. Turn into well greased loaf tin and stand for 15 minutes before baking in a moderate oven for ¾ to 1 hour. Best kept a few days before slicing and spread with butter.

SNOW PANCAKES

For the Snow Country

Mix and beat the flour and milk as usual, leave it to stand for half an hour. At the last minute fold in a dessertspoon of melted butter. Put a pan over a low heat to warm, and sally forth, well wrapped up, with a spoon and cold basin in hand to find one level tablespoon of clean snow to replace each egg normally used. Lightly fold snow into the batter with a fork, and cook immediately. The snow will remain crystalised and will make the pancakes light and fluffy.

The secret is to keep the snow crystalised when cooked, so if you make a large number it is better to divide the batter into four-person portions and get the snow at the last minute.

BUTTERMILK ROUNDS

2 cups plain flour; 1 teaspoon bicarbonate of soda; ¼ teaspoon salt; ¼ cup sugar; 3 dessertspoons butter; 1 dessertspoon treacle; 1/3 cup buttermilk; ½ cup currants.

Sift together flour, bicarbonate of soda and salt, stir in sugar. Work in the butter with one of your hands until well blended. Add treacle, buttermilk and currants, knead until smooth. Roll out on a lightly floured surface to ½ inch thick, cut into rounds with a floured 2 inch scone cutter. Put on a greased, floured tray, bake in a moderate oven 20 minutes or until lightly browned. Serve warm with butter.

JELLIES

Jellies used to be made from hartshorn or Isinglass, being a preparation of fish gut, the best of which came from sturgeons. John Farley, who in 1783 was master cook at the London Tavern, said the best jelly was made from Rhenish wine, lemon juice, hartshorn shavings, strained through a swan's skin (a kind of smooth flannel) jelly bag into a basin. It was also made laboriously from calves feet too, being boiled 5-6 hours. Next was sheet gelatine, which also had long hours of preparation.

Before powdered gelatine was manufactured there was isinglass. This was in a sheet and had to be soaked in water to melt it.

One ounce of isinglass to set a quart of jelly.

Isinglass should be put into invalids' tea, a good pinchful for a teacup. It should be introduced as much as possible into the food of the weak, as it is most strengthening.

To clarify Isinglass — break an ounce of isinglass small, pour over it half a pint of boiling water, and set over a gentle heat to dissolve. When dissolved take off the scum or strain it through a cloth.

SHERRY SNOW

An attractive cold sweet to serve in individual goblets (4 to 5).

8 oz. cup of cold water
2 barely level dessertspoons gelatine
2 ozs. castor sugar
1 tablespoon sherry
½ teaspoon vanilla essence
A little whipped cream
Some half glace cherries for decoration
3 eggs

Put the gelatine into a cup and cover with a little of the cold water. When softened, empty the remaining water into a small saucepan. Add the sugar, bring to boil and remove from heat. Stir in the gelatine. Blend until thoroughly dissolved.

Separate yolks and whites of eggs, whisk yolks until frothy. Then gradually add the hot syrup, beating all the time. Stir in vanilla and sherry and beat again.

Put aside until just showing signs of setting. At once whisk egg whites until really stiff. Take a fork and beat egg yolk mixture until smooth. Fold in egg whites. Blend evenly. Divide between the goblets. Chill before serving.

FRUIT AND NUT JELLY

"The 101 degrees in the shade" Christmas Pudding.

¼ lb. muscatel raisins (stoned), 3 ozs. (when shelled) walnuts (broken roughly), 2 ozs. blanched almonds (split), 2 ozs. candied cherries (each cut in four), ½ nutmeg (grated), ¼ teaspoon cinnamon, ⅛ teaspoon spice, 1 pint nicely flavoured amber jelly, with plenty of fruit juice or wine and fruit juice in it.

Wet mould. Pour 2 tablespoons of dissolved jelly in.

Let it set. Put two sprays of the stoned muscatels (still on the stalks) on. These muscatels can be "stoned" without being removed from the stalks. Put almonds into all the spare spaces.

Put liquid jelly on (with a teaspoon) till just covered. Set firm. Then set 1 inch of jelly.

Mix all the nuts and stoned muscatels and cherries and spices and remains of the jelly together (reserving a couple of tablespoons). When it beings "to jell" pour into the mould. Pour the 2 tablespoons in to fill in any little spaces there may be. Delicious eaten with whipped cream or custard.

CHOCOLATE MOUSSE

4 teaspoons powdered coffee
8 ozs. semi-sweet chocolate
6 eggs — 6 tablespoons sugar
½ cup cream — 2 tablespoons butter

Melt chocolate over low heat, add coffee. Stir in 4 tablespoons of the sugar, cook 10 minutes. Allow to cool. Add egg-yolks and softened butter, mix well. Whip cream with balance of sugar, fold into chocolate mixture. Lastly fold in stiffly beaten egg-whites. Fill into serving dish, chill until set.

PORT WINE JELLY

3 rounded teaspoons gelatine
2 tablespoons lemon juice
4 tablespoons sugar to taste
¼ pint hot water ½ pint port wine

Dissolve the gelatine in hot water. Add sugar and stir until thoroughly dissolved. Add strained lemon juice and wine. Pour into a mould and chill. When set, roughly fork into tall glasses. If preferred, serve with cream.

LEMON SOUFFLE

3 eggs 6 ozs. castor sugar
2 small lemons ½ oz. gelatine
½ gill water (2½ ozs.) 1½ gills cream (7½ ozs.)
A little extra cream
Finely chopped toasted almonds

Prepare souffle case, capacity 1¼ pint, or straight sided container, by tying double band of greased paper around dish on the outside with string, extending 2 inches above the edge.

Separate eggs and place yolks, sugar and grated lemon rind in basin and beat until thick. Heat lemon juice, add to mixture, then beat until mixture is firm enough to hold a double-eight shape.

Lightly whip cream and fold in mixture. Dissolve gelatine in water over heat and stir in mixture. Whisk egg whites until stiff, set bowl containing souffle mixture on ice or in cold water and fold in egg whites. As the mixture starts to thicken, pour into prepared souffle case and chill until set.

Remove paper, spread a little cream around sides and gently press on nuts, blanched and toasted for a few minutes in a hot oven until golden. Decorate top.

CARAMEL CREAM MOUSSE

5 eggs 2 ozs. castor sugar
½ oz. gelatine juice of 1½ lemons
cream chopped nuts

Caramel Syrup:

6 ozs. sugar ¼ pint water

Caramel Syrup:

Put sugar with half the water in saucepan. Stir over low heat until sugar is dissolved. Increase heat, cook until golden brown without stirring. Very gradually add remaining water, stirring well. Put syrup aside to cool.

Mousse:

Break 3 eggs into bowl, separate remaining 2, add their yolks, sugar to bowl also. Soften gelatine in lemon juice. Dissolve over gently boiling water. Whisk eggs and sugar over hot water until foamy and light in colour. Mixture should be firm enough to keep its shape. Remove from heat, continue whisking until mixture is cool; gently whisk in caramel syrup. Stir in gelatine mixture, leave in cool place until semi-set. Whisk egg-whites until stiff, carefully fold into mixture. Turn into serving bowl or large 2-pint mould. Top with whipped, sweetened cream and chopped nuts. Chill before serving.

PRUNE MOUSSE

Soak ½ lb. prunes overnight in cold tea and cook until tender without sugar. Stone the prunes and blend them. Sieving is tedious, but essential, to get rid of all skin. Fold the prunes into ½ pint of whipped cream flavoured with brandy, then add 3 stiffly beaten egg whites.

Serve it cold with extra cream.

PARTY ORANGES

4 large oranges ½ pint whipped cream
5 level tablespoons castor sugar
1 liqueur glass Maraschino liqueur
2 dessertspoons fresh orange juice
3 ozs. blanched and chopped almonds

Cut off top section of each orange and very carefully scoop out the sections without bruising the skin. Beat in a bowl the cream with the castor sugar and when stiff mix with the Maraschino liqueur, fresh orange juice and the finely chopped almonds. Add the orange sections and refill the fruit cases with this mixture.

Replace the tops and decorate each orange with a couple of orange (or small lemon) leaves. Chill thoroughly before serving.

IRISH CHERRIES

2 lbs. black cherries
3 tablespoons red currant jelly
½ pint claret ½ teaspoon cinnamon
3 cloves 1 tablespoon sugar
Whipped cream Brandy

Simmer the cherries, claret, cinnamon, cloves and sugar over a low heat till the cherries are soft. Remove the fruit and reduce the syrup till fairly thick. Stir in the red currant jelly.

Chill the fruit and sauce separately. When ready to serve, pour a little syrup over each dish of cherries and top with slightly sweetened cream flavoured with brandy.

ORANGE-PRUNE WHIP

1 cup cooked, sieved prune pulp
1 stiffly beaten egg white
1 tablespoon lemon juice or sherry
½ teaspoon grated orange rind
1 cup cream, whipped stiffly
½ cup sugar ½ cup orange juice

Beat egg white until stiff, then beat in the sugar. Add the prune pulp and mix well, then add orange juice, grated rind and sherry or lemon juice. Fold in the whipped cream. Chill. Garnish with whole cooked prunes.

HOW TO MAKE AGAR-AGAR JELLY FROM SEAWEED

After heavy winter storms, great banks of seaweed are usually left heaped along the beaches.

This provides an opportunity for anyone living along the coast of Victoria, to secure a supply of Gracilaria lichenoides, the seaweed from which the valuable agar-agar jelly can be prepared.

The botanical description of this marine plant is: Fronds growing in tufts from a basal stem. These fronds are round in section, still and tapering to points. The cysts containing the spores from which new plants grow, are thickly clustered on the branchlets. The plants are usually between fifteen inches and two feet in length.

A further aid in indentification, is the light purple colour of the plant and the way in which the fronds resemble thin rods of raw gristle.

The plants should be washed in fresh water, dried thoroughly and stored in calico bags, hung in a warm, dry place.

To use it, a handful of the dried plant is soaked in water until it swells to its original size, then it is boiled, sugar is added and for flavouring either a pure fruit juice or raw fruit cut into small pieces may be employed.

The really remarkable thing is the small quantity of the soaked seaweed required. One part of the plant, boiled in one hundred times the volume of water, will set into a firm jelly when cold.

GOLDEN SOUFFLE

Boil 2 tablespoons golden syrup. Allow to cool a little. Dissolve ½ teaspoon gelatine in as little hot water as possible. Whip whites of 3 eggs stiffly. Pour golden syrup on to these gradually, beating all the time, then add melted gelatine slowly. Pour into a mould to set. A squeeze of lemon juice may be added, if desired.

Sauce:

Whip ¼ pint cream and add 3 beaten egg yolks and 3 tablespoons of golden syrup.

NOUGAT FROMAGE

4 eggs 2 ozs. sugar
½ pint cream 1/5 cup gelatine

Nougat:

3 ozs. sugar
1½ ozs. walnuts or almonds

Melt sugar in pan, add chopped nuts. Leave to set. Crush. Beat eggs and sugar well. Add gelatine, crushed nougat and vanilla. Decorate with cream.

PRUNE AND ALMOND MOULD

Take ½ oz. of gelatine, dissolve in a little warm water, stew ½ lb. of prunes till soft and take out stones, add a little sugar and the juice of a lemon, then add the gelatine to it and half a pint of prune juice. Put ¼ lb. of finely chopped almonds at the bottom of a mould, then pour in the prunes. When cold turn out and serve with whipped cream. This makes a delicious cold sweet.

MINT SHERBERT

A palate refresher between courses. Can be used instead of an ice at the end of a meal. For five persons.

Leaves of 12 tender sprigs of mint
2 rounded teaspoons gelatine dissolved, cold
1 teaspoon grated lemon rind
¾ cup lemon juice ¾ cup sugar
2¼ cups water 2 egg whites
pinch salt

Strip sprigs of mint of their leaves and chop leaves. Boil sugar with water for 10 minutes. Add gelatine in cold water to syrup. Steep chopped leaves in this for 1 hour. Strain, then add lemon juice and rind. Chill until mixture begins to solidify. Put in a chilled bowl, whisk until fluffy with pinch of salt. Have ready separately whipped egg whites. Fold these into lemon mixture lightly. Chill for at least 4 hours. At intervals, work fruit mixture forward with a fork, to prevent egg whites from separating. Just before serving, whip again with a wire whisk. Serve in tall glasses, with a mint leaf.

NOTES

BEVERAGES

CRAIG'S ROYAL HOTEL — BALLARAT

Passing drovers, bullock-drivers, curious travellers and the shepherds from William Yuille's station, all found that the best place to camp was at the very edge of the plateau, at the top of the gully which ran down to the Yarrowee River. Here they were safe from the floods, though close to water, and from the heights of the plateau they had a clear view across the flat to the two peaks of Warrenheip and Buninyong. It was on this high ground in 1853, that Thomas Bath built his hotel — "The Ballarat".

The township of Ballarat had been proclaimed about the middle of 1852, and the first sales of Ballarat land were held soon after at Geelong. In May, 1853, the wood and iron structure was completed, and in June, Thomas Bath acquired the first local publican's licence. That December he had decided to add a two-storey section. It was built of local stone and timber cut from the crater on the western slope of Mount Buninyong. A tower was added which carried the first public clock in Ballarat — a fact of which Henry Handel Richardson made use in "The Fortunes of Richard Mahony". The clock is said to be still operating in the Clunes Town Hall. This fact is still to be verified. By 1854 the official name of the hostelry had fallen to disuse, it had become known as "Bath's". In August 1857, Bath sold the hotel to Walter Craig and retired to his splendid estate "Ceres" at Lake Learmonth.

Walter Craig had the humble single storied building of iron and timber transported to Soldiers' Hill, where it remained at the corner of Doveton and Macarthur Streets until 1897. In Lydiard Street he erected the three-storey south wing which stands today. This new wing was completed in the early 1860's. In less than five years, major additions were necessary.

In 1867 the Hotel was elaborately decorated for the visit of Prince Alfred, Queen Victoria's second son. During this year Craig rented the splendid stables behind the Hotel to a young man named Adam Lindsay Gordon, who conducted a livery and letting business on the site of the present bottle shop. The two men shared a passion for horses. Gordon made mention of Craig in his poem, "The Banker's Dream". Gordon left Ballarat late in 1868.

By Courtesy of the Management.

THE BILLY

Old Billy — battered, brown and black,
With many days of camping,
Companion of the bulging sack,
And friend in all out tramping:
How often on the Friday night —
Your cubic measure testing —
With jam and tea we stuffed you tight,
Before we started nesting.

ICED TEA

About an hour or two before it is to be served, brew a pot of strong tea. After 3 minutes, pour off the tea. Into a tall jug, put the juice of 1 orange, 1 lemon, 1 lime, 8 sprigs of tender mint (chopped), 4 rounded dessertspoons of sugar. Stir well and set aside to blend. Just before serving, fill the jug two-thirds full of ice and pour the tea over.

BILLY TEA

Boil the billy over the camp fire, putting a twig across the open mouth, to prevent smoking. When boiling, throw in several generous spoonsful of tea, then take the billy handle and quickly describe circles several times, so that the leaves are sent to the bottom of the billy.

HARVEST DRINK

Put 6 ozs. sugar, ¼ lb. very fine oatmeal, and half a lemon, sliced thinly, into a large jug or pan. Stir well together, gradually adding just enough water to dissolve sugar.

Then add a gallon of boiling water, stir, and leave to get cold.

SIMPLE BARLEY WATER

Put 3 tablespoons of pearl barley in a two-quart saucepan. Just cover the barley with cold water. Bring to the boil. Strain off the water. Fill saucepan with fresh cold water. Bring to boil again. Simmer 10-15 minutes.

In a deep earthenware bowl have ready the very finely cut golden rind (no pith) of two oranges and three lemons with the strained juice of the fruit and half a cup of sugar. Strain in the boiling barley water. Leave overnight to cool. Strain out the rinds. Serve well chilled. This is an excellent thirst quencher.

DANDELION COFFEE

Dandelion roots to be used for coffee must be gathered in the autumn. In the spring the roasted roots have very little flavour. Wash the roots, but neither pare nor scrape them for the flavour is chiefly in the skins. Bake them in the oven to the colour of roasted coffee berries. When cold grind and use like coffee.

BEEF TEA BRACER

Into a cup of hot beef tea put a wineglass of sherry, previously heated, but not boiled, and serve immediately.

HOLIDAY TEA

½ stick cinnamon	3 teaspoons tea
5 whole cloves	Juice of ½ lemon
3 strips orange rind	Juice of 1 orange
3 cups water	Lump sugar

Tie cinnamon and cloves in a cheese-cloth bag. Drop bag and orange rind slices into water. Simmer on low flame for 10 minutes. Add tea, lemon juice and orange juice, steep for about 3 minutes. Strain into 4 cups. Serve with lump sugar.

Add a bunch of mint leaves to a pot of hot tea. When cold, strain into glasses and chill.

MINT TEA

Use two sprigs of mint for each cup. Cut it rather finely into the teapot. Measure in the tea, and set the pot where it will gradually become warm. When the water boils, brew for about 3 minutes.

Now stir the fire, and close the shutters fast,
Let fall the curtains, wheel the sofa round,
And, while the bubbling and loud hissing urn,
Throws up a steamy column, and the cups,
That cheer but not inebriate, wait on each,
So let us welcome peaceful ev'ning in.

Cowper

TODDY

"Sit roun' the table well content
An' steer aboot the toddy."

TODDY

Whisky Sugar Hot Water Lemon (if liked)

Pour boiling water slowly into a tumbler till half full. Let it remain until the crystal is thoroughly heated, then pour out. Put in loaf sugar to taste with a glassful of boiling water. When melted pour in ½ glass of whisky and stir well, add more hot water and another ½ glass whisky — stir, serve hot! Can be flavoured with lemon if wished.

IRISH COFFEE

Pour one jigger of Irish whisky in each whisky glass, which you place on a warmer. Turn the glass over the flame and ignite the whisky.

While the whisky is still burning in the glass, which you have placed on the table, pour in the coffee, (hot and strong, prepared in advance).

Pour over semi-stiff cream, which should not combine with the coffee. (Pour the cream over a teaspooon which you hold upside down.)

ORANGE WINE

13 oranges	1 lb. of sugar
1 gallon of water	sugar

Wipe the oranges and cut into slices; take out the pips. Put into an earthenware bowl and pour boiling water over them. Cover and leave for a week, stirring every day with a wooden spoon. Strain through a jelly bag, measure the juice and add sugar — 1 lb. to the gallon. Put in a cask and bung up after seven days.

FARMER'S MARKET

½ cup tomato juice	Dash curry
½ cup cold buttermilk	Dash spice

Mix. Serve very cold in 1 glass.

The wines of Australia proper obtained a high meed of praise at the French Exposition, the Camden wines being much prized, and no one can deny that our Gallic friends are the best judges.

The South Australian wines are the Shiraz, the Verdeilho, the Pineau, the Muscat, the Riesling and the Montura.

The South Australian grapes are the largest in size of any of the Australians; but the finest fruits do not ferment the best wines.

The wines made in New South Wales are free from acidity, fruity in flavour, devoid of spirit and mellow on the palate.

Although no poet has spoken their praise, they will soon force themselves on public notice.

We have used M'Arthur's Camden, Blake's Kaludah and Cawarra, and cannot decide which is the superior; but it is only justice to the latter to say that the manufacturer was awarded a first-class medal at the last International Exhibition.

SLOE GIN

1 gallon gin — 2½ lbs. white sugar
4 cloves — 1 cup brown sugar
3 quarts sloes or prunes
1 teaspoon of almond essence

Put in crock for 3 months. Shake two or three times a week. Strain. Bottle carefully.

ELDERBERRY WINE

2 heads of elder flowers in full bloom picked on a dry day
1 gallon cold water
2 tablespoons white vinegar
1½ lbs. loaf sugar — 2 lemons

Squeeze the juice out of the lemons. Cut the rind into four, put this with the elder flowers, sugar and water into a large basin. Pour on the cold water and steep for 24 hours. Strain off and bottle in screwtopped lemonade bottles. Keep for three weeks before using.

OR

7 lbs. of elderberries, picked on a sunny day
3 gallons water
To each gallon of liquid, add 3 lbs. of good loaf sugar
½ teaspoon brewer's yeast
1 lb. raisins — ¼ pint brandy
6 cloves — ½ oz. ground ginger

Strip the berries from the stalks, pour the water, quite boiling, over them, let them stand for 24 hours, then bruise well and drain through a hair sieve or jelly bag. Measure the juice obtained, put it into a preserving pan with sugar, raisins, ginger and cloves in above stated proportions. Boil gently for about 1 hour and skim when necessary. Let the liquid stand until milk-warm, then stir in the yeast and turn the whole into a clean dry cask. Cover the bung hole with a folded cloth. Let the cask remain, undisturbed, for 14 days, then stir in the brandy and bung tightly. In about 6 months, the wine may be drawn off into bottles, tightly corked and stored.

ATHOL BROSE

Tablespoon barley meal,
2 tablespoons whisky,
1 tablespoon honey (melted).

CINNAMON HOT CHOCOLATE

1 cup water — ¼ cup sugar
3 cups milk
2 ozs. cooking chocolate
1 dessertspoon finely grated orange rind
a few drops of vanilla or almond essence cinnamon sticks

Melt the chocolate in basin over hot water. Put sugar, milk, water and essence in a saucepan and heat slowly stirring to dissolve the sugar. Pour into the saucepan the hot melted chocolate and stir well to mix. Bring to boiling point and stirring all the time simmer for several minutes.

GOOD COFFEE

It is hard to make enough coffee to go round at larger parties and cold coffee re-heated loses its flavour. However, coffee made earlier and strained into a large flame-proof pot to stand in a pan of hot water over a low heat, will be ready to bring just under the boil, when coffee time arrives. 1½ gallons of coffee, from 18ozs of ground coffee, pours 40 good cups.

Coffee and tea can be served black, with a thin slice of lemon in the cups.

TONIC STOUT

Tonic stout was made always with dried nettles. It was taken as a restorative and stimulant and was administered in all cases showing declining vitality or general weakness. It is a true beer and can be drunk at once.

8 ozs. black, or burnt malt
1 oz. dried stinging nettles
¼ oz. black liquorice 1 oz. hops
1 oz. yeast 2 potatoes
2 ozs. brown sugar 10 pints water

Bring the water to the boil and add to it the herbs, malt, hops, liquorice and potatoes, cut into pieces. Simmer all gently together for an hour, then strain into a pan, upon the sugar. When all is at blood-heat, stir in the yeast and cover the pan closely. Let it stand for twenty-four hours, then skim well, bottle and cork only lightly for another twelve hours. Then drive in the corks, leave for two days and the beer will be ready for use.

Long quaffing maketh a short lyfe.
John Lyly

MILK AND MOLASSES

1 tablespoon molasses (or black treacle)
½ cup boiling water
½ teaspoon ginger ½ cup hot milk

Mix molasses or treacle with ginger in saucepan. Pour boiling water over mixture and continue to boil for 1 minute. Add milk. Serve in mug.

CHOCOLATE RUSSE

2 cups of hot chocolate and 2 cups of strong coffee. Beat together. Top with sweetened whipped cream flavoured with almond.

ALMOND MILK

Put blanched almonds through a nut-mill or the smallest grinder of a mincer. Mix the meal with warm water made the consistency of milk. Let stand for at least two hours. Strain. Use as a drink or with fruit. It should be used the day it is made.

ORANGE HONEY MINT

6 oranges 1 cup water
½ cup honey
1 bunch crushed mint leaves
3 pints ginger ale or soda water

Grate the rinds from the oranges. Place in saucepan with water, mint leaves and honey. Bring to the boil. Cook for five minutes. Strain through a fine wire strainer or piece of muslin, add the orange juice, chill. Serve in tall glasses with ginger ale or soda water, crushed ice, cherry, mint sprigs.

EGG-NOG

1 white of egg 1 tablespoon cream
1 tablespoon sherry or brandy sugar to taste

Put the wine or brandy into a tumbler, add the cream and sugar and mix very thoroughly. Whisk the egg white to a stiff froth, and stir it lightly into contents of tumbler. Serve at once.

BLACKBERRY WINE

Cover blackberries with briskly boiling water and stand all night. Strain, sieve into a crock and let ferment for 15 days (not too warm or too cold). Add 1 lb. sugar and a pint of brandy to every gallon of juice. Bottle.

HONEY WINE

Take one quart of honey to a gallon of water and boil together for one hour, adding, during the boiling, not more than half an ounce each of ginger, cinnamon and cloves, and a small piece of bruised nutmeg. (If preferred, the spices can be omitted and the juice of a lemon, or an orange, with the thinly peeled rind, used instead.) The must is then allowed to cool and the spices taken out. Ale yeast is added, and, if a wide-necked vessel is used for the fermentation, the yeast should be spread upon a slice of toast and floated upon the surface. When the first ferment has subsided strain again to remove the toast and put all into a stone jar, or cask, and keep for a while in a warm place, lightly corked, until all visible ferment has ceased. Then cork securely and finish in a cool place. Honey wine can be bottled off and used within six months of its making, but it will improve if kept.

Within this hive,
We're all alive,
Good liquor makes us funny,
So if you're dry,
Come in and try
The Flavour of our honey.

WALNUT MEAD

To every gallon of water put three and a half pounds of honey and boil together for three-quarters of an hour. To each gallon of liquor obtained put two dozen walnut leaves and pour the liquor boiling hot upon them. Let them stand all night and then take out the leaves and put in a spoonful of yeast. Let it work for two or three days and then make up the quantity to fill the cask. Let it stand for three months, then bottle.

DANDELION WINE

Two quarts of dandelion flowers; cover with half a gallon of water, and boil; strain, and when lukewarm add three lemons, two pounds of white sugar and one-quarter royal yeast-cake; let it stand about ten days, or until done working, then strain, bottle and seal.

One sip of this
Will bathe the drooping spirits in delight,
Beyond the bliss of dreams.
Milton

PARSLEY WINE

To make parsley wine, take one pound of parsley to every gallon of water. Put the leaves into a crock and pour the water boiling on to them, leaving them to infuse for twenty-four hours. Then put into a pan four pounds of sugar or honey, with the juice and rind of two lemons and two oranges. Strain the infusion on to this and stir until the sugar has quite melted, then put in half an ounce of yeast and stand the vessel in a warm place for four days. When the tumultuous ferment has passed, bottle or cask the wine and keep the cask well topped up with boiling water. This wine can be drunk at once but will improve with keeping.

Good wine maketh good blood,
Good blood causeth good humours,
Good humours cause good thoughts,
Good thoughts bring forth good works,
Good works carry a man to Heaven,
Ergo, Good wine carrieth a man to Heaven.
Anon.

DRINKING

Three cups of wine a prudent man may take,
The first of these for constitution's sake;
The second to the girl he loves the best;
The third and last to lull him to his rest;
Then home to bed! but if a fourth he pours,
That is the cup of folly, and not ours.
Loud, noisy talking on the fifth attends;
The sixth breeds fueds and falling-out of friends;
Seven beget blows and faces stain'd with gore;
Eight and the watch patrol breaks ope the door;
Mad with the ninth, another cup goes round,
And then the swill'd sot drops senseless to the ground.

"Eubulus". Poetical fragment quoted by Athenaeus, turned into English verse by Cumberland.

ORANGE BRANDY

Take rinds of 3 lemons, 8 oranges, peeled very thin and 3 lbs. sugar finely pounded. Steep the whole in gallon of brandy, stirring it frequently. Filter and bottle.

MARROW RUM

One ripe tough-skinned marrow. Cut off stem end and scoop out the pith and pips with long handled spoon. Fill cavity with sugar and grated rind and juice of 2 oranges. Before replacing the top pour in ½ oz. of bakers' yeast creamed with a little warm water. Seal the top well and sling the marrow in butter muslin stem end upwards from a book in a warm room. Place a bowl underneath. Leave for 3 to 4 weeks until marrow begins to drip. Then tap it and draw off liquid into the bowl. Pour the liquid into a storage jar, one with a small neck for preference, and add a handful of raisins. Cover with three layers of clean cotton material and leave in warm room to finish fermentation, then syphon off and bottle when fermentation is complete. Keep for at least a year.

COFFEE-BRANDY

Place brandy, coffee beans, and sugar into a small bowl. Stir until sugar dissolves. Cover, stand overnight. Strain off coffee beans before using.

(A hot drink is as good as an overcoat.
Petronius)

PARSNIP WINE

To each gallon of water take 3 lbs. of parsnips; 3 lemons; 1 orange; 3 lbs. of white sugar; ½ oz. yeast.

Cut the raw parsnips into ½ inch pieces and cut the lemons and orange into small pieces. Boil all these until the parsnips are soft. Put the sugar into a bowl and pour the parsnip mixture over it. Stir until the sugar is dissolved and bottle while the liquid is warm. Place a small piece of yeast, about the size of a marble, in each bottle and leave it to ferment. When fermentation has stopped, cork tightly and wire the corks on to the bottles. Don't drink this wine when it is too fresh, leave for at least six months.

DAMSON WINE

To each gallon of damsons, add 1 gallon of boiling water. To each gallon of liquor obtained from these, add 4 lbs. of loaf sugar and ½ pint of French brandy.

Remove the stalks, put the fruit into an earthenware bowl. Pour in the boiling water and cover with a cloth. Stir the liquid 3 or 4 times daily for 4 days, then add the sugar and brandy, and when the former is dissolved, turn the whole into a clean dry cask. Cover the bung hole with a cloth, folded into several thicknesses, until fermentation ceases, then bung tightly and allow the cask to remain undisturbed for 12 months, in a moderately warm place. At the end of this time it should be racked off into bottles. The wine may be used at once, but if well corked and carefully stored in a cool, dry place, it may be kept for years.

"And Noah he often said to his wife when he sat to dine,
I don't care where the water goes, as long as it doesn't get into the wine."

ENGLISH BISHOP

Take an orange — stud with cloves — dip it in Cognac and dust with brown sugar. Brown well before a fire — held on a skewer. Cut into quarters. Take a saucepan, put in a quart of red port wine, simmer until tightly covered, for 20 minutes. Add 2 jiggers of Cognac just before pouring.

GRAPE WINE

Mash sound ripe grapes with your hands in an earthenware pan, or with a tasteless stick. Do not crush the seeds; strain the liquor into a cask; gently squeeze the pulp, pouring the remainder of the juice (strained) into the cask. Let stand for a fortnight, then draw it off into another cask, covering the bung-hole with a piece of slate till all fermentation has ceased. Bottle. In 6 months, cork and seal. Drink in 12 months time.

Merry met, and merry part,
I drink to thee with all my heart.
Old Cup Inscription

BOSTON CREAM

Pour three quarts of boiling water on two pounds of sugar and two ounces tartaric acid and the beaten white of one egg. Mix thoroughly and add two and a half teaspoons essence of lemon; strain and bottle. When drinking put a large tablespoonful into a tumbler of cold water and stir in a quarter of a teaspoon of carbonate of soda. Drink while effervescing.

TALL CLOVE PURPLE

2/3 glass ginger ale — 1/3 cup grape juice
Dash powdered clove — Shaved ice
Slice of orange — Several whole cloves

Stir together ginger ale, grape juice and powdered clove. Strain. Pour over shaved ice in 1 tall glass. Garnish with orange slice stuck with whole cloves.

SHERRY PUNCH

Juice ½ orange — 2 dashes lime juice
4 tablespoons dry white wine
4 tablespoons good dry sherry

Combine ingredients, sweeten to taste. Fill tall glasses one-third with crushed ice, add the mixture, stir well and serve.

SPICE CUP

2½ cups orange juice — 6 cloves
¼ cup lemon juice — ½ teaspoon cinnamon
2 cups water — ¼ teaspoon allspice
½ cup sugar — 3 pints ginger ale
grated rind 1 lemon — 1 tablespoon honey
½ teaspoon grated nutmeg

Combine orange, lemon and pineapple juice, water and sugar. Add the grated lemon rind, honey, cloves, nutmeg, cinnamon and allspice. Mix well and allow to stand for 3 hours. Strain through a fine cloth. Add the ginger ale. Stir briskly and serve in tall glasses with ice.

GINGER WINE

3 pounds of loaf sugar
3 ounces of root ginger, well bruised
½ pound stoned raisins
1 gallon water — 1 lemon
A quarter of a pint of brandy may be added when the wine is finished.

Boil all the ingredients together for one hour, skimming carefully any feculencies which rise. When the liquor is quite clear, strain it into the jar or tub, and when it is cool, add a tablespoon of yeast. Stir the mixture every day for a fortnight, adding another half pound of raisins if they are to be had. At the end of that time strain the wine into a cask, add the brandy and cork down when all hissing sound has ceased. It will be ready in a few weeks, but will improve if kept.

In Somerset and Devon, where cider is made at home, the ginger-wine was always made with cider instead of water, and this made a very superior wine indeed.

SUPREME CUP

1 cup orange juice
3 slices lemon
1 small apple sliced
12 cherries
1 thinly sliced peach
½ large orange cut into slices
3 slices pineapple cut into dice
2 large bottles lemonade
2 large bottles dry ginger ale

Place prepared fruit into a large jug with a large piece of ice. Allow to stand till thoroughly chilled. Just before serving, add bottled drinks, mix well and serve over cracked ice in tall glasses.

SUNDOWNER CUP

3 bottles sauterne
1 sliced lemon
3 pints soda water
1 small sliced cucumber
2 doz. white grapes
mint
1-1½ cups marnique (Australian quince liqueur brandy)
3 tablespoons castor sugar

Stir the castor sugar into the wine in a mixing bowl. Add marnique. Pour into punch bowl over cracked ice. Add sliced lemon, and cucumber, and float white grapes on top. Add soda water just before serving, top glass with mint.

God made the Vine
Was it a Sin
That Man made Wine
To drown Trouble in?
Herford

BURGUNDY PUNCH

Boil up for a few minutes a cup of apple juice, 6 tablespoons of sugar, a stick of cinnamon, 10 or 12 cloves, and a few slices of lemon. Strain this into another pot, pour in a bottle of burgundy, heat it gently (it must not boil) and serve in mugs with a dash of nutmeg.

TEA PUNCH

Before preparing a punch for 40 people, it is advisable to calculate the expected consumption and prepare accordingly. The following recipe will make about 4 quarts of punch or about 40 punch glasses. Double, triple or quadruple the stock recipe accordingly.

Stock Recipe:

2 pints strong tea, 1 cup diced peaches, 1 cup lemon juice, 1½ cups sugar, 3 cups orange juice, ½ pint brandy.

Combine brandy, peaches and fruit juices and stand overnight. In the morning make tea, add sugar, combine with fruit mixture and pour into quart jugs. Before serving, put 2 or 3 large pieces of ice into a punch bowl and add 1 quart iced champagne, 1 bottle iced hock, ½ bottle brandy, 1 bottle ginger ale, 1 bottle lemonade. Decorate with strawberries, pitted cherries, or seedless grapes, depending on availability. As more punch is required, add to each additional quart of the stock mixture a like amount of champagne, hock, etc. as above.

STRAWBERRY RASPBERRY DREAM
(English country recipe)

1 lb. of both fruits, ½ lb. granulated sugar, 2 quarts boiling water, a few redcurrants or juice of 2 lemons and some ice.

Put raspberries, strawberries and redcurrants (if used) in a big bowl with the sugar. Mash with a fork. Pour on the boiling water. Stir and cool. Strain at once. Add lemon juice (if no redcurrants). Chill.

WELSH NECTAR

Boil 2 gallons of water, let cool. Add 1 lb. raisins, 2 lbs. sugar, juice of 3 lemons and rinds thinly pared. Stir all for 4 days. Strain through a jelly bag. Bottle and cork.

LEMON POSSET

Steep the rind of a lemon, thinly pared, in a pint of sweet wine, 2 hours before required. Add to it the juice of a lemon and sugar to taste. Put in a bowl with a quart of milk or cream. Whisk in one direction until very thick. Serve in glasses. Orange likewise.

LEMON FROTH

¾ glass (6 ozs.) ginger ale
3 teaspoons lemon-and-lime syrup
3 teaspoons crushed ice
Beaten egg white
Slice of lemon
Glace cherry

Shake together ginger ale, syrup and ice. Strain into 1 tall glass. Stir in egg white. Garnish with lemon slice and cherry.

RHUBARB SHERBET

Boil 6 or 8 sticks of rhubarb for 10 minutes in a quart of water. Strain liquor into jug in which thinly pared lemon peel is placed and 4 tablespoons sugar. Let stand 5-6 hours before drinking.

WINTER PUNCH

1 quart water — 1 cup orange juice
½ teaspoon nutmeg — ½ cup lemon juice
½ teaspoon cinnamon — Ice
½ teaspoon allspice — 1½ cups superfine sugar
1½ heaped tablespoons tea
1 quart chilled raspberry or loganberry juice
1 quart chilled soda-water

Bring water to a boil in a saucepan. Remove from the heat. Immediately add tea, nutmeg, cinnamon and allspice. Brew 4 minutes. Stir. Strain into a punch bowl containing sugar and orange, lemon and other juices. Just before serving, add crushed ice and soda-water. Yields about 40 punch cups.

NEGUS

A drink of hot port wine, spiced with sugar, nutmeg and lemon juice.

"*To drink is a Christian diversion,*
Unknown to the Turk or the Persian."
Congreve

SACK POSSET

"*From fam'd Barbadoes on the western main*
Fetch sugar ounces four; fetch sack from Spain
A pint; and from the Eastern Indian coast
Nutmeg, the glory of our northern toast,
O'er flaming coals let them together heat,
Till the all-conquering sack dissolves the sweet;
O'er such another fire put eggs ten,
New born, from tread of cock and rump of hen.
Stir them with steady hand and conscience pricking
To see the untimely fate of ten fine chicken;
From shining shelf take down the brazen skillet,
A quart of milk from gentle cow will fill it.
When boiled and cold, put milk and sack to eggs,
Unite them firmly like the triple league,
And on the fire let them together dwell
Till Miss sing twice, "You must not kiss and tell".
Each lad and lass take up a silver spoon,
And fall on fiercely like a starved dragoon."
Sir Fleetwood Shepherd

SIMPLE HOME MADE CIDER

3 lbs. apples — 2 lemons — 2 lbs. sugar

Mince the apples. Put in earthenware crock. Stir twice a day. Strain. After a week add lemon juice. Leave a day then bottle. Leave 3 months before drinking.

FRUIT DRINK

6 large oranges — 2 pints boiling water
1 lemon — 5 lbs. sugar
2 ozs. tartaric acid — 1 oz. citric acid

Make syrup. Add orange and lemon juice, when syrup is cool.

"*What makes the cider blow its cork*
With such a merry din?
What makes those little bubbles rise
And dance like harlequin?
It is the fatal apple, boys,
The fruit of human sin."
Christopher Morley

HOMEMADE APPLE CIDER

4 lbs. over-ripe, bruised, or spotted apples
6 pints cold water — 1 cup sugar

Wash and dry apples, cut into ½ inch slices; place in large crockery basin, cover with cold water. Cover with cloth and allow to stand 10 days, stirring daily. The mixture will ferment and bubble. After 10 days, drain apples and discard, reserve liquid. Stir in sugar, stirring until dissolved. Strain through several thicknesses of fine muslin. Bottle into clean dry bottles and allow to stand, uncorked but covered with cloth, for 14 days. The cider will continue to bubble in the bottle, the bubbles becoming smaller and less frequent towards the end of this period. If necessary, re-strain into clean dry bottles to remove sediment. Cork securely, label and date. Keep for 3 months before using. Makes 3 pints.

HOT MULLED APPLE JUICE

Combine 1 quart apple juice, 2 inch stick cinnamon, broken; 4 whole cloves and ¼ cup sugar. Bring to boil, cover and simmer 10 minutes. Strain. Serve hot.

SPICED CIDER

Half cup brown sugar, ¼ teaspoon salt, 2 quarts cider, 1 teaspoon whole allspice, 1 teaspoon whole cloves, 3 inch stick cinnamon, dash nutmeg.

Combine brown sugar, salt and cider. Tie spices in small piece of cheese-cloth; add. Slowly bring to boil, simmer, covered, 20 minutes. Serve hot or cold. If desired, float a few clove-stuffed orange slices and cinnamon sticks in punch bowl.

SCOTTISH TREACLE ALE

Melt two pounds of treacle into a gallon of water, and when cool, add an ounce of yeast spread upon a brown toast. Cover and leave for three days. Skim and bottle the ale, and wire the corks, as this ale should be very effervescent.

CHILLI BEER

Boil for half an hour twenty three chillies (tied in a muslin bag) in two quarts of water. Take off fire and add eight quarts cold water, two pounds sugar, two ounces cream of tartar, two tablespoons essence of lemon, quarter cup yeast. Mix thoroughly, bottle and cork.

"He had his beer
From yeare to yeare
And then his bier had him."
Anon.

POOR MAN'S BEER

Shells of green peas contain a considerable portion of saccharine matter. Fill a boiler with pea pods. Cover with water until it is ½ inch above pods. Simmer 3 hours.

Strain. Add a strong decoction of wood-sags or hops. Ferment in the usual manner.

BEER FROM TREACLE

Put 2 lbs. of treacle to 4 gallons of water (boiling), add ½ dozen bay leaves, ½ oz. ground ginger. Boil all for ½ an hour. Ferment with yeast.

LAMB'S WOOL

In days of yore this was a favourite liquor with working people, and was composed of roasted apples and ale; the pulp of the apples worked up with the ale till the mixture formed a smooth beverage, with the addition of sugar and spice to taste, 1 teaspoon nutmeg if liked.

Now crown the bowle
With gentle lamb's wooll;
Add sugar, and nutmegs, and ginger.
Herrick

COOL TANKARD

Put to a quart of mild ale a wine-glassful of white wine, the same of brandy and capillaire, the juice of a lemon, and some of the rind. Add a sprig of balm of borage, some toasted bread, and nutmeg grated on the top. Borage is said to impart coolness to this drink.

ORANGE AND LEMON CORDIAL

Grate rind and squeeze juice of two large lemons and two large oranges. Add 2 lb. sugar, 1 oz. citric acid, 1 oz. Epsom salts, and ½ oz. tartaric acid. Pour on two and a half pints BOILING water. Cool. Bottle next day.

RASPBERRY VINEGAR

Put a pound of fruit into a bowl, pour upon it a quart of the best white wine vinegar; next day strain the juice on a pound of fresh raspberries, and the following day do the same. Bottle and cork well.

LEMONADE

3 lemons	3 cups sugar
4 cups boiling water	½ oz. citric acid
½ oz. tartaric acid	1 oz. epsom salts

Grate the lemons in basin and squeeze. Add sugar, salts and other things and pour 4 cups boiling water and leave until cold. Strain and then bottle.

Where is the wine I used to find?
Where is it now?
Gone with the wind?

NOURISHING LEMONADE

1½ pints of boiling water

The juice of 4 lemons	The rinds of 2 lemons
4 eggs	½ pint of sherry

6 ozs. of loaf sugar

Pare off the lemon rind thinly, put it into a jug with the sugar, and pour over the boiling water. Let it cool, then strain it. Add the wine, lemon juice, and eggs, previously well beaten, and also strained, and the beverage will be ready for use. If thought desirable, the quantity of sherry and water could be lessened and milk substituted for them. To obtain the flavour of the lemon rind properly a few lumps of the sugar should be rubbed over it, until some of the yellow is absorbed. Average cost is 1s. 3d. (1856).

LEMONADE FOR INVALIDS

½ lemon — Lump sugar to taste

1 pint of boiling water

Pare off the rind of the lemon thinly, cut the lemon into 2 or 3 thick slices and remove as much as possible of the white outside pith, and all the pips.

Put the slices of lemon, the peel and lump sugar into a jug; pour over the boiling water; cover it closely and in two hours it will be fit to drink.

It should either be strained or poured off from the sediment. Average cost 2d.

TEWAHDIDDLE

A pint of small beer, a tablespoon of brandy, and a teaspoonful of brown sugar, a little grated nutmeg, and a roll of thin lemon-peel.

1½ pints of good ale mixed with 1 bottle of effervescing ginger beer is refreshing. The ginger corrects the action of the beer.

Their beer was strong, their wine was port;
Their meal was large; their grace was short.
Matthew Prior

GINGER BEER

To make plant:

Squeeze the juice of two lemons and 1 teaspoon of pulp into airtight container. Add 4 teaspoons sugar, 2 teaspoons of ground ginger and 2 cups of water. This will start to ferment in about three days, then add 4 small teaspoons of ginger and 2 of sugar every day for a week. Pour off liquid and put into a large pan.

To make ginger beer:

To the ginger liquid add 4 small cups sugar, juice of 2 lemons, 10 cups of hot water. Stir well to dissolve the sugar, then add 18 cups of cold water and strained lemon juice. Bottle and seal.

To renew the plant:

After straining off liquid, divide plant in two. Throw half away and to the remainder add ¾ pint cold water. Each day for 6 days, add 1 heaped teaspoon of ginger and one of sugar. Bottle on the seventh day.

RUBY GLOW

½ cup sugar
1 cup lemon juice
1 bottle claret
3 cups iced water
lemon to garnish

Place the sugar and lemon juice into a jug and stir well until the sugar is dissolved. Add well-chilled claret and iced water. Mix thoroughly and serve in tall iced jug with slices of lemon.

COFFEE AND WINE CREAM

Put into top of a double saucepan 2 eggs, ¼ cup sugar, 2 tablespoons brandy and ¼ cup white wine. Moselle, the slightly sweet white wine is good for this, or a dry white wine such as a riesling is also suitable. Then beat over simmering water until mixture rises in a creamy cloud to top of saucepan. It takes about 3 to 4 minutes beating. Fill coffee cups about three-quarters full of steaming hot coffee. Then spoon about 3 to 4 tablespoons of the wine-cream on top of the coffee.

RODGROD

1 lb. 10oz. Redcurrants; 1 lb. 10 oz. raspberries; 2½ pints water; vanilla pod; 2 tablespoons castor sugar; 3 ozs. potato flour; blanched almonds; cream.

Simmer the fruit and water with the vanilla pod, skimming the pan carefully and thoroughly until the juice is clear. Take off 1 gill (5 fluid ozs.) of juice and put aside to cool. Sieve the remainder of the fruit through a fine sieve. Sweeten to taste and return puree to the heat. When puree boils again stir in 3 ozs. potato flour dissolved in the reserved fruit juice, and immediately remove pan from heat. Continue stirring off heat until puree is thick and clear. Pour it into a glass dish. When almost set, decorate with a few blanched almonds. Serve with thick cream.

ORANGE WINE

For 26 oranges allow two gallons of boiling water, and to each gallon of liquor, allow 2 lbs. sugar. Wipe the oranges and cut in slices, removing the pips.

Place in a tub and cover with the boiling water. Cover up and leave for a week, stirring each day with a wooden spoon. Then strain through a fine sieve, allowing the liquid to drip through of its own accord. Measure and add sugar in proportion. Put in a cask and bring up after a week. It will be ready in three months.

Carre and Co.'s patent economical freezing apparatus, for which the prize medal was awarded by the Exhibition of 1862, as well as a gold medal by the French 'Societe d'Encouragement', will produce a pound of ice at an expense of less than a farthing; will cost (including packing and accessories) not more than £6, and is invaluable in warm climates.

An apple a day keeps the doctor away.

FOR THE PANTRY SHELF

CANDY HIGH MARMALADE

Candy high sugar is sugar boiled to the point where it begins to form great slow blistery bubbles just the instant before it recrystallises.

Marmalade made this way is very full of flavour. Seville oranges are best, but others can be used. Thinly pare the skins without any pith or zest. Boil them until tender, changing water several times. Put them on a chopping board and slice as finely as possible. Put a pound of sugar into a saucepan, barely moistening it with water. Boil it candy high. Wait at all after the critical time and the sugar will be crystallised hard. At the exact moment when it reaches candy height — big sticky bubbles appear on top — put in your sliced peel. Boil gently for half an hour. During this time peel the pith off the oranges, slice them thinly, remove the pips. Then mix the orange pulp with the juice of two lemons. When the skins have boiled in the sugar for half an hour, add the rest of the pulp and pith and gently boil for quarter of an hour.

Orange flowers, violets or rosemary dropped into candy high sugar (boiled preferably with spring water) retains their perfume.

LEMON MARMALADE

6 lemons, 5 lbs. sugar, 6 pints boiling water

Cut lemons finely. Pour boiling water on and leave overnight. Simmer until lemons are cooked — about an hour. Add the sugar and boil quickly until it jells when tested on a cold saucer. Put in small knob of butter about the size of a walnut.

Put about half a dozen small marbles into the preserving pan when cooking jam, to prevent sticking.

BRANDIED GOLDEN ORANGE MARMALADE

6 small carrots　　1 lemon
Sugar　　1 cup brandy
3 medium sized oranges

Peel the oranges and lemon and soak the skins in water overnight. Next morning chop the skins and discard the water.

Cut the orange and the lemon pulp into wafer-thin slices, scrape the carrots and grate them finely.

Place the fruit, chopped peel and grated carrot into a large pan, just cover with water and bring to the boil.

Continue to cook until the carrots and fruit are quite soft — it can take up to 1 hour. Measure the pulp and juice together and for every 3 cups add 2 cups of sugar.

Bring to the boil and cook rapidly until a little will set when tested. Add the warmed brandy and continue to boil for a further 3 minutes.

Allow to become almost cold, bottle and seal.

POOR MAN'S MARMALADE

2 breakfast cups minced orange peel
2 medium size lemons
2 pints water　　2 lbs. sugar

Keep peels from oranges used for other purposes. Soak overnight in boiling water. Add lemon rind as well as juice but remove rind before adding sugar. Add sugar after cooking peel until tender. Boil fast after sugar is dissolved. Test for setting. This marmalade can stand a long cook when it looks and tastes like vintage marmalade.

SPICED VINEGAR

Two quarts vinegar, 1 small teaspoon cloves, 1 tablespoon peppercorns, 1 tablespoon allspice, and several pieces of bruised ginger. Boil together for 10 minutes. While still boiling pour over walnuts.

TO PICKLE EGGS

16 eggs, 1 quart of vinegar, ½ oz. of black pepper, ½ oz. of Jamaica pepper, ½ oz. of ginger.

Boil the eggs for 12 minutes, then dip them into cold water, and take off the shells. Put the vinegar, with the pepper and ginger, into a stewpan, and let it simmer for 10 minutes. Now place the eggs into a jar, pour over them the vinegar etc., boiling hot, and when cold, tie them down with a bladder to exclude the air. This pickle will be ready for use in a month.

PICKLED WALNUTS

Pick nuts when they can be easily pierced with a needle. Prick well and put into crock, rejecting any that feel hard when pricked. Cover with brine and allow to soak for 8 days. Throw away brine, cover with fresh brine and resoak for 14 days. Wash and dry nuts well and spread them out, exposing them to air until they turn black. Have sufficient spiced vinegar to cover them, put into wide mouthed jars and cover when cold.

On the table spread the cloth
Let the knives be sharp and clean
Pickles get and salad both
Let them each be fresh and green
With small beer, good ale, and wine
O ye gods! How I shall dine!
Johnathan Swift

PICKLED BEETROOT

Sufficient vinegar to cover the beets,
2 ozs. of whole pepper,
2 ozs. of allspice to each gallon of vinegar.

Wash the beets free from dirt, and be very careful not to prick the outside skin, or they would lose their beautiful colour. Put them into boiling water, let them simmer gently, and when about three-parts done, which will be in 1½ hours, take them out and let them cool. Boil the vinegar, with pepper and allspice, in the above proportions, for 10 minutes, and when cold, pour it on the beets, which must be peeled and cut into slices about ½ inch thick. Cover with bladder to exclude the air, and in a week they will be fit for use.

SPANISH ONIONS — PICKLED

Onions, vinegar, salt and cayenne to taste.

Cut the onions in thin slices; put a layer of them in the bottom of a jar; sprinkle with salt and cayenne; then add another layer of onions, and season as before. Proceeding in this manner till the jar is full, pour in sufficient vinegar to cover the whole, and the pickle will be fit for use in a month.

PICCALILLI

2 cauliflowers	1 lb. onions
1 quart vinegar	1 oz. whole spice
¼ lb. sugar	½ oz. ground ginger
1 oz. mustard	½ oz. tumeric

2 medium sized cucumbers
16 French Beans (young)
1 medium sized marrow
1 tablespoonful flour

Cut the vegetables into small pieces, lay on a dish and sprinkle with salt. Leave for 12 hours. Drain off water, boil nearly all the vinegar with the spice, then strain. Mix the other ingredients, with the remaining cold vinegar, into a paste; then mix with boiled vinegar. Pour into saucepan, add vegetables, and boil for 15 minutes.

BLACKBERRY PICKLE

1 quart blackberries	1 pint vinegar
1½ lbs. sugar	1½ ozs. allspice

½ oz. ground ginger

Put blackberries in a bowl, sprinkle with sugar and leave for 12 hours.

Bring vinegar to boil, add berries and sugar and boil for an hour. Allow to cool and when quite cold, add allspice and ginger. Mix well with a wooden spoon and cook for a further 10 minutes. Pour into jars and cover when cold.

MAKING BUTTER

Beat or churn the cream until the cream separates. The butter will form into a lump and the butter-milk can be poured off.

Measure the butter-milk and add the same quantity of icy-cold water to the butter.

Knead this clean water through the butter and strain off. Using fresh water, repeat this washing process until the water is clear.

With a heavy wooden spoon, force as much water as possible from the butter, draining off water as it occurs.

Add salt to taste (about 1 teaspoon to each 1 lb. of butter), kneading this well into the butter. Pat into shape.

Using boiled water, make a brine with salt (until it will float an egg). Have butter in lots of 1 lb. or similar size, and wrapped separately in butter paper.

Put the brine into a barrel, crockery or earthenware container, and when brine is quite cold, put the butter in with a weight on top to keep it under the liquid.

The butter must be kept under the brine. It will stay fresh for six months without absorbing salt.

More brine can be added to the container if necessary.

When you want to use some of the butter, take out 1 lb. without letting air into the rest.

MAKING CHEESE

There are many different types of cheeses which, as you know, are milk in a highly concentrated form.

Milk into a clean bucket, then strain the milk and stand overnight in a clean, cool place. In the morning stand the bucket in a tub of warm water in summer or 86 deg. in cold weather, and stir.

Dissolve rennet tablets according to directions in cup of water and of the same temperature and add to the milk, stirring well.

Let the milk stand for three minutes, when it should thicken. Then break up the curd with the hand or a large fork and it will settle down.

Press the curd into a lump and put into cheese-cloth to drain. Having drained off the whey, in 10 minutes break up the curd again with the hand.

Drain and repeat, thus working over three times in 30 minutes. Warm up the whey to about 100 deg. and pour over the curd a few times until it toughens, and will squeak when rubbed.

Drain and cut up again into small pieces. Salt at about 1 oz. to the pound. Put into tins without ends or small boxes without tops or bottoms and place under weight.

In 24 hours it should have set. It can be neatly bandaged and put into press again for a few hours. Grease all round and stand in a cool place for a few weeks to ripen.

Grease daily in warm weather, or twice weekly in colder weather. Before re-bandaging in cold weather, plunge cheese into water at 115 or 120 deg.

Keep cheese for about three months.

Buy only small amounts of rennet for thickening, as it loses its strength when stored.

BUTTERMILK CHEESE

Any amount of buttermilk, boiled and allowed to stand to cool, then placed in a heavy linen bag until the whey has drained off. Salt to taste, and spice if wished, thoroughly mixed.

Weigh and add a tablespoon of alcohol to each 1 lb. of mass, again mix well and knead and form into cheese any size or form.

The cheese is then dried in the open air and wrapped in linen cloth that has previously been soaked in the hot whey. Pack in a well covered cask, and store in a warm place. Can be used any time after four days.

TO DISTINGUISH MUSHROOMS FROM POISONOUS FUNGI

Sprinkle a little salt on the spongy part or gills of the sample to be tried. If they turn yellow, they are poisonous, if black they are wholesome. Allow the salt to act before you decide on the question.

False mushrooms have an astringent, styptic and disagreeable taste. When cut they turn blue.

MUSHROOM POWDER

Wash half a peck of large mushrooms, while quite fresh, and free them from dirt and grit with a flannel. Do not use any that are worm-eaten. Put them into a stew-pan over the fire without water, with two large onions, some cloves, a quarter of an ounce of mace, and two spoonfuls of white pepper, all in powder.

Simmer and shake them till all the liquor be dried up, but be careful they do not burn. Lay them on tins or sieves in a slow oven till they are dry enough to beat to powder, then put the powder in small bottles, corked and tied closely and keep in a dry place.

A teaspoonful will give a very fine flavour to any soup or gravy or any sauce, added just before serving and one boil given to it after it is put in.

TO POT MUSHROOMS TO KEEP THREE MONTHS

Choose large buttons or such whose inside is not yet the least brown. Peel and wipe out the fur of the larger ones, and to every two quarts put half a drachm of pounded mace, two drachms of white pepper, and six or eight cloves in powder; set them over the fire, shake and let the liquor dry up into them. Then put to them 2 ozs. of butter and stew them in it till they be fit for eating. Pour the butter from them and let them become cold. Pack them close into a pot, making the surface as even as possible, add some butter lukewarm, and then lay a bit of butter over them, and pour clarified suet upon it to exclude the air.

TO DRY MUSHROOMS FOR FLAVOURING

Gather the mushrooms on a dry day. Peel them and scrape the stalks. If the stalks are not firm remove them. Take a bodkin of strong darning needle, threaded with very coarse thread or fine string and pass it through the centres of the mushrooms and stalks. Put these strings of mushrooms in a hot oven for twenty minutes to kill any bacteria, etc. Then hang in a very warm place till quite dry. Store in air-tight tin boxes. All edible fungi can be stored in this way. When the mushrooms are required for use, soak them for twenty-four hours in water. Then cut them up very small and soak them again in the same water for twelve hours. Add milk and simmer till tender. Then season to taste and use in soups or sauces.

In regard to storing the dried mushrooms in a tin as described in this recipe, there is one infallible method of testing whether any dried vegetables or fruits of any kind have been properly dried. Put a crisp biscuit in the tin with the dried fruits or vegetables and close the lid tightly. If, after 24 hours the biscuit is soft, it indicates that there was moisture in the dried stuff.

VINEGAR PLANT

Put in a large jar 2 lb. coarse sugar,
2 lbs. treacle and 3 quarts of water.

Cover closely and keep in a warm place for three months.

The scum-like fungus that forms on top is the "vinegar plant". It will thicken during the process, adding a new layer on the under surface. Do not discard, but peel off the layer to use again indefinitely.

The liquid below is the vinegar. Pour it off, bring to the boil, strain and bottle.

VINEGAR FROM FRUIT

Take ripe fruit, such as plums or pears — over-ripe will answer perfectly well. Crush it with the hand, and put it into a stone or wooden vessel. Cover the fruit with water and mix well, then leave it to ferment. When fermentation begins let it stand for three or four days, stirring twice daily, then strain through a jelly bag. Put the liquid into a wide-mouthed jar, and the muslin over the top to keep dust and insects out. The more freely the air can get to it the sooner it will turn into vinegar. It is a good plan to put the jar out in the sunshine, on a verandah where it is out of reach of possible rain. Any soft fruit can be treated in the same way. Sweet fruit like plums and pears need no sugar. The less water used the richer the vinegar. Vinegar made in this fashion is so strong that it requires to be diluted with water before using.

CHEAP AND GOOD VINEGAR

To eight gallons of clear rain water add three quarts of molasses; turn the mixture in to a clean tight cask, shake it well two or three times and add three spoonsful of good yeast, or two yeast cakes; place the cask in a warm place and in ten or fifteen days add a sheet of common wrapping paper, smeared with molasses and torn into strips and you will have good vinegar. The paper is necessary to form the "Mother" or life of the vinegar.

POTATO AND HOP YEAST

Over a good pinch of hops pour a cup of boiling water. Let it cool, then strain. In its jacket boil a potato the size of a tea-cup. When cooked, peel and mash with a teaspoonful of the cooking water, let cool and then mix with the hop liquid. Pour into a clear glass bottle and tie down the cork, leave in a cool place for 2 or 3 days, then pour off all but 2 or 3 inches of the yeast. Make a second brew and add to it this remaining yeast to act as a primer. Always save 2 to 3 inches of the brew to add to the next lot made.

CAULIFLOWER PICKLED

Lay pieces of cauliflower in a brine of salt and water for 7-10 days. Then put them into a saucepan of water. Boil 10-15 minutes. Drain on coarse cloth in sun till free of moisture. Put into jars. Pour over them cold, a pickle of vinegar, to which mace, peppercorns, pinch allspice, have been simmered. Close up. Add vinegar as it becomes absorbed.

DRIED APRICOTS, PEACHES, NECTARINES

Select firm fruit just on the turn, remove stones and weigh fruit. To every 1 lb. put 1 lb. sugar. Cover fruit with sugar and let it stand all night. Next day simmer it for ¼ hour, then pour into dish and leave for 3 days.

Now take fruit out and dry it in the sun. Do not leave in damp air, bring indoors at night. Do not throw syrup away as it can be used as many as three times and afterwards strained and used for fruit bottling. A wonderful way to use fruit at a time of the year when there is an excess.

CANDIED LEMON OR ORANGE PEEL

Cut peel into quarters. Cover with salted water and allow to soak for one week. Put in fresh water and boil gently for two hours. Make enough syrup to cover the peel, using 1 lb. sugar to one breakfast cup water. Boil syrup 5 minutes, drain peel, pour syrup over. Allow to stand one week. Place peel and syrup in pan and simmer half hour. Drain peel and put in warm place to dry.

VERY FINE WALNUT KETCHUP

Boil a gallon of the expressed juice of tender walnuts, and skim it well; then put in 2 lbs. of anchovies, bones and liquor, 2 lbs. shalots, 1 oz. each of cloves, mace, pepper, and one clove of garlic. Let all simmer till the shalots sink; then put the liquor into a pan till cold; bottle and divide the spice to each. Cork closely, and tie a bladder over. It will keep twenty years, but is not good the first. Be very careful to express the juice at home; for it is rarely unadulterated, if bought.

GOOD MUSTARD

Take of mustard seed 1 part, of weak wood vinegar 2 parts, macerate for a fortnight, then grind the whole into a paste in a mill, and put into pots. Lastly thrust a red hot poker into each of them.

TO DRY HERBS FOR WINTER USE

On a very dry day, gather the herbs, just before they begin to flower; if this is done when the weather is damp, the herbs will not be so good a colour. (It is necessary to be particular in little matters like this, for trifles constitute perfection, and herbs nicely dried will be found very acceptable when frost and snow are on the ground. It is hardly necessary, however, to state that the flavour and fragrance of fresh herbs are incomparably finer.)

They should be perfectly freed from dirt and dust, and be divided into small bunches, with their roots cut off. Dry them quickly in a very hot oven, or before the fire, as by this means most of their flavour will be preserved: be careful not to burn them; tie them up in paper bags, and keep in a dry place.

This is a very general way of preserving dried herbs.

A FEW LINES ON FLAVOURINGS

One occasionally finds oneself without certain flavourings.

The combinations of rose and almond give a flavour very like sherry; grated orange or lemon rind may be used instead of the essence. In steamed pudding or fruit cake, orange marmalade will take the place of candied peel; it keeps the cake moist also.

TOMATO SOUP (for bottling)

12 lbs. tomatoes, washed and halved
¼ bunch celery plus leaves, cut small
6 large onions, cut in pieces
2 large carrots, cut in rings

Put in pan and boil gently until all vegetables are tender. Put in colander and press pulp through. Return pulp to pan and add 4 bay leaves, 12 cloves, 12 whole spice, sugar and salt to taste. Simmer gently for about 1 hour. Just before taking off stove and while pulp is still boiling, add ½ teaspoon carbonate soda. Press through fine sieve, bottle, and sterilise for 2 hours at 170°F.

BOTTLING CHERRIES

To every pound of fruit for tarts through the winter, add six ounces of loaf sugar. Fill the jars with fruit; shake the sugar over, and tie down with two bladders, as there is danger of one bursting through the boiling. Place the jars in a boiler of cold water, and after the water has boiled, let them remain three hours; take them out, and when cool, put them in a dry place, where they will keep over a year. We have tried this recipe for several years, and never knew it fail. The fruit makes delicious puddings.

SPICED PRUNES

1 lb. prunes — 1 pint cold water
1 cup sugar — ¾ cup burgundy
Strained juice 1 orange and ½ lemon
3 tablespoons wine vinegar
¼ teaspoon ground cloves
Grated rind 1 orange and 1 lemon
Small piece of cinnamon stick
¼ teaspoon ground allspice

Place prunes in preserving pan with water, wine, juices and rinds and spices. Bring slowly to the boil. Simmer for 30 minutes. Add sugar and vinegar. Simmer for 10 minutes longer. Remove cinnamon stick and pour into clean jars and seal. Serve with meats. Makes 1½ pints.

HERB POWDER FOR FLAVOURING
(When fresh herbs are not obtainable)

1 oz. of dried lemon-thyme
1 oz. of dried winter savory
1 oz. of dried sweet majoram and basil
2 ozs. of dried parsley
1 oz. of dried lemon peel

On a very dry day, gather the herbs just before they begin to flower. They should be free of dirt and dust and be divided into small bunches, with roots cut off. Dry them quickly in a hot oven. Tie them in paper bags and keep in a dry place. Pick the leaves from the stalks, pound them, and sift them through a hair sieve; mix in the above proportions, and keep in glass bottles, carefully excluding the air. This we think a far better method of keeping herbs, as the flavour and fragrance do not evaporate so much as when they are merely put in paper bags. Preparing them in this way, you have them ready for use at a moment's notice. Mint, sage, parsley, etc., dried, pounded, and each put into separate bottles, will be found very useful in winter.

ROWAN BERRY JELLY FOR GROUSE

Wash the Rowan berries and put them in a pan with an equal quantity of windfall apples and just enough water to cover. Simmer till soft. Strain the juice through a fine sieve or cloth but do not press any fruit pulp through, as this makes the jelly cloudy. Add 1 pound of sugar per pint of juice. Heat the liquid and stir it until the sugar has melted, then boil it rapidly until it sets. Pour it into warm jars.

APPLE JELLY SPICE (for cold meats)

Wash apples and cut them up roughly, barely covering with a mixture of 3 parts vinegar and one of water. Cook until soft. Strain through a sieve. Put liquid back in the pan and add to it a little stick of cinnamon and some cloves and whole ginger, according to taste. Boil all together for about 15 minutes. Strain and add ¾ cup sugar to each cup of liquid. Boil rapidly until setting stage is reached.

MINT JELLY

1 quart apple juice, made as for the apple jelly, 1½ lbs. sugar, 1 bottle pectin, a little green colouring — breakfastcupful of Mint leaves packed tightly. Strain the juice into a preserving pan, add the Mint leaves and bring to the boil. Strain out the Mint leaves and let the liquid cool slightly, add the sugar and stir until it is dissolved, then add the pectin and colouring and bring to a full boil for two minutes. Leave for a minute and then ladle into small hot jars and tie down at once. Makes about 3 pints of jelly.

PRESERVED CRABAPPLES

A delicious preserve with all dishes of this kind can be made with Crabapples preserved whole in a clear red syrup.

Put 1½ lbs. sugar in a pan with a pint of water, bring this slowly to the boil stirring it until the sugar melts, then boil it rapidly to make a thick syrup. Strain it and let it cool. Put the fruit into a pan, leaving about 1 inch stalk on each apple, add the cold syrup and let them simmer on a low heat, very, very gently indeed, nearly all day until tender. They must never be allowed to boil, as the skins will then crack. When cooked, take out each little apple carefully with a wooden spoon, and pack them into warm jars. Pour the syrup over them slowly. Leave them until cold before putting on the covers.

PLUM SAUCE

6 lbs. dark plums — 3 lbs. sugar
1½ pints vinegar — 1 handful cloves
6 teaspoons salt
1 teaspoon white pepper
1 small teaspoon cayenne pepper
1 ozs. whole ginger (bruised)

Put all ingredients in pan and boil until plum stones fall out. Strain through a colander, pour into wide necked bottles and seal.

If too thick, a little more vinegar may be added before taking mixture off the heat.

MARINATED PLUMS

1 pint water — 1 cup white vinegar
1½ cups sugar — 2 lbs. plums
2 tablespoons ground cinnamon
1 teaspoon whole cloves
½ teaspoon whole black peppercorns

Bring sugar and water to boil, stirring constantly. Boil approximately 10 to 15 minutes without stirring. Add vinegar, cinnamon, cloves, and peppercorns, reduce heat, simmer gently further 15 minutes.

While marinade is simmering, prepare plums. Plums should be firm, ripe and without blemish if possible. Pale fleshed plums are best for this recipe. Wash plums, prick each 7 to 8 times with fine skewer or needle. Pack into sterilised jars, pour hot marinade over to cover plums; seal. Let stand 6 to 8 weeks before using. Serve with meat dishes.

CATCHUP

Take a gallon of strong stale beer — the stronger and staler the beer is, the better will be the catchup. 1 lb. of anchovies (salted) anchovies from the barrel), 1 lb. of shallots, peeled, ½ oz. of mace, ½ oz. of cloves, ¼ oz. whole pepper — 3 to 4 large ginger roots, 2 quarts of large mushroom flaps rubbed to pieces. Cover all this close and let it simmer till it is half wasted, then strain through a muslin or flannel bag. Let it stand till it is quite cold, then bottle it.

A spoonful of this to a pound of fresh butter, melted, makes a fine fish sauce.

PEAR CATSUP

Stew 1 quart of pears, mash, and rub through a sieve. Add 1 cupful of sugar, ½ cupful vinegar, 1 teaspoon salt, ½ teaspoonful each of pepper, ground cinnamon and ground cloves.

Boil gently until thick, then put into bottles and seal tightly.

APPLE CHUTNEY

4 lbs. apples, ½ lb. sultanas, ¾ lb. stoned raisins, ¼ lb. mustard, 6 ozs. ground ginger, 1 lb. brown sugar, 4 ozs. salt, ¾ oz. cayenne.

Chop the fruit up finely, raisins as well as apples, mix and boil together, and put into preserving pan with 2 quarts of vinegar. Boil until soft. If liked the chutney can be run through a sieve to make it smooth. The proportion of sugar, salt, mustard, and cayenne may be altered slightly to suit the tastes of the maker.

APPLE AND ONION CHUTNEY

2 lbs. green apples   1 lb. onions
1 tablespoon salt   2 tablespoons raisins
1 lb. sugar
1 teaspoon ground spice
¼ teaspoon cayenne pepper

Peel apples and onions. Put all through mincer. Cover with vinegar (about 2/3 pint). Boil about ½ hour. Bottle.

UNCOOKED FRUIT CHUTNEY

1 lb. stoned dates   3 medium green apples
1 lb. sultanas   1 lb. onions
1 teaspoon salt   ¼ teaspoon pepper
1 cup brown sugar, firmly packed
1 pint brown malt vinegar
1 teaspoon whole allspice
1 teaspoon whole cloves
1 dessertspoon chopped green ginger

Mince dates, peeled and cored apples, sultanas, and peeled and roughly chopped onions (or chop all ingredients very finely). Place minced mixture in bowl, add sugar, vinegar, salt, pepper, mix until well combined. Tie allspice, cloves and ginger in muslin bag, add to fruit mixture; mix well. Cover, stand for 24 hours, stirring mixture occasionally. Remove muslin bag. Bottle and store.

"He may live without books,
What is knowlege but growing?
He may live without hope —
What is hope but deceiving?
He may live without love —
What is passion but pining?
But where is the man
Who can live without dining?"

GOLDEN CHUTNEY

1 pint apple pulp   3 good sized shallots

Simmer in ¼ pint of vinegar till thick. Remove from stove and add 1 teaspoonful of each, ginger, mustard, curry powder, tumeric mace, salt and 2 tablespoons of sugar.

Mix well, turn into a bowl and bottle when quite cold. This is liked by those who cannot take anything really hot, being quite mild.

RHUBARB RELISH

1 bunch chopped rhubarb, 1½ lbs. onions chopped finely, 3 cups brown sugar, 1 tablespoon salt, ½ cup sultanas, 1 pint vinegar, cayenne pepper, ½ teaspoon mixed spice. Boil all ingredients together for 2 hours. When cool, bottle. This relish makes a delicious filling for sandwiches and is good with meat.

UNCOOKED RELISH

2 large apples   1 large white onion
1 cup seeded raisins   1 teaspoon salt
2 tablespoons white vinegar
1 teaspoon sugar   1 red pepper

Peel apples and onion. Chop finely. Cut pepper in half. Remove seeds. Put pepper and raisins through mincer or chop finely. Mix all ingredients together. Add vinegar, salt and sugar. Spoon into jars and cover. Leave 24 hours before serving.

APPLE JAM THAT WILL KEEP FOR YEARS

Weigh equal quantities of brown sugar and good sour apples; pare, core and chop apples fine; make a good clear syrup of the sugar. Add the apples, the juice and grated rind of 3 lemons, and a few pieces of white ginger. Boil it till the apple looks clear and yellow; this resembles foreign sweetmeats. On no account omit the ginger.

QUINCE JELLY

Wash and wipe the quinces and cut up roughly. Do not peel or seed. Place in a preserving pan and just cover them with water. Boil gently until soft — about 45 minutes. Strain and measure.

For every cup of strained liquid add an equal measure of sugar as well as the juice of two lemons. Boil rapidly until the jelly will give the jell test. Bottle and seal.

PUMPRICOT JAM

Wash and soak 1 lb. dried apricots in water to cover for 24 hours. To 2 lbs. pumpkin (cut small) add 1½ lbs. sugar and let stand overnight. Put into preserving pan the apricots and water in which they were soaked. Add pumpkin and 2½ lbs. sugar.

Use a little less sugar if the pumpkin is very sweet. Add a pinch of salt and boil all together for about 2 hours, until it thickens. Then bottle in the usual way. A delicious jam.

ROSEHIP JAM

Fill a pint measure with rosehips (fully ripe). Snip off the dead flower ends. Wash and drain the hips. Put into 2 pints of boiling water. Reduce heat and boil gently until hips can be crushed with a wooden spoon. Mash well and turn contents of the pan into a freshly scalded jelly bag. Leave to drip overnight. Great care must be taken to strain the hips carefully through the jelly bag and never to press or squeeze during the process. The tiny hairs on the hips, must be eliminated or they can cause irritation to the mucous membrane of the stomach.

Measure juice next day and make up to 1½ pints, with water. Meanwhile, wash, dry and chop up 1 lb. or less of cooking apples (green). Put in a saucepan with water just to cover. Stew (lid on pan) until apple is a soft thick pulp. Rub through a sieve. Mix with rosehip juice. Bring nearly to boiling point. Stir in 2 lbs. sugar. When dissolved boil until setting stage (test on a cold saucer). Bottle and seal at once.

MINCEMEAT

Grate the rinds of three large lemons, squeeze out the juice and strain it, and then boil the remainder of the lemons until tender enough to pulp or chop very finely. Add to this the pulp of three large baked apples without the core and skins, add 1 lb. stoned raisins then 8 ozs. currants, then 1 lb. shredded suet, mixing it well as you go. Add 2 lbs. moist sugar, 1 oz. sliced candied citron, 1 oz. sliced candied orange peel, 1 oz. sliced candied lemon peel, then add 1 teacupful of brandy and 2 tablespoonsful orange marmalade, mixing everything very well together. Put the mincemeat into stone jar with a closely fitting lid. In a fortnight it will be ready for use. Unless it is liked very bitter, all or part of the pith of the lemon should be omitted. It can be stored in jars also.

ROSE PETAL JAM

1 lb. red rose bud petals	Juice of 2 lemons
1 pint water,	3 lbs. sugar

Cut petals into thin strips: arrange on plates and sprinkle with lemon juice. Stand overnight. Put in saucepan with the water. Bring to boiling point. Strain. Keep aside half of the petals. Return water to saucepan, add sugar and remaining lemon juice. Add conserved petals. Simmer gently for 30 minutes. Cool a little before bottling.

The rule is, jam tomorrow and jam yesterday — but never jam today.

Lewis Carroll

LEMON HONEY

2 cups parsley	2 lemons
3 pints water	1½ lbs. sugar

Wash parsley, do not remove stalks. Slice lemons and remove pips. Cover parsley and lemons with water and boil gently until parsley is yellow and liquid reduced to half the quantity. Strain through scalded jelly bag. Add sugar and boil until mixture jells slightly, when tested on a cold saucer.

LEMON CURD

1 lb. sugar — 4 ozs. butter
6 eggs, well beaten
grated rind and juice 2 lemons

Melt the butter in double saucepan, stir in other ingredients. Keep stirring all the time on the stove until the consistency of cream or honey. It must not come to the boil. Pour into pots. This Store will keep for months and is a nice filling for sandwich cakes or cheese cakes.

ESSENCE OF CELERY

This is prepared by soaking for a fortnight, half an ounce of the seeds of celery in a quarter of a pint of brandy. A few drops will flavour a pint of soup or broth equal to a head of celery.

GINGER BEER

1 oz. compressed yeast 1 dessertspoon sugar
1 despn. ground ginger 1 pint warm water

Stir all together and keep in a warm place. Daily for 1 week add 1 teaspoon ginger and 1 teaspoon sugar.

To Make Beer:

½ cup lemon juice — 2-3 cups sugar
4 quarts warm water

Add liquid from plant, strain and bottle, adding 1 raisin to each bottle. Cork well. Leave 3-5 days before using.

After using liquid from plant replace with same quantity of warm water and continue with daily sugar and water as above.

CLARET CUP

80 ozs. Claret
30 oz pineapple and orange juice (mixed)
26 ozs. ginger beer
2 small bottles soda water
26 ozs. lemonade

Mix all together and any mixed fresh fruit (such as bananas, passionfruit, strawberries and mint) may be added together with ice cubes.

LEMON SYRUP

Juice of 12 lemons — 3 pints boiling water
Rind of 8 lemons — 7 lbs. sugar
Juice of 2 oranges — 1 oz. epsom salts
3 ozs. citric acid

Put all ingredients in large bowl, stir till sugar dissolves, bottle. Keeps indefinitely. Fill glass with either water or lemonade add to this a little of the syrup.

PARTY TIME PUNCH

1 bottle fruit juice — 1 lemon
16 ozs. fruit salad — 52 ozs. ginger beer
4 passionfruit — 26 ozs. lemonade
1 cup strawberries — 13 ozs. white wine
2 oranges — Ice

Combine in punch bowl, the fruit juice, fruit salad, passionfruit pulp, strawberries, orange and lemon juice. Place in cool place until ready to serve. Add ginger beer, lemonade and wine.

LEMON SQUASH

2 lbs. sugar — 1½ pints boiling water
1 oz. citric acid — Grated rind of 2 lemons
1 despn. epsom salts — Juice of 6 lemons

Pour over sugar, citric acid and epsom salts, boiling water. When cool, add rind and juice. Bottle. Will keep for some time.

NOTES

THE PICNIC

PIC-NICS

The origin of pic-nics has been traced to Charles, Prince of Wales, afterwards Charles I., who, in the year 1618, gave such a party, and invited the marquises, lords, knights, and squires to bring every man his dish of meat.

'History'

A TASMANIAN PICNIC

Anon he led that Royal pair
And goodlie companie
Into a tent, where stood a board
So filled, you plain mote see
That master cook had mastered well
His task of cookerie;
For there was store of viands good —
Beef, mutton, lamb and veal;
And tongues, and hams, and sucking pigs;
As fat as e'er did squeal.
There hens and cocks, and bubly-jocks
Were plucked, and stuffed, and trussed;
And puddings crammed so full of plums,
The cook "was sure they'd bust!"
And on a lordly dish, upraised,
The lure of every eye,
In tempting glory was displayed
A noble warden-pie.

WITCHETTY GRUBS

Those fat, white grubs found in the damp rotting bark of old trees, are delicious cooked in honey. Wild honey can sometimes be found in the bush.

TERRINE DE LAPIN

Cut the rabbit flesh from the bones in strips, season with salt and black pepper and place into a bowl and cover with a liqueur glass of brandy. Leave to marinate for an hour or two. Meantime, prepare some forcemeat with 6 ozs. of dry breadcrumbs, grated lemon peel, thyme, sage, chopped fat of pork, salt, black pepper and a couple of finely chopped shallots. Bind together with one egg.

When the rabbit strips have marinated the required time, pour off the brandy and add to the forcemeat. Render the fat from 4 rashers of bacon; when cool, grease a large terrine with the fat. Cut about 6 rashers of streaky bacon into strips and line the dish with some of them. Spread a layer of forcemeat. Top with some more strips of bacon. Place some rabbit fillets over the top and again cover with a layer of forcemeat. Continue in this manner until the rabbit and forcemeat have been used up, finishing with a layer of forcemeat. The terrine (which should be earthenware), should now be three-quarters full. Cover the top with thin slices of fat bacon, sprinkle with a little powdered thyme and allspice, and place a couple of bay leaves on top. Cover dish with greaseproof paper and tie down, and place into a shallow baking dish into which some warm water has been poured. Cook in moderate oven for 1½ hours. Remove bay leaves, cool and serve.

(If you want to keep a terrine for any length of time, then some pure lard should be prepared, melted, and poured over the surface as soon as it is completely cold.)

There, on a slope of orchard, Francis laid
A damask napkin, wrought with horse and hound,
Brought out a dusky loaf, that smelt of home,
And, half cut down, a pasty, costly made,
Where quail, and pigeon, lark and leveret, lay
Like fossils of the rocks, with golden yolks
Imbedded and injellied.

Tennyson

WILD DUCK TERRINE

Cut the flesh into strips or dice. Leave them overnight in 3 ozs. of brandy or madeira, the juice of half an orange and some grated orange rind, plus salt, pepper and thyme. When ready to cook, mix ½ lb. of minced veal with ½ lb. of minced pork, bind with a raw egg, and season.

Line your terrine with strips of pork fat, place half the minced meat into it, then a layer of duck meat. Chop up the liver and the heart and dot over the duck meat, plus a chopped truffle if you have one. Cover with remaining minced meat, top with thin strips of pork fat, cover with lid or foil and cook for two hours in a slow oven in a shallow pan of water. Cool for some hours without removing the lid. Then coat top of the terrine with a layer of lard and it will keep a long time in a cool place.

AUNT SARAH'S CAMP PIE

1½ lbs. shin of beef, free from fat and gristle
½ lb. bacon with rind cut off, pinch of mace,
nutmeg, thyme (leaves only)
pepper to taste.

Mince meat and bacon finely through mincer, add seasonings, blend thoroughly with one egg, pack into a small billy. Put lid on tightly and steam for two hours. Remove from billy when cold and garnish. Splendid for picnics.

STUFFED GOOSE NECK

(To be served sliced, cold, as an appetiser)

The skin of a goose-neck
2 tablespoons lard or goose-fat

1 egg	¾ lb. minced veal
1 clove garlic	Black pepper
2 cups stock	Salt

Carefully remove the inside flesh and bone under the skin. Sew up one end with strong cotton. In a bowl put the minced meat, mix with an egg, season with salt, pepper and one minced clove of garlic. Work the mixture into a smooth filling. (You may like to mix the meat with rice, in which case take 4 ozs. of minced meat and ½ cup uncooked rice.) Stuff this mixture inside the neck, similar to stuffing a sausage. Sew up the top end. Place this sausage in a saucepan, add stock, cover and simmer for one hour. Take out the sausage, drain and roast in a hot oven in fat until golden and crisp on all sides. Let cool overnight. Serve as thin slices.

The same recipe for turkey-neck can be used.

BEUREE DE JAMBON

4ozs. lean cooked ham
3 ozs. thoroughly creamed butter
A mean 1 oz. of crustless bread
1 fluid oz. dry white wine
¼ of a small peeled, crushed garlic clove
1 tablespoon double cream
A generous pinch of freshly-milled black peppercorns

Chop up the ham and emulsify everything together. The yield fills 10 little pots or egg cups.

HERB BUTTERED BREAD

Cut a 10 or 12 inch loaf of French Bread into 1½ inch slices but do not cut all the way through the bottom crust. Spread one side of each slice with butter that has been blended with fresh minced parsley, thyme and a little salt. Wrap tightly in greased paper and chill for an hour before putting in hamper.

OLD DEVONSHIRE RABBIT BRAWN

1 large rabbit	Pepper
2 pig's trotters	Spice
Salt	Water

Put 2 pig's feet in a saucepan with cold water to cover and boil gently for 1½ hours. Then put in with them a rabbit which has been prepared and soaked in salted water for ½ hour to whiten the flesh. Boil all together for 2 hours, or until the flesh is tender and leaves the bones easily; adding more water in the meantime, if needed. Remove from the fire, and when cool enough, take out all the bones, cut the meat in small pieces, and season with salt, pepper and spice to taste. Boil all up together, then put into 2 moulds or pudding basins, previously rinsed with cold water, let it stand overnight, turn out, and serve with a dish of lettuce and tomatoes.

This makes a very good meat course for luncheon or supper, and is fit to put before any one — as the saying is.

CHEESE POTS

3 lbs. cheddar cheese	¾ cup sherry
½ lb. butter	Salt and pepper

Roughly grate cheese and place over moderate heat with butter, stirring continuously until cheddar and butter have melted. If mixture separates, remove from heat and beat well. Beat in sherry and salt and pepper to taste. Pour into small pots, allow to cool and set. Use to spread on savouries or bread.

HERB BUTTER

Chop very fine parsley, chervil, chives, basil and French sorrel. Take two heaped tablespoonsful of this mixture, cream well with one pound of butter; form into shape and place in cool room to set. Allow a few hours for flavours to blend.

QUANTITIES FOR 100

3 1/3 large bread
2½ lbs. butter
½ oz. eggs (minced)
2 lbs. tomatoes
½ lb. cheese (minced)
3 lbs. cornfeef.

SANDWICH SPREAD

Boil a ham, using 2 parts water and 1 part cider to cover it, adding 2 bay leaves, 8 or 10 peppercorns and 4 or 5 whole cloves, simmering until ham is tender. Then in this same stock, boil a fowl, simmering until it is tender, then drain it well.

The stock is cooled and the fat collected from the top, and this is mixed with an equal amount of fresh butter, this butter being used to spread the bread for the chicken sandwiches.

The same stock, reinforced when necessary with a little more cider, can be used to cook more than one fowl, thus uniting the cider and ham flavours with the chicken.

CHEESE BALL

In a bowl, combine 1 lb. finely grated cheddar cheese, 2 tablespoons chopped shallots and 4 ozs. chopped ham. Stir in ½ cup mayonnaise and 1 teaspoon lemon juice. Shape into a ball. Roll in ½ cup finely chopped parsley or walnuts. Chill until firm. Serve with savoury biscuits or bread.

PATE DE FOIE GRAS

1 lb. lambs fry   ¼ lb. butter
1 teaspoon ground mace
1 teaspoon black pepper
1 saltspoon cayenne pepper
1 teaspoon ground cloves

Put all through the mincer. Cook in a double boiler for 3-4 hours.

STEAK PASTE

1 lb. steak, fat free
1 tablespoon anchovy sauce
1 teaspoon salt, pepper
½ teaspoon nutmeg   pinch cayenne
¼ lb. butter   ½ teaspoon mace

Mince steak. Put all ingredients on top of double saucepan. Cook for three hours.

PATE MAISON

¼ lb. chicken livers   6-8 ozs. butter
1 medium onion   Seasoning
1 small bouquet garni   2-4 tablespoons brandy

Chop the onion and garlic finely and soften in 1 oz. of the butter until just turning colour. Add the liver, herbs and seasoning and fry together for about three minutes. Chop finely or pass through a sieve and add to the well-creamed butter. Add the brandy, fill into a china pot; smooth the top and cover with a layer of clarified butter.

SANDWICH FILLINGS

Tongue and Apple

1 cup of finely sliced tongue, ½ cup chopped apple, seasoning. Mix and spread with shredded lettuce.

Savoury

Mince some boiled bacon or ham and cooked chicken liver. Spread on brown bread with lettuce.

Cheese and Prune

Mix equal proportions of raw chopped prunes with cream cheese. Add a sprinkling of grated lemon rind.

Bacon

Mix ½ lb. lightly fried bacon, 1 shallot chopped very fine, 1 cucumber, celery chopped fine, and seasoning. Mix these ingredients with mayonnaise and spread.

Brain and Nut

Soak a set of sheep's brains in salt and water for a few hours. Boil a few minutes in salted water. When cold mash with chopped walnuts, salt, pepper and a little lemon juice.

Celery and Walnut

Finely dice celery and add to finely chopped walnuts, salt and pepper.

OUTDOOR SANDWICHES

A wonderful sandwich idea for a picnic is to use a whole loaf — or even two or three if numbers warrant it. Cut the loaf in halves lengthwise and scoop out the soft centre (keep this for breadcrumbs for another dish), then spread the insides with butter or cheese spread. The inside can be filled with any mixture you like, such as chopped eggs, chopped beef, or sausage mixed with chopped tomatoes, gherkins, or grated raw carrot, the whole then covered with crisp lettuce leaves and wrapped up carefully to keep fresh until picnic time. Cut into thick slices to serve.

GRANDMOTHER'S LIVER PASTE

1 lb. baby beef liver   ¼ lb. fat of bacon
4 anchovies, drained   1 cup rich milk
2 teaspoons salt   ½ teaspoon pepper
⅛ teaspoon allspice   2 eggs
¾ lb. unsalted fresh pork fat
1 medium sized white onion
2 teaspoons potato flour
2 tablespoons melted butter
¼ teaspoon ground cloves

Soak the liver in milk for ½ hour, dry, and with a sharp knife or scissors cut away skin and sinews, and cut into small pieces; cube ½ pound of the pork fat, saving the remainder to line the baking-dish; chop the bacon.

Mix the eggs, and milk; stir in the potato flour and the seasonings, and feed into the mincer with liver, pork fat, bacon, onion, and anchovies. Blend small portions at a time, apportioning the liquid and solids so as not to overload the machine. Force the pureed mixture through a coarse-meshed sieve to catch the bits of sinew the scissors miss. Mix all together and add the melted butter. Stir well.

Slice the remaining pork fat thinly and line the baking-dish; pour in the liver mixture, seal with wax paper; set the dish in hot water and bake in a very slow oven, 275°, about 1¼ hours, or until the blade of a knife inserted into the paste comes out clean. Cool well, turn out, and remove the strips of fat.

The paste will be slightly grainy. It keeps well if chilled. Over the top of any to be stored, pour melted bacon fat, to seal.

SAVORY TURNOVERS

½ lb. short crust pastry
½ cup mashed fish
2 small peeled tomatoes
2 hard-boiled eggs
1 tablespoon finely diced onion
2 tablespoons soft white breadcrumbs
Salt and pepper to taste

Drain mashed fish, removing as much oil as possible, then mash. Skin tomatoes and chop into small pieces. Cut up eggs. Add these to the sardines with onion, breadcrumbs, salt and pepper. Drain any extra moisture out.

Roll pastry out thinly on a well-floured board, cut into 4 inch squares, place some mixture on each square, moisten edges and fold over. Pinch edges together, glaze with milk and bake in hot oven 20-25 minutes. Serve cold.

CHICKEN LIVER PATE

The pate can be made in great quantities and stores well if kept as cold as possible. Melt a quarter of a pound of butter in a pan, put in 1 lb. of chicken livers, 1 grated white onion, a bay leaf, garlic, fresh herbs or a sprinkle of dried thyme, peppercorns and 3 anchovy fillets.

Simmer and stir gently until the livers have changed colour, but are only lightly cooked. Ladle them and the juices into the chopper, add ¼ lb. butter, in chunks and 2 tablespoons of brandy.

Mince until smooth, pour into bowls to set. If this is a long-term project, you can seal the pots with clarified butter, but for immediate party use, give the pates a touch of elegance. Place a baby bay leaf or sprig of fresh herbs on top.

MEAT ROLL

½ lb. minced veal
¼ lb. steaky bacon
1 egg
¼ lb. pork sausage meat
2 cups beef stock
3 hard-boiled eggs
¼ oz. gelatine
3 ozs. fresh breadcrumbs
seasoning including herbs

Mix together meat, chopped bacon, breadcrumbs and 2 tablespoons of stock. Stir in beaten egg and seasonings. Press half the mixture into a greased tin, shell eggs and put down centre, then top with remaining mixture. Wrap securely in greased greaseproof paper and simmer in large saucepan for 2 hours. Remove paper, replace with fresh, and press well, overnight. For the glaze, mix the gelatine with a little cold consomme, heat the rest in a small saucepan, stir into gelatine and allow to thicken. Take the roll from the tin. Stand roll on a rack and brush with the glaze. When set, brush again and serve, sliced, with salad.

ABERDEEN SAUSAGE

1 lb. buttock steak, 6 ozs. rather fat bacon, 2 small cups breadcrumbs, all run through the mincer; ¾ teaspoon salt, pepper to taste, ¼ nutmeg (grated), 1 egg (beaten), 1 dessertspoon Worcestershire sauce.

After meats come through the mincer, add all other ingredients. Tie (like a sausage) in a greased cloth. Boil 2 hours, or steam 2½ hours in a buttered basin (covered).

BACON AND EGG PIE TO EAT COLD

Steep a few thin slices of bacon in water to take out the salt, lay the bacon in the dish, beat eight eggs with a pint of thick cream, put in it a little pepper and salt, and pour it on the bacon. Lay over it a good cold paste. Bake in a moderate oven the day before you want it.

CHEESE, BACON AND ONION TART

½ lb. shortcrust pastry

Filling:

1 lb. onions, 2 bacon rashers, 2 eggs, 1 small cup cream, 3 ozs. grated cheese, salt and pepper.

Line deep pie plate with rolled-out pastry, trim and flute edges, prick base lightly with fork.

Cook peeled and sliced onions in very little salted water until soft, drain well and chop. Trim bacon, cut into small pieces, mix with onion. Beat eggs lightly with 1 tablespoon cream, season with salt and pepper.

Put onion mixture in pastry case, pour over beaten egg. Sprinkle top with grated cheese, pour over rest of cream. Bake in a hot oven for about 30 minutes.

A LARGE HERBED CHEESE BALL
is economical.

Place 1 lb. of cottage cheese in a large bowl, add 1 teaspoon cayenne pepper, 3 chopped shallots, chopped fresh herbs, salt and pepper and pound and beat, adding a little cream to smooth the texture.

EGGS IN BREAD CASES

8 slices of bread — ½ cup bacon fat
4 eggs — salt and pepper
4 rashers of bacon

Spread fat on slices of bread. Top each with a second slice, from which an inner circle has been cut with a scone cutter. Spread fat on top slice and break egg into each circle. Sprinkle with pepper and salt. Place rasher of bacon, grilled, on top of egg. Bake in hot oven for seven minutes or until egg is set.

BUSH CAKE (Long keeping)

1 lb. honey; 1 lb. sugar; 4 ozs. butter; ½ lb. wholemeal flour; ½ lb. plain flour; ½ lb. oats; 1 lb. mashed potatoes; 5 teaspoons baking powder; 1 teaspoon cinnamon; 2 tablespoons cocoa; 1 lb. raisins; 4 ozs. finely chopped nuts; 2-3 eggs; juice and grated peel of a lemon.

Melt honey and sugar together. When cooled a little add the butter. Mix together sieved flours, spices, raisins, nuts and potato. Make a hole in the centre of mixture and add the honey mixture gradually and evenly, then add the eggs and lemon. Put into bread baking tins with oiled greaseproof paper. Bake for 1¼-1½ hours in a slow oven.

METRICS IN THE KITCHEN

1 kilogram is a little more than 2 lb.

½ kilogram is the nearest convenient measure to 1 lb.

½ kilogram	=	500 grams
1 kilogram	=	1000 grams
1 lb	=	454 grams (approximately)
2 lb	=	907 grams (approximately)

ASCERTAINING WEIGHT OF CATTLE

Measure the girth close behind the shoulder, and measure the length from the fore part of the shoulder-blade along the back to the bone at the tail, which is in a vertical line with the buttock, both in feet. Multiply the square of the girth, expressed in feet, by five times the length, and divide the produce by 21; the quotient is the weight, nearly, of the four quarters, in stones of 14 lbs. avoirdupoise. For example, if the girth be 6½ feet, and the length 5¼ feet, we shall have 6½ multiplied by 6½ equal to 42¼, and 5¼ multiplied by 5 equal to 26¼; then 42¼ multiplied by 26¼ is equal to 1,109 1/16th, and this divided by 21, gives 52 4/5ths stones nearly, or 52 stones 11lbs. It is to be observed, however, that in very fat cattle the four quarters will be about 1/20th more, while in those in a very lean state they will be 1/20th less than the weight obtained by the rule. The four quarters are little more than half the weight of the living animal; the skin weighing about the eighteenth part, and the tallow about the 12th part of the whole.

NOTES

11th October 1851.

Sketch of The Ballaarat Gold-Field.

Commissioner's Tent.
Alfred Clark's Tent was afterwards erected here.
Golden Point
Lomas' Claim.
Kavanah's claim yielded £3000.
Oddie's Tent.
Macdonald, Sister & Co Claim.
Willis's Claim.
Macdonald Suter & Thompson's claim.
Highett's Claim.
Oddie's claim.
ISLAND
McLeod's Tent
Cradle
Macdonald's
Macdonald's Tent.
YARROWEE
RIVER
RICH OPEN FLAT
Present Site of the
TOWNSHIP of BALLAARAT WEST
1867.

Note

.... Indicating approximate extent of present Gold field (1851)

-.-.-.- do do — do — at present covered with Tents.

Copied from a sketch made by A. S. Macdonald -